"Kwok Pui-lan's *Postcolonial Politics and Theology* expands the horizons of political theology that are steeped in Eurocentric theories and Western colonial legacy by shifting theological locus to the geopolitical and social realities of the Global South. This comprehensive book could not come at a more relevant time. It is a must-read for anyone who is interested in what radically reimagined contours of political theology have to offer from postcolonial and transnational perspectives."

—Nami Kim, Professor of Religious Studies, Spelman College

"A stunningly accessible and comprehensive map of postcolonial thought and global theology. With this text, Kwok Pui-lan gives us the gift of nourishing and insightful analyses of postcolonial geographies of race, class, gender, and sexuality that 'challenge the Eurocentric preoccupation of political theology.' Essential reading for those interested in anti-imperialist ways of thinking about and doing theology."

—Traci C. West, Professor of Christian Ethics and African American Studies, Drew Theological School

"Kwok shows how theology is deeply entwined with politics and vice versa, whether in the Black Lives Matter and ecological movements, the struggle for democracy in Hong Kong, or the fight against the COVID-19 pandemic. Deeply rooted in wide-ranging scholarship yet lucidly written, this book also brings theoretical reflections to bear on theological pedagogy, preaching, and interreligious dialogue. This book, which represents the culmination of Kwok Pui-lan's theological scholarship, is a must-read for anyone interested not only in following her theological journey and development but also in understanding how postcolonial Asian feminism can contribute to the construction of a just society. I enthusiastically recommend it to the widest circle of readers."

—Peter C. Phan, The Ignacio Ellacuria Chair of Catholic Social Thought, Georgetown University

"In the midst of political upheaval caused by the authoritarian tendencies of global superpowers, Kwok asks how one does theology in the shadow of colonialism. Is it even possible to separate Christianity from its colonizing roots? Kwok leads us in an exploration of how to reimagine theology through the political lens of the Global South, interrogating the dominating views of both 'Make America Great Again' and a 'China Dream.' This book is a must-read for those wishing to expand and build on the political theology discourse while paying close attention to the changing geopolitical situation in Asia Pacific and its impact on Sino-American competition."

—Miguel De La Torre, Professor of Social Ethics and Latinx Studies, Iliff School of Theology

"As much of theology is trying to figure out its relation to the political, Kwok moves the discussion forward by substantially expanding the horizons of the conversation. As the political engages the colonial and postcolonial, imperialism, as well as race, gender, sexuality, and class in global perspective, fresh theological insights emerge here in conjunction with specific practices that are bound to make a difference."
—Joerg Rieger, Distinguished Professor of Theology, Cal Turner Chancellor's Chair in Wesleyan Studies, Vanderbilt University Divinity School

Postcolonial Politics
and Theology

Postcolonial Politics and Theology

*Unraveling Empire
for a Global World*

KWOK PUI-LAN

WESTMINSTER
JOHN KNOX PRESS
LOUISVILLE · KENTUCKY

First edition
Published by Westminster John Knox Press
Louisville, Kentucky

21 22 23 24 25 26 27 28 29 30—10 9 8 7 6 5 4 3 2 1

Unless otherwise indicated, Scripture quotations are from the New Revised Standard Version of the Bible, copyright © 1989 by the Division of Christian Education of the National Council of the Churches of Christ in the U.S.A., and are used by permission.

Excerpt from *Call Me by My True Names* (1999) by Thich Nhat Hanh is used with permission of Parallax Press.

See page ix, "Acknowledgments," for other permissions information.

Book design by Sharon Adams
Cover design by Lisa Buckley

Library of Congress Cataloging-in-Publication Data
Names: Kwok, Pui-lan, author.
Title: Postcolonial politics and theology : unraveling empire for a global world / Kwok Pui-lan.
Description: First edition. | Louisville, Kentucky : Westminster John Knox Press, 2021. | Includes index. | Summary: "The book invites readers to recognize both the inherent political nature of theological study and how it has propped up the values of domination and the necessity of reimagining political theology through a postcolonial lens"-- Provided by publisher.
Identifiers: LCCN 2021046362 (print) | LCCN 2021046363 (ebook) | ISBN 9780664267490 (paperback) | ISBN 9781646982301 (ebook)
Subjects: LCSH: Postcolonial theology. | Christianity and politics. | Christianity and culture.
Classification: LCC BT83.593 .K96 2021 (print) | LCC BT83.593 (ebook) | DDC 261.7--dc22
LC record available at https://lccn.loc.gov/2021046362
LC ebook record available at https://lccn.loc.gov/2021046363

To the teachers and students of the Theology Division (now Divinity School),
Chung Chi College,
the Chinese University of Hong Kong,
where I began my theological journey

Contents

Acknowledgments

This book was brought to fruition in the midst of the Hong Kong protests, the COVID-19 pandemic, and Black Lives Matter demonstrations in the U.S. in 2020. Public protests and social movements in many parts of the world in 2019 and 2020 convinced me that political theology must take into consideration changing geopolitics in the world, especially in Asia Pacific. I would like to thank Pacific, Asian, and North American Asian Women in Theology and Ministry for providing a forum for the exchange of ideas for more than thirty-six years.

I had the privilege of sharing some of the contents of this book at the Korean Association of Christian Studies in Seoul, Korea; Johannes Gutenberg University in Mainz, Germany; Boston University School of Theology; St. Mary's College in Notre Dame, Indiana; and an annual meeting of the American Academy of Religion. I want to thank the hosts at the various institutions, including Kim Jeong Joon, Volker Küster, David Schnasa Jacobsen, and Arlene F. Montevecchio for their hospitality during my visits. I learned from conversations with the group of scholars who collaborated to produce the book *Teaching Global Theologies: Power and Praxis*. I want to thank Federico Settler, Lilian Siwila, and Charlene van der Walt for their kind invitation to speak at the Religion, Gender, and Sexuality in Africa conference at University of KwaZulu-Natal in Pietermaritzburg, South Africa, in 2018. The conference sharpened my thinking on postcolonialism, racism, and sexuality. I benefitted from dialogues at the De-provincializing Political Theology: Postcolonial and Comparative Approaches conference at Ludwig Maximilian University of Munich, Germany, in 2019. I am very grateful to the organizers Vincent Lloyd and Robert Yelle for delicious food and wonderful conversations.

Colleagues and students at the Episcopal Divinity School and Candler School of Theology at Emory University have encouraged and supported my teaching and research over many years. Candler School of Theology has provided funds for research assistance, and I am very grateful. I want to thank my research assistant Ryan Washington, who has combed through the manuscript with meticulous care and helped make the book more readable and consistent. His probing questions and comments urged me to be more precise in my language and to be clearer in my thoughts. I want to pay tribute to my editor Julie Mullins at Westminster John Knox Press, who has provided excellent editorial comments when I pondered how to put the chapters together to form this book. The book is much improved because of her careful editing. She has been a source of support and encouragement and has shepherded the book through its various stages. I want to thank Daniel Braden for his careful copyediting, and Julie Tonini and the production team at the press for their professionalism and efficiency. Finally, I am very grateful to my spouse, Wai Pang, for his steadfast support of my scholarship and for the love and care he has shown during the pandemic.

Earlier versions of many chapters have appeared in various publications. I am grateful to the editors who have worked with me and to the publishers for allowing me to reproduce and use the materials. They have been included in this book with revisions, and several have been updated and expanded with new materials.

The Introduction draws from "Doing Contextual Theology: Feminist and Postcolonial Perspectives," in *Wrestling with God in Context: Revisiting the Theology and Social Vision of Shoki Coe*, ed. M. P. Joseph, Po Ho Huang, and Victor Hsu (Minneapolis: Fortress Press, 2018), 65–80.

Chapter 2 is a revised and expanded version of "Empire and the Study of Religion," *Journal of the American Academy of Religion* 80 (2012): 285–303.

Chapter 3 incorporates material from "Touching the Taboo: On the Sexuality of Jesus," in *Sexuality and the Sacred*, ed. Marvin M. Ellison and Kelly Brown Douglas (Louisville, KY: Westminster John Knox Press, 2010), 119–34; and "Body and Pleasure in Postcoloniality," in *Dancing Theology in Fetish Boots: Essays in Honor of Marcella Althaus-Reid*, ed. Lisa Isherwood and Mark D. Jordan (London: SCM, 2010), 31–43.

Chapter 4 draws on my essays "Christianity, American Empire, and the Global Society," *Journal of Commonwealth and Postcolonial Studies* 15, no. 1 (2008): 109–21; and "Postcolonialism, American History, and World Christianity," *The Ecumenist* 48, no. 1 (2011): 1–7. The journal is now titled *Critical Theology*.

Chapter 5 was published as "Postcolonial Theology from an East Asian Perspective," in *Proceedings of the Conference on "Response to 1919: March First Spirit and the Future of the Church"* (Seoul: Korean Association of Christian Studies, 2018), 25–48.

Chapter 6 is a slightly revised version of "Fishing the Asia Pacific: Transnationalism and Feminist Theology," in *Off the Menu: Asian and Asian North American Women's Religion and Theology*, ed. Rita Nakashima Brock et al. (Louisville, KY: Westminster John Knox Press, 2007), 3–22.

Chapter 7 is an updated and expanded version of "Introduction," in *Hong Kong Protests and Political Theology*, ed. Kwok Pui-lan and Francis Ching-wah Yip (Lanham, MD: Rowman and Littlefield, 2021), 1–12. All rights reserved. Chapter 8 is a slightly revised version of "Teaching Theology from a Global Perspective," in *Teaching Global Theologies: Power and Praxis*, ed. Kwok Pui-lan, Cecelia González-Andrieu, and Dwight N. Hopkins (Waco, TX: Baylor University Press, 2015), 11–27. Copyright © Baylor University Press, 2015. Reprinted by arrangement with Baylor University Press. All rights reserved.

Chapter 9 is an updated version of "Postcolonial Preaching in Intercultural Contexts," *Homiletic* 40:1 (2015): 8–21.

Chapter 10 uses material from "Religion and Peacebuilding: A Postcolonial Perspective," Contending Modernities Initiative, Kroc Institute for International Peace Studies, part of the Keough School of Global Affairs, University of Notre Dame, October 21, 2019, https://contendingmodernities.nd.edu/theorizing-modernities/religionandpeacebuildingpostcolonial/.

Chapter 11 draws from "Sustainability, Earthcare, and Christian Mission," in *Creation Care in Christian Mission*, ed. Kapya J. Kaoma (Oxford: Regnum Books, 2015), 213–28. ISBN: 978-1498290869.

Introduction

Postcolonial Reflection on
the Political and the Theological

To make vulnerable the political and the theological through engagement of text and context is the intellectual labor of political theology. Critique and defense are the tools of the polemicist and the demagogue. The vocation of the academic, by contrast, is to expose what is taken for granted, to make vulnerable.

Vincent W. Lloyd[1]

In 2019, the protests against an anti-extradition bill in Hong Kong captured the world's attention as millions took to the streets in the former British colony, and many people took part in rallies in cities around the globe to support their struggle. Toward the end of that year, a mysterious disease broke out in the city of Wuhan, the capital of Hebei Province in the People's Republic of China. Soon, the novel coronavirus began to spread in Europe, the U.S., and other parts of the world, with many people ending up in intensive care units and dying from the disease. In early spring of 2020, President Donald Trump tried to downplay the seriousness of the pandemic. Later, he used the term "Chinese virus" to refer to the coronavirus, despite calls from global health officials to avoid labels associating the disease with a particular nation or group of people. Trump's references to the coronavirus as "Chinese virus" and "Kung Flu" intensified the tensions that already existed between China and the U.S. as a result of a trade war and other competition between them.

As I looked for theological resources to help make sense of the changing geopolitical situations in Asia Pacific and to address rising concerns about the stigmatization of Asian Americans, I found a dearth of material. The majority of books on politics and theology focus on Europe, the U.S., or the North Atlantic,

1

and there are few resources on Asia Pacific, though the twenty-first century has been dubbed the Pacific Century.[2] While China loomed large in presidential politics and foreign policy debates, many theologians acted as if they were living in a time capsule, sealed off from the changing world politics around them. When I looked at recent publications in the field of political theology, I found that most remained steeped in a Eurocentric mindset and had not caught up with the current moment.

In order to address this gap in the literature, I gathered and revised several of my articles published over more than a decade to form the foundation of this volume. This book employs postcolonial theory to challenge the Eurocentric preoccupation of political theology, proposing instead a postcolonial and comparative approach that addresses the realities of the majority world. It points to the ongoing need to use a postcolonial lens to critique the alignment of the study of religion and theology with empire and to reimagine political theology more broadly from a global perspective. Challenging a Eurocentric genealogy of political theology that often begins with Carl Schmitt's *Political Theology*,[3] I argue for uncovering the diverse origins and multicultural genealogies of the discipline. A contrapuntal and comparative reading of different political theologies opens possibilities to explore overlapping political struggles in the past and present—for example, between the Hong Kong protests and the Irish struggle for independence.[4]

A special focus of the book will be on the changing sociopolitical realities of American Empire and Sino-American competition. The tensions between China and the U.S. are encapsuled in Donald Trump's slogan of "Make America Great Again" and Xi Jinping's hope for a "China Dream." The shifting of U.S. and Asian relationships provides an exemplary case through which to look at political theology globally. First, it shifts attention from the Atlantic to the Pacific; this change in context provokes new questions and issues for political theology. Second, the U.S. has been a key player in Asian politics and has fought a number of wars in Asia since the late nineteenth century, a longstanding involvement that demonstrates how political theology can benefit from using a transpacific lens. Third, many Asian countries, like the rest of the majority world, have experienced the trial and tribulation of postcolonial nation building. Eurocentric political theology, based largely on the experiences of liberal democracy, cannot address the kinds of issues arising in the postcolonial world. Fourth, Asia, with more than half of the world's population, is multicultural, multilingual, multiracial, and multireligious. In the past several decades, the religious landscape in the U.S. has become increasingly more diverse and pluralistic as well.[5] Political theology in both the Asia Pacific and U.S. context cannot privilege Christianity and must adopt a comparative approach and include discussion of religious plurality and diversity.

In my own work, the political has impinged on the theological ever since I began to study theology in Hong Kong in the early 1970s, during the heyday of worldwide student protests. I had the privilege of participating in Asian contextual theology and Asian feminist theology when these theological currents emerged in the 1970s and 1980s. Later, I became one of the pioneers exploring the implications of postcolonial theory for biblical studies and theology. The Hong Kong protests in 2019 brought my memory back to my college years, when I first pondered what Christian theology had to say to the Hong Kong and Chinese people. In order to show how the political and the theological have transversed and intersected in my theological thinking in the past five decades, I want to chart and share my intellectual trajectory. This recollection is necessarily selective, for as Edward Said writes, "any autobiographical document . . . is not only a chronicle of states of mind, but also an attempt to render the individual energy of one's life."[6] But I believe my experience helps demonstrate the need to reconceive political theology as it intersects with global, postcolonial contexts, where this scholarly work is, in fact, already happening.

I was born in the former British colony of Hong Kong and began to study theology in 1971, as a college student at Chung Chi College, the Chinese University of Hong Kong. The 1960s and 1970s were a period of ferment and protest around the world. In Hong Kong, students took to the streets to fight against corruption and to demand that the Chinese language be used as a second official language. For, even though 98 percent of the people in Hong Kong were Chinese, English was the only official language until 1971. Many people came to Hong Kong from south China as refugees and spoke no English. They had to rely on others to explain to them government notices and help them fill out official forms. While in college, I had the privilege of joining a small travel seminar organized by the Student Christian Movement, which brought us to the Philippines, Korea, and Japan. I remember talking with progressive students at the University of the Philippines who told us that they took turns going to prison to fight against the Marcos dictatorship. In Seoul, the Park Chung Hee government was so repressive that we had to change the place we met for fear that the room was bugged. Surrounded by the serene and beautiful shrines of Kyoto, we heard about the peace movement Japanese Christians had initiated and their vow to never forget the crimes perpetuated by their government during World War II. These Asian Christian leaders were involved in the struggle for democracy, human rights, demilitarization, and economic justice. During the trip, my heart felt very heavy when I saw the suffering and struggles of Asian people, but I also glimpsed what Bonhoeffer had said about the cost of discipleship and the grace of God.

LIBERATION THEOLOGY AND CONTEXTUAL THEOLOGY

I was taught theology in Hong Kong mostly by missionaries from Canada, the U.S., Germany, and Australia, and we read works by Tillich, Barth, Bonhoeffer, and the Niebuhr brothers. But it was Latin American liberation theology, particularly Gustavo Gutiérrez's *A Theology of Liberation*, that captured my attention.[7]

This book helped me fathom the vocation of a theologian, even though the colonial situation in Hong Kong was very different from that of Gutiérrez's native country Peru or the wider Latin American society. For Gutiérrez, theology is a critical reflection of praxis, and he suggests that theology without action is dead. Gutiérrez emphasized God's preferential option for the poor, the structural dimensions of sin, and people as the subjects of history. His book integrates theology with a political reading of the people's social and economic history and summons the church to listen to the cries of the people.

While Latin American theologians developed liberation theology, using insights and tools from Marxism, Asian theologians engaged in contextualization so that their theological reflections could speak to their Asian social and political realities. It was Shoki Coe, a Taiwanese theological educator, who coined the term "contextualizing theology" in the early 1970s. For him, contextualization "responds to the Gospel itself as well as to the urgent issues in the historic realities, particularly those of the Third World."[8] After the 1960s, most Asian countries had regained political independence, but the continent suffered from poverty, military dictatorship, government corruption, and serious violations of human rights. Asian theologians had to address the issues of democratic participation, economic justice, cultural autonomy, and human dignity. *Minjung* (meaning the people or masses) theology was developed in Korea, Homeland Theology in Taiwan, and Theology of Struggle in the Philippines. I was inspired when theologians from these areas visited Hong Kong and described their participation in the fight for democracy. I was particularly impressed by a few *minjung* theologians who lost their positions as university professors and were detained by the police or put in jail for daring to speak out against Park's dictatorship in Korea.

Two Asian theologians, who challenged Eurocentric dominance in theology, helped in the process of decolonizing of my mind—Choan-seng Song from Taiwan and Aloysius Pieris from Sri Lanka. Song argues that the theological journey from Israel to Asia must be undertaken all over again. In the past, the trip was predetermined in the West and had to make too many intermediary stopovers, with too many attractions and interruptions. The travelers spent too much time visiting Gothic churches and cathedrals and consulting with learned scholars of Western Christianity, to an extent that they have come dangerously close to "disowning [their] own cultural heritage as having no useful meaning in the design of God's salvation."[9] To remedy this, Song insists that the journey must make fewer stops and allow changes of itinerary or rerouting when occasions demand. Song also insists the travelers must work out the itinerary themselves, instead of relying on others.

Song uses the term "transposition" to describe this journey from Israel to Asia. Transposition means a shift of time and space. For him, Christian faith was transposed from Palestine to the Greco-Roman world, and eventually to the West. Although it has been transposed to Asia and other parts of the Global South by the missionary movement, it has not taken root because Christianity has not "become flesh" in the native cultures. Transposition is not simply a translation into another language, style, or expression, but requires "theological discussion to shift to different subjects, to face new questions, and to discover alternative approaches."[10] Song's theological hybrids use stories from many Asian societies, ancient and modern, to illuminate and uncover the meaning of the biblical tradition.

Through his writings and his leadership role in the Programme for Theology and Cultures in Asia, Song has inspired generations of Asian theologians to recover their own cultural and spiritual resources for doing living theologies in Asia. His work has facilitated the development of story theology in Asia, cross-textual hermeneutics, and creative indigenous approaches to theology. It supports and guides Asian Christians in the border passage of rediscovering their cultural roots after a long period of colonialism. Influenced by Song's work, I published one of my first essays on Asian feminist theology, "God Weeps with Our Pain," using women's stories as resources.[11] Yet Song's approach is not without drawbacks. First, coming from a Reformed tradition, Song's theology is very Bible-centered. His biblical interpretation is rather traditional, drawing primarily from mainline male scholars and paying little attention to newer methods. He is more reluctant than other Asian theologians, especially the feminists among them, in critiquing the biblical texts. Second, though Song has very open and inclusive attitudes toward people's cultures and stories, his theology remains Christocentric. Third, scholars have questioned whether Song has created too sharp a binary between Asia and the West and whether such bifurcation is still useful today.[12]

If Song's theology accents on symbols, stories, and people's movements, Aloysius Pieris highlights Asian religiosities and spiritualities. As a Jesuit, Pieris argues that the Western models of inculturation are not suitable for Asia. The Latin model of "incarnation in a non-Christian *culture*," and the Greek model of "assimilation of a non-Christian *philosophy*" cannot be easily adapted to contemporary Asia. Instead, he advocates the monastic model, which is the "participation in a non-Christian *spirituality*."[13] For too long, he argues, Christianity has adopted the attitude of "Christ-against-religions." The inculturists have advocated "Christ-of-religions," but have often separated religion from liberation struggles.[14] A Third World theology of religions, for Pieris, must link spirituality with the liberation of people from poverty.

Pieris has been criticized for generalizing religion and poverty as the two distinct characteristics of the Asian continent and flattening many differences among the peoples and cultures in the continent. He tends to make very broad generalizations for his theological schema and typologies, which can be misleading at times. For example, his differentiation of Asian religiousness as cosmic and metacosmic may not do justice to the vast varieties and nuances of Asian traditions and practices. His broad generalization that Western religiosity is agapeic and Eastern religiosity is gnostic,[15] though helpful in a certain sense, does not pay sufficient attention to the differences within Asian traditions, say between Confucianism and Buddhism, and the enormous diversities within each of the traditions. His opting for a monastic paradigm may also reinforce the colonial stereotypes of the mythic, passive, religious "East" versus a progressive, active, and secular "West."[16] Despite these criticisms, the works of Song and Pieris prompted me to explore a different style of doing theology using Asian resources and to search for my own theological voice in the midst of a changing political situation in Hong Kong.

As a student and later a junior faculty, I had the benefit of attending different ecumenical gatherings, as Hong Kong was and continues to be Asia's primary traffic hub. There were vibrant exchanges of ideas and debates about the church's mission in the rapid sociopolitical changes taking place in Asia. In the climate of developing contextual theologies that met the challenges of the time, theologians in Hong Kong began to reflect on their social and political situation. In the early 1980s, when Britain and China started the negotiation about the future of Hong Kong, I edited the book *1997 and Hong Kong Theology*, the first book on the subject, which discussed the history and role of Hong Kong and the identity of the people of Hong Kong. It offered biblical and theological reflections and recommendations for local churches and Christian schools to prepare for the political transition when Hong Kong would be returned to China.[17]

Although Asian male theologians have made important contributions to the contextualization of theology in Asia, women's issues were not their primary concern. Some of them, like Song,[18] have written on women's oppression, but gender analysis was largely missing in their theologies or were rendered secondary. The Asian feminist theological movement began in the early 1980s in response to Asian women's struggle for dignity and full humanity, and I have had the privilege of participating in it since the beginning.

ASIAN FEMINIST THEOLOGY

I was fortunate when I was a teenager to have a woman as the vicar of my Anglican church in Hong Kong. Deacon Hwang Hsien-yuin was ordained as one of the first female priests in the worldwide Anglican Communion in 1971, when I began to study theology. She used to lead a short meditation before our choir practice each Sunday, and I heard from her the important message that women and men share equal responsibility in leadership and ministry. She offered me much encouragement when I decided to study theology and helped me secure a scholarship. During my college years as a theological student, the Cultural Revolution (1966–1976) was raging in China. Mao Zedong had advocated that women hold up half the sky, and the Red Guards smashed feudalistic and bourgeoise values in society. Women and men wore the same muted blue, green, or grey Mao suit, or clothes that were serviceable and sexless. While women's movements in the West were advocating for women's liberation and individual freedom, women in China had to sacrifice their individuality in order to fit into the collectivity and the revolutionary fervor for a classless society.

Although I did not have a single female professor in my theological training in Hong Kong, I was exposed to feminist theologies and the works of Mary Daly and Rosemary Radford Ruether by my professor Raymond Whitehead. I was interested in their works because the Cultural Revolution had brought into sharp relief the patriarchy entrenched in Chinese society. I participated in one of the first conferences devoted to Asian feminist theology held in Suka-bumi, Indonesia, in 1981. The conference was organized by Elizabeth Tapia, who worked for the Women's Desk of the Christian Conference of Asia at the time. Mary John Mananzan from the Philippines left a strong impression on me as she astutely analyzed the sociopolitical causes of women's oppression in Asian societies.

Asian women theologians were keenly aware of the ways that social and economic changes had affected women's lives. Although industrialization had enabled an increasing number of women to work outside the home, their jobs were often insecure and their working conditions were poor. The economic take-off of countries around the Asian Pacific Rim accorded women more educational opportunities and participation in the public and corporate sectors. However, these advances did not significantly change stereotypical gender roles, and women still had limited power in both the domestic and public spheres. The Vietnam War had brought unspeakable suffering and a devastating impact to Southeast Asian countries. War, militarism, guerilla fighting, and violence affected women and children disproportionately. Prostitution around the American military bases and the development of insidious forms of sex tourism in the Philippines, Thailand, and neighboring countries exploited women's sexual labor. Mananzan was one of the pioneers to write about sexual exploitation of women and violence against women in Asia.[19]

For Asian feminist theologians, attempts at contextualization were inadequate if they failed to take into serious consideration the intersection of patriarchy with poverty, militarism, gender violence, and political discrimination. They criticized male contextual theologians when they overlooked the androcentric elements in both the Bible and Asian cultures. I have pointed out the limitations of contextualization: "First, it takes the content of the Bible and the Gospel for granted, without seriously challenging the androcentric biases both in the biblical texts and in the core symbolism of Christianity. Secondly, it identifies with Asian culture too readily, often failing to see that many Asian traditions are overtly patriarchal."[20] Thus, Asian feminist theologians had to engage in a double critique and reconstruction. While they criticized the patriarchal teachings and practices in the Buddhist, Confucian, Shinto, and Hindu traditions, they also wanted to recover their liberating potentials. For example, some feminist theologians have recovered feminine images and metaphors of the divine in both the Asian and biblical traditions. They pointed out that many Asian religious traditions emphasize the interplay between the feminine and the masculine, yin and yang, heaven and earth, and challenged the predominant usage of male metaphors and images in liturgy, theology, and preaching in Asian churches.

As several pioneers in Asian feminist theology were active in the Ecumenical Association of Third World Theologians (EATWOT), they adopted EATWOT's theological methodology. This methodology could be conceived as a spiral process that included the following steps: critical analyses of the social, cultural, and political contexts; questioning biblical and theological traditions from the perspectives of the oppressed; reformulation of theological doctrines and traditions; and concrete action and social praxis to change social systems and promote justice. But Asian feminist theologians took care to adapt this methodology specifically to the Asian situation. Virginia Fabella from the Philippines surmised that Asian feminist theologians had to take into consideration both their Asianness and their womanness. She writes: "By 'womanness' is not meant a mere conglomerate of biological and psychological factors but an awareness of what it means to be a woman in the Asian context today. . . . Women's experience is basic to our theology."[21]

Since the Bible occupies a pivotal place in church life, the interpretation of the Bible from women's perspectives is crucial for theology. Many Asian women emphasize the liberating heritage of the Bible by lifting up women such as Ruth and Naomi, Hannah, Miriam, Deborah, Mary Magdalene, and Mary the mother of Jesus as role models. Others have reclaimed the tradition of oral interpretation of Scriptures in Asian cultures to retell, dramatize, and perform stories of biblical women, thereby giving them voice and subjectivity. Reading the Bible through the lenses of sociopolitical analyses and cultural anthropology, Asian women theologians demonstrate the commonalities of struggle shared by biblical and Asian women. My participation in women's Bible studies and conversations about the impact of the Bible in Asian churches led to my sustained interest in biblical interpretation and later the publication of my book *Discovering the Bible in the Non-Biblical World*.[22]

After teaching for a few years as a junior faculty member in Hong Kong and introducing feminist theology to my students, I embarked on my doctoral studies at Harvard Divinity School in 1984. I had the privilege of studying with Mary Daly, Elisabeth Schüssler Fiorenza, and Sharon D. Welch. Although I later criticized Daly's work, I have great respect for her scholarship and admiration for her righteous anger against gender discrimination.[23] Schüssler Fiorenza had recently published *In Memory of Her* at the time, and I learned from her methodologies about constructing women's history and critical feminist hermeneutics.[24] Welch broadened my knowledge in critical theory, especially the work of Michel Foucault. I also took courses with Gordon Kaufman on theological methods and with Harvey Cox on liberation theology. During my doctoral studies at Harvard, I had the opportunity to read and reflect on Chinese culture and history, and the lectures and seminars at Harvard's Fairbank Center provided much intellectual stimulation. Living for the first time abroad and learning from Benjamin Schwartz, Paul A. Cohen, and Tu Weiming gave me new insights to look at China and Asia from a much broader perspective than before. Instead of taking many regular courses, I took several independent studies and spent my time going to lectures and brown-bag luncheon discussions at the university. My lifelong intellectual curiosity was nurtured at Harvard because I had followed a self-directed education, and I was able to pursue my own questions and interests.

The year before I went to the U.S., I met Letty Russell when she was invited to deliver a few lectures on feminist theology in South Korea. In the fall of 1984, Russell gathered a group of Asian and Asian American students and ministers who were studying and working in the Northeastern U.S. to meet in her house. Together we formed the group called Asian Women Theologians and held our first conference in 1985. As the group expanded to include a plethora of women from different nationalities and backgrounds, the name was changed several times. The current name is Pacific, Asian, and North American Asian Women in Theology and Ministry (PANAAWTM).[25] The gatherings of PAN-AAWTM make me keenly aware that Asian and Asian American women have very different life experiences, which affect our theological interests and outlooks. Asian women are concerned about their national history and want to connect with their Asian cultures and histories, which have been downplayed because of colonialism or their Western theological training. Asian American women are concerned about racism and their hyphenated identity in a white dominant society.[26] PANAAWTM provides an invaluable community of discourse to discuss feminist politics from a transpacific lens. Over the years, the group has published pioneering works and made significant contributions to the development of Asian and Asian American feminist scholarship in theology, religion, and leadership.[27]

The mid-1980s was an exciting period to study feminist theology in the U.S. because different racial and ethnic minority groups of women began to articulate their theology and ethics by taking into consideration the multiple oppressions of race, gender, and class. Katie Geneva Cannon, a pioneering womanist ethicist, received her doctoral degree in 1983 and began teaching in Boston. For several years, she gathered a small group of women of color who were students and church workers involved with different ministries to discuss our work and the issues we faced in both the church and the academy. Womanist scholars formed a Womanist Approaches to Religion and Society group at the American Academy of Religion (AAR) in 1985 and began publishing womanist works.[28] Hispanic and Latina women and Native women also began to develop their theologies and religious scholarship. Conversations with women from other racial and ethnic minority groups helped me look at American politics and women's oppression through the inflections of race and class.

POSTCOLONIAL FEMINIST THEOLOGY

My foray into postcolonial theory began in the 1990s, when intellectuals and theologians in Hong Kong began to talk about preparing for the imminent changes in the postcolonial period. Even though I had begun teaching in the

U.S. at the time, the return of Hong Kong was a significant moment in my personal life and in the history of the Chinese people. *Postcolonial* is a contentious term, and the meaning of the prefix "post" has been vigorously debated. Some find the prefix problematic, since it might suggest that the colonial situation is over, and we have entered a postcolonial period. They point out that the colonial legacy remains strong in many countries, while neocolonialism continues to dominate the world. But the prefix "post" denotes not only a temporal period or a political transition of power but also reading strategies, practices, and actions that challenge colonialism and its legacy. I have defined postcolonial imagination as "a desire, a determination, and a process of disengagement from the whole colonial syndrome, which takes many forms and guises."[29] Engaging the postcolonial means to participate in a community of discourse and in actions of resistance. This engagement can be traced to the anticolonial period and continues into the present. Postcolonial theory began initially with the study of literary texts and history by pioneers such as Edward Said, Gayatri Chakravorty Spivak, and Homi Bhabha and has since been applied to many different fields in the humanities and social sciences. Postcolonial theory has raised our consciousness in the politics and rhetoric of empire in the Bible and theological tradition, in Eurocentrism and colonialist assumptions, in hidden and submerged voices, and in the plurality and diversity within Christian traditions.

Postcolonial theory entered theological fields through biblical studies in the mid-1990s. R. S. Sugirtharajah writes, "What postcolonial biblical studies does is to focus on the whole issue of expansion, domination, and imperialism as central forces in defining both the biblical narratives and biblical interpretation."[30] The Hebrew people and early Christians lived under the shadows of Egyptian, Assyrian, Babylonian, Greek, and Roman empires. The Bible lends itself to postcolonial and intercultural studies because it deals with the themes of travel, space and spatial construction, movement, boundaries, borderland, border-crossing, crossroad, indigenized women and populations, ethnic formation, diasporic communities, displacement, transplantation, international power relations, and globalization processes.[31]

My first attempt to apply postcolonial theory to biblical studies was a reading of the Syrophoenician woman (Matt. 15:21–28; Mark 7:24–30) using insights provided by Spivak. In this piece published in 1995, I discussed the representation of a gentile woman in the Gospels, the intersection of anti-Judaism, sexism, and colonialism, and the politics of reconstructing women as subjects of history.[32] I also contributed a chapter questioning the preoccupation of the historical quest for Jesus in one of the early texts in postcolonial criticism, *The Postcolonial Bible*.[33] As more scholars began to show interest in postcolonial criticism, several of us organized a New Testament Studies and Postcolonial Studies Consultation at the Society of Biblical Literature in 2000. Some of the papers presented with additional contributions were published in an anthology exploring the intersections between postcolonial biblical interpretation and feminism, Marxism, poststructuralism, and racial and ethnic theories.[34] During this time, I was also interested in the use of postcolonial theory by scholars who studied different religious traditions. With Laura E. Donaldson, I coedited a pathfinding volume: *Postcolonialism, Feminism, and Religious Discourse,* published in 2002.[35]

Though I was interested in the use of postcolonial theory in the study of the Bible and religious traditions, I had little awareness of how to do postcolonial theology, since the field was uncharted. In 2003, I attended a transdisciplinary theological colloquium with the theme "Com/Promised Lands: The Colonial, the Postcolonial, and the Theological" at Drew University. There were only a few theologians as presenters because the discussion was so new in the field.[36] On the surface, the intersection between the postcolonial and the theological appears to be tenuous. After all, most postcolonial theorists harbor negative attitudes toward religion in general and Christianity in particular. For Edward Said, it was Christian Europe that constructed an inferior and negative image of the "East" for the sake of control and domination. As a humanist and a champion for secular criticism, Said insisted that critical consciousness can only flourish and criticism can only be conducted freely without the imposition of political and religious dogmas. Postcolonial theorists influenced by Derrida, such as Spivak, are allergic to anything that smacks of ontotheology.

But I have contended, then and now, that if Christianity has played such an important enabling role in colonialism and empire building, the study of the postcolonial will not be complete without engaging the theological. The theological also needs the critique and contribution of the postcolonial because the theological enterprise has been laden with imperial assumptions and motives ever since Christianity became the state religion of the Roman Empire. Postcolonial theology is not an exercise in nostalgia, of trying to recuperate a pristine Christianity that has not colluded with empire. As theologian Catherine Keller has reminded us, there is no "pre-colonial Christianity": "When [Christianity] opened its young mouth to speak, it spoke in the many tongues of empire— nations and languages colonized by Rome, and before that Greece, and before that Babylon, which has first dispersed the Jews into imperial space."[37] It is delusive to find a particular moment or an Archimedean point in the Christian tradition that was not enmeshed in the power dynamics of the time. Precisely because of the prolonged imbrication of Christianity with empire, postcolonial critique is not only necessary but also indispensable in the reconceptualization of the theological discipline and the articulation of an alternative politic.

Postcolonial theory remains attractive to me because it offers a critical lens to look at the world and inculcate a habit of thought that takes the colonial legacy seriously. As globalization has built on the colonial legacy and enables rapid movements of capital, labor, and resources, the former binary conceptualizations of the world, such as colonizer/colonized, First World/Third World, and "the West and the rest" are no longer adequate to describe the new global relations. Postcolonial theory emerged in the late 1970s and provided a new theoretical impetus to examine culture and economy different from the Marxist approach. With the phenomenal economic development in China, India, and other countries in the Asia Pacific, Asia increasingly occupies a key geopolitical position in the global political economy. The postcolonial approach illumines our current political and theological realities, and this book intends to demonstrate the ongoing insidiousness of empire, as exemplified in the Asia Pacific, and also within the U.S., context.

As I read more in postcolonial theory, I began to see the limitations of the liberationist paradigm, though I continue to appreciate its commitment to economic justice. One important critique of liberation theology is that it has been done primarily by male theologians and is very androcentric. The focus has been on the preferential option of the poor, without adequate gender analysis. I am glad to see that works by feminist liberation theologians and by second-generation liberation theologians have increased. Gustavo Gutiérrez argues that Jesus has come to bring political liberation, the liberation of human beings throughout history, the liberation from sin and communion with God. Other versions of Christ as the liberator can be seen in various Black theologies and feminist theologies. The image of Christ as the liberator dispels the myth of a gentle and meek Jesus often preached in the middle-class churches. But postcolonial and queer theory has led me to question this masculinist portrayal of the savior who intervenes in human history, because very often a concomitant critique of such a patriarchal and heterosexist image of Christ is missing.

In 2003–2004 when I collected and revised my essays to be published as *Postcolonial Imagination and Feminist Theology* (2005),[38] I recognized that I had been slowly doing postcolonial feminist theology all along. It is only in hindsight that I became aware that I have used postcolonial insights to interrogate some of the categories and assumptions of (white) feminist theology: women's experience, the gender of divinity, the question of whether a male savior can save women, and the relation between women and nature. While many white women insist that feminist theology begins with women's experience to contest androcentrism in traditional theology, they have often forgotten that they are not only victims of patriarchy but also imperial subjects who benefit from colonialism and its legacy. The intersection of gender and imperialism has not been theologized, even though many white women are now more conscious of their racial privilege than before. The attention given to inclusive language and the gender of divinity overlooks the fact that in other languages, masculine pronouns for God may not be a problem. In Chinese, for example, there is a separate pronoun for God, different from he and she. The question of whether a male savior can save women is an important one, but many cultures have both male and female saviors, and the emphasis of Jesus as male overlooks the fact that many cultures have come up with different expressions of the hybrid Christ: Christ as the Corn Mother in Native American culture, Christ as the feminine Shakti in India, and the Bi/Christ in queer cultures. Many Western feminist theologians argue that women are subordinate to men as nature is to culture. But in Asian traditions, nature is not subordinate but glorified in poetry, paintings, and other artifacts. I have argued that feminist theology cannot be defined by one culture but must be global and intercultural because "different cultures are not isolated but intertwined with one another as a result of colonialism, slavery, and cultural hegemony of the West."[39]

After the book was published, I was delighted to see the publication of a growing number of books on postcolonial theology and that some younger scholars and doctoral students are interested in the discourse. A highlight was meeting and conversing with Gayatri Chakravorty Spivak in 2007 at the "Planetary Loves: Postcoloniality, Gender, and Theology" colloquium at Drew University. Clad in a light blue sari, she engaged theologians and scholars in a spirited discussion on the development of her thought and its possible intersection with religion and theology.[40] When Donaldson and I coedited our book *Postcolonialism, Feminism, and Religious Discourse* in the early 2000s, we had a hard time recruiting contributors who engaged postcolonial theory in religious studies. Today it would be much easier to find potential contributors. There is a group called "Religion, Colonialism, and Postcolonialism" at the AAR. A cursory reading of the programs of the AAR in the past few years shows that scholars across different religious traditions have shown far more interest in colonial and postcolonial issues than before. Given that colonialism has shaped so much of modern experience and left an indelible impact in the study of religion, this critical engagement is welcome and long overdue.

ABOUT THIS VOLUME

Some might wonder if postcolonial theory is outdated because globalization and neoliberalism have exacerbated the neocolonial control of the world. Even Spivak has criticized postcolonial theory for focusing too much on colonial domination in the past, often using the history of South India as a model.[41] The old model, she notes, was basically "'Asia' plus the Sartrian 'Fanon,'" and it would not be sufficient to deal with the heterogeneity of imperialism on a different and much larger scale.[42] This might be true if we only concentrate on the works of Spivak, Bhabha, and Subaltern Studies in India. But if we cast the net wider, we will see that many scholars have discussed and contributed to postcolonial theory out of French, Belgian, Japanese, Chinese, and American colonial experiences. Continuing the work of the pioneers, scholars have brought postcolonial inquiry to bear on globalization, neoliberalism, science and technology, queer theory, cinema, and a whole range of other topics.[43]

In this book, I want to explore the connections between postcolonial politics and theology as I bring postcolonial theory to bear on the current critical issues faced by human beings and our planet. From within the theological discipline, postcolonial theory helps to illuminate the colonial imaginary[44] employed in theology and the collusion of theology with empires of different periods. Following Edward Said's advice to pay attention to the "worldliness" of the text,[45] postcolonial theology examines the sociopolitical context from which theology emerges and to which it responds. It discusses how theologians in different periods have colluded with, lent support to, or resisted and subverted empire.[46] The late postcolonial queer theologian Marcella Althaus-Reid uses the term "unveiling" to describe the process of exposing colonial and heteronormative underpinnings of traditional Christian theology.[47] In so doing, she issues a clarion call to us to unravel other imperial logics that have sustained theology and given it legitimacy.

From without, the theological has returned with a vengeance and many disciplines, such as philosophy, political science, literature, history, critical theory, and psychoanalysis, have felt the impact of its return. Creston Davis attributes this return to the collapse of Communism and the advent of capitalist nihilism, with the consumerist mentality infiltrating so much of modern life. Some have found religion an ally to discuss the deeper meaning of life and to find ways to resist individual will-to-power.[48] Scholars as diverse as Jacques Derrida, Jean-Luc Nancy, Julia Kristeva, Terry Eagleton, Slavoj Žižek, Gorgio Agamben, and Alain Badiou, among others, have engaged theological ideas to discuss justice, religion and politics, subjectivity, psychic life, religious moral imperative, and universalism. These discussions are timely and helpful to broaden the scope and subject matter of theology and to push its boundaries. Given this resurgence of the theological in critical theory, it is now more crucial than ever to examine how postcolonial theory continues to challenge some of these theoretical discourses.

This book presents my theological reflection on postcolonial politics understood in a broad sense, which goes beyond the usual juridical-institutional understanding. This is important because the emphasis on the juridical-institutional sense of politics usually focuses on male leadership and actors, while leaving out the voices and participation of women, subalterns, and other marginalized people because they do not have equal access to power. The discussion of postcolonial politics needs to take into consideration the ways race, class, gender, sexuality, culture, and religion intersect with political narratives, structures, institutions, and movements. The postcolonial turn in political theology enlarges our moral and political imagination by articulating the hopes and desires of the majority of the world's people, who have been impacted by colonialism and continue to struggle for freedom. The political horizons of this book are shaped by theorists who have reflected on colonialism from the underside: Aimé Cesaíre, Albert Memmi, Frantz Fanon, Edward Said, Gayatri Chakravorty Spivak, Homi Bhabha, Partha Chatterjee, Dipesh Chakrabarty, Arjun Appadurai, Rey Chow, Lisa Lowe, Chen Kuan-hsing, Stuart Hall, Achille Mbembe, Anibal Quijano, Walter Mignolo, and María Lugones.

This work also reflects my increasing engagement with practical theology, as I have been invited to speak to theological fieldwork educators, practical theologians, and homileticians since the early 2010s. The growing interest in postcolonial studies in practical theology reflects a collective consciousness of the limitations of ecclesial practices and ministry shaped by colonial Christianity.[49] For even though the Christian demographic has shifted to the Global South,

Christian practices, especially in mainline denominations, are still much shaped by European or Euro-American theological underpinnings and cultural experiences. If postcolonial theology is going to have a future, it must be embodied in new religious and social practices in our heterogeneous and richly textured social worlds, in which the local intersects with the global. These practices are counter-hegemonic, creative, and subversive, poised to produce new forms of beings and institutions in our church, community, and society.

This book is divided into three parts. Part 1, "Contesting Empire," argues for a political theology of postcoloniality that is decolonial and comparative, with a focus on the social and political realities of the majority world. It contests the ways "religion" has been conjured and studied to further colonial interests; explores the relation between race, sexuality, and empire; and elucidates Christianity's complex relations with the American Empire. Part 2, "Political Theologies from Asia Pacific," discusses the colonial backgrounds of the formation of "Asia Pacific," the long involvements of the U.S. in Asian politics, and the rise of China and changing geopolitical relations in the region. Using the case study of Asia Pacific, I want to show that the circumstances specific to this region and current developments can serve as a live example to shed light on how postcolonial theology can make an intervention in imperialist politics and theology in and beyond the Asia Pacific context. This part highlights the development of postcolonial theology from East Asia, the emergence of Asian and Asian American transnational feminist theology, and the difficulties of constructing postcolonial subjectivity in the intersection of the local, the national, and the global in the protests in Hong Kong. Part 3, "Practices," suggests how postcolonial theory can be brought to bear on teaching and religious practices in faith communities. While postcolonial theory has been introduced to the fields of biblical studies and theology for some time, it has also impacted practical theology, though this has been far less studied thus far. These chapters explore teaching global theology for the education of global leaders, preaching in intercultural contexts, religious solidarity and peacebuilding, and the need to reimagine Christian mission and planetary politics in the age of the Anthropocene.

This book argues that postcolonial theology functions as a training of the imagination and an attempt to construct a religious worldview that promotes justice, radical plurality, democratic practices, and planetary solidarity. In his much-quoted essay on globalization, anthropologist Arjun Appadurai speaks of the role of imagination as a positive force that encourages an emancipatory politics in the globalized world. By imagination, he is not so much concerned about the work of an individual genius or a dimension of aesthetics. Rather, he is interested in imagination that is popular and social, the faculty "through which collective patterns of dissent and new designs of social life emerge."[50] Spivak similarly invites us to consider the profoundly democratic possibilities of imagination and the critical roles that art, the humanities, and literary studies can play in cultivating profound feeling and engendering critical thinking that go beyond the logic of capital.[51] The study of theology through the wider lens of postcolonial theory will hopefully safeguard us from the tyranny of common sense and nurture habits of thought that challenge dominant religious imaginaries and imperialist social and political orders. In doing so, theology can contribute to the process of collectively imagining a different world in which justice and freedom prevail.

PART ONE
CONTESTING EMPIRE

Chapter 1

Toward a Political Theology of Postcoloniality

The relationship between religion and politics—whether in democracies or in so-called theocracies—has always been a necessary yet impossible relationship. Each encounter between the political and the religious has always ended up reconstituting each domain anew.

Achille Mbembe[1]

In October 2019, I participated in the De-provincializing Political Theology: Postcolonial and Comparative Approaches international conference at Ludwig Maximilian University of Munich, Germany.[2] The conference brought together some twenty scholars from religious studies, theology, history, politics, and law. This was the first time I took part in a conference on political theology billed as "postcolonial and comparative." The majority of the participants teach in Europe and the U.S., with a few racial and ethnic minorities among them, and two work in India and Colombia. The participants are scholars who study diverse religious traditions, and I was one of the few participants who specializes in Christian theology. I benefited from the papers presented and the questions raised by scholars from other disciplines and religious traditions. In one poignant moment, for example, we discussed what "politics" means in Islam. The conference prompted me to imagine what a political theology that accounts for the postcolonial condition and also religious plurality would look like.

Political theology has enjoyed a renaissance in recent times as books about the topic have been published and conferences on it have been held regularly, oftentimes drawing hundreds of people.[3] This phenomenon can be attributed to several factors. Since September 11, 2001, religion has been on the forefront in

discussions around the war on terrorism, peace and violence, and conflict resolution. There has been an attitudinal shift in both the secular state and, also, in
the public domain with respect to the enduring influences of religion, religious
actors, and religious communities. Scholars have discussed, animatedly, a post-
secular world and talked about the "permanence of the theologico-political."[4]
Interest in political theology has also been prompted by crises of liberal democracy in both the U.S. and Europe, as displayed by recent, and accelerating,
populist and right-wing nationalistic movements, which support white hegemony, anti-immigration, homophobia, and misogyny. Scholars and critics have
called attention to the dangers of fascism, totalitarianism, and tyranny in the
past and the present.[5] While democratic structures have been threatened, mass
protests and assemblies in public spaces have become central in the fight for
political change, economic equity, racial justice, and queer people's rights. The
most notable of these was the Occupy Movement, which spread to more than
900 cities in the world. In 2020, rallies to support Black Lives Matters were
seen in many parts of the world, not just on U.S. soil, where the movement was
founded. These recent events and protests call for serious theological reflections
on emerging political subjectivity and an imaginary that connects the local with
the global.

As more people become interested in the relationship between the political
and the theological, it is worthwhile to pay attention to a question posed by
Corey D. B. Walker. In his introduction to a collection of essays titled "Theology and Democratic Futures," Walker asks, "What is the fate of theology in
a post-theological moment?"[6] By "post-theological," he does not mean we are
"entering an age devoid of theology," because the strong influence of religious
fundamentalism in political and theoretical discourses persists.[7] Rather, Walker's term points to the fact that traditional theological discourse can no longer
hold the breadth and depth of what animates current intellectual discussions
on theology and politics emerging from many disciplines and quarters. The
return of theology to public discourse and to the North Atlantic academy means
that intellectuals, whose training may not be in theology, and whose interests
far exceed that of the "theology" proper, are seriously thinking about theology today. Their exploration, Walker says, overflows the categories, concepts,
languages, and frameworks of theology, thereby making them inadequate to
contemplate both the negation of traditional theological formulations and their
(re)emergence in new forms.[8]

This "post-theological" moment opens theology to interdisciplinary inquiries
and critical scrutiny that has gone beyond the traditional parameters of theology. As new questions are being broached, postcolonial theology contributes
to this moment by exposing colonial imaginaries embedded in theological systems and frameworks by showing theology's complex and ambivalent relations
to empires. Postcolonial criticism challenges Eurocentric biases in the conceptualization of political theology as a field of study, which has so far not taken
seriously political questions from the majority world. Instead of a Eurocentric

genealogy of political theology, I argue for transnational and multicultural origins and genealogies, using developments in Asia as an example. I then discuss the scope and contours of postcolonial politics, which goes beyond the usual juridical-institutional understanding of politics. In the final section of this chapter, I outline a postcolonial and comparative theology of postcoloniality.

WHITHER POLITICAL THEOLOGY?

In their introduction to the second edition of *Wiley Blackwell Companion to Political Theology* (2019), William T. Cavanaugh and Peter Manley Scott define political theology as an "analysis and criticism of political arrangements (including cultural-psychological, social, and economic aspects) from the perspective of differing interpretations of God's way with the world."[9] In this sense, political theology has existed since the beginning of Christianity. Jesus preached the Kingdom of God and contrasted life under God with life under Caesar. He died a condemned political prisoner under Roman imperial rule. Paul's relation to politics has been up for debate. On the one hand, he encouraged Jesus' followers to be subject to the authorities (Rom. 13:1), but on the other hand, he challenged the lordship of the emperor by calling Jesus "Lord."[10] In keeping with Paul, Augustine wrote his *City of God* when the Roman Empire was threatened, in which he contrasted the city of God with the earthly city. He defended Christianity against its critics and saw the history of the world as a contest between God and the devil. He refused to sacralize any human-made state (the City of the World) and argued that human society only finds completion in the realm of God.[11] In the medieval period, the relation between the church and the state became thorny as a result of power struggles between the papacy and secular rulers. During the Reformation, Martin Luther proposed his theory of "two kingdoms." These two kingdoms consisted of the spiritual regiment, concerned with the soul and the inner person, and the worldly regiment, concerned with the body and the world. After many years of war, the Treaty of Westphalia (1648) marked the end of "Christendom" by giving secular authorities the power to determine matters of religion in their own state. The authority of the church was further challenged during the Enlightenment, when philosophers attacked religion and pushed to separate religion from public affairs. Later, Max Weber would characterize modernity as the "disenchantment of the world."[12]

Many scholars trace the development of modern political theology to the book *Political Theology* published by German conservative jurist Carl Schmitt (1888–1985) in 1922.[13] This controversial figure penned his book during a time of political crisis after World War I. He saw the legitimacy of the Weimar Republic being undermined by atheism, capitalism, and political radicalism. He argued that these social and political currents denied a place for transcendence in modern society which had been provided for by religion. Concerned about the need for a stable social order, Schmitt proposed a particular account of sovereignty, which I will discuss below. From Schmitt, scholars have traced the development of political theology through Johann Baptist Metz, to Jürgen Moltmann, and Dorothee Sölle after World War II, before moving on to the present theological turn in political discourse on both sides of the North Atlantic.

Such a (white) genealogy of modern political theology traces its origin to Europe as it grappled with the political crises of the two world wars. This genealogy foregrounds the works of European and Euro-American theologians, placing their reflections on politics at the center of inquiry. Two introductory texts on political theology written from different viewpoints illustrate this bias. Elizabeth Philips' *Political Theology: A Guide for the Perplexed* (2012) is a text based on traditional theological approach.[14] The book offers a Eurocentric development of political theology, citing Schmitt, Augustine, Calvin, Yoder, and Hauerwas, before discussing topics such as the church and the political, the politics of Jesus, violence and peace, and liberalism and democracy. Although she includes the discussion of oppression, marginalization, and liberation, she does not discuss liberation theology adequately and mentions women theologians from the Global South only in passing. The audience she has in mind are primarily white students living in Western democratic countries.

In contrast to Philips, British political theorist Saul Newman offers an introductory text that we can call a "secular" political theology. His book *Political Theology: A Critical Introduction* (2019) follows the convention of beginning with Schmitt, before moving on to critical figures such as Bakunin, Stirner, Freud, Hobbes, Benjamin, Foucault, and Agamben.[15] Newman's various chapters explore sovereignty, psychology, economy, spirituality, and the politics of the profane. His book traces from Freudian psychoanalytic politics, through the reimagination of power by Foucault, all the way to power relations in the current form of capitalism. He does not assume any belief in God, nor does he dwell on theology, for he argues that "political theology is not so much a problem of religion in modern societies as a problem of *power*."[16] On the surface, Newman's secular approach is very different from Philips' book. However, though they cite different registers of thinkers, they both draw primarily from Western sources, especially canonical figures in their respective fields. The problematic that the two authors want to address arises from crises and tensions within liberal democracy.

If an introductory text by a single author is limited by the author's horizon, multi-authored companion volumes on political theology do not fare better. In the second edition of *Wiley Blackwell Companion to Political Theology*, Cavanaugh and Scott write that they have paid more attention to the growth of Christianity in the Global South.[17] This edition improves over the first by including a few more chapters on the Global South, with additional chapters on postcolonialism and grassroots social movements. Yet only seven out of forty-three chapters focus explicitly on issues and figures from outside the North Atlantic. While Schmitt, Barth, Bonhoeffer, Moltmann, Metz, Hauerwas, and Milbank each have their own chapter, political theologies from Asia and Africa are each given only one chapter, and Latin American liberation theologies are given two. The majority of the contributors are either Europeans or Euro-Americans. *The Cambridge Companion to Christian Political Theology* (2015) is even more problematic.[18] Out of fourteen chapters, only one chapter is on liberation theology and one other chapter covers postcolonial theology. The book lacks a global perspective, and the issues discussed do not touch on many political concerns from the majority world.

This Eurocentric bias in many books about political theology reveals the field is outdated and fails to catch up with the changing geopolitics of our time. Since the meteoric rise of China and its growing global political impact, Asia Pacific has become a strategic region poised to shape the future of the twenty-first century. The U.S. government has spoken about the "pivot" to Asia and Asia Pacific as a key military theater for the U.S. The Sino-American trade wars, the tech cold wars, and the rush to control space have rattled the world's economic and political orders in recent years. It was ironic to see Chinese President Xi Jinping defend globalization and world trade, while President Donald Trump resorted to protectionism and economic nationalism. In the midst of shifting global politics, there exists a time lag between political theology that continues to focus on the Atlantic and the world we live in today.

To combat Eurocentric biases, we have to reject the notion of a single, originating moment, or a singular tradition, of political theology. Instead, I propose a transnational and multicultural articulation of the origins and genealogies of political theology. Edward Said has taught us to read histories contrapuntally and to see histories as intertwined and overlapped.[19] Around the time when Schmitt was writing *Political Theology*, a different kind of political crisis emerged on the horizon in China. On May 4, 1919, students in Beijing took to the streets to protest the transfer, to Japan, of Germany's rights over China's Shandong peninsula at the Paris Peace Conference after World War I, even though China had entered the war on the side of the Allied powers. Germany had previously obtained the right to build a naval base in Qingdao in 1898 and occupied territories in Shandong to extend its military power in the Pacific. After the protests in Beijing, a mass movement swept through the country, denouncing Western imperialism and demanding democracy alongside radical cultural reforms.

The year 2019 marked the centenary of the May Fourth movement. As we look back over the past hundred years, we find that political theology can be traced to different genealogies. A largely white and male genealogy traces its modern origin to Schmitt and is concerned about religion and the state, secularism and the postsecular world, church and politics, and liberalism and democracy. The other genealogy deprovincializes the Eurocentric approach by placing political theology in the struggles against colonialism, neocolonialism, dictatorship, authoritarianism, militarized violence, and religious and ethnic strife in the majority world. In China, Schmitt's contemporary Wu Yaozong (1893–1979) advocated in the 1930s that only a social revolution would save China and transform the world. He urged other Christians to embrace a revolutionary

Christianity because, for him, Christianity should not only attend to people's spiritual lives, but should also care for their social condition. He wrote, "A true revival of the Church will come only when it has awakened to its social task and begins to tackle it fearlessly and sacrificially."[20] Chastising the exploitation of European capitalistic powers, Wu was increasingly attracted to socialism and saw China's only way out as via a social revolution.[21] His appeal to Marxist critique and his criticism of idealist Christianity anticipated liberation theology that came decades later.

After World War II, many countries in Africa and Asia regained their political independence. This transfer of power did not usher in peace and stability but often led to dictatorships, military coups, and concentrations of power among national elites. Amid Asian revolutions and transformations, Indian theologian M. M. Thomas wrote *Christian Participation in Nation-Building* (1960) and *The Christian Response to the Asian Revolution* (1966).[22] Similar to progressive Indian scholars at the time, Thomas challenged Western imperialism and argued that the gospel should not be equated with Western culture. The Asian revolution showed that the gospel transcends all cultures since God is at work in people's histories. His understanding of Jesus was anticolonial, for he contrasted the messianism of a conquering king with the crucified servant Christ. Jesus is seen as the model of new humanity, bringing renewal and fulfilment of all humanity.[23]

In the 1970s and 1980s, as will be discussed in chapter five, different political theologies were developed in Asia, including Korean *minjung* theology in response to Park Chung Hee's dictatorship. *Minjung* is the Korean word for "the masses" or "people." Korean theologians argued that Jesus identified with the *minjung* and not with the political elites or religious leaders of his time. In Taiwan, Homeland Theology was developed to address its increasing isolation after China was admitted to the United Nations. Taiwanese theologians argued that Taiwan belongs to the people of Taiwan and not to successive colonizers or the Chinese Nationalist government that came to the island after 1949. During the Marcos era, theologians in the Philippines developed Theology of Struggle to articulate Filipinos' demand for democracy, identity, and peoplehood. Interpreted through the suffering Filipinos, Christ was seen as a liberator who was in solidarity with the people's struggles.[24] In India, Dalit theology was developed to address the dehumanization of about 200 million people who were treated as societal outcasts and were previously labeled as "untouchables."[25]

As these examples have shown, the context for political theology in Asia is postcolonial and deimperial. This reality stands in sharp contrast to the postmodern and growing populist and nationalistic political climate of the North Atlantic. Political theologies in Africa, Latin America, the Middle East, and other parts of the world have their own beginnings, pioneers, and developments because of their diversity of histories and political struggles. Political theology does not have one beginning, but many diverse origins and multicultural genealogies. Theological reflections arising from anticolonial struggles and postcolonial realities must be included in the scope and historical memory of political theology. These reflections have a broad understanding of politics and address political situations very different from those defined by Western liberal democracy. As an interdisciplinary project, political theology can learn much from the insights of postcolonial studies, subaltern studies, critical race theory, and transnational and global studies. A contrapuntal and comparative reading of different political theologies enables us to grasp overlapping struggles in the past, decipher the dense politico-theological of the present, and envision a future for the survival of humans and the earth.

POSTCOLONIAL POLITICS

As the above discussion has shown, postcolonial politics cannot be separated from anticolonial and independence struggles because the colonial legacy and imperial administration continue. Beginning in 1492, the European "discovery" and conquest of the Americas ushered in a new global order that eventually led to the imperialistic powers' occupation of most of the global landmass by World War I. In his magisterial *Postcolonialism: An Historical Introduction*, Robert J. C. Young writes, "If colonial history, particularly in the nineteenth century, was the history of the imperial appropriation of the world, the history of the twentieth century has witnessed the peoples of the world taking power and control back for themselves. Postcolonial theory itself is a product of that dialectical process."[26] The bulk of his book is devoted to the history of national liberation movements from the continents of Latin America, Africa, and Asia and thinkers and politicians such as José Carlos Mariátegui, Fidel Castro, Aimé Cesaíre, Léopold Senghor, Frantz Fanon, Mao Zedong, and Mahatma Gandhi. Young argues that Marxism, as it has been appropriated in different contexts, has played a paramount role in anticolonial movements. It is noteworthy that Edward Said, who has often been hailed as the founder of postcolonial theory, has said that the artists and writers in the Bandung era in the 1950s were, in fact, the first-generation of postcolonial scholars. "The earliest study of the post-colonial" he writes, "were by such distinguished thinkers as Anwar Abdel-Malek, Samir Amin, and C. R. J. James; almost all were based on studies of domination and control made from the standpoint of either a completed political independence or an incomplete liberation project."[27]

However, several Marxist-leaning scholars have charged that postcolonial theory emerging from the late 1970s has been depoliticized, focusing more on text and discourse and less on history and political movements, and therefore pandered to the interests of the neoliberal academy.[28] Aijaz Ahmad accuses postcolonial studies of shifting the theoretical paradigm from Third World nationalism to postmodernism.[29] Benita Parry mounts a materialist critique and charges that although Said has tried to combine Western theory with historical and political struggle, the "linguistic turn" in postcolonial theory has dwelled on the instability of the subject and indeterminacy of meaning. As a result, she says, "the material and experiential worlds of colonialism addressed by historians, social scientists, and cultural materialists have receded from . . . purview."[30] Neil Lazarus argues that the consolidation of postcolonial studies in the academy in the 1980s and 1990s took place during a period of retreat by Third World insurgency and revolutionary anti-imperialism. He surmises that postcolonial studies can be seen as a complex intellectual response to this defeat. Lazarus criticizes postcolonial theorists, such as Homi Bhabha, for treating Marxism as obsolete and for dismissing the grand narratives of revolution or imperialism. Lazarus calls this "the postcolonial unconscious," adapting the title of Fredric Jameson's book *The Political Unconscious* published earlier.[31]

These charges are significant and demand serious attention. It is important to stress that the struggle on the cultural front had been an important part of anti-imperialist movements and should not be seen as apolitical. Cesaíre, Fanon, and Mao understood this well as they wrote poetry, literature, or plays, in addition to political writings during revolutionary struggles.[32] Young astutely observes: "Cultural politics is itself the product of the notion of cultural revolution first developed by Third World socialists and communists—by Connolly, Mariátegui, Mao, Fanon, Cabral—as a strategy for resisting the ideological infiltrations of colonialism and neocolonialism."[33] In *Orientalism*, Said demonstrates that cultural representation is not apolitical, since the West has created an allegedly inferior and backward "Orient" for the purpose of political control and domination.[34] Furthermore, Said's involvement in postcolonial theory cannot be separated from his longstanding scholarship and activism on behalf of Palestinian people. Bhabha's work cannot be said to be apolitical, though he does not follow Marxist theory or want to reduce complex social and political problems to class antagonism. He traces the postcolonial project to Third World struggles and argues against a simple, binary construction of the colonized and colonizers, the subjugated and the dominant:

> Postcolonial perspectives emerge from the colonial testimony of Third World countries and the discourses of "minorities" within the geopolitical divisions of East and West, North and South. They intervene in those ideological discourses of modernity that attempt to give a hegemonic "normality" to the uneven development and the differential, often disadvantaged, histories of nations, races, communities, peoples. . . . As a mode of analysis, it attempts to revise those nationalist or "nativist" pedagogies that set up the relation of Third World and First World in a binary structure of opposition. The postcolonial perspective resists the attempt at holistic forms of social explanation. It forces a recognition of the more complex cultural and political boundaries that exist on the cusp of these often opposed political spheres.[35]

Bhabha's work provides the language of ambivalence, mimicry, and hybridity to describe colonial agency and colonial culture.[36] These concepts have spawned numerous discussions in many fields, including religious studies. His depiction of colonial agency and subjectivity as ambiguous, hybrid, and heterogeneous is important because in any colonial situation, there is both the possibility to resist and also the temptation to collaborate with the colonial regime. While the Marxists want to speak of the class consciousness of the proletariat, their analysis has limited purchase in traditional agrarian societies, in which a sizeable proletariat did not exist, as members of the Subaltern Studies collective have pointed out.[37]

Furthermore, postcolonialism and Marxism are not always on antagonistic terms. In *Orientalism*, Said draws not only from Michel Foucault's concepts of discourse and power/ knowledge, but also from Marxist philosopher Antonio Gramsci's notion of hegemony to challenge colonialism and literature for dehumanizing and denying the rights of colonized people. Although Said keeps a distance from Gramsci's discussion of class and class struggle, the concept of hegemony refers to ways that the state and the bourgeoisie use media, universities, and cultural institutions to maintain power. The idea of a counterhegemonic struggle has broad appeal in social and political movements. Gayatri Chakravorty Spivak is a feminist Marxist deconstructivist and wants to push each of these theories to the limits.[38] She was influenced by Marxism long before she encountered Derrida's work.[39] Her prolific writings include the discussion of theory of value in Marx and a critique of "the Asiatic mode of production" and the notion of the "value-form" in Marx's thought.[40] But in the Western academy, her scholarship has been selectively appropriated, with more attention being paid to her literary criticism in the "linguistic turn" in the humanities than to her engagement with Marxism. Her combination of Marxism, social theories, and cultural politics is not new, since Western Marxists have paid much attention to the Frankfurt School and the British cultural materialists.[41] A rejoinder between postcolonial and Marxist thinkers would further explore the lack of a substantial theory of politics in Marxism, which has opened it to appropriation by authoritarian governments.

Criticism of postcolonial studies' alleged depoliticization emerging in the 1990s focused on literary study because postcolonial criticism first took root in English and Commonwealth literature departments. But postcolonial criticism has since made an impact in other fields in the humanities and in social sciences. Olivia U. Rutazibwa and Robbie Shilliam, coeditors of the *Routledge Handbook of Postcolonial Politics*, have noted that engagement with postcolonial critique among students of politics has grown significantly in recent years. They use "postcolonial" as "a heuristic device that sensitivises the thinker to the multiple, contending and overlapping legacies of colonial rule and imperial administration that inform contemporary global politics."[42] Routledge also produces a Postcolonial Politics book series that has published fourteen titles. The aim of the series is to "help us read culture politically, read 'difference' concretely, and to problematise our ideas of the modern, the rational and the scientific by working at the margins of a knowledge system that is still logocentric and Eurocentric."[43]

Scholars interested in postcolonial politics look at Western liberal political thought with suspicion because even as human rights, equality, democracy, and representative government were seen as important for citizens of the empire, they were consistently denied to colonial subjects. This caution is important because when Western political theologians discuss state, politics, and power, they often draw from the liberal political tradition developed since the Enlightenment. They are concerned about individual rights, the social contract, the rule of law, equality and justice, democracy, representative government, and the balance of power. A postcolonial turn in political theology needs to challenge the hypocrisy of liberal political theory, because Western modernity could not be separated from the colonial project. Many Western political theologians have conveniently ignored this connection and their work is therefore one-sided and incomplete.

Partha Chatterjee, an Indian political scientist and anthropologist who is affiliated with Subaltern Studies, offers an insightful critique of Western political theory. He shows how Western thinkers attempted to rationalize their lofty Enlightenment ideals of freedom and equality with the dark realities of colonialism. He argues that when Europeans conquered Asian countries in the second half of the eighteenth century, the existing political institutions in these kingdoms posed thorny questions for the colonizers. In India, for example, the question arose as to whether the colonized peoples should be ruled by British principles or as the Indian situation demanded. Chatterjee notes that philosophers such as Jeremy Bentham developed new ideas to justify colonial rule. First, there was the norm of deviation, which took the English society as both the norm and the measure of all other societies. For example, Orientalist despotism found in many countries was considered feudalistic and backward. Since the structure and government in these countries were inferior, they could be brought closer to the norm through colonial rule and tutelage over time. Chatterjee writes, "The norm-deviation structure has provided, from the nineteenth century to the present day, an enduring framework for addressing policy questions of improvement, progress, modernization, and development."[44]

Second, there was the principle of colonial exception, which justified why universally valid norms did not apply to the colonies. Bentham saw the colonies as vastly different from Europe not only in terms of climate and geography, but also in terms of manners, customs, and religion. Therefore, while democracy, freedom of speech, and the secular state might be universally desirable, they could be suspended in countries where prevailing practices deviated from the norm. This norm-exception structure affected colonial rule and policy, while also shaping how Christian missionaries encountered diverse cultures and customs. For example, when missionaries faced polygamy in Asia and Africa in the nineteenth century, heated debates broke out whether such a practice should be allowed to continue. Some missionaries saw polygamy as deviant from the Christian norm of monogamy and argued for its abolition. Others argued that since polygamy was widely practiced and a long-held tradition, it would be too difficult for missionaries to demand change without alienating the local populace. Therefore, these missionaries argued that an exception had to be made to accommodate indigenous practices.[45]

After the former colonies became independent, Western forms of liberal democracy did not take root in many postcolonial nations. Because of their sense of superiority around their political systems, many Westerners assume that non-Western peoples are not ready for self-governance. Others claim that there are deficits in non-Western cultures, which hinder the development of democratic ideas and rule. They argue that democracy has been developed in the West because of the influences of Christian culture. Western Christianity understands human beings to be sinners with a propensity for egotism and self-aggrandizement. Therefore, the mechanism of checks and balances developed in democratic structures to limit the use of power is necessary. Chatterjee cautions us not to take liberal democratic theory as the norm or presume deviation from it as "the sign of philosophical immaturity and cultural backwardness."[46] It is important to pay attention to what is happening on the ground to investigate how postcolonial political and legal structures have taken shape since the colonial period. Chatterjee notes that in many colonies, civic social institutions and representative politics were restricted to a small section of the colonized population. After independence, the conservative regimes in Africa left the traditional sphere of customary law largely intact. In India, although the new republic was founded on liberal democratic principles, there was a split "between a narrow domain of civil society where citizens related to the state through the mutual recognition of legally enforceable rights and a wider domain of political society where governmental agencies deal not with citizens but with populations to deliver specific benefits or services through a process of political negotiation."[47] Chatterjee gives the example of squatters in India, who occupy land illegally while also enjoying certain governmental services and welfare. Chatterjee's study of postcolonial democracy challenges political theologians not to construct simple binaries between Western liberal thought and "Asian values" or "Islamic principles." Instead, we should look at how the legacy of colonial government and administration has been adapted, modified, negotiated, or resisted in particular postcolonial contexts.

Scholars interested in postcolonial politics must pay attention to colonial differences and the diverse experiences of different peoples and nations under colonialism and imperialism. Social scientists and philosophers from Latin America and those in diaspora have developed a rich body of literature on decolonial theory, written in Spanish and Portuguese. In opposition to postcolonial studies, decolonial theorists have challenged the dominance of the study of colonization and decolonization processes in Asia, Africa, the Middle East, and the Caribbean during the nineteenth and twentieth century. They argue that the modern colonial project started much earlier, with the conquest of the Americas from the sixteenth century onward. Building on Immanuel Wallerstein's "world-systems analysis," decolonial theorists argue that the conquest of the Americas enabled the formation of the modern world system through the spread of the capitalist world-economy.[48] Peruvian sociologist Anibal Quijano writes that the conquest of Latin America "began the constitution of a new world order, culminating, five hundred years later, in a global power covering the whole planet."[49] He introduced the term "coloniality" to underscore the hidden side of modernity while arguing that modernity in Europe is so imbricated in colonial structures that the two cannot be separated, hence modernity/coloniality. Coloniality of power refers to the complex processes of European control, the expansion of labor and capital, the construction of racial differences and enslavement of African people, and the establishment of one global cultural order revolving around European or Western hegemony.[50] In the late 1950s, scholars and politicians in Latin America used dependence theory to explain how resources from poorer countries have been channeled to richer countries via integration of those poorer states into the world system. Poverty, environmental disaster, governmental corruption, political instability, and war and violence have forced many to leave their countries to become migrants, refugees, or asylum seekers.

Decolonial theorists also pay attention to the plight of indigenous peoples of the Americas, and elsewhere, in their long struggles for sovereignty and recognition in legal and political systems. In settler colonialism such as in the Americas, indigenous peoples and tribes continue to fight for their tribal lands, sacred sites, civil rights, and cultural and economic survival. The knowledge systems and worldviews of indigenous peoples and marginalized groups are often treated as inferior and subordinate to the form of colonial rationality reinforced by European hegemony. Decolonial theorist Walter D. Mignolo has developed the concept of "border thinking," first used by Gloria Anzaldúa, by arguing that rich traditions of theory and knowledge exist at the borders of the colonial matrix of power.[51] Mignolo and others have argued for decolonization of knowledge, which involves delinking our thinking from the rhetoric of modernity and the logic of coloniality. This decolonial epistemic shift involves paying attention to the sources and geopolitical locations of knowledge, delinking from colonial structures of knowledge, and learning from modes of knowledge that have been denied or suppressed.[52] The decolonial theorists want to recover and re-articulate the knowledge of the subalternized groups, which emerge from alternative forms of justice and ways of living.

While postcolonial and decolonial theorists emerged from different contexts and have diverse dispositions and approaches, they can enter into critical dialogue to understand colonial difference and global coloniality in more comprehensive ways. As Gurminder K. Bhambra has said, both postcolonial and decolonial thought "take the historical processes of dispossession and colonialism as fundamental to the shaping of the world and to the shaping of the possibilities of knowing the world. The very creation of what we understand the global to be . . . are created in the context of dispossession and appropriation."[53] I agree with Bhambra that we need to connect subversive knowledge, developed in different geopolitical locations, in order to understand the present global politics and to build coalitions of resistance.

In this book, postcolonial politics is understood broadly and not limited to the discussion of the state, sovereignty, government, and political economy, etc. I pay attention to how race, gender, and sexuality is reconfigured through the colonial encounter, because colonization changed social patterns and disrupted gender relations. My approach has been developed in conversation with decolonial thought. As a Latina, María Lugones has extended Quijano's theory to develop the concept of coloniality of gender. She argues that Quijano has not contested gender constructions and heterosexism imposed by modernity/coloniality. This imposition sought to erase diverse conceptualizations of gender, sex, and sexuality that existed before the European modern/colonial gender system. It especially erased the voices and agencies of colonized women from social life and knowledge production.[54] Spivak has also written about the relation between reproductive heteronormativity and nationalism and government control. She discusses the role of mothering and the importance of mother tongue in cultivating belonging to a culture and a people. According to Spivak, women hold the future of the nation since they reproduce future citizens. This is why control of women's sexuality is related to nation building.[55] Therefore, we must adopt an intersectional approach to analyze the multidimensional facets of postcolonial politics.

The *Routledge Handbook of Postcolonial Politics* uses a transnational and transregional approach because the local and the global intersect both in colonialism and neocolonialism. It includes many topics such as indigenous knowledge, sociology of the tribe, struggle over land, coloniality of gender, racial and ethnic politics, queer resistance, migration control, statelessness, human security, postcolonial diplomacy, global environmental crisis, and international relations. In this book, I also conceptualize postcolonial politics broadly and will discuss religion as it intersects with race, gender, sexuality, anticolonial movements, social protests, educational practices, peacebuilding, and the fight for climate justice.

A POSTCOLONIAL AND COMPARATIVE POLITICAL THEOLOGY

Even though colonialism and globalization have brought different religious traditions into close proximity with one another, most books on political theology focus on Christianity alone and seldom include other traditions. Michael Jon Kessler's *Political Theology for a Plural Age* is an exception because it includes the Abrahamic faiths of Judaism, Islam, and Christianity.[56] Kessler explains that we live in a highly pluralistic world with contrasting political and moral values, competing ideologies, and different political formations and legitimations. In order to find solutions to global challenges humanity faces in the twenty-first century, he says, we have to engage in dialogue to better understand the comparative religio-ethical dimension of political phenomena and undertaking.[57] To understand political theology in this way, he argues, is to cast it as a comparative exercise that involves not just reflection and clarification of one's own views but also the encounters with others who are citizens of other political orders, and with those who hold different normative viewpoints. For him, the goal of comparative political theology is:

> identifying particular similarities and differences in normative ideas and practices across plural political traditions in order to advance understanding of existing political realities and possibilities, to sharpen and expand our own positions vis-à-vis other positions, and to thereby deepen understanding in a way that improves upon the outcomes of political interactions between diverse individuals and groups.[58]

While I affirm Kessler's recognition of the need to dialogue with and learn from others, I argue that a postcolonial turn for political theology must go beyond the liberal recognition of diversity and religious pluralism, precisely because that recognition does not pay sufficient attention to power asymmetry and cultural hegemony rooted in colonialism. A comparative approach that goes beyond dialogue to acknowledge this asymmetry is needed because religious difference plays a critical role in colonialism, postcolonial nation building, and globalization. A postcolonial and comparative political theology that recognizes unequal power dynamics opens Christian political theology to wisdom from other traditions and learns from complex interactions between religion and politics in diverse colonial and postcolonial situations.

Since a comparative approach to political theology is quite new, we can learn from those who have worked in comparative theology for some time. The work of John Thatamanil is especially important because he has challenged the ways Asian "religions" have been studied under colonial influences. Like others before him, Thatamanil argues that "religion" has been constructed as a universal concept imposed by the West, based on the understanding of Christianity, onto other cultures and traditions.[59] He points out that most of the traditions that have been labeled "Hinduism," "Buddhism," "Confucianism," and "Sikhism" have "no conceptual analogue to 'religion' prior to modernity."[60] The notions of "religion" and "religions" have been constructed and institutionalized for particular purposes at particular times. The global discourse of world religions, he says, "emerges . . . precisely at the moment when Western colonialism and globalization brought traditions into ever greater proximity."[61] On Thatamanil's account, different "religions" are seen as self-enclosed religious systems distinct from one another, which can be nicely fitted into the different boxes of "world religions." In fact, religious traditions have existed alongside each other and interacted in numerous ways. Thatamanil argues that religious identity is not pure or singular, but "hybrid and polyphonic."[62] He further notes that there is a power differential in the study of religion because Asian religious traditions are mined for data for Western theory, while they are not allowed to furnish conceptual resources for theoretical work, such as in philosophy of religion or theology. He writes, "Asian religious traditions are to be thought *about*. They are not what we think *with*."[63] He points out that Christian theology has hitherto remained quite insular and oblivious to claims of other religious traditions, except in the subfields of theology of religions and the newer comparative theology. Comparative theologians are self-conscious of being rooted in the Christian tradition and yet open to the wisdom of other traditions. Comparative theology is interreligious and dialogical; in the words of Francis Clooney, it is "a theology deeply changed by its attention to multiple religious and theological traditions; it is a theology that occurs truly only *after* comparison."[64]

A postcolonial comparative political theology can use insights from other traditions to think *with* some of the categories and ideas that are important in the field. I will illustrate this by discussing the debate on secularism, Carl Schmitt's notion of sovereignty, and Foucault's concept of governmentality.

Secularism is an important topic in postcolonial politics because Western liberalism has assumed that the separation between the religious and the secular is important for the development of modern democracy. As Peter van der Veer has noted, "notions of progress, liberty, tolerance, democracy, civil society, and the public sphere converge in an all-embracing notion of secularity."[65] This leads to the view that the politicization of religion, whether it is in the Islamic states or in Christian fundamentalism, is against reason and liberty. People respond to the rise of so-called political Islam, the fatwa against Salman Rushdie, the terrorist attacks of September 11, 2001, in the U.S., and subsequent attacks in Europe with scorn and condemnation. The distinction between religious/secular has impacted political discourse about immigration in the U.S. and Europe, and, for some, strong religious influences in the immigrant populations are symptomatic of the "backwardness" of these communities. Thus, secularism deserves to be a serious topic of scrutiny in postcolonial critique.

Postcolonial critics and their allies have different positions on secularism. Edward Said was a staunch supporter of secularism and has cast a long shadow in the field. He has criticized both the ideology of Zionism,[66] the politics of the Islamic countries, as well as the Palestinian Liberation Organization. From his vantage point as a Palestinian American, religion has caused too much bloodshed and innumerable massacres.[67] Spivak is also a secularist and is equally suspicious of the so-called great religions of the world. She writes, "the history of their greatness is too deeply imbricated in the narrative of the ebb and flow of power."[68] But anthropologist Talal Asad has argued that diverse cultures and societies have understood "the secular" differently by pushing back against Western liberal ideology of secularism. Asad uses a multi-pronged approach to study "the secular," investigating its relation not only to religion but also to modernity, democracy, nation-state, and civilization. Using Foucault's genealogical method, Asad shows that historical and political factors have caused shifting understandings of secularism in the modern West and Middle East. The production of "secularism" as a Western political project developed at a certain period, so secularism's supposed connection to rationality or modernity should neither be taken for granted nor universalized for all societies.[69] As ideas and frameworks of governance have their own contexts, a Western model cannot be taken as normative for other societies.

The discussion of religious/secular can benefit from thinking *with* the cultural and religious traditions in China, especially with regard to the Confucian tradition. Wilfred Cantwell Smith observes that the named "religions," such as "Buddhism" (1801), "Hindooism" (1829), "Taouism" (1839), and "Confucianism" (1862), were formulated no earlier than the nineteenth century.[70] But Westerners have been fascinated with Confucius and his teaching for some time. Enlightenment philosophers, such as Voltaire, Rousseau, Montesquieu, Comte, Leibniz, and so forth, mentioned Confucius in their emerging social, political, and theological criticisms against the old political order and the church. Confucius would symbolize different things for these thinkers, reflecting European debates about self, society, and the sacred during the inception of the nation-state. As Lionel Jensen says, in the late eighteenth century, during a time of "conflict between the *anciens* and the *modernes*, the image of the Chinese ancient helped shape the self-image of the [Western] modern."[71] It was later, in the nineteenth century, when the comparative study of religion was instituted at Oxford as a new field, during the heyday of British colonialism, that Max Müller and his colleague James Legge constructed "Confucianism" as a world religion among other religions like Buddhism, Islam, Hinduism, etc.[72]

Even though the Confucian tradition has had pervasive influences in Chinese culture, it was not construed as a religion, but more as moral philosophy. The Chinese did not have an equivalent of the modern concept of "religion" and followed the Japanese way of translating the term "religion" as *zongjiao*, which originally meant the teachings of a particular sect.[73] In the early twentieth century, when the last imperial dynasty was overthrown, and the republic was formed, some Chinese intellectuals proposed having a national religion to strengthen the national and cultural identity of China on the world stage. The scholar Kang Youwei proposed having the Confucian tradition as a state religion. In his encounters with the West, Kang noted that Western countries had Christianity as the foundation of their civilization and argued that the Confucian tradition could be a force in the reform and modernization of China.[74] His attempt was unsuccessful and was considered reactionary by other radical reformers. The conversation about whether Confucianism is a religion has not died in China; instead, it has changed with the vicissitudes of Chinese politics and the government's attitudes about religion. In the late 1970s, a prominent scholar Ren Jiyu suggested that Confucianism should be considered a religion, like Buddhism and Daoism, and that the religious components of Confucianism have been harmful to the long history of China. But in the 2000s, with liberalization, some scholars have argued for a more positive view of Confucianism as a religion in order to criticize and contest the traditional Marxist treatment of religion.[75]

Thinking *with* the Confucian tradition shows that the religious/secular controversy has been tied to a more institutionalized understanding of religion (membership, priesthood, structure, and organization). Chinese religious life is more diffuse than in some other religious contexts since religious activities are performed in the family and other settings. Thus, the boundary of the religious/ secular, or sacred/profane, is not so clear-cut and defined. The above discussion also shows that both in the West and in China, the debate on religious/secular changed over time depending on social, political, and cultural factors. While there has been pressure to conform to Western notions of modernity, as defined by secularism and the separation between the church and state, other constructions of religious/secular suggest other ways of constructing global modernities that are not confined to one, single model.

Another concept that is key to political theology is sovereignty. Carl Schmitt, who penned *Political Theology*, famously wrote, "Sovereign is he who decides on the exception."[76] Exception, he argued, is that moment when the sovereign can suspend the juridical order in a state of emergency. The sovereign can decide who is included and excluded in the juridical order. Those who are included in the body politic are citizens with full rights; those who are excluded are nonmembers who have no rights. He argues that the political is based on the distinction between friend and enemy—that is, who is in the body and who is out of the body.[77] His understanding of the political and sovereignty is very different from liberal thought. Classical liberalism assumes the autonomy of self-sufficient individuals and conflicts as faulty social arrangements that need to be resolved to bring about prosperity and peace. Schmitt believes in the primacy of conflict, and that the most basic instinct of human beings as political persons is to differentiate between friend and adversary. Classical liberalism regards sovereignty as given to individuals who can build legitimate political institutions by themselves. Schmitt treats sovereignty as ushered in by an arbitrary self-founding act by a leader or a nation.[78]

Schmitt has said, "All significant concepts of the modern theory of the state are secularized theological concepts not only because of their historical development—in which they are transferred from theology to the theory of the state, whereby, for example, the omnipotent God became the omnipotent lawgiver— but also because of their systematic structure."[79] He sees the parallel between the absolute authority of the sovereign and the absolute authority of God. The sovereign has the power to decide the exception because he stands outside of the law, just as the transcendent God is outside the universe but can intervene and suspend the natural order (what is called a miracle). The state stands above the law and the law is not unbreakable, just as God can decide to transgress the natural order. Schmitt's conception of the state and sovereignty is also related to his understanding of human nature. Liberalism has a more positive outlook of human nature and believes in individual sovereignty and limiting the power of the state. Schmitt, however, is more pessimistic and sees the corruption of humans and their capacity for evil. Thus, on his account, strong governance is necessary to bring out the better nature of humans. Instead of seeing society as made up of autonomous individuals with semi-autonomous spheres—such as the economy, culture, and religion—Schmitt emphasizes the priority of society as a common whole (his ideal is medieval Catholicism). The state is to protect

the interests of the whole. Therefore, self-preservation and protection from enemies are crucial tasks of the state. Schmitt supported the Weimer Republic and
thought a strong state for Germany was important coming out of World War I.
His collaboration with the Nazis was severely criticized.

Schmitt's decisionist account of a sovereign, analogous to a transcendent
God who stands outside the universe, can hardly find a parallel in traditions such
as Buddhism and Daoism, which do not presume such a transcendent being. A
more productive comparison to think *with* would be Islam, a member of the
Abrahamic tradition. Shāh Muḥammad Ismāʿīl (1779–1831), a South Asian
Muslim reformer in the early nineteenth century, offers a Muslim political theology with a notion of sovereignty very different from Schmitt's. Ismāʿīl wrote
a Persian text *Manṣab-i Imāmat* (Station of Leadership) during a time of crisis
of sovereignty, when South India transitioned gradually from Mughal to British
rule. According to SherAli Tareen, this text shows "a vision of Muslim political
thought and understanding of sovereignty that exceeds and subverts the modern
privileging of a territorial conception of the nation-state as the centerpiece of
politics."[80] For Ismāʿīl, sovereign power has less to do with defending physical
borders and more to do with the maintenance of public markers of Muslim
identity, especially in the public performance of everyday religious life.

Ismāʿīl offers a theory or framework of an ideal form of political orders and
leaders. He contrasts two different forms of politics: salvational politics and
imperial politics. Salvational politics is based on the principle of abundant love
and its goal is to strive for moral reform and the elevation of salvational prospects for a community. Imperial politics is for the personal gains and desires
of the ruler and neglects the responsibilities of shepherding the moral lives of
one's subjects. Ismāʿīl, in contrast to Schmitt, does not see imperial sovereignty
as a mirror of divine sovereignty. The ideal ruler, for Ismāʿīl, is one who fears
God, respects the boundaries of sharīʿa, and reigns in his egoistic desires. It is
the responsibility of the ruler to lead his people to submit to divine law and
to follow the prophets' teachings. Ismāʿīl attacks the aristocratic practices and
extravagances of the Mughal elite as well as popular superstitions, such as the
veneration of the saints. Similar to Schmitt, Ismāʿīl sees the human propensity
to deviate from the path of the prophets and the demands of the law. Therefore,
Ismāʿīl's political theology emphasizes the integration of political power and
dominance with religious piety and salvation. He advocates that political leaders
should model everyday performance of religious life in a way that preserves the
sovereignty of divine law.[81] Schmitt distinguishes between friend and enemy.
For Ismāʿīl, the ruler could become the enemy when he becomes arrogant and
immersed in earthly pursuits, thereby showing brazen contempt for divine sovereignty. In this situation, rebellion against the king to remove him is called for.
Ismāʿīl does not think the monarch has absolute power and offers an understanding of sovereignty based less on juridical power than on piety and faith
displayed by the ruler and his ability to maintain public markers of Muslim
religious identity and life.

The third concept of political theology I want to explore briefly from a comparative perspective is governmentality. Michel Foucault uses "governmentality" to refer to the act of government and the techniques of power used to manage populations and control the conduct of people. Instead of focusing on centralized sovereign rule, as Schmitt did, Foucault is more interested in the "diffuse and decentered techniques of governance,"[82] such as schooling, policing, and other measures adapted to preserve or control the body politic. Foucault suggests that the Christian pastorate formed the basis of modern governmentality.[83] As God takes care of his flock, the pastor, as their shepherd, has the responsibility to care for and watch over the lives of members of the congregation. Foucault's historical study and his genealogical method have yielded astute analyses of modern statecraft and details about the exercise of power, but he has been criticized as Eurocentric and silent on colonialism. Critics challenge whether his analyses of Western governmental reason and techniques of power are equally applicable to a colonial context. As we have seen above, Chatterjee has pointed out that democracy, though valued in Europe, was not practiced in colonial India. The adaptation of Western mechanisms of governance in the colonies was not easy and was often met with suspicion and resistance. Peter Pels observes that there were complex negotiations and struggles between colonial and Western frameworks, as well as selective adoption, which gave rise to "alternative governmentalities."[84]

The issue Foucault raises of the relationship between religion and governmentality in a Eurocentric framework—the model of a pastor overseeing a congregation—can be studied comparatively outside the Western context. Patrice Ladwig, for example, has studied how the monks and monasteries in Theravāda Buddhism have played certain roles in establishing religious and monastic governmentality in Southeast Asia.[85] He argues that the boundary between religious and secular is much more porous and permeable in Laos or Thailand. For instance, monasticism is much more widespread in Southeast Asia than in the Christian West, and boys and men can be ordained temporarily, staying a short time in the monasteries. The Buddhist monk once served as "peasant intellectual" and taught children reading and writing before the arrival of the state school system. Temples were the only places where education was offered before the colonial era. The French built the colonial school system by extending the networks of Buddhist monasteries. Furthermore, the monasteries continue to play important roles in the community for social and political cohesion. Recognizing the crucial roles Buddhism plays in Laos and Cambodia, the colonial government patronized Buddhism through helping to build temples and monasteries, print books, and provide higher education for monks. At the same time, it regulated religious organizations, including the recruitment of leaders, the duties of monks and novices, the travel of monks, and the construction and renovation of religious buildings.[86] The French also adapted Buddhist state rituals in Laos, which were formerly used to symbolize the nobility's alliance to the Laotian kings, to the new context of the king and his vassals pledging loyalty to the French in a form of "ritual government."[87] Whereas in the Western context, Foucault argues that the government has assumed the pastoral functions that the church used to perform, in the colonial context, the French worked through existing religious institutions and rituals to bolster its legitimacy and governmentality. Thus, Ladwig concludes: "in Laos and Cambodia Buddhism was crucial for establishing an 'alternative governmentality' beyond the religious-secular divide."[88]

To conclude, a political theology of postcoloniality is an interdisciplinary project that pays attention to political and social theories emerging out of anticolonial protests, nation formation after political independence, and social movements against the exploitations of economic globalization and neocolonialism. It challenges Western political theorists and theologians when they overlook the close connections between modernity and coloniality and fail to acknowledge the darker side of modernity. Modern Western political ideas did not emerge in a vacuum but were developed in societies whose political economy and social institutions benefitted from colonialism. Postcolonial politics *is* global politics because colonial legacy and imperialistic administration continue to shape our world today, from responses to the COVID-19 pandemic, to the worldwide refugee crisis, to climate change. A political theology of postcoloniality needs to be transnational and interreligious, committed to thinking *with* people of other religious traditions to build solidarity and alliances across boundaries for our common future. Given the resurgent interest in the connection between religion and politics across disciplines, it is vital for postcoloniality to pose this critique of the continued centering of Western modernity in *both* politics and the study of religion and theology. Even postmodern theories and discourse reflect this preoccupation of Western modernity. By reading Western modernity not as a teleological promise and by challenging the edifice of modern theology that justifies empire, the postcolonial turn in political theology would open up spaces for incipient theology and the emerging public.

Chapter 2

Empire and the Study of Religion

By retaining religion as a key term, while paying attention to the imperial, colonial, and indigenous mediations in the production of knowledge about religion and religions, we will gain insight into the expanding but unstable empire of religion.

David Chidester[1]

As the British Empire expanded to cover vast areas of the earth, Max Müller (1823–1900), a professor of comparative philology at Oxford, was busy directing the publication of the fifty-volume *Sacred Books of the East* (1879–1910). Widely regarded as the leading European Sanskrit scholar of his time, he published the first Sanskrit edition of the *Rig Veda*, with support from the French government, the Prussian government, and the East India Company. As a German-born philologist and Orientalist, Müller was credited as a founding figure of the science of comparative religion. Though he had never set foot in India, he helped create a "textual India" through his voluminous output, and he also played a role in fetishizing the Vedas. Prior to Müller "textual India," most Indians encountered the Vedas through the oral medium.[2]

The construction of "religion" as a field of study is not innocent as it has been shaped by the social and political forces in Europe and the U.S. and by the cultural imaginary of empire. This chapter traces the development of the field from 1600 to 1800, to its institutionalization in the second half of the nineteenth century, to its coming to the U.S. in the early twentieth century and argues that the field needs to radically change to address the postcolonial situation. Three promising developments in the field include more sophisticated conceptualization of racial construction and hierarchy in religious studies, the comparative study of religion and economics, and international developments in the study of religion in academia.

For some time, some scholars in the field, such as Talal Asad, Timothy Fitzgerald, Tomoko Masuzawa, Richard McCutcheon, and Jonathan Z. Smith, have questioned the fundamental concepts of the field such as "religion," "world religion," "ritual," and "the sacred."[3] Inspired by the work of Edward Said, some have used postcolonial theory to scrutinize the ways Islamic, Hindu, Buddhist, Christian, and Native American traditions have been studied.[4] A new generation of bright and adventurous scholars has broken new ground in exploring the intersections among race, gender, sexuality, culture, religion, and colonialism.

The origin and development of the study of religion have been shaped by imperialism in the past and empire in the present. Some scholars in the field have supported the status quo, served imperial interests, and shown inertia and resistance to change. The study of religion has been marginalized in the humanities and in American higher education. As more students want to pursue fields that are marketable, fewer students and their parents want to invest in a discipline that may not lead to profitable careers. At the same time, membership in mainline Protestant denominations has been declining while seminaries and divinity schools have seen dwindling financial support. The coronavirus has impacted the financial stability of universities both in Europe and the U.S. with some schools being forced to cut faculty and staff, and in some cases, the entire religion department.[5] Facing such financial stress, it is critical to ask: Does the study of religion matter? Why has the study of religion taken the form it has taken?

I want to examine the cultural imaginary of empire and how it has shaped the development of the field. In *Culture and Imperialism*, Edward Said shows the intricate links between empire building and the cultural imaginary.[6] Taiwanese scholar Chen Kuan-hsing says the cultural imaginary "structures the system of ideology, links to the concrete experience of daily life, and forms the direction and boundary of the psychological space."[7] Decolonizing the cultural imaginary, of which religious studies is a part, is a daunting task, since it has shaped both the colonized and the colonizing subjects. Chen suggests the following steps: (1) placing colonialism at the center of analysis; (2) exposing hidden Eurocentrism so that a more balanced account of the formation of other regional spaces of the world can emerge; and (3) emphasizing the relative autonomy of local history and insisting on the specificities of the historical and the geographical.[8] Following Chen's suggestion, I will trace the rise of the new science of religion in the seventeenth and eighteenth centuries, its institutionalization in the nineteenth century, and the field's coming to the U.S. Such a sweeping review will leave out many details. My goal is to offer some suggestions for the field so that it can change into a positive force both against empire and for human flourishing.

CLASH OF EMPIRES AND THE ORIGIN
OF THE NEW SCIENCE OF RELIGION

The French historian of religion Daniel Dubuisson argues that "religion" is a Western construct that supplies "the nucleus about which the West has constructed its own universe of values and representations." In this capacity, it has influenced the totality of Western "ways of conceiving and thinking about the world."[9] The concept is too Eurocentric, he says, and too much based on Christian experience to be useful for a comparative discipline.[10]

Many people have traced the root of "religion" to its Latin word *religio* (the *relegere* of Cicero and the *religare* of Lactantius). But Dubuisson said that a term's etymology does not offer us its timeless meaning and essence. The archaic Latin word has gone through its classical usage by Cicero, its progressive acceptance by Christian writers, and its adaptation as an anthropological and universal concept in the modern period, influenced as it was by Christianity.[11] The term "religion" has been hotly contested since Wilfred Cantwell Smith published his classic *The Meaning and End of Religion* in the 1960s. Smith says Westerners have reified "religion" as if it is an object. Religion has generally been taken to mean the belief in god or some transcendent subject. Such misconception fails to understand the living and variable ways and traditions by which religious faith presents itself in the world.[12]

Not only do scholars have no consensus on what religion is, they also debate when the field actually began. In *A New Science*, Guy S. Stroumsa traces the origin of the new comparative study of religion to the age of reason, from 1600 to 1800.[13] Three significant events created a crisis in Europe that prompted a new intellectual development: (1) the encounters with the New World and religious traditions of South and East Asia; (2) the Renaissance and its direct consequences, such as the new interest in antiquity and in philological study; and (3) the religious wars in the wake of the Reformation, which caused devastation and turmoil.

The conquest of the New World changed forever the cultural imaginary of Europe. The decisive battles with the Aztec and Incan empires allowed the Spaniards to conquer a vast territory and peoples. Europeans' contacts with the religious practices and beliefs of the native peoples challenged the biblical view of the unity of humankind and one true religion. At first the Europeans wondered if the Indians were human beings and had souls. After deciding that the Indians were human beings, they compared the religious practices of the New World with Greek and Roman rituals and with Islam. Using the old concepts available to them, they considered the Indian rituals as idolatrous, as serving the devil.[14] This rudimentary comparison of different traditions, though completely biased, was an important step toward the establishing of the field as a new science.

The Europeans' clash with the Chinese Empire in the seventeenth century led to very different results—to the expulsion of Catholic missionaries and to what Lionel Jensen has called "manufacturing Confucianism."[15] The focal point of the debate was how to interpret the Chinese rituals venerating the ancestors and Confucius. While Matteo Ricci (1552–1610) and his fellow Jesuits argued that these rituals were social customs with no religious implications, the Dominicans and Franciscans condemned the rituals as idolatrous.[16] When Pope Clement XI sided with the Dominicans and Franciscans and Chinese Emperor Kangxi sided with the Jesuits, the ecclesial empire clashed directly with the Chinese Empire. In 1706, the Chinese emperor became furious that foreigners were attempting to interpret his country's rituals. He expelled the missionaries who did not accept Matteo Ricci's approach.[17]

Ricci learned the Chinese language and respected Chinese customs. He had written that Christianity had similarities with and could augment Confucian teachings. Chinese scholars were incensed by such ideas, and they learned Ricci's writings in order to denounce them.[18] On the European side, theologians and intellectuals had to learn something about Confucius and Chinese rituals in order to adjudicate between the Jesuits and the Dominicans and Franciscans. The Rites Controversy, as the debate was called, reached its high point when the matter was brought before the theology faculty of the Sorbonne, who decided against the Jesuits' efforts at accommodation. The controversy led to the comparative study of Christianity and the Confucian tradition in both China and Europe.

Although the Jesuits did not prevail, they left great impact on Europe's intellectuals. Stroumsa writes: "they had launched, much beyond the Catholic hierarchy, the deep and long-standing attraction to all *chinoiseries* among European intellectuals that would be so evident throughout the eighteenth century and would lead to the birth of sinology."[19] As the Enlightenment philosophers were looking for an alternative to the divine revelation and dogmas espoused by Christianity, Confucianism, as a Western construct, became an exemplar of rational and natural religion. Confucius had great appeal because his tradition did not worship idols and had no false gods. In fact, Confucius was against superstition and idolatry. For the West, Confucius became an "iconic representation of Chinese native otherness," as Jensen says.[20] Confucius appeared in the writings of Enlightenment figures as diverse as Voltaire, Rousseau, Comte, Diderot, Bayle, and Leibniz, who were fascinated by an idealist view of China.[21]

In sum, the new science of religion was born during the religious wars within Europe and the clashes with other empires. Western encounters with beliefs and rituals in the New World and in East and South Asia revealed that Christianity was only one among a plurality of religious traditions. The Catholics first used the plural form "religions" as early as 1508.[22] Religion became a generic concept that described a crucial aspect of society, and it had different historical expressions.[23] The comparative study of Christianity with these other practices and beliefs gave rise to the origin of the study of religion.

EXPANSION OF EMPIRES AND INSTITUTIONALIZATION OF COMPARATIVE STUDY OF RELIGION

The institutionalization of the field took place during the second half of the nineteenth century with the formation of new chairs in the general and comparative study of religion in European universities. The availability of new materials and religious artifacts as a result of colonialism greatly facilitated the field's development. The cultural imaginary of this period of rapid European expansion was defined by the promotion of the Indo-Aryan myth, the application of evolutionary theory to society and religion, the racist construction of the "primitive man," and the belief in science and progress and in the civilizing mission of the West.

If the Enlightenment thinkers were attracted to Confucianism, German Romantics and the English Orientalists had fallen in love with Sanskrit and Indian myths.[24] Max Müller developed a genealogy of language, based on the work of William Jones (1746–1794), who discovered the commonalities between Sanskrit and European languages. He traced the origin of Indo-Europeans to India, the birthplace of human cultures and religions,[25] and hypothesized that the Europeans and the Indians had come from the same stock because of their linguistic affinities, and that they were distinct from the Semites. As an enlightened Christian, Müller had hoped that such affinity might lead to better treatment of the Indians under the British. But the essentialized dichotomy between the "Indo-Aryans" and the "Semites" contributed to a racist construction of the world, especially during the rise of German nationalism.

Anti-Semitism, racist ideology, and the belief in progress found their ways into the study of ancient Jewish history and Christianity. The French philologist Ernest Renan (1823–1892), a friend of Müller, introduced Orientalism to the study of the New Testament. In his bestseller *Vie de Jésus*, first published in 1863, he argued that Jesus had infused a new spirit into Judaism and into the Mosaic law. His portrayal of Jesus was modeled after the bourgeois: a man who was willing to face risk, competition, and conflict.[26] Christianity became an Aryan religion by getting rid of the vestiges of Judaism. In his other works, Renan asserted that the Semites were inferior to the Aryans because the progress of the human mind toward truth, science, and philosophy was foreign to them.

French and German scholars created the historical Jesus according to their own images. In 1879, the Jewish artist Max Liebermann's portrayal of the twelve-year-old Jesus in the temple was condemned as blasphemous because he was too Jewish-looking. In response to the uproar, Liebermann transformed Jesus into a blond-haired boy characteristic of contemporary German taste.[27] As Suzannah Heschel has shown, the de-Judaization of Christianity since the 1860s led to the dehistoricization of Jesus, fueled anti-Semitism, and contributed to the controversy that Jesus was an Aryan because he had come from Galilee.[28]

Racist ideology by this time had been rampant in the construction of the "primitive man" since the Enlightenment.[29] The "primitive" and non-Western peoples were depicted as sexually promiscuous and lustful, as opposed to the Victorian ideal of sexual restraint. The earliest use of the term "homosexuality" can be traced to the late 1860s, about the same time when the study of religion was institutionalized. "Homosexuality" was regarded as an inversion, which represented a historical and cultural regression to pre-Christian moralities.[30] To show Christianity's superiority, as I will explore further in the next chapter, Jesus was depicted as a bourgeois gentleman, devoid of passion and fully capable of controlling his desires and appetites. The sexuality of Jesus was a taboo subject. This taboo, as I have shown, "served not only to discipline individual sexual behavior, but also to maintain racial boundaries and cultural imperialism to facilitate the expansion of Europe. Jesus' sexed body provided a provocative site for the inscription and projection of powerful myths about sexuality, race, gender, and colonial desire."[31]

Racism shaped the classification of religion in this new discipline in the modern university. Racial discrimination and slavery were justified by appealing to so-called scientific theories of the different sizes of skulls for Caucasians, Mongols, and Africans. Racist ideology and social Darwinism also found their way into the study of religion. David Chidester, a professor at the University of Cape Town in South Africa, notes that Europeans initially did not recognize Africans as having religion because their religion did not easily fit into the norms of Christianity. It was only after colonial supremacy was established that the Africans were credited as having religion, though their religion was considered primitive.[32] In *Empire of Religion*, Chidester shows the complex relation between European imperialism and the modern study of comparative religion.[33] Power and knowledge were intimately related, as the knowledge of religion was mediated through indigenous informants, colonial collaborators (missionaries and officials), and imperial/metropolitan scholars. African religion loomed large in the development of the field by providing data for discussing crucial concepts such as animism, myth, ritual, and magic. Race was formative in the development of the field as seen by the maintaining of the divide between savagery and civilization. In the modern university, there is division of labor with the anthropology department studying "primitive" religions and the religion department studying world religions.[34]

AMERICAN EMPIRE BUILDING AND RELIGIOUS STUDIES

The study of religion in U.S. colleges and universities began in the early twentieth century, shortly after the Spanish-American War. Since then, the fortune of the discipline has been much linked to American wars and foreign interests. The cultural imaginary of the American empire has been shaped by beliefs in American exceptionalism, white supremacy, the defeat of Communism, and increasingly, hegemony through military power.

Richard McCutcheon notes that the kind of sociopolitical changes that took place in the U.S. in the early twentieth century could find certain parallels in the changes in Europe four hundred years ago. In the 1500s, the transition of feudalism to the early stage of modern states required small social groupings to join to form larger entities. In the early twentieth century, the U.S. came out of its policy of isolationism and began to exert a nascent worldwide influence. In both cases, different groups competed for control over the rhetoric of religion and the public authority that came from such control. McCutcheon believed that "there is a link between managing an emerging empire and the rhetoric of religion."[35]

In Europe, the Reformers attacked Catholicism and strove to form their national churches. In the U.S., the challenges of science and Darwinism, biblical criticism, and the belief in freedom and progress attacked the fortress of orthodoxy. The spirit of liberal Protestantism allowed spaces for nonsectarian inquiry and the introduction of the comparative study of religion. The teaching of the Bible and religion was to inculcate values and morality in the sons and daughters of the middle class[36] and to offer a sense of unity across an increasingly fragmented university curriculum. The National Association of Biblical Instructors in American Colleges and Secondary Schools, the forerunner of the American Academy of Religion (AAR), was formed in 1909.

The comparative study of religion declined in the 1930s because of the rise of neo-orthodoxy, the depression, and both world wars. It was reborn after the U.S. Supreme Court decided in 1963 that public schools could teach religion in the *Abingdon v. Schempp* case. During the Vietnam War, the U.S. government saw the study of "non-Western cultures" as a national defense strategy. Different areas of strategic interest to the U.S. were carved out and area studies was born. Lyman H. Legters, who was in charge of the National Defense Education Act language and area studies program at one time, said the study of religion could help these programs understand the "spiritual engines of other civilizations and societies."[37] He said the establishment of departments of religion in universities was a positive step.

In addition to the world religions model, scholars could follow the area studies model and speak of the religion of China and Japan, the religion of South Asia, the religion of the Middle East, and the religion of the Americas.[38] These were areas of special interest to the U.S. in the twentieth century. With the availability of funds, American students of religion could go to their "fields" to study foreign language and cultures, and not be limited to textual studies. The use of anthropology and other social scientific methods, in addition to the phenomenological approach to religion, became one of the major directions of the study of religion in North America.

"Culture" became a buzzword in the academy, not only in religion, but also in other disciplines. As former colonies regained their political independence after World War II, new ways to imagine the difference between the West and the rest became necessary. Étienne Balibar has argued that the nineteenth-century associations of race with nature and biology and a concept of racism based on uncrossable boundaries of bloodlines were by this time no longer acceptable. The former notion of biological difference has since been displaced into the realm of culture. The insurmountability of cultural identity, or cultural difference, is used to justify modern racism.[39]

It was no coincidence that Clifford Geertz would publish his tremendously influential essay "Religion as a Cultural System" in 1966.[40] Religion was defined as a system of symbols that generates powerful moods and motivations by formulating conceptions of a general order of existence and clothing these conceptions with an aura of factuality. I was very impressed by Geertz when I first read the essay as a graduate student in theology. Only later did I find out that Talal Asad has accused Geertz of basing his definition on a modern, privatized Christianity.[41] Geertz gave priority to belief and the cognitive aspect of religion, while overlooking how humans' social life shapes and gives meaning to the religious symbolic system.

The 1980s saw the introduction of cultural anthropology to the study of the New Testament and early Christianity. Bruce Malina and other scholars reminded us that Jesus was not born in San Francisco and that the Mediterranean culture was distinct from American culture.[42] According to James Crossley, the focus on Mediterranean culture and especially on the Middle East in the early 1980s coincided with a time when the region became crucial to American foreign interests. Crossley found it disturbing that scholars have made blanket statements about the ancient Mediterranean world based on contemporary anthropological studies of the Middle East.[43] Scholars generalized that Mediterranean culture was characterized by honor and shame, patronage and clientele, and dyadic personality. As such, so these scholars said, it was very different from our own culture. Crossley notes that this "us" versus "them" rhetoric cohered with Anglo-American foreign policy interests in the Middle East.

The introduction of social-scientific study of the New Testament has prompted scholars to ask a new set of questions about Jesus: What did Jesus eat and who shared the table with him? What were the living habits of itinerant leaders? Did Jesus know how to use medicine or even magic? Such fascinating questions and inquiries led to a new parade of images for Jesus: a wandering charismatic leader, a Jewish rabbi, an eschatological prophet, a millennial rebel, a Jewish peasant cynic, a social radical, a spirit-filled person, a healer, and a magician.[44] Even though some of these images would appear shocking and even blasphemous to the nineteenth-century gentleman, they were and are acceptable to our contemporaries because Jesus, as a Mediterranean native, is supposed to be culturally different from "us." Jesus has gone native in our time.

The Middle East was a focal point in the rhetoric of the war on terrorism and the axis of evil soon after September 11, 2001. Colleges and universities rushed to hire an expert on Islam. Books on Islam flooded the bookstores and became bestsellers. The media looked for talking heads that could answer President George W. Bush's question, "Why do they hate us?" Some scholars, notably Bernard Lewis, seized the opportunity to dissect the crisis of Islam and what went wrong in the Middle East.[45] Others, including many members of the AAR, argued that the action of small group of Muslim extremists should not be taken to represent the whole of Islam.[46] It seems that whenever the U.S. has gone to war in the last fifty years, the stock of Religious Studies has gone up. Religion has enjoyed a "resurgence" in the public square, with some speaking of a theological turn in our political discourse.[47] What will the future look like?

LOOKING FORWARD

Daniel Dubuisson has said the study of religion in the nineteenth century was both "captive and witness to its time."[48] I wonder, a hundred years from now, how will future historians describe what we have accomplished? Will the cultural imaginary of empire continue to shape the study of religion? If we look at the history of the AAR, the world's largest scholarly society devoted to the study of religion with more than 9,000 members, we will see that many of its program units grew out of the world religions model (e.g. Buddhism, Hinduism, Islam, and Christianity) and the area studies model (e.g. African Religions, North American Religions, Religion in Europe, and Religion in South Asia).[49] Added to this mix is a variety of identity groups according to race, gender, and sexuality. It is important to stand back and ask whether the old classification systems and identity politics have run their course. We must imagine new ways of studying religion that will promote cross-cultural understanding while strengthening the desire and resolve to fight for a better world. The newer program units such as "Religion, Colonialism, and Postcolonialism," "Religion and Politics," and "Class, Religion, and Theology" show promise since they use interdisciplinary approaches to study the relationships between religion and larger issues in political economy.

As race has played such a formative role in the imperialist study of religion, it is important to scrutinize how racial constructs have shaped the ordering of the world and the ways we portray peoples and cultures in religious studies. Two recent, award-winning books deserve special attention because of the scope of their works and the methodologies employed to unveil racial constructs in the context of religion. Geraldine Heng's *The Invention of Race in the European Middle Age* challenges our assumptions that race and racism began in the modern era.[50] She shows that racial thinking, racial laws, and racial practices existed between the twelfth to fifteenth centuries in medieval Europe even before the vocabulary of race emerged in the fifteenth century. Through the study of the interaction of Christian Europe with Jews, Muslims, Africans, native Americans, Mongols, and Gypsies, she demonstrates that religion was one of the chief categories used in the demarcation of human difference and the distribution of different positions and powers to diverse human groups. Her research uses a wide variety of resources, including media, maps, stories, saints' lives, architectural features, literature, and religious commentaries. Her study shows that "race-making" contributed to the emergence of *homo europaeus* and the identity of Western Europe in this time. She argues that, by not using the category of "race," we inadvertently destigmatize and absolve the Middle Ages of the errors and atrocities committed in that period. Her groundbreaking volume has caused debates among scholars interested in medieval studies and in the study of race. Heng is also the founder and director of the Global Middle Ages Project, an ambitious project of an international collaboration of scholars to look at the period 500–1500 C.E. from global, comparative, and interactive perspectives. This collaboration will provide rich resources for the study of religion's interaction with state, language, culture, social institutions, and law.[51]

J. Lorand Matory's *The Fetish Revisited: Marx, Freud, and the Gods Black People Make* links nineteenth-century Europeans' fantasies about Black people

and their worship of fetishes with the development of Marx's historical materialism and Freud's psychoanalysis.[52] He shows that "fetish" was widely used
as a metonym for the superstitious and irrational thinking of the "savages" or
"primitives" during a time of intense colonization of Africa. Marx and Freud, as
secular Jews living in Europe that did not fully accept Jewish people, deflected
their anxiety and stigma of irrationality and psychological immaturity onto the
African peoples. Though both appropriated the idea of the fetish, they have
plucked it out of the meaning and context of transatlantic Black religion, and
by doing so, suppressed the brutal facts of slavery and subjection of African
peoples. What is original in the book is that Matory not only criticizes the European theorists, but enables the Afro-Atlantic priests, who make use of fetishes,
to "talk back." Matory presents fascinating ethnographical data of West African Yoruba and Fon, Central African Kongo and Yaka, Brazilian Candomblé,
Cuban Santería/Regla de Ocha, and Haitian Vodou and their religious objects.
He shows that Afro-Atlantic priests were not primitives, but contemporaries of
Marx and Freud, who were thinkers and actors trying to create meaning and
assert ideas about social order and hierarchy through physical objects. His book
includes pictures of these religious objects, and there is an informative website
"The Sacred Arts of the Black Atlantic" with images and audiovisual materials.[53]

    In addition to debunking racial ideologies, we need to pay more attention
to the relation between religion and economics, since contemporary empire has
increasingly taken the form of economic and financial control and domination.
Michael Hardt and Antonio Negri use the term "Empire" to describe the globalization of capitalist production and the declining sovereignty of nation-states.
Empire is different from the imperialism of the previous era when Europe controlled distant lands and peoples. Today, Empire is all-pervasive since it has no
territorial center of power and does not rely on fixed boundaries.[54] Proponents
of neoliberalism assume that only Western capitalist modes of free-market, competition, the rule of the law, and limited government intervention can lead to
economic development and prosperity. They argue that societies that are steeped
in traditional culture and religion lag behind because of the difficulty of inte-
grating them into the global economy. Because of the "war on terrorism" and
persistent Orientalism, there are frequent commentaries on the perceived sad
and backward state of "Islamic" economics and finances. Yet there are a spate of
books that have contested such assumptions and pointed to Muslims' long history of contributions to modern economics, including "discussions of ideas on
taxation, market regulation, usury, permissible economic behavior, wages, prices,
division of labor, money as media of exchange and unit of account, admonition
against debasement of money, coinage, price fluctuations, and, finally, ethical
prescription regarding observance of the mean."[55] Scholars contrast Western
capitalism and Islamic economic systems by analyzing the foundations, institutions, and operation of Islamic economics at the macro- and microeconomic
levels. They also study the principles and instruments of Islamic capital markets,
Islamic rules of exchange, the roles of the state, and social and fiscal policies in

shaping Islamic economic development.[56] They levy the critique that unbridled capitalism and corporate greed have led to wide and growing income and wealth disparities, recurrent and disruptive financial crises, the neglect of societal well-being, and environmental degradation.[57] Instead of advocating a laissez-fare market economy, some of these scholars look to resources in Islam for principles in guiding economic behaviors. Hossein Askari and Abbas Mirakhor, who have written on Islamic economics, finance, and government, argue that justice is at the heart of Islam and the principal mission of all prophets has been to bring justice to their communities. They study the development of the concept of justice in Islam over the centuries, lament that justice is missing in many Muslim societies, and offer insights on how this can be remedied.[58]

In Christianity there is renewed interest in the study of money, economics, and class in Christian thought and practice with a desire to undo how Christianity has been bound up in the values of Empire and capitalism. For example, Devin Singh's book *Divine Currency: The Theological Power of Money in the West* argues that the Christian imagination has been infused with economic ideas, practices, and traditions since the patristic periods, when some of the foundational Christian doctrines about God, Christ, and salvation were formulated.[59] He shows that centuries before Max Weber connected Puritan ethics to the spirit of capitalism, early theologians such as Eusebius and the Cappadocian fathers had discussed ancient capital in the forms of money, currency, debt, circulation, exchange, and re-distribution. Kathryn Tanner's *Christianity and the New Spirit of Capitalism* argues that contemporary capitalism is finance-dominated, which is drastically different from the economic constellations during the rise of capitalism that Max Weber has described.[60] Capitalism has become a quasi-religion by placing totalizing demands on people's time, energy, and commitment while simultaneously infusing the private and public spheres of life. She argues that Christian beliefs and values can form the basis of a counternarrative to capitalism by highlighting: the Christian view of history, with a focus on God's redemptive action in Christ; commitment to God instead of to Mammon; God's abundant love instead of scarcity; confidence in the future because of God's grace and the hope for resurrected life; salvation's not hinging upon one's achievement; and a Christian way of being in the world that does not follow the logic of the work ethic of capitalism. While Singh and Tanner focus on Christian thought, other scholars and activists study social movements against domination and economic inequality. Theologian Joerg Rieger and labor organizer Rosemarie Henkel-Rieger argue that the church must move from advocacy to deep solidarity. Deep solidarity is possible when people recognize that their destinies and struggles are interconnected, despite differences among them.[61] They cite Jesus as an example because Jesus grew up as a carpenter—a construction worker—and throughout his ministry, he formed deep solidarity with working people, fishermen, and tax collectors and even reached out to some wealthy and prominent people. Jesus was committed to forming new communities and bringing out positive changes to society. [62] They argue that Christians, following Jesus, need to forge connections between faith and work, learning to organize to bring about social and economic changes.

Alongside subverting racial ideologies and capitalist assumptions, in our globalized world, the study of religion cannot be parochial and must value transnational and cross-cultural collaboration. Many American universities have established centers and branches in other parts of the world while colleges and divinity schools have set up various international partnerships. The field of religion will have to move beyond European and American domination to become global in nature by asking questions about new ways of conceptualizing "religion" and about religion's roles in changing global culture and social and economic life.

It is important for those of us who live and teach in European and North American contexts to get out of our comfort zones to learn what our colleagues in other parts of the world are doing. Scholars from Japan to Argentina would not be considered fully equipped to teach religion if they have never heard of the theories of Marx, Freud, or Durkheim. Yet many of us know far too little of the history of religious studies and current research interests in other countries and regions, especially in the Global South. One such example is the Southern Knowledge Conference held at the University of Cape Town and which I attended in 2015, which focused on postcolonialism and religions in the Global South.

One of the areas that we need to pay special attention to is the study of religion in China. It is worth noting that China has invested a lot of resources into the study of religion in the midst of its economic boom and its so-called "peaceful rise." Taiwanese scholar Tsai Yen-zen describes the rapid increase of the number of departments of religion and research institutes in China funded by the Communist government.[63] Naomi Thurston studies the emergence of Sino-Christian studies and how theology plays a part in it. She also shows how scholars of Christianity in China negotiate the nexus between scholarly inquiry, cross-disciplinary investigation, and religious belonging.[64] It is apparent that the Marxist theory of religion no longer dominates the study of religion in China. Since the liberalization process began in the late 1970s, many Western theories of religion have been introduced in China. According to Zhuo Xinping, Director of the Institute of World Religions at the Chinese Academy of Social Sciences, Chinese scholars now have a more comprehensive view of religion. The majority of them recognize the positive social functions of religion in socialist China, including identity formation, social cohesion, psychic accommodation, and socialization of individuals.[65] Since China occupies such an important position in the world economy and politics today, it will be fruitful for European- and North American-based scholars to have cross-cultural dialogues on religion and the Sino-American empire, religion and civil society, and ethnic minorities and religious rights with Chinese colleagues.

At a time when the arts and humanities are not viewed to be as important as the sciences and technology, I want to conclude with the words of Homi Bhabha, who says,

There was always a sense of crisis in the humanities. . . . But where there are large-scale transformations within society, the humanities have a major guiding role to play in the diverse conversations of mankind [sic]. They raise very important issues about the place of culture, the place of art, the place of ethics, the place of morality, the place of subjectivity—the place of the whole world of the imagination and of the emotions, in private and public life.[66]

I hope scholars of religion will take a critical role in such animated conversations, for religion has shaped so much the development of art, culture, and morality in human societies, and the collective impact of these fields on contemporary politics cannot be ignored.

Chapter 3

Race, Colonial Desire, and Sexual Theology

In theology, as in love, this quest is a spiritual one, which requires continuing to the Other side of theology, and the Other side of God.
Marcella Althaus-Reid[1]

The Uganda Anti-Homosexuality Act of 2014 caught the world's attention because of the death penalty clauses in the original version. It was signed into law with life imprisonment substituted for the death penalty. Around that time, homophobic people circulated a notice of one hundred of the most wanted Ugandan lesbian and gay leaders and activists, like a witch hunt. Although the Constitutional Court of Uganda later ruled the Act invalid, the "Kill the Gay Bill," as it was called in Western media, helped to revive the myth that Africa is a "dark continent" and "barbaric." In fact, same-sex relations have been outlawed in Uganda because of British colonial rule, as they have been in many African countries. Before the new law was passed, homosexual acts were punishable by up to fourteen years in prison. The new, even more draconian law was proposed to shore up support for Ugandan conservative politicians, who denounced same-sex relations as a threat to African families and traditional marriages.

It is worth noting that, in the nineteenth century, it was polygamy that caught the ire of Western missionaries and colonial officials in Africa. Influenced by their Victorian sexual mores, missionaries found African sexual practices incompatible with their teaching of Christian monogamous marriage. They vigorously debated whether polygamous persons could be baptized and accepted into the church.[2] Times have changed, and in the twenty-first century the issues have become homosexuality and African attitudes toward same-sex relations. Whereas many Western countries have become more open to accepting queer persons, African nations' intolerance toward homosexuality is seen as disputable and antiquated. Sexuality once again serves as a clear marker of cultural difference, and African attitudes toward sex have been taken as symptomatic of the inferiority of African cultures. Furthermore, as Christian demographics have shifted to the Global South, Western Christianity is seen as being under threat from the spread and growth of conservative Christianity. In his book *The Next Christendom*, Philip Jenkins points out that the fastest-growing churches in the Global South are evangelical and Pentecostal, which are adapting to the so-called "indigenous" cultures. In terms of theology and moral teaching, these churches are conservative in outlook, often authoritarian, and highly patriarchal.[3] Many scholars have criticized Jenkins' use of the trope of "Christendom" when describing southern Christianity as superfluous and ill-advised.[4]

Race and sexuality intersect and constitute an essential part of the colonial discourse, for colonial domination depends not only on political and military might, but also on the control of sexuality and the repatterning of desire. Thus, postcolonial theology cannot deal with the social and the political while leaving the sexual regime intact. Using the lens of queer theology, this chapter explores the intersections between race, colonial desire, and sexual theology. It begins with queering Jesus' sexuality by focusing on the asexual Jesus and colonialism. It continues by queering the constructions of the poor and the female subaltern as theological subjects, which have often left heterosexism and heteronormativity intact. After an exploration of queer issues from a cross-cultural perspective, the chapter concludes with queering phallic pleasure by arguing that the disciplining power of the one phallic God reinforces male domination and colonial power.

QUEERING JESUS' SEXUALITY

In order to bolster the moral superiority and sexual purity of the European bourgeoisie, peoples of foreign lands were often portrayed as promiscuous, lustful, and polygamous in medical, missionary, and anthropological literature in the nineteenth century. Anthropologists furnished much data about the "strange" courtship and marriage customs among the so-called "primitive" peoples. Havelock Ellis and others, writing in the nineteenth century, found that there was a widespread natural instinct toward homosexual relationship among the "lower races."[5] The discourse on sexuality was much imbued with racial obsession, the technologies of power policing the bourgeois self, and the boundaries of the "civilized" European nations. Anne Laura Stoler writes, "Bourgeois identities in both metropole and colony emerge tacitly and emphatically coded by race. Discourses of sexuality do more than define the distinctions of the bourgeois self; in identifying marginal members of the body politic, they have mapped the moral parameters of the European nations."[6] How did nineteenth-century discourse on sexuality, imbued as it was with racial obsessions and polemics, influence scholars' construction of the sexuality of Jesus, who was seen in liberal thought as the moral teacher and as the embodiment of human ideals?

Ernst Renan begins his best-selling *Vie de Jésus* (1863) by placing Jesus in the history of the world as a kind of evolutionary framework. He says that man distinguishes himself from the animals by being religious. Renan traces the belief in sorcerers in Oceania to the degeneration of the "hideous scenes of butchery" in the ancient religion of Mexico. He posits that African peoples did not go beyond fetishism and their belief in material objects and the supernatural powers those objects possessed. On Renan's account, though the civilizations of China, Babylonia, and Egypt represented some progress, their contributions to human civilization were not important. For him, the religions of Babylonia and Syria never "disengaged themselves from a substratum of strange sensuality" and these religions continued to be "schools of immorality" and "only threw into the world millions of amulets and charms."[7] Although Renan did not discuss explicitly the sexuality of the natives, the sexual overtones in his condemnation of the world's other religions could not be mistaken. Renan then went on to contrast these religions with the soul, faith, liberty, sincerity, and devotion of Christianity, which emerged out of the two races—the Aryans and the Semites—with the Aryans finally superseding the Semites.

With such a highly charged racial and sexual rhetoric, Renan's "Jesus" fits the projected image of a self-controlled, restrained, and morally superior bourgeois gentleman. Renan says that "an infinite charm was exhaled from his person," and that Jesus showed an amiable character. Renan alleges there was a common spirit felt among Jesus' followers and the brotherhood of men—as sons of God—were seen as having moral accountability. Renan's Jesus demanded perfection, beyond the duties of the Law, and espoused the Christian virtues of "humility, pardon, charity, abnegation, and self-denial."[8] He preached about loving and forgiving one's enemies, being merciful, giving alms, doing good works, and showing kindness and charity to others. With such refined and sweet qualities, Jesus was celebrated and loved by many around him. But Renan says that Jesus never allowed human affection to interfere with his ministry and calling. In one particularly telling passage that touches on Jesus' sexuality, Renan wrote:

> Jesus never married. All his power of loving expended itself on what he considered his heavenly vocation. The extremely delicate sentiment which one observes in his manner towards women did not interfere with the exclusive devotion he cherished for his idea. Like Francis d' Assisi and Francis de Sales, he treated as sisters the women who threw themselves into the same work as he did; he had his Saint Clare, and his Françoise de Chantals. However, it is probable that they loved himself better than his work; he was certainly more beloved than loving. As happens frequently in the case of

very lofty natures, his tenderness of heart transformed itself into an infinite sweetness, a vague poetry, a universal charm.[9]

Renan's Jesus sublimated his sexual desire to pursue his real vocation. Even his relations with the women of doubtful character, though free and intimate, were of an entirely moral nature and were a means to carry out the will of the Father. Jesus evolved a religious ethic based not on outward behavior, but rather on the purification of the individual human heart. He was content with praying, meditating, and maintaining a close relation with God. The Jesus inscribed on the pages of *Vie de Jésus* was neither value-neutral nor scientifically reconstructed from the Gospels but was heavily imbued with the bourgeois values and morality of Renan's high French culture.

While Renan's *Vie de Jésus* attracted a large audience, Albrecht Ritschl's liberal understanding of Christology cast a long shadow on German theology. Karl Barth charged liberal Protestant thought in general, and Ritschl in particular, as "the very epitome of the national-liberal German bourgeois of the age of Bismarck."[10] Ritschl believed that Jesus was the founder of the perfect religion, in contrast to all other religions. He regarded Judaism as politically nationalistic and Buddhism as a kind of cosmology which does not balance the ethical and religious aspects of faith. For Ritschl, these non-Christian religions are secondary and incomplete, for the life of Jesus provides the truest source for knowledge of God:

> Christianity, then, is the monotheistic, completely spiritual and ethical religion, which, based on the life of its Author as Redeemer and as Founder of the Kingdom of God, consists in the freedom of the children of God, involves the impulse to conduct from the motive of love, aims at the moral organization of mankind [*sic*], and grounds blessedness on the relationship of sonship to God, as well as on the Kingdom of God.[11]

Ritschl sought to combine the historical-critical study of the New Testament with his dogmatic theological interests to present the Christian faith intelligibly within the context of nineteenth-century German thought. His Jesus is a moral exemplar who embodies the highest ideals of human life. According to Ritschl, Christians should strive for Christian perfection that corresponds to the example set by Jesus himself. In his instruction on Christian life, Ritschl commended the virtues of obedience to God, humility, patience, fidelity to one's vocation, self-control and conscientiousness, and love of one's neighbor.[12] Such a morally superior, diligent, and self-denying Jesus met the ideals of the German bourgeoisie who were playing an important role in the expanding power of Prussia, a political move that Ritschl supported.

Ritschl devoted much of his last decade to the study of the history of pietism, including an interesting comparison of Catholic piety with Protestant piety under the influences of Lutheranism and Calvinism. Ritschl penned a lengthy and detailed exposition of Bernard's sermons on the Song of Songs, which he said epitomize the Catholic approach. He noted Bernard's use of erotic language such as the kiss of the Lord' feet, hands, and mouth to describe the union between Christ and the individual soul. Bernard described love for God as sensuous, passionate, and powerful. Just as Luther disapproved of Bernard's interpretation of the Song of Songs, Ritschl wrote that Bernard's perspective on the love of Christ was, from its very beginning, alien to Protestant piety. He said that this kind of mystical union might be expected of monks who did not have to face the temptations of the secular world. On Ritschl's account, Protestant Christians had to conduct their everyday life through their trust in God and in the redemption of their sin and guilt. Thus, for Ritschl, Catholic piety allowed for more "sentimental pathos" and "sentimental desire" for the unity of the spirit with Christ, while Protestant piety, influenced by Lutheran and Calvinism, tended to be more austere and ascetic because of a different understanding of grace. He writes: "the certainty of reconciliation as it is expressed in trust in God is the necessary presupposition of sanctification for the protestant Christian, whereas for the Catholics the enjoyment of redemption in tender intercourse with the redeemer is a possible appendage to their sanctification."[13]

In Britain, the theological climate was quite different from that on the European continent; British theologians had not produced influential texts about the life of Jesus as had Renan, D. F. Strauss, and Albert Schweitzer. But this does not mean that they were not concerned about the historical-critical study of the Bible. In fact, one of the dominant concerns in Anglican theology at the turn of the twentieth century was incarnation, as theologians tried to harmonize the Christ of dogma with the picture of Jesus presented by the historical study of Scriptures. John Robert Seeley was credited with producing the first English book on the life of Jesus, *Ecce Homo: A Survey of the Life and Work of Jesus Christ*, first published in 1865. Seeley obviously has the model of the British Empire in mind when he talks about the kingdom of God and the ministry of Jesus. Emphasizing the royalty of Jesus, he argues that Jesus was the founder and legislator of a new theocracy, a new Christian Commonwealth. Through obedience to his laws and teachings, his followers can become subjects or citizens of the Christian republic.[14] Although this Christian Commonwealth is universal and open to all, Seeley believes that human beings are not all equal and gifted. He upholds the authority of the father over the child and the husband over the wife and defends Christianity's tacit approval of slavery's existence because of the belief that not everyone was able to live in a free condition. Seeley also justifies British colonial rule in India by arguing that Indians were not capable of ruling themselves and would revert to instability and anarchy if the British left.[15]

Writing less than a decade after British suppression of the formidable Indian national struggle in 1857, Seeley portrays Jesus as an enlightened king with royal pretensions and power, which he exercised with patience and restraint. He writes: "For the noblest and most amiable thing that can be seen is power mixed with gentleness, the reposing, self-restraining attitude of strength."[16] Seeley's Jesus was also full of sympathy and appreciation, and this combination of greatness and self-sacrifice had great appeal to his followers. Jesus did not win them over by power and might but through moral example, benevolence, and the relief of their suffering. Just as the British did not conquer India, as Seeley would argue, but ruled over the Indians because of the moral superiority of the British, he asserts that "in Christ's monarchy no force was used, though all power was at command; the obedience of his servants became in the end, though not till after his departure, absolutely unqualified."[17]

Seeley discusses the pursuit of pleasure and bodily gratification in Jesus' legislation for the new kingdom. He says the sensualist would make bodily comfort and pleasure his goal for life, while forgetting that he also possesses a soul. The Stoics and the ascetics, on the other hand, seek discipline and coercion of the body. Seeley argues that Jesus did not deprecate the life of the body since he healed the sick, attended weddings and banquets, and his disciples were sometimes accused of indulgent behaviors. Yet Jesus redirected their attention toward seeking the kingdom of God first rather than worldly pursuits. For Seeley, temperance and moderation are necessary to safeguard against what he called sensualism and excessive pursuit of pleasure.[18]

At the end of the nineteenth century, Anglican theologians were preoccupied with the issue of incarnation, being prompted in part by theories of evolution and partly by critical study of the Bible. Commenting on that particular era of Anglican theology, Arthur Michael Ramsey remarks: "The Incarnation was the centre of a theological scheme concerning nature and man, in which Christ is both the climax of nature and history and the supernatural restorer of mankind (sic)."[19] Charles Gore's Bampton Lectures, published as *The Incarnation of the Son of God* in 1891, laid down some of the basic questions that were explored over the next several decades. Gore was concerned with the question: How could the fully human Jesus be the incarnated Son of God? Gore went to great lengths to defend the full humanity of Jesus and dismissed any form of Docetism: "He passed through all stages of a human development, willing with a human will, perceiving with human perceptions, feeling with human feelings."[20] Defending passionately the doctrine of Two Natures, Gore maintained that God the divine creator humbled himself to take the form of the creaturely life of man.

Gore and his contemporary theologians, however, were more interested in the preconsciousness of Jesus in their kenotic theory of incarnation than in the embodiment of a fully enfleshed Jesus. The debate focused on the idealistic discussion of whether Jesus had to give up his divine knowledge and consciousness when he assumed the personality and nature of a human being. Gore insisted that Jesus is fully human with human consciousness and reveals what mankind should be: "We contemplate Jesus Christ, the Son of man, in the sinlessness, the perfection, the breath of His manhood, and in Him we find the justification of our highest hopes for man."[21] Jesus' sinlessness was seen in his exercise of moral freedom over temptations including lust of the flesh, worldliness, and pride. Gore's Jesus is the perfect example for sinners for he overcomes "the tyranny of passions, the disorder of faculties, the inward taint and weakness."[22] The body, desire, and passion were once again seen as obstacles and hindrances that must be suppressed in order to become an ideal, perfect human person.

The taboo around Jesus' passions and sexuality in the nineteenth-century quest for the historical Jesus served not only to discipline individual sexual behavior but also to maintain racial boundaries and cultural imperialism, which facilitated the expansion of Europe. Jesus' sexed body provided a provocative site for the inscription and projection of powerful myths about sexuality, race, gender, and colonial desire. As the humanity of Jesus was emphasized and the superiority of Christianity as an ethical religion was touted, human perfection was closely linked to the "cultivation of the self," a task Michel Foucault sees as the defining feature of the nineteenth-century bourgeoisie. Contrasted with sexualized natives and the lower classes, Jesus was seen as exemplifying the bourgeois ideals: controlling his passions, managing his desire, and sublimating his bodily needs. Such ethical demands guaranteed the hygiene, purity, and health of the bourgeois body. Control of the body and of sexuality must be consistently placed in its larger social, economic, and political contexts. A transgressive reimagining of the sexuality of Jesus calls for simultaneous emancipation of the multiple others: the sexual other, the racial and ethnic other, and the religious other. This can only be done through a vigorous analysis of how Christianity's most powerful symbol—Jesus—has been deployed to provide for religious sanctification of heteronormativity, capitalism, and colonialism in the past, and new forms of oppression in the present.

QUEERING THE POOR AND THE FEMALE SUBALTERN

Latin American liberation theology arose in the 1960s to challenge European bourgeois theology that supports the status quo and oppresses the poor and the downtrodden. Proponents argue for God's preferential option for the poor and emphasize the poor as theological subjects. In her groundbreaking book *Indecent Theology*, Marcella Althaus-Reid charges that these theologians have created the poor as a homologated category.[23] The poor can be imagined as a rural peasant in Peru, or someone living in a shantytown demanding a job. But the poor, she says, cannot be imagined as someone who enjoys a carnival centered on a transvestite Christ, as leather dykes who subvert gender norms, or as Latinas who would not leave their rosaries at home when going to the salsa bar.

Althaus-Reid's charge should make feminist theologians wonder: How have we constructed the "poor woman"? Have we thought of her as asexual, just as many male theologians have done? For a long time, feminist theologians from the Global South have written about the broken body of women as victims of domestic violence and abject poverty, migrant workers in foreign lands, prostitutes and sex-workers serving American GIs and businessmen, women and girls raped and mutilated in wars, and illegal immigrants in borderlands. But can we imagine the poor woman as someone other than a victim, a survivor, a person under multiple oppressions, or an object for our compassion? Can we imagine women as sexual subjects with their own desires? Do we have anything to say about body and pleasure in postcoloniality, especially from feminist or queer theological perspectives?

Althaus-Reid's work is indispensable in helping to explore these questions. What distinguishes her work from those of other queer theologians is her post-Marxist, postcolonial stance. If postcolonialism is a process of decolonizing the mind, *Indecent Theology* demonstrates the arduous process of unhinging our habits of thought from heterosexist theology and heteronormativity. By shattering all taboos and laying out her truths with such tenacity, she illuminates for us, by way of example, the fierce battle for truth and for freedom of thought.

A memorable figure in postcolonial discourse is that of the female subaltern described in Gayatri Chakravorty Spivak's controversial essay, "Can the Subaltern Speak?"[24] Bhubaneswari Bhaduri, a young Indian woman of sixteen or seventeen, hanged herself in North Calcutta in 1926 while she was menstruating. It was later discovered that she was a member of a group involved in armed struggle for Indian independence. She was given a task associated with a political assassination and, unable to confront the task, she killed herself to show her loyalty. Bhaduri took care to prevent her death from being seen as the result of an illicit pregnancy, which is why she committed suicide during menstruation. Yet, this fact was soon forgotten, with her family members, even women, treating her suicide as a case of illicit love. Out of despair and disappointment, Spivak famously declares: "the subaltern cannot speak."

"Can the subaltern speak?" became one of the most hotly debated subjects in postcolonial discourse in the wake of this article. Some have accused Spivak, because of her elitist position, of not allowing the subaltern to speak or for failing to listen to her even when she speaks. As a result of harsh criticisms, Spivak has clarified and revised her position. She argues that even if the subaltern speaks, she would not be listened to because there is no infrastructure to allow her to be heard.[25] Yet it seems that no one has pointed out that the female subaltern described by Spivak was a very conventional figure in the nationalist discourse—politically subversive, but sexually innocent. Given these circumstances, feminist liberation theologians would have no problem embracing the subaltern and giving her voice in their theology. Spivak further notes the teenager was "no doubt looking forward to good wifehood"[26] while waiting for her menstruation. In other words, Bhaduri remained faithful to patriarchy and heteronormativity in Indian society. One might wonder whether she would have had many sympathizers—those who rushed to defend her and give her speech—if Bhaduri had somehow disturbed the heterosexist closet.

Althaus-Reid begins her *Indecent Theology* with female subalterns who are much less sexually innocent than the Indian teenager. She tells of the women lemon vendors, who sit on the pavement of the streets of Buenos Aires, selling fruit, flowers, and fresh herbs. These indigenous women, with lustrous black plaits, give off the odor of sex and perhaps do not have their underwear on while

they sit there. Althaus-Reid's theology is populated with these colorful charac-
ters who have not been given voice and remain invisible in traditional theology—the queer, the bisexual, the transgender, the leather community, the drag
queens in carnivals, and those who dream of French-kissing God. Her inclusion
of these figures challenges the construction of a universalized theological subject,
the fiction of stable sexual identity, and the mono-relational patterns in church
and society. The bodies of the sexual Other and the excluded force us to look at
theology from the Other side and to encounter a Queer God "as a stranger at the
gates of Hegemonic Theology."[27]

If women theologians from the Global South have called the intervention of
women in liberation theology the "irruption within an irruption,"[28] Althaus-
Reid calls for a further irruption. She writes, "theology needs to confront the
irruption of the sexual subject in history, in the same way that liberationists confronted the irruption of the Church of the poor or the 'underdogs of history.'"[29]
The emergence of new theological subjects—whether the poor, the female subaltern, the Black, or the Dalit—is threatening and polemical. As formerly silenced
theological subjects, they have been unrepresented and unrepresentable by a
Christian symbolic that excludes them as the Other. The irruption of the Other
always challenges existing episteme and theological methodologies and "consti-
tutes the revelatory horizon of the Church."[30]

Although postcolonial theology has interrogated the intersections of race,
gender, and class within the contexts of nation, empire, colonialism, and diaspora, not much has been said about heterosexism and heteronormativity except
for in the works of Althaus-Reid and a few others. Some postcolonial and liberation theologians still assume that attention to sexuality will distract us from the
most important economic and political issues. I have heard one Chilean theologian ask, "If we talk about God in the gay bar, what about God in the torture
chamber?" Althaus-Reid argues to the contrary that every economic and political theory has explicit or implicit assumptions about gender and sexuality such
that changes in sexual ideologies would help transform mechanisms of control
and power. She writes: "postcolonial theology needs to take seriously the sexual
gestures of difference which inform the Sacred, while allowing the same sexual
different to participate in the construction of new ecclesiologies and a different
concept of marriage."[31]

TONGZHI LOVE FROM A CROSS-CULTURAL PERSPECTIVE

The struggle of queer people for dignity cannot be separated from the colonial
legacy and the continuing fight for human rights. Many writings on queer issues
arise out of a Christian and white American context. Regrettably, they have
seldom touched on the relation between colonialism and sexuality, tending to
separate sexuality from other social and political forces. For people from the
majority world, it is imperative to look at how sexuality has been impacted by

colonial discourse and policy. As a former British colony where the majority of the population is Chinese, Hong Kong offers a good case study. On August 17, 2003, members of the Rainbow Action gay rights group disrupted Sunday Mass at a Hong Kong Cathedral to protest the church's stance against same-sex unions as set out by a statement from the Vatican. Although gay rights groups in Hong Kong had held rallies and demonstrations, it was rare to confront the church during Mass. The Catholic Church in Hong Kong had been known for its progressive stance, speaking out for many social justice issues. During the turnover of Hong Kong to China in 1997, the Catholic Church was outspoken about the protection of human rights, democracy, and the rule of law in Hong Kong. It has been disappointing that the Catholic Church in Hong Kong cannot see same-sex love as a human rights issue but, rather, continues in its homophobic biases.

As a former British colony, Hong Kong, similar to Uganda, inherited the British common law system, which was influenced by the Victorian prejudice against male homosexuality. Hong Kong criminalized homosexual acts between two male adults, and the highest penalty was a life sentence. This draconian law was not abolished until 1991 after almost ten years of struggle and resistance.[32] Since the late 1980s, lesbians and gay people in Hong Kong have called themselves "*tongzhi*," and the word has spread to Taiwan, mainland China, and other overseas communities. The word *tongzhi* has many meanings and interpretations and literally means "common goals and aspirations" in Chinese. It does not refer to a particular gender or fixed identities, such as homosexual, heterosexual, or bisexual, but is more fluid. It problematizes the notion of identity as fixed or natural and destabilizes the homogeneity and simple identification of "being gay."[33] As Rose Wu has pointed out, the use of the term *tongzhi* is a postcolonial gesture, indicating that sexual minorities in this context want to have their own name, different from those used in the West.[34] Moreover, *tongzhi* is the term used by Chinese Communists to mean "comrade" and carries negative connotations in postcolonial Hong Kong. Queer people have reclaimed the term and given it positive meanings and an interesting twist. We can see some parallel in the reappropriation of the term "queer" in the West.

Scholars who study ancient Chinese tradition point out that there has been a long homosexual tradition in China, and homo-, bi-, and transgendered practices were well documented.[35] It also spanned a range of social classes, from emperors and aristocrats to impoverished laborers. When some missionaries first came to China, they were shocked by the variety of sexual practices and the tradition of homosexuality in Chinese culture.[36] Transvestitism and transsexuality could be seen among the cross-dressing male actresses, and eunuchs performed the role of lover and comforter for emperors. In the 1980s, during debates to change the sodomy laws inherited from Britain in Hong Kong, evangelical Christians strongly opposed the decriminalization of male homosexual acts to protect Christian marriages and Chinese family structure. The supporters of decriminalization argued that Chinese culture had been more tolerant of homosexual behaviors than these opponents assumed. They surmised that it was the colonial sexual discourse, shaped by Christian biases, that had superimposed homophobic attitudes and laws on people in Hong Kong.

In traditional China, sexual intercourse is called *jiaohe*, which means joining together, or *fangshi*, which means things one does in one's room. The related term *se*, has many different meanings, which can refer to color, beauty, sexual sensation, or pleasure. Both Confucian and Daoist traditions regard sex as human nature that need not be repressed. Chinese religious and medical discourses include instructions about sexual techniques and bedchamber arts for vitality, bodily health, and circulation of energy.[37] According to Chou Wah-shan, same-sex activities were portrayed in social, rather than sexual terms, such as *xiang gong* (male prostitute), *fen tao* (shared peach), *jinlan zimei* (golden orchid sisters) and *qidi* and *qixiong* (adopted brothers).[38] The terms used to describe same-sex activities are rather poetic and without social and moral condemnation, including *mo jing* (polishing mirrors), *mo doufu* (grinding bean curd), *hou ting hua* (the backyard flower), *dui shi* (paired eating), or *chui xiao* (to play a vertical flute). The Chinese have a broad and relational view of sexuality and do not confine it narrowly to sexual activities. The body has many pleasurable zones, which are not limited to genitalia.

Although China has a very rich cultural understanding of sexuality and a long tradition of same-sex love, we must avoid an Orientalist approach commonly found in missionary and colonial discourses that sexualizes "the East." We also need to include a gender analysis in assessing the role of the erotic in this complex tradition. Historian Charlotte Furth has pointed out that Chinese religious and medical discourses on bedchamber arts were meant for male readers for their health and vitalization, and the erotic itself was gendered. She writes, "The erotic could be seen as a vehicle for social reproduction and the conception of descendants or for individual self-transformation and sagehood. Both of these alternatives require women to serve male goals."[39] China has a lesbian tradition, especially the *tzu shu nü* in Shunde, in Guangdong Province, who vowed not to marry and lived in a community house. Some of them lived together as married couples and made public vows in an official ceremony. More research has been done to understand female same-sex relationships in modern China and in urban settings, including the use of ethnography and the study of literature and visual culture. These studies offer fresh perspectives on the intersection between female same-sex love, modernity, gender and sex identity, and the politics of recognition in global times.[40]

QUEERING PHALLIC PLEASURE

Theology has much to say about gender and sex and about which bodies and bodily acts are acceptable, and which are not. Feminist theologians have argued that, in Christianity, patriarchy is justified by and coheres around the symbol of the phallic God. Without debunking this phallic symbol, a vibrant and life-giving postcolonial sexual theology cannot be written. The power of the phallus is found not only in Christianity, but also in other religious traditions and practices. For example, Chinese ancestor worship reenacts patrilineal and patriarchal structures and powers. Some Chinese scholars who have studied the etymology of the Chinese character for ancestor (祖) believe that it originally referred to the phallus.

Why does society have such in investment in the phallus, and what gives it such sustaining power? In the chapter "God's Phallus" in his award-winning book *On the Postcolony*, Cameroonian theorist Achille Mbembe writes about the phantasm of power and the phantasm of the One.[41] In the Jewish and Christian traditions, this is represented by the monotheistic God, who has no equals, whose power is total and whose commandments must be obeyed. In the Bible, the phantasm of the One coincides with the political discourse associated with the concepts of kingship and sovereignty, and the exclusionary logic of the "elected nation." Later, when Christianity became a state religion, this phantasm further evolved to include not just one God, but also one church and one salvation. The logic of the One excludes plurality and imposes homogeneity and conformity. Ever since Europe encountered the diversity of cultures and peoples, the colonial logic of one God and one faith has been contested. In the East Asian tradition, for example, the symbol of yin and yang challenges the closure of the One, for it embodies a logic that is dialectical, relational, and ever-changing.

The one phallic God has disciplining power over women's sexuality, because the definition of sex and the propriety of sexual acts have been constructed in relation to the phallus. The Christian church traditionally had only two sexual roles for women, both defined vis-à-vis the phallus: virgins and mothers. All other sexual relationships were outlawed, and even today many people still have a hard time imagining two women having sex. Even though many poor countries can ill afford to support more children, the Catholic Church continues to propagate the ideology of global, compulsory motherhood by enlisting the figure of Mary the Mother of Jesus as an accomplice. As Althaus-Reid has pointed out, the church can accommodate Mary as the Mother of the poor, but Mary as the "Mother of faggots" must be shunned and kept in the closet.[42]

The phallic God severely limits and restricts women's sexual pleasure and enjoyment to such an extent that many women internalize this, treating sex as taboo. In contrast, men's phallic pleasure is boosted, if not glorified. In a colonial setting, the colonial masters have sexual access to indigenous women, slaves, and people of the lower classes. In fact, sexual violence is a form of colonial domination and control. People who are not white or possess phallic power lack the socioeconomic power and access. Social ethicist Miguel De La Torre notes, "Communities of color, who have been castrated and lack the power, privilege, and profit afforded by the phallus symbol, occupy the position where both their bodies and minds are forcefully and violently raped. They are relegated to primitive and exotic spaces to be enjoyed by those who have proven their misogynist authority."[43] What is more troubling is that sexual domination does not only take the forms of rape, assault, and coercion but also in the generation of sexual desire and lure. Frantz Fanon has analyzed the psychodynamics of why Black women desire white men over Black men in a racist, colonial context, because of the inequality of power that exists between white and Black people.[44] Although critics challenge Fanon's position as chauvinistic,[45] the question of who can express their colonial desire and have access to phallic pleasure is a political and ethical one that cannot be ignored. Some gay theologians have tried to recover the beauty of gay sex and phallic pleasure. Although I am sympathetic to the recovery of gay sex, which has long been a taboo subject, I detect vestiges of phallic worship, especially with regard to Jesus. Some gay theologians have observed how the naked and erotic body of Christ on the cross has elicited titillating homoerotic desire and pleasure in male believers. Others argue that Jesus was neither asexual nor heterosexual, but rather that he had intimate and erotic relations with the beloved disciple in John's Gospel. Robert Goss traces a long tradition of homoerotic devotion to Jesus, which can be seen in the poetry of John Donne and George Herbert. To subvert the normative borders of heteronormativity, he imagines Jesus to be a penetrated male, a bottom violating the usual construction of phallic domination and male penetration.[46] Although this Jesus figure would be iconoclastic, we need to point out that the bottom is not without pleasure in gay sexuality and literature. In his queer studies of John's Gospel, Tat-siong Benny Liew points out that in the passion narratives, John depicts Jesus' masculinity "with a body that is being opened to penetration."[47] Jesus says that the Father is with him throughout the process. Liew suggests that when Jesus' body is pierced and penetrated, he might be imagining his passion experience as a masochistic sexual relation with his Father. In Freudian terms, the pleasure and death principle come together at that moment.

Jesus' death on the cross has been an intense site of contention in the controversy on violence, suffering, sacrifice, and redemption. Feminist theologians Rita Nakashima Brock and Rebecca Ann Parker reject the idea that redemption is brought about by Jesus' innocent suffering.[48] Throughout history, countless women have been taught to imitate Jesus' example and to sacrifice and suffer silently in the face of abuses and injustice. But if we look at the death of Jesus from the phallic pleasure principle, a different picture of the cross appears. Achille Mbembe connects Jesus' suffering not with pain but with ecstasy and links salvation with the ejaculatory power of God's phallus:

> At the final point of his calvary, the victim's body became fixed in a posture of ecstasy in suffering. In his death, erective power and ejaculatory power came together to cancel each other and form one flux, the salvatory flux. The god demonstrated an extraordinary ability to discharge salvation in the very act of dying. To that extent there is something orgiastic about his death.[49]

After the bodily implosion and tension abates, Jesus' body returns to a state of felicity in the magic act of resurrection. During the Renaissance, some artists depicted the resurrected Jesus with an erect penis as a sign of life and proof of virility and vitality.[50] Therefore, the cross and resurrection are not just associated with God's love, but with the incarnated God's sexual physiology as well. If the central salvific symbols of Christianity are predicated on male physiology and sexuality, it is not surprising that the Vatican repeatedly declares that women cannot be ordained, because women cannot be *persona Christi*. It is not just a matter of Jesus' male gender, as feminist theologians have long questioned, but his masculine sexuality too.

Mark D. Jordan has written about what he has called the paradox of the Catholic Jesus: "the paradox created by an officially homophobic religion in which an all-male clergy sacrifices male flesh before images of God as an almost naked man."[51] If the half-naked Jesus symbolizes not just terror and suffering, but also ejaculatory power, people cannot come close to this power, because it is taboo. In many religions, sexual relations often play a role in magical orgies, but the Hebrew religion strictly forbade any form of cultic prostitution. In the Christian church, believers can meditate on the half-naked Jesus, but any erotic and sexual feeling about him is taboo. It seems to me that the Eucharistic liturgy might contain, at least subliminally, some rudimentary elements of phallic worship, since male flesh is consecrated and distributed. For a Catholic priest to represent Jesus at the altar, he is required to be celibate and keep his phallic power in check. He is not supposed to use his ejaculatory power for his own sexual pleasure, but to work for the church and the salvation of humankind. It is indeed paradoxical when sexuality, ejaculation, and ecstasy are so much linked with Christology and redemption that the church would be so anti-body and anti-sex.

POSTCOLONIALITY AND SEXUAL THEOLOGY

Postcolonial discourse challenges the binary, hierarchical, and patriarchal construction of identity and difference. Postcolonial sexual theology must debunk the convention of Presence-God-Phallus in order to recover the body and sexual pleasures in their numerous forms. This is not an easy task, as Trinh T. Minh-Ha has noted, "The refusal of a *dualistic* and *thing-oriented* philosophy is a work of *endless* locating and undermining."[52] Althaus-Reid challenges us to experiment with thinking bisexually, which refers to a critical epistemological stance, rather than the theologian's individual sexual identity.[53] In doing so we might be less prone to thinking in heterosexual dyad, which has dominated the theological tradition for so long. Her challenge to think bi- or poly-amorously is an invitation to look at human desire and pleasure in their myriad forms, to embrace the searing beauty as well as vulnerability in our search for love and for God.

Sexual theology has a relatively short history in Asia, and many Asian churches still find it embarrassing to discuss sexual issues in public. A range of new sexual subjects has entered theological discussion, including lesbian and gay people, butches/femmes, Filipino domestic workers, female sex workers, and older women.[54] A key issue is reexamining body and sexuality from both the Christian tradition and the rich cultural heritages of Asia. While women's sexuality has been discussed in Asian churches primarily within the bounds of monogamous marriage and procreation, feminist theologians are bold to explore other manifestations of women's passion and desire. For example, Pushpa Joseph from India articulates a Shakti theology, which links the creative power of eros with the divine energy of Shakti in Tantric philosophy.[55] She wants to move from the dualism of intellectualistic patriarchal theologies to an embodied theology, which celebrates eros, fertility, and life. Sharon A. Bong from Malaysia turns to Judith Butler's queer theory and Carter Heyward's theology as resources for her queer revisions of Christianity.[56] Using the images of the lesbian mother, lesbian nun, and butch/femme, she speaks of the autoerotic pleasure of women, the conflation of sex/gender/desire, and the church's indoctrination of compulsory heterosexuality and motherhood. In her recent work, she interviews queer people from different religious traditions in Singapore and Malaysia to understand different ways of being spiritual and religious in postcolonial and multireligious contexts. She shows how queer people have both challenged and reconstructed elements of their religious traditions for survival.[57]

From a postcolonial context, these feminist theologians do not treat sexuality narrowly through a gender/sex framework, but place it within the larger cultural, political, and economic contexts. They are keenly aware that sexuality is shaped by the changing cultural ethos, such as modernization, as well as by globalizing forces. The availability of a woman's body for pleasure is determined not by her desire alone, but also increasingly by market forces, such as migrant labor, sex trafficking, patriarchal workplaces and business practices, and a consumerist culture. Lest we forget, the capitalist market is a keen promoter of women's sexual freedom and adventures. Thus, simply reclaiming women's sexual agency, without a concomitant economic analysis, will easily benefit those marketing perfume, fashion, lingerie, and other consumer goods. While the French feminists talk about *jouissance*, the majority of the world's women may not yet enjoy this class privilege.

It is Althaus-Reid's astute materialist analysis of society that makes her sexual theology significant to addressing the postcolonial condition. Although she shared poststructuralist theory's assumption about the instability of identity, and has created a playful and sarcastic sexual vocabulary, she cared deeply about the poor and remained close to her working-class roots. I hope that future sexual theologies will not run with her queerness without paying attention to her concern for the postcolonial. We will be remiss if we only take one or two of her famous concepts, such as the Bi/Christ or indecency, without grasping that indecent/ing is a process to rethink sexuality within the whole matrix of social power and its disciplining apparatuses. My fear is that we have so trivialized her "indecent" project that it will become cliché. While "indecency" gains currency as something trendy, the risk is that it will be evacuated of its subversive meanings. For Althaus-Reid, even gay, lesbian, and queer theologies need the process of indecent/ing, when the modes of thoughts and writing protocols have become stale and no longer surprising.

Postcolonial sexual theology must also address how race is sexualized and sex is racialized in the colonial discourse. As Kelly Brown Douglas has pointed out, the construction of whiteness is based upon the views and attitudes that dehumanize Black people and other people of color.[58] In particular, Black bodies and sexuality have been portrayed with stereotypes and false images, such as the "Black mammy," "Black Jezebel," and the hyper-libidinous "Black buck." Partly because of the hyper-sexualization of Black bodies in the dominant white culture, the Black church and community have avoided talking about sexuality issues. Douglas faults Black theology for its silence about sexuality and the Black churches for their heterosexism. Black lesbians, she says, have been especially targeted, for they are seen as a threat to Black families. Douglas wants to develop a theology of Black sexuality based on a sexual discourse of resistance. Such a discourse must promote an awareness of the complex history of Black people's responses to sexual issues and affirm sexual pluralism in the Black community. A more open discussion about sexuality in the Black churches, she says, will promote healthier sexual attitudes and will be helpful in addressing issues of male and female relationships, heterosexism, teenage pregnancy, and HIV/AIDS in the Black community.

Several years ago, I taught a course on "Christology and Cultural Imagination," and my African American student La Ronda Barnes wanted to find images of Christ that she could identify with and in which she could see Black womanhood as fully reflected in the image of God. Barnes writes, "I believe that in order to experience, envision, and be in intimate relationship with God as Christians, we must be willing to embrace Christ as more than a male and more than a being with black or white skin or any other color or characteristic that we have categorized as human."[59] She referred to the paintings of artists such as Angela Yarber, Megan Clay, and Janet McKenzie, each of whom envisioned a Christ who is a person of color and who is female.[60] She also discusses the icon "Neither" by David Hayward that shows a Black Christ who is neither male nor female.[61] She explained why these images are important to the faith formation and spirituality of Black women:

> To see a black female as Christ, whether on the cross or as a symbol of daily companionship, renewal, or transformation, is to see black females, in all our shapes, hues, and backgrounds, as beings created in the image of God. It is to see black females as connected to the strength, interconnectedness, and wholeness of body, mind, and spirit that emanates from what is holy and sacred.[62]

Barnes' work shows much more can be learned about race, body, sexuality, and Christ through visual arts and other sources. Because of her untimely death, Althaus-Reid left behind a very important project of mutual learning and cross-fertilization of people in "innumerable Queer religious and political diasporas."[63] Her work is not without critique though. For example, Jane Nichols has challenged that Althaus-Reid still harbors a bio-essentialist view of a woman. She has used the figure of transvestite to subvert assumptions about gender but does not talk much about transgender or transsexual women.[64] Transsexual women who reject biological sex as controlling and challenge a gendered regime that places them at odds with their initially perceived and assigned category have much insight to offer us about gender and sexual identity, motherhood, reproduction, and family, as well as a more inclusive sexual theology.

In Althaus-Reid's later work, she had increasingly turned to Latin American cultural resources and literature for theological insights. As we have seen, there are also resources for the construction of sexual theology in the Chinese traditions and in cultures historically not dominated by the Christian symbolic and imaginary. Patrick S. Cheng, an Asian American gay theologian, draws resources from Asian American queer theory and literary works to reconstruct the Christian doctrines of sin and grace.[65] He highlights the importance of the postcolonial concept of hybridity in decolonizing Asian American theologies with regard to sexuality and in decolonizing queer theologies with regard to race. As we have more queer theologies from diverse cultural, racial, and linguistic backgrounds, we will liberate God from the hegemonic Western closets and hear God speak in different queer tongues.

Can the subaltern enter the discourse of sexual theology? Spivak's challenge remains when we try to talk about the sexual life and experiences of the poor and the subaltern as middle-class theologians. As Mario Costa, Catherine Keller, and Anna Mercedes have warned: "The theopolitical eros of the poor differs significantly from any 'love the poor' where the poor are the subject of the love of the rich; it is rather the poor's own love, the brawny love born in the place of poverty itself."[66] There is a certain ingenuity and courage in the persistence of those experiencing poverty to love and live against all odds. Remembering the subalterns, theologians must continuously push their theological envelope and stand in solidarity with those who struggle to love on the Other side. This work is not only life-giving but also politically subversive, for it undermines the heteropatriarchal colonial regime. In *The Wisdom of Fools?* Mary Grey says that revelation does not happen one-on-one but is a communal experience shared through "epiphanies of connection."[67] It is in forming new matrices of relationships and connections that we offer each other the gift of touching the "Other side of God."

Chapter 4

American Empire
and Christianity

*Inevitably the social and political order in which men [sic] find security is
given a higher sanctity than their own interests and opinions. It is derived
from the divine logos or reason and attributed to the divine will.*

Reinhold Niebuhr[1]

*We are not trying to make America great again; we must be about making
America better than it has ever been.*

Emilie M. Townes[2]

During his 2016 presidential campaign, Donald Trump used "Make America
Great Again" as his campaign slogan. He wanted to take American foreign policy in a radically new direction by bombing the Islamic State, strengthening
the military, building a wall between the U.S. and Mexico, deporting undocumented persons, banning Muslims, limiting refugees, and renegotiating trade
agreements. In his campaign rallies, candidate Trump repeatedly charged that
other countries were taking advantage of the U.S. and that the country was in
serious trouble. This was rather disingenuous, considering the U.S. is the most
powerful nation on earth. The U.S. economy is the world's largest in terms
of GDP. In 2019, the GDP in the U.S. was $21.4 trillion, which represented
17.65 percent of the world economy.[3] When Trump was running for the highest office in 2016, the U.S. defense budget was around $597 billion, almost as
much as the next fourteen countries put together and accounted for more than
a third of global defense spending.[4]

After four years of Trump's presidency, the country's democratic values and
institutions were severely threatened. Trump interfered with the Justice Department, pressured the Ukrainian government to investigate his political opponent,
and obstructed Congress. His administration was incompetent and utterly failed

71

to lead the country amid multiple crises: the coronavirus, economic devastation because of the pandemic, and a national reckoning of racial injustice. After the death of George Floyd, an unarmed Black man who was killed in police custody, protests erupted in many cities around the country while Trump threatened to send the military to quell the unrest. Demonstrators at a peaceful protest at Lafayette Square were forcefully dispersed with tear gas so that Trump could pose for a photo-op holding up a Bible in front of a church. After he lost reelection in 2020, he and his enablers spread baseless lies that the election was fraudulent, and he even refused to concede for months. He incited the crowd who violently stormed into the nation's Capitol on January 6, 2021, and became the only president to be impeached twice. Democracy barely survived, and Trumpism will continue to cast its spell on many Americans even though Trump is gone from the White House.

Trump could not have ascended to power without the support of the Christian Right. As Reinhold Niebuhr warned almost sixty years ago, empires require gods to give them an aura of higher authority and ultimacy. Trump tried to put on the face of a bona fide Christian to appeal to conservative Christians. Religious rhetoric describing the current political climate as an apocalyptic showdown between good and evil has been employed to justify American hegemony. The Christian Right has supported America's imperialistic agenda for decades through their talk shows, TV evangelism, megachurches, religious propaganda, and political clout. To galvanize support, conservative Christians have fought prolonged cultural wars against abortion and homosexuality in the name of "family values." About 81 percent of white evangelicals voted for Trump in 2016 and about 75 percent in 2020.[5] Given the enormous political influence of the Christian Right, it is critical to scrutinize its deployment of religious rhetoric to further white nationalism and imperialistic causes.

Scholars of religion have examined the historical and religious roots of American imperialism and its newer manifestations. Some have drawn insights by comparing the religious ethos of the Roman Empire with that of contemporary American empire.[6] Others have scrutinized the religious and political ideologies of neoconservatives and the Religious Right to understand their formation of a theology of empire.[7] The number of American religious scholars interested in postcolonial studies has been growing, and the concerns of postcolonial critics—such as imperialism, expansionism, conquest, slavery, diaspora, hybridity, colonial violence, and globalization—can be found in the discussion of religion and American empire. In this chapter, I discuss the relationship between Christianity and empire, generally, before focusing on the American context, specifically.

CHRISTIANITY AND EMPIRE

Christianity cannot be understood apart from empire. We cannot understand the Bible without knowing something about the struggles for survival of the

Hebrew people under the Babylonian, Assyrian, Persian, Greek, and Roman Empires. Christianity began in the Roman Empire, in which Jesus and the early disciples lived as colonized peoples. Jesus died on the cross, which was a symbol of state terrorism and a form of torture and punishment for political rebels. Yet the connections between empire and Christianity have not received sufficient attention until fairly recently. Theologian Joerg Rieger notes:

> These connections were either taken for granted or simply overlooked. What was lost in the process was not only a clearer understanding of how the forces of empire impact us all, consciously or unconsciously, but also a sense of how Christianity can never quite be absorbed by empire altogether and which of its resources push beyond empire. One of the key purposes of the study of Christian theology in the context of empire has to do with a search for that which cannot be co-opted by empire, and thus inspires alternatives to empire, based on what I have called a "theological surplus."[8]

Before we explore Rieger's "theological surplus" and alternatives to empire, we have to ask why Americans have not been comfortable with seeing connections between empire and Christianity. One of the main reasons is that many Americans have been brought up to see religion and politics as separate from one another. Middle-class American Christianity has so successfully adapted to the individualistic culture of the U.S. that religion has become a privatized affair. The Christian messages of sin, atonement, justification, and salvation have been thoroughly individualized, if not psychologized, such that they have relatively little social import. We look at Jesus primarily as a religious figure, separated from the highly politicized and volatile situation of his time, an era filled with periodic popular revolts and protests against Roman rule. New Testament scholar Richard Horsley denounces this attempt to depoliticize Jesus, saying, "It is difficult to continue to imagine that Jesus was the only figure unaffected by his people's subjection to the Roman imperial order."[9] This depoliticization of Jesus is rooted not only in American individualism, Horsley says, but also in the so-called scientific quest for Jesus in our day, which reduces the Gospels to religious bits and pieces and Jesus to a religious teacher uttering isolated parables and sound bites. In some of this historical reconstruction, Horsley writes, Jesus was not a prophet but "rather a wisdom teacher, like the wandering Cynic philosophers in Hellenistic cities, teaching an alternative hippie-like lifestyle to a bunch of rootless nobodies."[10]

In addition to depoliticizing Jesus, Christianity has held very ambivalent attitudes toward empire. On the one hand, some churchgoers believe that the Roman Empire was beneficial to Christianity and helped prepare the way for the spread of the gospel to the many nations it had brought together. The Romans built roads and infrastructure, which allowed missionaries such as Paul to travel and preach the gospel. The conversion of Constantine in the fourth century elevated Christianity from a persecuted sect to a state religion. Since then, Christianity has cast its enormous influence on the development of Western societies and cultures. On the other hand, there are those who see the relationship between empire and Christianity as more paradoxical. Constantine's conversion brought protection of the Christian churches but also ushered in an endless power struggle between the church and the state. Some also point to the Crusades in the Middle Ages and the Spanish conquest of the Americas as examples of how the church either justified or served the interests of empire.

To clarify the complex relation between Christianity and empire, I coedited *Empire and the Christian Tradition* to investigate the interconnections between the two throughout the centuries, and to explore resources for resistance to empire.[11] The volume demonstrates that the relationship is more dialectical, as Rieger notes, "there might be a theological surplus even in the theologies that shaped up under the conditions of empire, and . . . there are traces of empire even in those theologies that consider themselves resistant to or independent of empire."[12] For instance, while Augustine contrasted the city of God with the earthly city and did not sacralize any worldly power, his theological justification for imperial violence and intervention against Donatism raised problematic questions for political theology. Later, the Spanish Dominican priest Bartolomé de Las Casas (1484–1566) spoke vehemently against the torture and unjust treatment of Amerindians. Yet, at the same time, he supported Spanish colonial rule and the conversion of the Native peoples. In the case of the U.S., Christianity has both colluded with imperial interests and provided insights for challenging empire. As early as 1930, Reinhold Niebuhr published his essay "Awkward Imperialists," in the *Atlantic Monthly* to warn that the U.S. was not prepared for the responsibilities associated with imperial power. Niebuhr noted that because of World War I, the U.S. was suddenly thrust into the position of an imperial power thanks to her new-found economic clout. Yet American imperial power was "administered with singular awkwardness" because American economic and political structures had not prepared for it.[13] Niebuhr concluded: "No one knows what the future may hold in store for us. The fate of imperialists is always uncertain, and awkward imperialists run a double hazard."[14] America's road to become the world's superpower was marked by torturous wars in Asia and the Middle East with the tragic loss of many lives, economic exploitation and financial control, and military domination throughout the world. American ascendency and hegemony have been propelled by a strong belief in America's Manifest Destiny and the nation's mission to change the world.

MANIFEST DESTINY AND CHRISTIANITY

The notion of Manifest Destiny in U.S. history has strong religious roots in Christianity. From the beginning of American history, empire and Christianity were closely intertwined. Spain, France, and England each claimed that they were the elect nation with a divine mandate when they created their colonies in America and expanded their imperial control. The formation of the U.S. as a nation and subsequent expansion into the western "wilderness" were based on strong religious beliefs that America was chosen by God for a special calling and destiny. The Puritans believed that they were God's New Israel, the new elect people, and America became the new "Promised Land." The continental expansion of the U.S. could not be treated as a separate phenomenon from European colonialism and must be seen as an interrelated form of imperial expansion. Novelist Russell Banks notes in his book *Dreaming Up America*: "Our earliest conquest of the western half of North America. . . bore an astounding resemblance to European colonization of Africa and elsewhere" and "the path to the American Dream has become a tortured path. It has led to our building an empire."[15]

This belief in "New Israel" and in the newly elect nation gave rise to the notion of American exceptionalism. According to historian James Hudnut-Beumler, this exceptionalism has two interrelated meanings. The first meaning is the sense of being more fortunate than others, because of a superabundance of good land, minerals, natural resources, waterways, and hardworking people. The second is that America is God's favored nation. This view goes all the way back to John Winthrop's speech to his fellow Puritans aboard the *Arabella* on their way to found Massachusetts Bay Colony. America was considered chosen by God, and God had great expectations for a holy commonwealth. Winthrop said: "Wee shall be like a Citie on a Hill."[16] Christianity provided and continues to provide the religious sanction for the belief in Manifest Destiny of the American people, such that they have the mandate to expand territorial control from the Atlantic to the Pacific coasts and to fill the whole continent. On this view, Americans are virtuous people and have the unique mission to demonstrate to the world a superior form of government and a religious calling to redeem the nations.[17]

The American myth of chosenness provided religious legitimization for the dispossessing of Native lands, forced conversion, numerous and repetitious warfare, and genocide of the Native peoples. Unlike external colonialism, in which a group of colonists occupy the land and exercise control over a large indigenous population, the American expansion is sometimes called "domestic imperialism" or "internal colonialism." In internal colonialism, Cherokee scholar Jace Weaver explains, "the native population is swamped by a large mass of colonial settlers who, after generations, no longer have a *métropole* to return to. Today, Native American life is characterized by the same paternalistic colonialism that has marked it for over a century. The heavy hand of federal plenary power still rests heavily upon their affairs."[18] Because this internal colonialism has shown no signs of abatement, Weaver questions whether postcolonial theories, based largely on the experience of external colonialism, are applicable to the American situation. He further argues that colonialism is not dead in much of the Two-Thirds World and "the post-colonial moment for Native Americans will not yet have arrived."[19]

Even though Weaver has justifiably expressed reservations, Andrea Smith does not treat "postcolonial" in a chronological sense and has found elements of postcolonial theory helpful, especially the works of Edward Said and Homi Bhabha, for her analysis of how the colonizers in the U.S. context needed a strategy of "assimilating the colonized in order to establish colonial rule."[20] She points to the roles played by Christian missionaries and faults the missionary boarding schools for separating Native American children from their families to receive Christian "civilizing" instruction. After studying the work of several missions, George E. Tinker of the Osage Nation also concludes, "The missionaries were guilty of complicity in the destruction of Indian cultures and tribal social structures—complicity in the devastating impoverishment and death of the people to whom they preached."[21]

Smith agrees with postcolonial critics who argue that colonial asymmetry of power is often exhibited in the intersection of race, gender, and sexuality. For her, sexual violence against Native women was and is an insidious form of colonial control and a tool of genocide. Native scholars have pointed out that Native peoples are often compared to the Canaanites in the Bible, who personify sexual perversity and were the descendants of unsavory relations. As a result, Native bodies are considered "dirty," sexually violable, and "rapable," and they are not "entitled to bodily integrity."[22] If white women are symbols of purity and sexual prudence, then "Native women, as bearers of a counter-imperial order, pose a supreme threat to the imperial order. Symbolic and literal control over their bodies is important in the war against Native people."[23] In the past, cultural genocide often included the suppression of Native cultures and the prohibition of performing religious rituals. Today, this has taken a different turn as Native rituals and spirituality have been misappropriated and commodified in new ways.[24]

The notion of Manifest Destiny has also been reinforced by a racial imaginary, which justified white supremacy and the horrors of chattel slavery. Slavery began not long after the English settlement in Virginia in 1607 and lasted as a legal institution for centuries until 1865. In the Middle Passage, Africans were brought from their African homeland in exchange for raw materials and resources in the Americas in the ludicrous Atlantic slave trade. Traders from Spain, Portugal, the United Kingdom, Netherlands, France, Denmark, Sweden, Brazil, and North America reaped plenty from this triangular trade. Christian slaveholders used the curse of Ham (Gen. 9:18–27) and other passages in the Bible to justify slavery. As Willie James Jennings has shown, the modern Christian imagination has been infused with a racial hierarchy, and Christianity's socialization process has contributed to the creation and maintenance of segregated communities. He writes, "Christian theological imagination was woven into processes of colonial dominance. Other peoples and their ways of life had to adapt, become fluid, even morph into the colonial order of things."[25] But slaves did not passively acquiesce to this racist and brutal modern/colonial system, as clearly evinced by slave narratives, spirituals, and autobiographies. They assembled secretly to sing their songs, pray for their freedom, and retain elements of their African religious culture. In *Shoes That Fit Our Feet* and other works, Dwight N. Hopkins has mined the rich depository of slave religion as a resource for constructing Black theology.[26] Hopkins' theological concerns have led him to study traditional African religions in slave religions and turn to African traditions as resources for his construction of theology.

The belief in Manifest Destiny was also used to validate continental acquisitions in the Oregon Country, Texas, New Mexico, and California. Roberto S. Goizueta says Hispanics and Latinos continue to be "a people exiled in a foreign land" because they had lived on this land long before the Pilgrims "settled" here. He writes, "Exile in our own land, we speak the languages, pray to the gods, and sway to the rhythms of the Native American and the Spaniard, the African and the Anglo."[27] Because of their mixed cultures, languages, and backgrounds, they are often treated as "aliens" and "outsiders." President Trump's anti-immigrant rhetoric and policies and his building a wall on the U.S.-Mexican border targeted especially immigrants and refugees from Central and Latin America. The Hispanic and Latinx community has resisted his border wall and his harsh treatment of undocumented immigrants, including the Dreamers who came to the country as minors. As the largest racial and ethnic minority group in the U.S., Hispanic and Latinx people comprise an estimated 18 percent of the population. Already they have changed the face of the American Catholic Church and make up 52 percent of Catholics under thirty.[28] They are a social and political force to be reckoned with in American politics.

The racial imaginary can also be seen in the treatment of Asian Americans as perpetual foreigners and "strangers from a different shore."[29] American Orientalism works in tandem with American exceptionalism in constructing ontological and epistemological differences about the "West" and its non-Western "Others."[30] Asians are seen as strangers, partly because of the diverse cultures and religious traditions they have brought with them to the U.S. Asian religious traditions are seen as incompatible with Christianity, which is considered to be the only true religion. Indian American scholar Khyati Y. Joshi says, "Christianity dominates by setting the tone and establishing the rules and assumptions about who belongs or does not belong, about what is acceptable and not acceptable in public discourse."[31] The racist color-metaphor "yellow peril" has been used to describe the peoples of East Asia as an existential danger to the nation and to the Western world. The Chinese Exclusion Act of 1882 was the first federal law that proscribed entry of a national group. During World War II, about 120,000 Japanese Americans were sent to internment at isolated camps. Later, the myth of Asian Americans as "model minorities" has created a wedge between Asian Americans and other racial and ethnic groups. This farce does not take into consideration the plight of working-class Asian Americans and newer Asian immigrants who are struggling to survive in a foreign land.

THEOLOGICAL CRITIQUE OF AMERICAN EMPIRE

After September 11, 2001, the ideology of Manifest Destiny was revived as the U.S. sought to impose American values and institutions on the world, by military might if necessary, in the war against terrorism, and in the name of liberty and democracy. Biblical scholars have compared this emerging *Pax Americana* to the *Pax Romana* and pointed to their commonalities and differences. New Testament scholars, in particular, have used the theme of empire as a critical lens to reinterpret selected biblical texts. Books began to appear that bear the words "empire" or "imperial" in their titles, such as Horsley's *Jesus and Empire* and his edited volume *Paul and the Roman Imperial Order*; John Dominic Crossan's *God and Empire*; Warren Carter's *Matthew and Empire*; and Stephen D. Moore's *Empire and Apocalypse: Postcolonialism and the New Testament.*[32] Among the authors of this growing scholarship, Richard Horsley stands out because of his voluminous output on New Testament and Roman Empire.

With a postcolonial sensibility, Horsley analyzes the interlocking structures of the Roman imperium, such as the Emperor-cult, the patronage pyramids, the flow of resources to the imperial metropolis, the glorification of conquest, the maintenance of national security through terror and military force, and the use of client rulers and religious leaders.[33] Even though the *Pax Romana* seemed to be all-pervasive, the empire was not uncontested, as popular resistance and rebellions erupted in Judea and Galilee, as well as in Spain, Gaul, and North Africa. For Horsley, Jesus' movement was one such resistance movement which could be compared to the kind of anti-imperial "nationalist" movements of our own time. This is particularly true in the description of Jesus' ministry and work in Mark, a Gospel that Horsley has studied in great detail. He writes, "Reading Mark from a postcolonial perspective may enable the recovery of Mark as a narrative of imperially subjected peasantries forming a movement of revitalized cooperative social formations based on their own indigenous traditions."[34] From such a postcolonial optic, Jesus was evidently not a passive religious leader, but an insurrectionary whose movement took an uncompromising stance against the Roman Empire and its client Judean and Galilean rulers, Antipas and the high priests. Horsley believes that once Jesus' anti-imperial message and the political nature of his movement are understood, they can provide a sound basis for a theological critique of imperial ideologies and structures, whether of Rome or of the contemporary U.S.[35]

While biblical scholars such as Richard Horsley and Fernando Segovia[36] have taken the lead in decolonizing biblical studies, several theologians have also applied postcolonial insights to their critical work. Mark Lewis Taylor, for instance, has identified the scope and tasks of postcolonial theologies in the specific context of the U.S. He surmises that this postcolonial approach needs not start from scratch but can draw from other available sources. The first source is the kind of work that Richard Horsley and others have been doing, which seeks to bring into sharp relief the counterimperial character of the origins of Christianity. The Jesus movement aimed to form anti-imperial communities and a new ethos to resist the colonizing and imperial powers. The second source consists of Latin American liberation theologies, Black theology, feminist theology, and other theologies from the margin, which offer alternative paradigms to mainstream, white, Eurocentric theology. The third consists of the religious revolutionary tradition in the North Atlantic, which challenges colonialism, capitalism, and imperial power. The Levellers and Diggers in England and the sanctuary movement that sheltered Central American refugees in the 1980s are examples of this tradition. The fourth resource can be drawn from the work of interreligious coalitions that come together to struggle for political and social changes. For example, religious leaders of different traditions have gathered in ceremonies and attended events for major political mobilizations for justice.[37]

Taylor argues that postcolonial theologies in the U.S. must address the *Pax Americana's* nationalism and militarist exploitation. This requires nothing less than a "spiritual awakening" among U.S. theologians, he stresses, so that they will develop a counterimperial critique and not just another liberal theology that tends to accommodate the empire and the neoliberal market. Since the U.S. has supported the repressive policies of the State of Israel in dispossessing Palestinian lands and violating the peoples' rights, postcolonial theologians must speak against these unequal policies that not only have hurt the Palestinians but also threatened the peace and security of Israelis. For a long-lasting peace in the Middle East, postcolonial theologies will need to foster solidarity with liberation movements within the Islamic tradition and take caution not to label all Muslim resistance groups as Islamic fundamentalism. Some of these groups have legitimate reasons to react against American imperialistic practices. Strategic collaboration with anti-imperial groups working for peace and justice will undermine the one-sided rhetoric of war on terrorism. Last but not the least, Taylor observes that American imperial aggression is found not only abroad but also at home. As examples, he cites the two million plus people in the 2000s being locked up in U.S. prisons and racial profiling that unfairly targets racial minority persons and other stigmatized groups such as Muslim, Arab, and South Asian immigrants. Given such political repression in the name of national security, postcolonial theologians will need to find allies across faith traditions and political groups to bring about change effectively.[38]

If Taylor lays out the tasks of postcolonial theologies in the U.S., Catherine Keller uses postcolonial theory to challenge the fundamental imaginary of God and power and its deployment to justify American imperialistic claims. She argues that ever since theology hybridized with Hellenistic philosophy in the Greco-Roman empire, theology has relied on philosophical abstraction to develop its mode of discourse and its concepts and vocabularies. Theological arguments have tended to focus on doctrinal purity and orthodoxy, to the neglect of the sociopolitical and material contexts from which these theological concepts were drawn: "Theology learned from the *metaphysics* of the empire how to abstract from the *politics* of empire. So, by positing the ahistorical propositions of Christian orthodoxy as its eternally true foundation, theology has less readily recognized its own complicity in the multiple layers of western colonialism."[39]

To overcome such colonial complicity, Keller implores theologians to examine the use of theological rhetoric to justify preemptive attack, omnipotence, and state-authorized terror and torture. She focuses on the Christian notion of apocalypse, which has been repeatedly deployed to legitimize unilateral use of power, violence, and imperial aggression. Christian fundamentalists have used the apocalypse to point to God's judgment against the apostasy of a secularized America, as well as against the evil enemies that threaten their God's favored nation. These right-wing groups draw the parallel that in as much as God does not refrain from using violence and torture in the Apocalypse, the U.S. is justified to use the tactics of "shock and awe" in seeking vengeance against its enemies, with or without weapons of mass destruction. The power of such an apocalyptic imagination is hinged on the construction of mighty binary opposites—us versus them, the righteous versus the wicked, and the insider versus the outsider. In the past, progressive theologians tended to dismiss a frightening and gloomy portrayal of an imminent Armageddon and adopt an anti-apocalypse posture. Keller argues that such a dismissal will not address the issue at hand. Instead, she says this violent portrayal of the apocalypse must be replaced by a counterapocalypse. The construction of this counterapocalypse can take its cue from postcolonial critics, such as Homi Bhabha, who have proposed an "interstitial perspective" and a "third space" or "in-between space."[40] Counterapocalypse of the interstitial does not dwell on rigid and irreconcilable boundaries and differences. In a fluid third space, national and self-identities are not bounded and frozen because, in it, histories and geographies are seen as intertwined and overlapped, and differences can be constantly renegotiated.

During the COVID-19 pandemic, the trope of apocalypse was revived, as the U.S. was the country most hard-hit by the coronavirus, with more than 700,000 people dead as of October of 2021. Keller and her colleague John Thatamanil reject a literal interpretation of apocalypse, but they think that the apocalyptic moment can serve as a wake-up call to examine the precarious world we have built, "a world that now stands exposed and tottering in the harsh light."[41] The global crisis, they write, demands that we pay attention to our inescapable interdependence with other humans and non-humans, the looming calamity as a result of climate change, and global inequity as a result of the neoliberal economy. But the double sense of the word "apocalypse," meaning both revelation and end-time, also signals hope for a new beginning—the new heaven and new earth—that we can all strive for.

An important element of the Christian apocalypse is the coming of the Messiah who will separate the good from evil, save the righteous, and punish the wicked. These images of the warrior-messiah, Keller warns, whether taking the forms of a crusader, cowboy, or one who is supposed to bring (white) civilization to the world, has led to cultural imperialism and wreaked havoc in the world on a global scale. Because this messianic imperialism lies at the heart of an American ideology of empire and the myth of Manifest Destiny, Keller urges theologians to "free the messianic from the imperial imaginary, divine and human."[42] Even liberation theologians, she charges, subscribe to a masculinist and anthropocentric image of a "messianic warrior-liberator" who intervenes in history.[43] These theologians often place their hope in an omnipotent and transcendent God who will judge the rich and vindicate the poor. Contrary to this anthropocentric interpretation of liberation, Keller opts for a more inclusive and feminist understanding of messianic hope, based on the depths of creation and radical relationality and love.

Keller's critique of a messiah-warrior is relevant now more than ever, as Trump has often claimed that only he can save America and bring back the nation's past glory in his nationalistic and populist rhetoric. The overwhelming support of white evangelicals for Trump challenged Christian communities to rethink their position vis-à-vis American politics, alternative facts and realities, and deep divisions in their country. Miguel De La Torre articulates three particular challenges in this context. The first challenge is that the 2016 election "was marked by self-proclaimed faith leaders rushing to proclaim Trump as God's faithful servant."[44] Christians need to think about whether or not the church has sold its soul to the highest political bidder. The church needs to be clear that no political party, whether Republican or Democrat, and no president, prime minister, or emperor is ordained by God. Second, De La Torre observes, we live in a time of alternate "truths," fake news, doublespeak, lies, and rants. It is important for Christian leaders and theologians, together with leaders of other faith communities, to serve as unmistakable voices of justice based on "true facts." Third, we cannot only criticize the present, without projecting a radical hope for the future: "Our call is to create a new America that moves beyond its oppressive racist, imperialist, and misogynist past toward a new possibility, a possibility that takes seriously the rhetoric of 'liberty and justice for all.'"[45]

As the nation faced the coronavirus and a summer of protests in support of Black Lives Matter in 2020, womanist theologian Kelly Brown Douglas spoke loud and clear during a season of national reckoning with systemic racism. For her, racial injustice and inequality defined by white hegemony have existed since the founding of the nation. But COVID-19 has shined a spotlight on racism because the pandemic had disproportionally affected Black and Latinx communities. The coronavirus has magnified the injustice of the prison system and the mass incarceration of Black people as well as discrepancies within the health care system. Douglas says that there were two health crises in the nation—the coronavirus and the virus of racism. Because the nation has not attended to the latter, the former has exacerbated the problem. The Black Lives Matter movement has called attention to systemic racism and assault on Black bodies. She says white supremacy was manifested in the spectacle lynchings of George Floyd and Ahmaud Arbery, which were examples of twenty-first-century-style lynchings. She laments that many other Black bodies have been killed, though those killings might not have been caught on tape or attracted our attention.[46]

To dismantle white supremacy, Douglas traces racism and anti-blackness to the religious roots of American exceptionalism and Manifest Destiny. She argues that American exceptionalism is shaped by the Anglo-Saxon myth that came to America through the English reformers. The Pilgrims and Puritans fled from the Church of England to build a society and religious institutions that were more fitting for Anglo-Saxon culture. They wanted to build an Anglo-Saxon nation, which to them was virtually synonymous with a religious nation. Thus, "the Pilgrims and Puritans not only ensured that the Anglo-Saxon myth was the defining piece of American identity, but they provided this myth with religious legitimation. They gave it sacred authority."[47] From the founding of the nation, America's political identity, form of government, and its understanding of democracy and freedom were expressions of Anglo-Saxon character. The promise of liberty was reserved for its white citizens, though the Constitution says, "We the people." Inasmuch as America lives out this Anglo-Saxon myth, it will remain God's "chosen nation" and a "light on the hill": "To be a chosen nation is to be an Anglo-Saxon nation. To be an Anglo-Saxon nation is to be a chosen nation. It is this constructed racial-religious synchronicity that makes America exceptional."[48] Furthermore, since God has a preferential option for Anglo-Saxons, who possess the highest culture, God by implication can only be Anglo-Saxon. This God blesses America. For Douglas, American exceptionalism has its roots in the "hypervaluation" of whiteness as cherished property and the denigration of blackness, which is constructed as sin and alienated from God.[49]

Douglas argues that the belief in Manifest Destiny was closely related to American exceptionalism and that they can be considered two sides of the same coin: "America's sense of Manifest Destiny was about the destiny of Anglo-Saxons."[50] They had a mission of expanding their Anglo-Saxon virtue, religion, and liberty across the U.S. and the world. "The civilizing project was an Anglo-Saxon project. To be civilized was synonymous with assimilation to Anglo-Saxon social, cultural, and religious culture."[51] Native Americans and Black people could not be assimilated, and they were treated as uncivilized or not fully human. The ideology of Manifest Destiny, grounded in beliefs of a New Israel and divine calling, had the devastating impact of the genocide of Native Americans. Blacks were condemned to becoming chattel property and to live in subservience. After emancipation, the war against Black bodies continued, and "white backlash" took the form of Black Codes, Jim Crow, lynching, the war on drugs, and the stand-your-ground culture that has killed Trayvon Martin and other Black bodies.[52]

Given this history of the suffering of Black people, Douglas does not see salvation as associated with a messiah-warrior or with a triumphant liberator. She emphasizes that in the Black church tradition, it is the suffering of Jesus on the cross that speaks to Black people. Along with James Cone and others, Douglas regards Jesus' crucifixion as a first-century lynching.[53] The cross signifies Jesus' solidarity with the crucified class of his time and his opposition to the imperial forces. Jesus was with the denigrated bodies, the social outcasts, and people on the margins. Jesus' resurrection shows his death was not the end, for God prevails over the crucifying powers of evil. Therefore, to follow Jesus means the church needs to listen to the cries of the crucified people of our time. Douglas laments that the church has not lived out its prophetic mission because it often sides with the status quo. She says that faith communities should lead the way in anti-racism work.

As many white evangelicals continue to support Trump, despite his bigotry and racist rhetoric, Christian ethicist David P. Gushee has taken up the burden of calling white evangelicals to repentance. For twenty-five years, Gushee identified himself as an evangelical but then came to feel that he could no longer do so. He writes, "I would say that white evangelicalism in America has largely retreated back to its whiteness, its social conservatism, and the Calvinist-tinged fundamentalism out of which (neo)evangelicalism was carved at mid-century."[54] Gushee argues that white American Christianity has always been rooted in colonial empire building dating back to the colonization of the "New World." He agrees with Douglas that white Christianity accompanied the founding of the nation: "There was no original innocence, the heresy of white supremacy and its resulting sins were there from the beginning."[55]

For decades, Gushee was considered the leading evangelical ethicist. He observes that, though evangelicals included abolitionists and suffragists like Charles Finney, most of the time evangelicals have been socially and politically conversative. With the birth of the Christian Right in the late 1970s, white evangelicals supported Ronald Reagan and became entangled with the modern Republican Party. They supported the GOP's hawkish foreign policy and its laissez-faire economics. In return, the GOP allowed them access to Republican officials and supported their conversative "family values" agenda. With the marriage between white evangelicals and the GOP having lasted for some forty years so far, it is not surprising that white evangelicals voted overwhelmingly for a thrice-married and womanizing reality TV-star in the 2016 election. The plausible reasons for them to support Trump, as for any other GOP president in this era, include: "antiabortion policies, the appointment of conservative judges, business-friendly tax and regulatory policies, efforts to protect American jobs, efforts to secure US borders, support for Israel, and . . . friendliness to conservative Christians and their religious liberty concerns."[56] But the strong white evangelical support for Trump—some even saw him as helping bring the nation back to Christian ways—troubled many evangelicals, especially Black evangelicals.

Gushee agrees with African American professor Eboni Marshall Turman, who has said that "White Christianity in America was born in heresy."[57] It is a heresy, because it is against the basic tenets of Christianity that everyone is created in the image of God and is a child of God. Gushee says that white evangelicals have missed every opportunity of rejecting this heresy and repenting for the sins of slavery and racism. During the Civil War era, many southern white evangelicals sided with slavery, even citing passages from the Bible to support their position. In the Reconstruction period, many white Christians resisted national and racial reconstruction and did not condemn forthrightly the Jim Crow laws, the suppression of Black political rights, the rise of the KKK, and the terrors of lynching. While the Social Gospel movement at the turn of the twentieth century espoused social and economic reforms, the leaders for the most part ignored the plight of Black people and the voices of prophetic Black leaders, such as Ida B. Wells and W. E. B. DuBois. In the 1940s, the leaders of the modern evangelical movement were all white men, and the institutions they led were segregated: Black and Hispanic evangelicals had to form their own separate associations. During the Civil Rights period, responses from white evangelicals were sluggish and woefully inadequate. Instead of advocating for swift changes to recognize Black people's rights, white evangelicals opted to go slow with the integration of white churches, in Civil Rights legislation, and in recognizing Black leadership. The election of Barack Obama led to resistance among white evangelicals, the escalation of racially charged rhetoric, and the rise of what has been called white nationalism.[58]

Gushee surmises that a post-white-evangelical democratic politics must be based on the repentance of racism, the abandonment of white supremacy, and the refusal to collude with power in the name of religion. This can only be achieved by a renewed understanding of Jesus and his politics. Gushee finds white evangelicals' emphasis on personal salvation limited and narrow and their espousal of a prosperity gospel to be against Jesus' teaching. Instead, he emphasizes Jesus as an apocalyptic prophet who came to proclaim the imminent coming of the Kingdom of God. Jesus' warnings of divine judgment were urgent and relentless as he often spoke of the final coming of the Lord (Matt. 16:27; 24:36–51; 25:31–46). While Keller has reservations about the apocalyptic language outlined above, Gushee argues that Jesus' radical apocalypticism was meant to call people to be awake, to repent, and to prepare. In addition, Gushee regards Jesus as the lynched God-man. Following James Cone, Gushee regards the murder of Jesus on the Roman cross as a lynching. He makes the connection between Jesus' lynching and lynchings in the U.S. because both violate the requirements of the law and both were basically mob-based murders, even when state authorities were involved. Yet Gushee confesses that the cross was not the end, for Jesus lives as the risen Lord, promising that life overcomes death. Similarly, lynching and racial terror will not have the final word, as justice and righteousness will prevail. Gushee argues this new understanding of Jesus as the lynched God-man demands white evangelicals to live watchfully, for they do not know when God's judgment will come. They must repent of their past sins of supporting racism and benefitting from a white status quo. They need to heed Jesus' prophetic call and stand in solidarity with Black and other oppressed people and work for justice for all.[59]

All of these American theologians who have challenged the expansion of American empire offer several important insights. The history of the nation cannot be separated from the modern/colonial system defined by the interests of Europe created during the fifteenth century. This system was bolstered by racism and the myth of the superiority of Anglo-Saxons, whose culture was defined by civil liberty and Christianity. The American beliefs of Manifest Destiny and American exceptionalism are rooted in the Christian notions of a "New Israel," and God's "chosen people," such that Americans have a unique mission to spread American values and systems across the world. Thus, a postcolonial theology for the U.S. must challenge white hegemony, American nationalism, discrimination against Muslims and adherents of other faiths, and militarism. During COVID-19, the sort of apocalyptic language that Keller warns against has been revived. During his presidency, Trump tried to project a sense of American exceptionalism that the virus would not affect the U.S. because the U.S. is a blessed nation, and that the virus would go away like a miracle. This messianic imperialism embedded in fundamentalist apocalyptic ideas extended to his label of the coronavirus as the "Chinese virus" and "Kung Flu," which not only led to increased incidents of anti-Asian racism but also put a spotlight on already tense Sino-American relations. It is important to discuss the Sino-American relationship right now from a postcolonial perspective because the contest between China and the U.S. will shape global politics in the twenty-first century. It also showcases how American Christianity has influenced U.S. empire building and foreign policies.

SINO-AMERICAN COMPETITION

The rise of China and its phenomenal economic growth over the past several decades have changed global economics and politics. After President Xi Jinping became the leader of China in late 2012, he began to popularize the slogan "China Dream," which signals the great rejuvenation of the Chinese nation, modernization and economic prosperity, and national glory. His "China Dream" has competed directly with Trump's "Make America Great Again." Trump initiated a trade war with China in 2018 by imposing a series of tariffs on Chinese goods. He was determined to correct the trade deficit between China and the U.S., which amounted to $345.6 billion in 2019.[60] In addition, he waged a tech cold war with China by banning Chinese tech-giant companies from the U.S. In return, China retaliated by imposing tariffs on U.S. goods. The coronavirus further tore the two countries apart.

Commentators have diverging forecasts about Sino-American relations: falling on a spectrum from a win-win situation to inevitable warfare. The first position argues that the opening of China to world trade and modernization will continue to bring China closer to Western systems and values. Privatization and marketization of the Chinese economy will put pressure on the Chinese political system, and, over time, it will turn China into a friendlier, more democratic country. Although some are disappointed that China has not turned more democratic, they insist that engagement with China is better than isolation.[61] From the Chinese side, Chinese leaders have argued that globalization is an inevitable trend, and any forms of economic nationalism or protectionism will hurt world trade and the global economy. Although the U.S. and China have many differences in terms of trade, security, and the South China Sea, leaders say that the two countries need to resolve their differences because their economies are so interconnected. They seek to find a "win-win" solution for both countries and to avoid a decoupling of the world's two largest economies. It remains to be seen whether China and the U.S. can find ways to cooperate with each other, given that the coronavirus and the production and distribution of vaccines have strained their relationships.

The second position falls somewhere between win-win and warfare and is proposed by journalist and commentator Fareed Zakaria. He suggests that the world is moving from the U.S. as the sole superpower to multipolar centers, with the economic development of Brazil, Russia, India, and China each on the rise. In *The Post-American World*, he insists that this does not mean the U.S. is in decline, but, rather, that this is the rise of everyone else. He considers this balance of power better for world peace and stability.[62] But there are many issues with this proposal. Would the U.S. be willing to give up its world hegemony and accept a multipolar world? Further, China has undoubtedly emerged as the key competitor to the U.S., becoming not only the second-largest world economy but also the world's second-largest military spender. Zakaria later modified his position to speak of a bipolar world, in which China and the U.S. dominate. For him, it is all the more necessary for the two countries to cooperate to achieve common goals instead of locking into a race of militarization of space, biotechnology, and weaponizing cyberspace, which would produce consequences that we can hardly imagine.[63]

The third position argues that China and the U.S. will fall into the Thucydides Trap and go into war. As the ancient Greek historian predicted, conflicts will inevitably occur between the ruling power and the rising power that seeks to replace it. Already, China and the U.S. have been competing for tech supremacy—artificial intelligence, robotics, and automatic vehicles—and the huge commercial and national security advantages that come with it. China's One Belt One Road initiative is a global infrastructure development strategy that aims to bolster Chinese influences among Eurasian countries and ensure Chinese corporations have a mighty presence in Africa. The U.S. and China are vying for dominance in the South China Sea, while Asian countries are forced to choose between siding with the U.S. or China. The escalation of conflict between these two countries has already had a serious impact on the global response to the coronavirus.

Americans' attitudes toward China have been influenced by Christian churches and their leaders and theologians. China used to be one of the largest mission fields for American missionaries in the first half of the twentieth century. After the Communist regime was established and missionaries were forced out, Christian churches and missions harbored negative attitudes toward the new China. A strong critic of Communism and a defender of America's containment policy was Reinhold Niebuhr. Though Niebuhr was once committed to socialism and warned against American imperialism, he had moved toward Christian realism in the 1930s. He began to criticize socialism's idealism and utopianism and emphasize the human propensity for sin and the need for realist politics. In 1944, he wrote *Children of Light and Children of Darkness*, and, for him, the American liberals were children of light, while the fascists and Stalinists were children of darkness.[64] After World War II, Niebuhr supported American efforts to confront Soviet Communism and defended America's cold war policy. Social ethicist Gary Dorrien writes that in the late 1940s and mid-1950s, Niebuhr "provided much of the rationale for cold war ideology by describing Soviet Communism as a perverted messianic religion with global ambitions."[65] Although Niebuhr's main target was the Soviet Union, China was also included in his containment policy. Niebuhr had negative views about ancient cultures like China and India, which he thought were stagnant, backward, and incapable of renewing themselves. Furthermore, he charged that these cultures could not form a cohesive and integral community because they lacked the technical means of communication.[66] Given the disparity of achievements, Niebuhr regarded colonialism as an inevitable stage of the development of civilizations. He also viewed empire as neutral and not necessarily immoral. He distinguished between old empires and new empires—the former were characterized by nationalistic imperialism, while the latter were superior because they were servants of the universal community.[67]

Niebuhr's theological and political positions were criticized by China's Wu Yaozong, a Christian leader who supported the Chinese Communist government and attacked Western imperialism. Writing in the early 1950s, Wu charged that Niebuhr belonged to the group of Christian scholars who supported imperialism. Niebuhr's Christian realism emphasizes that human beings are all sinful and only God is good. Since all human institutions are sinful, Niebuhr regarded Communism as sinful too and did not see some of the positive changes brought by Communism. Wu argued that Niebuhr and his group "want us to maintain the status quo and support exploitative capitalist and imperialist systems."[68] Wu's critique of Niebuhr anticipated liberation theologians' criticism of Niebuhr two decades later. Rubem Alves chastises Niebuhrian realism as an ideology in support of the American order by providing it with theological justification. Cornel West, too, charges that Niebuhr supported the superiority of European and U.S. culture, cold war militarism, and U.S. dominance in Latin America and other parts of the world. West regards realism as an ideology that functions to legitimate U.S. hegemony of the world.[69]

Neoconservatives who arose in the 1970s appropriated Niebuhr's anti-Communist ideology, though Niebuhr rethought his Cold War policy because of the nightmare of the Vietnam War, which he has spoken against. The neoconservatives were further bolstered by Samuel P. Huntington's hypothesis of the clash of civilizations. After the cold war era, Huntington predicted that future world conflict would no longer be determined by ideologies but by a clash of civilizations.[70] He forecasted that a major fault line would be between Western civilization and Islamic civilization. Western civilization, for him, is defined by white Christian culture, and he firmly rejects multiculturalism in the U.S. Although many critics such as Edward Said have challenged Huntington's reductive, static, and homogeneous views of civilization,[71] Huntington's hypothesis became in vogue after September 11, 2001, and during the war on terrorism. The other fault line, Huntington proposes, would be between Western civilization and Sinic civilization, which is influenced by Confucianism. Huntington's language of conflict and war, rather than dialogue and cooperation, was embraced by conservative ideologues and military hawks. People close to the Trump administration, including his former advisor Steve Bannon, believe in this model of the clash of civilizations and predicted that the U.S. will go to war with China in the South China Sea in the next few years.

Given the dangerous revival of Cold War rhetoric and Trump's China-bashing, especially during the coronavirus, Christian theologians and ethicists must not add oil to the fire by reinforcing an "us" versus "them" or good versus evil stance in their analysis of Sino-American relations. The traditional posture of Christianity against Communism is outdated because China is no longer a "pure" Communist country. China claims that the country is practicing "socialism with Chinese characteristics," which outside critics have simply dubbed "state capitalism." Since its joining of the World Trade Organization in 2001, China has become an integral part of the global neoliberal economy. China became the factory of the world, producing consumerist goods that the American middle-class craves. The neoliberal economic system as we know it today could not have been created without this symbiotic relation between China and the U.S., and decoupling would not be easy. Globalization and neoliberalism have produced a transnational capitalist class that dominates the economy and has a huge influence in politics, whether these people live in Washington or Beijing, New York or Shanghai, the Silicon Valley or Shenzhen. As a result, there is an alarming disparity between the rich and the poor in both China and the U.S. In 2017, the top 1 percent in China owned one-third of the country's wealth, while their counterparts in the U.S. owned 40 percent.[72] The top 1 percent of the world's population of that year owned more than half of the world's wealth.[73] This mass concentration of wealth and maximization of profit run against the common good as well as biblical teaching and must be challenged.

Many Christians are against the autocratic government of China because of its lack of democracy and transparency. Christian theologians and ethicists need to speak out against China's violation of human rights, persecution of religious and ethnic minorities, such as Tibetans and Uighur Muslims, and limitation of religious freedoms, including forcing churches to remove their crosses. The government has supported violent suppression of protests for democracy, in both mainland China and Hong Kong. At that same time, we must be vigilant about the decline of civil liberties and political freedoms around the world, and the U.S. is no exception. Michiko Kakutani, a longtime New York Times literary critic, notes that there has been an outpouring of recent books on the relations between democracy and autocracy, such as Edward Luce's *The Retreat of Western Liberalism*, Timothy Snyder's *On Tyranny*, and *How Democracies Die* by Steven Levitsky and Daniel Ziblatt. These books look at the troubling developments of the decline of democracy in countries such as Russia, Hungary, Turkey,

Poland, and Brazil. These countries serve as warnings to the U.S. because there were dangerous signs that, under Trump, the U.S. was similarly going down a slippery slope toward autocracy. The worrying signs that democracy was being undermined included sabotaging constitutions, sidelining legislative bodies in the name of representing the people, packing courts with loyalists, delegitimizing opponents and the election processes, attacking the free press, condoning or encouraging violence, and threatening to take legal action against political rivals.[74] It will take years to undo the damage that the Trump administration has caused.

Given these stark economic and political realities, theologians and ethicists must challenge empire—whether it is American empire, Chinese empire, or Sino-American empire. Our hope lies in the rising consciousness of the multitude and in social and grassroots movements around the world. In 2019 and 2020, we witnessed protests in Thailand, Turkey, Belarus, Hungary, and Brazil. In Hong Kong, the pro-democracy movement continues, albeit in a different form, because of government suppression and China's imposition of the national security law. In the U.S., the Black Lives Matter movement, spurred by three Black women, gained momentum in the summer protests in 2020, following the deaths of George Floyd, Breonna Taylor, and other Black men, women, and persons. The unprecedented strike by Black athletes, joined later by college professors, marked an important stage of a national reckoning with systemic racism in the country.

Since white American Christianity has been so intimately tied to empire building, reckoning and repentance are much needed. Douglas summons the churches to be the nation's moral conscience and claim a prophetic stance. She says, "to claim to be prophetic means partnering with God in mending the earth as we move toward a future that God has promised all."[75] Churches need to reclaim the liberating potential of Christianity and contribute to fostering a democratic culture in both church life and society. Some churches provided sanctuary to undocumented persons who might have been deported by the Trump administration. Others have sponsored forums to discuss racial justice and encourage their members in civic and political engagement. In this season of racial reckoning, a critical postcolonial lens will illumine the entanglement between theological ideas and the formation of the American Empire.

As white nationalism and populism obstruct people's quest for justice and freedom, the struggles ahead will be long and hard. Thus, we need to develop a fierce passion for justice and a spirituality of resistance to meet the tasks. Jewish philosopher and environmentalist Roger S. Gottlieb has said that a spirituality of resistance is needed to resolve the tensions between our search for peace and our rage at injustice; cultivating a forgiving heart and not being willing to let go of anger at evildoings; and accepting the world as it is while refusing to affirm a world that contains so much unjustified suffering.[76] We can be inspired by the long history of people's movements and struggles in Asia Pacific, to which I shall now turn. The ascendancy of the U.S. as a global empire cannot be separated from its political expansion in the Asia Pacific. In the second part of the book, I will argue that looking more deeply into the Asia Pacific region helps to further illuminate the kinds of work that need to be done to detach and disentangle Western theological studies from empire, through a postcolonial lens.

PART TWO
POLITICAL THEOLOGIES
FROM ASIA PACIFIC

Chapter 5

Postcolonial Theology from an East Asian Perspective

Imperialism cannot be eliminated without eliminating our own imperial desires. Imperial and colonial violence are conterminous and create histories of violence as well as resistance to it.

Nami Kim and Wonhee Anne Joh[1]

On March 1, 1919, thirty-three religious leaders—among them sixteen Christians—protested Japanese colonial rule in Korea. They read out loud the Korean Declaration of Independence and signed the document. The protest was inspired by U.S. President Woodrow Wilson's "Fourteen Points" statement at the Paris Peace Conference after World War I, which included the right of national "self-determination." Although the protesters were soon arrested, their resistance prompted a nationwide demonstration against the repressive Japanese rule. About two million participated in more than 1,500 demonstrations. Around 7,000 people were killed by Japanese police and soldiers and about 15,000 people were injured. Approximately 46,000 people were arrested, and a large number of them were convicted. In addition, 47 churches and 715 houses were burned down.[2] Although the protest was violently suppressed, what came to be known as the March First Movement became a significant symbol for the Korean people's resistance against colonial rule and government exploitation.

Two months after the March First Movement, on May 4, 1919, students in Beijing took to the streets to protest against the Treaty of Versailles, agreed upon at the Paris Peace Conference. The Allied Powers decided to transfer German rights over China's Shandong peninsula to Japan, instead of returning these rights to China. Protests soon broke out in many cities, and protesters denounced Western imperialism and the Chinese government's weakness in protecting its territorial integrity. The centenary of the March First and May Fourth movements in 2019 has provided a fitting backdrop to discuss postcolonial theology from an East Asian perspective. Postcolonial theology unmasks colonial epistemological frameworks in theology, contests mainstream and dominant biblical interpretation, and interrogates stereotypical cultural representations. Furthermore, postcolonial theory challenges theologians' potential complicity in reinscribing the colonial legacy through knowledge production and social and ecclesial practices. Postcolonial theologians and scholars share the vocation of an intellectual, whom Edward Said describes as "someone whose whole being is staked on a critical stance, a sense of being unwilling to accept easy formulas, or ready-made clichés, or the smooth, ever-so-accommodating confirmations of what the powerful or conventional have to say, and what they do."[3] In this chapter, I discuss the importance of decolonizing theology and explore critical themes in doing postcolonial theology from an East Asian perspective.

DECOLONIZING THEOLOGY

Ever since Constantine's conversion to Christianity and Christianity's adoption as the state religion of the Roman Empire, Christian theology has been infused with imperial language, metaphors, ethos, and mindset. Throughout the centuries, theologians have had to negotiate with and sometimes resist empire, conquest, colonization, and anticolonial struggles.[4] Decolonizing our theological imagination requires our disengagement with Christianity's complicity in the creation of Christendom and in the expansion of colonial and imperial powers. First, we have to investigate how Christian symbols and doctrines have borrowed from imperial cultures and in turn contributed to the production and reinforcement of empire. For example, the image of the cosmic Christ in the early centuries of Christianity was not politically neutral but could be used to bolster the imperial extension of the power of the Roman emperors as rulers on earth. Second, we must look for alternative sources and lift up forgotten, silenced, and repressed voices in the theological tradition. For too often, the canon of theology has emphasized the contributions of clergy, academic theologians, and the elites to the exclusion of the poor, laity, and the masses—especially women—in many parts of the world. Third, decolonizing theology needs to construct forward-looking, life-affirming, anti-imperial, and anti-oppressive theology that provides clues and guides for the future. This requires interdisciplinary collaboration, creative re-imagining, attention to indigenous and subversive traditions, and speaking truth to power.

Decolonizing theology requires overcoming Eurocentrism in our understanding and interpretation of Christian history and theology. The demographic of the Christian population has shifted, and the majority of Christians now live in the Global South. By 2050, only one-fifth of the world's three billion Christians will be non-Hispanic and white. Yet the teaching and reading of Christian theology and doctrine continue to be shaped by the Eurocentric and Western orientation of the church. Theologian William A. Dyrness writes, "This has had the unfortunate consequence of marginalizing not only what we call the Eastern tradition but the still vibrant Syriac, North African, and Asian strands of the larger Christian tradition, to say nothing of the newer traditions of Africa and Latin America."[5] It is important to remember that Christianity had a long history in Asia before missionaries came with colonial powers. Syrian missionaries from the Church of the East (often referred to as Nestorians) arrived in China in the seventh century along the Silk Road and established churches. A cross-cultural understanding of the Christian tradition broadens our theological imagination by pointing to the richness and diversity within Christianity.

In addition to expanding our historical and theological horizons, decolonizing theology requires a new theological hermeneutic that interprets the theological tradition globally and contrapuntally. Edward Said encourages us to interpret different experiences contrapuntally, like music with counterpoints, in order to better make sense of our histories, which intertwine and overlap because of colonialism.[6] For example, when we commemorated the 500th anniversary of Martin Luther's 95 Theses in 2017, few thought to ask about the relation between the Reformation and the so-called "discovery" of the "New World." I was surprised to see in an exhibit held in 2017 at Wittenberg that Luther had written about the peoples in the New World.[7] He said that the exploration of the New World would allow the gospel to be brought to these peoples. I wondered if his attitude would have changed if he had known of the complicity of the Catholic Church in the annihilation of the peoples and cultures of the Americas. In the past two hundred years, there has been quest after quest for the historical Jesus. These quests were billed as objective searches for the authentic Jesus. Yet Jesus in the nineteenth-century quest appeared as a genius and/or a middle-class, celibate, and self-controlled gentleman. This image was not value-neutral, as white European men fantasized about a Jesus made in their own image. Jesus was cast in sharp contrast to the images of racialized and colonized men that Europeans considered inferior and deficient. Such theological imagination, fueled by racism, classism, and heteronormativity, furthered the cause of empire and justified Europe's civilizing mission. Today, American right-wing Christians propagate a muscular, militaristic, and triumphant Christ to bolster their cultural imperialism, white supremacy, and religious intolerance.

Decolonizing theology and developing postcolonial theology share with and build on the legacy of liberation theology. Both projects are committed to social justice, solidarity with the oppressed, and social praxis aimed at changing the world. But there are also differences. One of the significant differences is that postcolonial theology wants to avoid simple, binary constructions of colonizers and colonized, the rich and the poor, and the West and the rest. Latin American liberation theology emphasizes the preferential option for the poor and posits that the poor are the subjects of history. Postcolonial scholars point to the dangers of homogenizing the poor and valorizing the colonized and the oppressed. They offer complex readings of the multilayered and fragmented subjectivity of the colonized. For example, Homi Bhabha discusses postcolonial subject formation through the lenses of hybridity, ambivalence, and mimicry.[8] Frantz Fanon investigates the complex psycho-social and sexual dynamics in the relationship between white and Black men and women.[9] Ashis Nandy discusses the loss and recovery of the self under colonialism in his book *Intimate Enemy*.[10] These studies point to the complex formation of the colonized and postcolonial subject, the double inscription of colonialism, and the psychological impact of colonialism, which cannot be easily characterized by the binary relation of the colonizer and the colonized.

Because of the lengthy colonial legacy and ambivalent postcolonial identity, theologians need to be vigilant about our complicity as academics and leaders of faith communities. Spivak has raised the uneasy question, "Can the subaltern speak?" and cautioned academics against serving as native informants and for speaking for the subalterns.[11] As middle-class academics, it is not easy to decolonize our minds because of the neoliberal market economy and the conservatism in many churches. Without active participation in social praxis and reading outside the confines of the theological field, we cannot engage in vigorous social analyses and maintain an alternative view of reality. We have to recall how progressive Asian theologians of the past generation, such as *minjung* theologians, risked losing their jobs and going to prison for their solidarity with the *minjung. Minjung* means people or the masses. At a time when conservative and populist leaders dominate the political scene and democratic institutions are under attack, it is imperative to create supportive networks and communities of discourse to nurture progressive and anti-imperial thinking.

Decolonizing theology also means taking seriously our vocation to teach the Bible and theology with a commitment to producing global citizens and leaders of faith communities who can understand the complex legacy of colonialism and the sociopolitical forces shaping our world. This requires what Latin American theologian Enrique Dussel calls an "epistemological decolonization of theology," which involves both the challenge of the universality of Eurocentric theology and the creation of fresh theologies. Dussel notes, "the epistemological decolonization of Eurocentric theology is a fact that began in the second half of the twentieth century, but which will occupy the whole of the twenty-first century."[12] Doing this important work will require changing theological curriculum, a search for alternative sources, and the development of transnational pedagogies and best practices.[13]

DOING POSTCOLONIAL THEOLOGY IN EAST ASIA

Doing postcolonial theology in East Asia needs to take into consideration the long and complex history of political control, imperial expansion, and colonialism in the region. Since the mid-nineteenth century, major Western countries vied for power in East Asia while Japan rose to dominance and sought to exert power over its neighbors. The East Asian region has experienced continuous political turmoil, international and civil wars, and the division of countries. It is difficult to pinpoint a particular "postcolonial" moment understood in a linear, chronological sense. For soon after World War II, civil war broke out in China. When the Nationalist Party lost the war to the Communists, it evacuated to Taiwan. The Taiwanese people regarded the Nationalist Party as a foreign and colonial force and fought for self-determination for decades. But for a long time, the Nationalist Party continued to claim that it was the legitimate government of China. In Korea, the defeat of Japan after World War II did not result in a smooth transition of power back to the Korean people. Instead, the Soviets occupied the northern part of the country, while the U.S. occupied the South. The Korean peninsula became the battleground for the Cold War and was divided into North and South after the Korean War (1950–53). Today, the war has not ended; open hostilities were ended only when a ceasefire was declared. With this complex social and political history in mind, I do not take "postcolonial theology" to mean theology done "after" political independence, since the struggle for political autonomy in the region is far from over. Instead, I trace postcolonial impulses in theological voices and movements that have revolted against foreign aggression, imperial ambitions, and political oppression, some of which date back to the anticolonial period.

China has long considered herself the "Middle Kingdom" and has exerted cultural, economic, and political influences and control over neighboring countries. For many centuries, Korea had to establish a tributary relationship with the ruling dynasty in China and regularly send tributary gifts to the Chinese court. After the Meiji Restoration in 1868, Japan developed economically and militarily and wished to replace China as the regional power. Japan's defeat of China in the Sino-Japanese War (1894–1895) resulted in the cession of Taiwan to Japan. About a decade later, Japan shocked the world by defeating Russia in the Russo-Japanese War (1904–1905), proving that its modernized military could combat European forces with success. These two victories paved the way for the Japanese colonization of Korea in 1910. Using the slogans "Pan-Asianism" and "the Greater East Asian Coprosperity Sphere," Japan claimed that it would "save" or "liberate" Asia from Western aggressors and emphasized racial and cultural affinities as "Asians" under Japanese rule.[14] But in reality, Japan used the slogans to further its imperial expansion and ruled its colonies with an iron fist, suppressing dissidents and protests.

As the March First Movement of 1919 attested, Korean people did not quietly acquiesce to Japanese rule but rather stood up against foreign aggression. Likewise, the May Fourth Movement in the same year represented an anti-imperialist, cultural, and political movement that grew out of student protests in Beijing. Social protests and people's movements prompted theologians to reflect on the relevance of Christianity for social reform and political salvation.

Early attempts at decolonizing theology focused on bringing Christianity into dialogue with Asian culture and religious traditions. The process of indigenization in China began in the 1920s, as theologians emphasized the role of Jesus as a social reformer and his mission as socio-political reconstruction. Zhao Zichen (1888–1979), the most prominent Protestant Chinese theologian, emphasized Jesus as a moral exemplar. Jesus was fully human just like us, but he was empowered by a profound consciousness of God. Salvation through Jesus, in Zhao's view, is a call to a renewal of moral life and society, modeled after Jesus' character. Influenced by Confucianism, Zhao saw moral reconstruction as the key for national salvation, and Christianity provided the spiritual force to do so.[15] In Korea, Choi Byung Hun (1908–2004) was a pioneer of the indigenization of the Christian message in the Korean Confucian and Buddhist traditions. Combining Eastern philosophies, the Bible, and the Wesleyan tradition, he argued that Christ was the fulfilment of all religious aspirations. While he did not want to denigrate Asian religious traditions, he aimed to introduce the gospel message for the salvation of the people and social reform.[16]

In the 1930s, facing Japanese invasion and continued foreign aggression, some Chinese theologians and Christian leaders were radicalized. They no longer saw social reform as a way to solve China's problems, as China's very survival was at stake. Wu Yaozong (1893–1979), who worked at the YMCA, argued that only social revolution could save China and transform the world. He urged other Christians to embrace a revolutionary Christianity, anticipating liberation theology by several decades. For Wu, Christianity should not only attend to people's spiritual lives but also care for their social condition. He wrote, "A true revival of the Church will come only when it has awakened to its social task and begins to tackle it fearlessly and sacrificially."[17] Chastising the exploitation of European capitalistic powers, Wu was increasingly attracted to socialism and saw China's only way out as being a social revolution.[18] After the founding of the People's Republic of China, Wu and other Christian leaders formulated a Christian manifesto, titled "Ways of Christian Efforts in the Construction of a New China," and sought ways to work with the new government. In 1950, the Chinese government launched the "Resist America, Aid Korea" campaign and cut off all financial relationships with religious and cultural organizations in the U.S. As a response, Christian leaders developed the Three-Self Patriotic Movement, emphasizing self-governance, self-support, and self-propagation, to remove foreign influences from the Chinese churches.[19]

In the 1960s, Park Chung Hee assumed power in South Korea, and his authoritarian policies prompted massive demonstrations and demands for human rights, democratic government, and economic justice. Korean progressive theologians responded by developing *minjung* theology to express solidarity with the people's movement. New Testament scholar Ahn Byung Mu (1922–1996) studied the *ochlos*—the crowd who followed Jesus from place to place in Mark's Gospel. The diverse groups of Galilean *ochlos*, coming from the lower class, were the audience whom Jesus' message addressed and formed the background of his activities (Mark 2:4, 13; 3:9, 20, 32; 4:1; 5:21, 24, 31; 8:1; 10:1). In contrast to the ruling class from Jerusalem, the *ochlos* frequently sided with Jesus against the ruling class. *Minjung* theologians argued that Jesus was part of the *minjung*, and his teaching must be interpreted in the context of the social aspirations of the people.[20] Using the social biography of the people as a critical lens, *minjung* theologians began to read the Bible together with the long history of suffering of the Korean people. Theologian Kim Yong Bock criticized Western dominance in theology, which assumes that the cultures of Asian people are discontinuous with the gospel and do not have any positive place in theological reflection.[21] In contrast, *minjung* theologians emphasized that people are subjects of history and recovered the liberating potentials of Korean's indigenous traditions, such as shamanism and the masked dance. Sebastian C. H. Kim said, "Minjung theology developed into a major contextual theology intended to address the problems of the poor and the exploited. . . . [It was] against the unjust system of modern and divided Korea on the one hand, and against conservative fundamentalist theologies on the other."[22]

Theologians in Taiwan developed "Homeland Theology" in their fight for self-determination against the Chinese Nationalist Party. After the Nationalist Party evacuated to Taiwan in 1949, martial law was declared, and Chiang Kai-shek's regime denied the people freedom of speech, arrested and tortured dissidents, and suppressed political movements. Taiwan faced international isolation in the 1970s, when the People's Republic of China joined the United Nations and Taiwan was expelled from it. The 1972 visit of President Richard Nixon to China paved the way for the normalization of relations with China. The Presbyterian Church of Taiwan issued three statements at the time, declaring that the homeland was a gift from God and that the Taiwanese people had the right to determine their destiny. In response to political change, theologian Wang Hsien-chih and others developed Homeland Theology, seeing parallels between the histories of Taiwan and Israel. The Hebrew people left the land of bondage in Egypt and crossed the Red Sea to enter the promised land. Trying to build a community, they insisted that the land belonged to God and not to the rulers and elites. Their prophets repeatedly condemned corruption and injustice and exhorted them to care for the poor and the marginalized. Just as in the exodus, many Chinese people crossed the Taiwanese Strait over the centuries to escape political oppression and seek better lives. In the face of isolation and uncertainty, homeland theologians insisted that Taiwan does not belong to the rulers or political parties, but to all those who live on and love the homeland. Taiwanese people have the right of self-determination for their future and destiny.[23]

In the several decades since *minjung* theology and Homeland Theology caught international attention, there have been rapid social, economic, and political changes in East Asia. Postcolonial theology in East Asia builds on anticolonial and antidictatorial social and theological movements in the past but must attend to the new situations. Economically, the region has experienced phenomenal growth, and some have dubbed it the "Asian miracle." South Korea, Taiwan,

Hong Kong, and Singapore were called the "four Asian dragons," as they underwent rapid industrialization and maintained high growth rates between the 1960s and 1990s. Since China adopted liberalization policies in the late 1970s, its economy has grown by leaps and bounds, and today it is the world's second largest economy, overtaking that of Japan. The East Asian model of development has been held up as a model for other developing countries to emulate. The so-called "capitalism with Asian characteristics," under the influences of neo-Confucianism, is seen as competing with the Western model.

While many Asian political leaders have hailed the phenomenal economic development as a source of pride, others have sounded alarm and caution. In *Asia as Method*, Taiwanese cultural critic Chen Kuan-hsing warns that integration into the global neoliberal market and capitalist accumulation has transformed former colonies, such as Taiwan and South Korea, into subimperial states (when compared to empires such as the U.S.), with the potential to exploit others.[24] He cites as example Taiwan's southward advance policy of economic expansion into Southeast Asia in the 1990s. The effort exhibited a "subimperial desire," driven by positioning Taiwan as a neocolonial power, with the danger of replicating the Japanese militarist discourse of the Greater East Asian Coprosperity Sphere. In South Korea, the big conglomerates have worked closely with the government to further its national interests and to exert its influence in other countries. South Korea mimics American transnational neoliberalism and its military imperial desires. Chen notes that in numerous countries, decolonization is followed by recolonization or neocolonization.[25] In East Asia, the legacy of the Cold War has drawn Taiwan and South Korea close to the American empire. But with the rise of China and President Xi Jinping's "China Dream," Japan, Taiwan, and South Korea must reposition themselves in the competition between the American and Chinese empires.

Because Asia is so linked to the global economy and has been greatly influenced by Western culture, postcolonial theologians have warned against a binary construction of "Asia" and "the West." Wong Wai-Ching Angela from Hong Kong notes that as Asian countries regained political independence, the nationalist rhetoric of formerly colonized countries gave rise to the collective "Asian" identity of Asian theologies. Asian theology has adopted an anti-imperial stance, positioning itself as anti-Western and challenging theologies that are complicit with colonial interests. These anti-imperialistic and nation-building themes can be seen in the work of many pioneering Asian theologians, such as M. M. Thomas, D. T. Niles, Aloysius Pieris, C. S. Song, Marianne Katoppo, and others. Although these theologians have not identified themselves as postcolonial theologians, Wong discerns postcolonial characteristics in their work. She writes, "When Asian theology set out to differentiate itself from its Western constitution and declared its commitment to a people's movement in Asia, it meant, in a similar way, a postcolonial construction of an autonomous religion of Christianity for Asian Christians as a colonial-resistance force and a moving spirit in national struggle."[26]

Wong notes that emphasis on national and regional identity in Asian theology has a positive effect because theologians have paid serious attention to the sociopolitical milieu of postcolonial Asia and formed a unified identity among themselves. Yet she argues that a binary construction of "Asia" and "the West" has problems and offers the following reasons. First, such a formulation has a tendency toward essentialization of both "Asia" and "the West," without attending to the tremendous heterogeneity in the two categories. Second, Asian theologians emphasize the use of indigenous Asian resources and cultures, and any theological discussion that does not engage indigenous resources or address concerns of people's movements is seen as irrelevant. This has limited the scope and development of Asian theology. Third, the Third World "postcolonial" subject is cast as one who is in opposition to autocratic Third World government supported by Western powers. He or she is understood in terms of a Western liberal subject, who demands freedom and control over the destiny of his or her country. As such, the "postcolonial" subject is constructed in a "Westernized" style. Fourth, the binary construction has collapsed the differences among "Asian" women in Asian feminist theology. Asian women are portrayed either as victims of multiple oppressions or heroines who fight for their fate and destiny against all odds.[27] Instead of understanding identity as fixed and in opposition to others, Wong encourages us to see identity as contingent and shifting. Following Homi Bhabha, she sees the potential to explore the hybrid and in-between spaces in which new identities and experiences can be narrated.

GENDER, SEXUALITY, AND EMPIRE

Many narratives about the March First Movement that I have consulted leave out the participation of women. I first heard about the involvement of a high-school girl through a former Korean female student. She attended the same school as Yu Kwan Sun, whose picture was hung in what is today called Ehwa Girls' High School, in memory of her leadership and sacrifice in the March First Movement. Yu was arrested and imprisoned for her leadership role in the demonstrations, was brutally tortured, and ultimately died in prison. In addition to Yu, other Korean women, among them several Christian women leaders, helped organize the women's March First Independence Movement. These women saw their struggles for dignity and gender justice as inseparable from the political fight for independence.[28] Korean feminist scholar Bae Hyun Ju writes, "As has been the case with the Third World women's movements in general, Korean women's commitment to their own liberation has been inseparable from their participation in movements that focus on sociopolitical oppressions other than sexism, such as colonialism, military dictatorship, labor exploitation, and ideological division."[29] However, the struggle for national liberation had been led by national elites with a patriarchal worldview, and consequently feminist concerns were treated as secondary. A postcolonial feminist theology needs to pay attention to the intersecting axes of gender, sexuality, militarism, and empire.

Postcolonial feminist theology in East Asia has to remember the victims of war, colonialism, militarism, and hypermasculinity. During World War II, around 200,000 women and girls from China, Korea, Taiwan, and other countries were kidnapped and forced or coerced into serving as "comfort women"— sexual slaves for the Japanese military. But owing to the national shame around this issue, it was not talked about for decades until some of these women courageously spoke out in the 1980s. Korean churchwomen leagues, sororities, and many individual women worked to address this issue and formed the Korean Council for Women Drafted for Military Sexual Slavery by Japan in 1992. These women leaders demanded that the Japanese government recognize the crimes committed against women by the Japanese military, punish the offenders, compensate survivors, and build memorials to educate the public.[30]

As Choi Hee An has noted, the rape and atrocities committed against Korean women's bodies were not just to satisfy the sexual needs of the soldiers but also to humiliate Korean men. She writes, "women's sexuality became nationalized, and it symbolized Korea's powerlessness at the hands of a controlling power."[31] This was the reason why the Korean government concealed the issue for fifty years, and the Japanese, having lost the war, did not want to bring it up. But Korean Christian women do not want to forget the atrocities inflicted upon the comfort women. Yang Mi Kang uses the example of the hemorrhaging woman in the Gospel of Mark (5:25–34) to show that the act of Jesus healing the woman could be a source of hope and courage for comfort women. The hemorrhaging woman was stigmatized and declared impure by the purity laws of society. Yet she defied the taboo and dared to touch Jesus for healing. Her bold action created an opening for Jesus to heal her spiritually and physically. Likewise, the wounds of the comfort women would be healed if they continue to demand justice with the support of the international community.[32]

Korean women scholars also look for clues in the Bible and in tradition for women's leadership and redemptive roles. For example, the exodus story has been seen as a foundational liberative event, and Moses has been remembered as a national hero who led the Hebrew people out of Egypt. Yet Lee Yeong Mee notes that "the exodus story can be an oppressive model for women if the interpretation emphasizes the role of the male hero, Moses, alone."[33] Instead of a male-centered and hero-centered reading, some Asian women propose to interpret the exodus narrative as a collective liberative movement of both male and female slaves to create a new community. Exodus 1–2 presents the story of women's collective struggle to lead their people out of suffering and into new lives. The two Hebrew midwives Shiphrah and Puah chose to resist the king's command to kill male newborns, choosing instead to save lives. They were the first victors in the confrontation between the Hebrew slaves and the king. After Moses was born, three other women contributed to the redemptive effort to save his life. His mother hid the baby against the king's command and placed him in a basket along the river. Moses's sister played a mediating role between the birth mother and the adoptive mother. Pharaoh's daughter went against her father's decree and adopted the baby even though she knew the baby was a Hebrew child. The cooperation of these women made the redemption of the Hebrew people possible, and they should be included in the collective memory.[34]

These examples show that Asian women scholars have used postcolonial and anti-imperial imagination in interpreting the Bible. Korean biblical scholar Kim Seong Hee argues that Korean postcolonial analysis should consider not only the colonialism of the past but also neocolonial situations in which Korea continues to be subject to the U.S. economically, politically, and militarily. There is also the task of the unification of South and North Korea. Kim identifies several characteristics of Korean postcolonial feminist interpretation, which can work toward the decolonization of the Bible and for the empowerment of women. First, the Bible is not value-neutral and has characteristics that could be either harmful or useful for women's liberation. Thus, the Bible should be read with a "hermeneutic of suspicion" to scrutinize its ideologies of colonization and suppression and their impact on readers. Second, the Bible was brought to Korea by missionaries, who denigrated Korean religious traditions and cultures. The Bible needs to be read in conjunction with Korean traditions to create a new Korean hermeneutic. Third, Korean Christianity is still dominated by a patriarchal and hierarchical system. Addressing this requires the decolonization of colonial/patriarchal ideology and theology that seek to perpetuate the patriarchal system. Fourth, because of globalization, Korean society has become diverse in terms of people, language, lifestyle, and culture. Biblical interpretation needs to be opened to diverse voices and to foreign people, such as migrant workers, who are minorities in Korean society. Fifth, identities have become more fluid and the formerly oppressed might become oppressors in changing circumstances. One should be cautious in idealizing certain individuals or models of social change.[35] In sum, Kim says, "Korean postcolonial feminist interpretation should seek for the decolonization and liberation so that Korean women and men recognize themselves as reading subjects and resist any kind of oppressive power and system."[36]

Japanese biblical scholar Hisako Kinukawa also finds postcolonial insight helpful in developing feminist interpretation of the Bible and theology. She acknowledges her complex location and subjectivity as a Japanese feminist and confesses, "I cannot practice my feminist theology without a critical analysis of my own cultural and social contexts in their relationships to Asian countries that Japan has invaded and colonized: in the past in the form of wars, and in the present as one of economic powers."[37] But she also acknowledges that Japan was under the strong political and military power of the U.S., and to some extent it can be considered as invisibly colonized by the U.S. Thus, Japan has been both "a colonizer and a colonized nation."[38] She offers a postcolonial reading of the Syrophoenician woman in Mark 7:24–30 by paying attention to the power relationship between the protagonists in the story. Jesus meets the woman with a daughter possessed by a demon in the vicinity of Tyre. Tyre was an urban city exploiting the Galilean hinterland for its wealth and was dependent upon the villages for food and other necessities. Jesus' hard words of not taking the children's food and throwing it to the dogs might refer to not taking poor people's food and giving it to the rich Tyrians in the city. But the Syrophoenician woman is from one of the villages of the hinterland of Tyre, so she might not be as rich as those living in the urban city. She insists that Jesus' harsh words did not apply to her and her daughter. While acknowledging the need to take care of the Galilean peasants, she retorts that there are other people who are in dire need too. For Kinukawa, Jesus decolonizes the relationship between those who wielded power in Tyre and the Galilean peasants. At the same time, the woman decolonizes the primacy that Jesus had limited to the Jews.[39] In her book, Kinukawa demystifies the notion that the Japanese society is monocultural and lifts up the struggles of women, aliens, and Koreans living as minorities in Japan. She uses the Syrophoenician woman's story to illustrate the ways that Jesus crossed boundaries to reach out to others. Jesus changes his mind, heals the daughter, and praises the woman's faith. Following Jesus' example, Japanese people should also treat Koreans and other groups living in Japan without discrimination.[40]

PEACE AND RECONCILIATION

In the current political situation in East Asia, postcolonial theology must address concerns surrounding militarism and the prospects for peace and reconciliation. There are continuous tensions between Japan and its neighbors concerning whether Japan has properly atoned for the deeds of its government and imperial army during World War II. The visits of Japanese prime ministers to the Shinto Yasukuni Shrine that honors Japan's dead warriors, including 14 war criminals, have been seen by Asian neighbors as a symbol of the nation's unrepentant militarism. Japan and other countries have debated about wartime history and atrocities committed. Japan has been accused of attempts to downplay the actions of its government and military during World War II in Japanese history textbooks. While Japan's constitution denounces war and limits its military to self-defense, Japanese politicians have proposed to alter the interpretation of their constitution to enhance military capacity.

Since World War II, there has been a strong peace movement in Japan led by peace activists, labor unions, and women's organizations.[41] Although the Christian community in Japan is small, it has worked for peace and denounced Japan's military aggression. Kosuke Koyama (1929–2009), a pioneer in Asian theology, recalled growing up in the post-war era and presented a stirring critique of the war in *Mount Fuji and Mount Sinai*.[42] Born in Tokyo, Koyama saw the city in ruins from constant bombings. He was sixteen when the atomic bomb was dropped in Hiroshima. His book is organized based on biblical themes and brought biblical messages to bear on Japanese history and the predicament of the people after the war. Unlike Korean and Taiwanese theologians, who read the Bible from the point of view of the oppressed, Koyama mines the Bible for its warnings to the powerful.

Koyama begins with Jeremiah's warning: "All its cities were laid in ruins before the LORD, before his fierce anger" (4:26). He says Japanese cities were destroyed because Japan had turned to worship the idols: the cult of the emperor, the confidence in military might, and the belief in Japan as a righteous empire to supervise other nations. He compares the symbolism surrounding Mount Fuji and Mount Sinai. Mount Fuji represents for many Japanese the cosmo-logical *axis mundi*, the primeval womb of the earth, and the union of the male and female principles. As the symbol of the security of the nation, Mount Fuji has also been associated with the emperor cult. In contrast, Mount Sinai was the place where the theophany of God took place. There was no veneration of Mount Sinai because the biblical God is a mobile God and is not fixed in one place. God who met the people at Mount Sinai would meet them again in other places and in other critical historical events.[43] Even though people repeatedly turn against God and create their own idols and symbols for devotion, God still forgives them and is passionately involved in history. Koyama argues that rec-onciliation is possible because of the cross, where the broken Christ healed the wounds of a world broken by idolatry.

Koyama's critique of idolatry and the worship of military power is very rel-evant today as East Asia continues to face military threats, the legacy of the Cold War, and new political challenges. Following the attacks of September 11, 2001, President George W. Bush launched the "war on terrorism." He declared that North Korea was a member of the "Axis of Evil," adding fuel to political and military tension in the region. In 2018, President Donald Trump even taunted the rogue state with threats to use nuclear weapons against it. Even though Trump and North Korean leader Kim Jung Un met in Singapore in June of 2018 and agreed to a peaceful denuclearization of the Korean Peninsula, the results of the meeting were far from certain. In addition, China has risen rapidly as an economic and military force, competing with the U.S. for hegemony in the region. Territorial disputes in the East and South China Seas have led to increased military presence and surveillance. Asian countries have tried to step up their military arsenals and to acquire the newest missiles and weapons.

Given the pivot of U.S. attention to Asia and increased military threat in the Asia Pacific, Nami Kim and Wonhee Anne Joh, editors of the pioneering vol-ume *Critical Theology against US Militarism in Asia*, encourage more theological reflections on militarism and militarized violence both locally and globally. They emphasize that the Jesus movement began in the context of Roman imperialism. The Roman Empire exercised power through political, economic, social, and religious forces, and used military power to keep its people in check. They write, "It is within militarized violence that the formation of the Jesus movement and the emergence of Christianity took place. As a movement that was, at its heart, a response to the legacy of militarized violence, it is critical that Christian theology offer an account of its relationship to militarized violence today."[44]

As a Korean American theologian, Joh uses postcolonial and trauma theories to analyze collective trauma as a result of war and militarized violence. Colonialism and militarism affect not only physical and material conditions but also leave an indelible impact on the psyches of the colonized. Postcolonial theory explores the ways that "structural and systematized colonization made legible in the interior psyche space of those who come within the reach of the colonizer and his/her world."[45] Joh studies the unrelenting grief and loss in people who have experienced devastating wars and traumas, such as Koreans in the Korean War. Such grief is deep and haunting and may pass on to the next generation, to those who have not directly experienced the war. When grief is suppressed and not adequately dealt with, it can result in immobilization, anguish, and depression. But grief can also be transformed into postcolonial "critical melancholia," in which the feelings of loss and melancholia can be channeled into survival and resistance after the war. Instead of social amnesia, people, though in grief, can bear witness to the collective trauma, memorialize the victims, and fight for a better world.

Joh uses this understanding of postcolonial grief to reinterpret the meaning of the cross. The central symbol of Christianity is a man tortured and dying on the cross. Crucifixion is a public spectacle in which the victim dies a slow death for people to see. Christianity has centered its attention on Jesus the tortured subject, but Joh asks us to also pay attention to the trauma created in the people who bore witness to the event, and to their collective subjectivity. The early Christian community came out of these people, who, though traumatized and in deep grief, carried on with the memory of Jesus' death and suffering to continue his mission. The cross became a site of terror, trauma, grief, and memory. Joh argues that the cross cannot be seen as a single event concerning a particular individual but should be expanded to encompass a broad experience of social suffering. Many people who have experienced trauma and suffering have found strength and solidarity in the symbol of the cross. Joh argues that grief and outrage over unbearable loss can have the potential to transform the world. As the followers of Jesus might have created funeral rituals to work through the mourning for his death, Joh encourages rituals of mourning for people to work through and support one another after collective trauma.[46]

One powerful way of addressing collective trauma and grief is to work for peace and reconciliation. The legacy of the Cold War created animosity between North and South Korea as families were divided and suspicion was sown among the people. There have been movements toward reunification in South Korea, while progressive theologians developed *Tongil* theology in the 1980s. The historical summit between South Korea President Moon Jae-in and North Korean leader Kim Jong Un in 2018 and the symbolic crossing of the line dividing the demilitarized zone brought glimpses of hope. The two pledged to form closer relations and work to formally end the Korean war.

Kim In Soo notes that there have been deep divisions among South Korean churches over the issue of peace and reconciliation in the peninsula. Conservative

Korean Christians have negative attitudes toward communist ideology and its antireligious stance. They remember the persecution of the churches by the government in North Korea and the lack of religious freedom. For them, free democratic values are important. Liberal Christians emphasize that people in the North and South share the same roots and consequently want to open channels for dialogue. The National Council of Churches in Korea has played a crucial role in the discussion of peace and unification of the Korean people. In a series of meetings under the auspices of the World Council of Churches, representatives from the North and South Korean churches met, worshiped together, and issued joint statements.[47]

Sebastian C. H. Kim suggests that Korean churches should work toward reconciliation because God reconciles Godself with us through Christ. He proposes three principles of working toward a theology of reconciliation.[48] The first is the jubilee principle found in Leviticus 25:9–55 (also in Lev. 27:16–25; Num. 36:4). "Jubilee" in the Bible means a sabbatical year, the restoration of the land, and the liberation of slaves. In the Korean context, this means "the proclamation of the liberation of Korean people from the bondage of ideological hegemony, and from political systems which hinder the formation of a common community."[49] The jubilee principle calls Koreans to search for a restored shared community, despite their separation for over 60 years. The second principle is overcoming *han* and building trust and hope. *Minjung* theologians have identified the division of the country as the *han* of Koreans. It is only through building trust among the divided people that reconciliation and peaceful reunification can be brought about. The third principle is bringing about reconciliation by forming shared identity. Drawing examples from the unification of Germany and reconciliation in South Africa, Kim highlights the importance of creating "cultural common memory." This means acknowledging loss, making new connections, and taking action to bring something new to the situation. Given the meetings between the leaders of North and South Korea in the last several years, I hope that new opportunities and avenues will be open for Christians in the North and South to contribute to the reconciliation effort.

As we commemorate the centenary of the March First Movement and the May Fourth Movement, we recall several generations of people in the past who have fought against foreign aggression, militarism, and colonialism in the East Asian region. Today, the work has not been completed, as new political and military threats continue to challenge peace and stability in the region. Japan and Korea have tightened their security alliances with the U.S. in response to the rise of China. The tensions across the Taiwan Strait have heightened since the election of President Tsai Ing-wen, while nuclear disputes on the Korean Peninsula remain unsettling. As cultural critic Chen Kuan-hsing has said, the region needs to engage the processes of deimperialization, decolonialization, and de-Cold War thinking to develop true democratic institutions and reconcile relationships.[50] Churches in the region have prophetic and reconciling roles to play—proclaiming the reconciling action of God and ushering in God's Shalom. Huang Po Ho,

a leader in theological education in Taiwan and in the Asian ecumenical movement, urges the churches to continue the decolonial process by "strengthening
contextual theological formation and theological education in the contexts of
Asia."[51] He hopes that the churches can work ecumenically to strengthen God's
oikoumene and offer hope in a divided world. He says the ecumenical movement
in Asia must be a "Christian movement for people which will strive for people's
security instead of the church's or even the nation's security. It must seek peace
for people instead of peace for the powerful and the rich."[52] As Asia Pacific
becomes a critical geopolitical area for world politics and peace, Christians and
churches need to respond to the challenges of the time. This can begin with a
postcolonial reckoning with the long history of imperial aggressions of multiple
empires in the region and a critique of subimperial desires, so that a theology of
decolonization and deimperialization might emerge and take root, enabling us
to face the future.

Chapter 6

Transnationalism and Feminist Theology in Asia Pacific

We endeavor to make sense and meaning out of the multiple social loca-
tions, the hybrid cultures, and the many powers of death and life that are
placed before us.

Rita Nakashima Brock[1]

A young Filipina was sexually assaulted by a U.S. marine in a van while three other marines watched and cheered him on. The twenty-two-year-old woman, identified with the pseudonym Nicole, met the marine in a bar on the former U.S. naval base at Subic Bay, near Olongapo City, about ninety kilometers northwest of Manila. According to the doctor who examined her, she suffered from bruises on her arms, legs, and genital areas, injuries consistent with rape.

The incident took place in November 2005, when the marines went for a night out after two weeks' counterterrorism exercises with Filipino troops. They belonged to a marine expeditionary force stationed in Okinawa, which hosted most of the fifty thousand U.S. troops in Japan. When the charge surfaced, the U.S. government refused to turn over the marines, citing provisions of a Visiting Forces Agreement between the two countries. The marines were placed under custody in the American Embassy in Manila.

During the trial, the accused marine admitted that he had had sexual inter-course with Nicole but declared he was innocent and that the sex was consen-sual. But according to a witness, Nicole was offered money to drop the charges hours after the alleged attack occurred. The case sparked anti-American protest in the former U.S. colony as feminist and civic groups mobilized to bring justice for Nicole. Some protesters and even legislators demanded the revocation of the country's security pact signed with the U.S. Others countered that the rape case has blemished the joint military exercises aimed at weakening al Qaeda-linked militants in the southern Philippines.

Nicole's case is not an isolated incident. It must be placed in the long, contentious relation between Asia and the U.S. For before Asia emerged as a market for U.S. global capital, Asia was seen as a war zone.[2] Beginning with the Spanish American War over the destiny of the Philippines, the U.S. has fought successive wars in Asia. During the Cold War, the U.S. pursued a containment policy against China and the former Soviet Union. Today U.S. hegemony in the region is maintained by the strategic deployment of American forces throughout the Pacific. The U.S. signed bilateral security pacts with Asian nations, creating a vast network of political influences comparable to a solar system, with the U.S. at the center. In America's so-called global war against terrorism, the collaboration of Asian allies becomes even more crucial.

Geopolitical conflicts with Asia always touch a raw nerve in the American psyche. The popular myth of the "yellow peril" surfaces again and again whenever the U.S. has tensions with Asian countries. The "Orient" has been constructed as barbaric, exotic, alien, and racially different from and inferior to the "West" in what Edward Said has called "Orientalism."[3] American Orientalism puts Asian Americans in a double bind—although they are Americans, they are perceived as perpetual foreigners whose loyalty is suspect and who can never be fully assimilated. As such, Asian Americans become easy targets and scapegoats during national crises, as the internment of nearly 120,000 Japanese Americans during World War II clearly reminds us. Transnational relations have direct bearings on racial formation on the U.S. home front. As Lisa Lowe comments:

> During the crises of national identity that occurred in periods of U.S. war in Asia—with the Philippines (1898–1910), against Japan (1941–45), in Korea (1950–53), and in Vietnam—American Orientalism displaced U.S. expansionist interests onto racialized figurations of Asian workers within the national space. . . . On the one hand, Asian states have become prominent as external rivals in overseas imperial war and in the global economy, and on the other, Asian immigrants are still a necessary racialized labor force within the domestic national economy.[4]

Lowe's astute observations point to the necessity of a transnational analysis of the intersections of race, labor, state, and gender in the age of global economy. To bring justice to Nicole, we would need a transnational scrutiny because of the complex configuration of powers in the case: the deployment of American troops involving three governments, the service industry surrounding military bases, the judicial systems and the bilateral agreements, the war against terrorism, grassroots people's movements, and women's international networks. It would have been simplistic to interpret her rape as another example of male violence or male domination over women. The rape of Nicole is an inscription on a Filipina's flesh and blood of the forces of transnational capital, masculinist military power, corruption of national government, and American imperialistic interests in the Asia Pacific. The case points to how globalization, supported by military and political might, has changed the configuration of social, economic, political, and juridical powers in the world. While globalization is a worldwide phenomenon, this chapter uses the Asia Pacific region as a critical lens to articulate the challenges of transnationalism to feminist theology specifically. Since I am using "Asia Pacific" as a framework to explore some of the critical issues that Asian and Asian American feminist theologians might address together, I begin with an analysis of the discourses on the Asia Pacific and critical interventions that feminist scholars and theologians on both sides of the Pacific have offered.

CONCEPTUALIZING THE ASIA PACIFIC REGION AND FEMINIST VOICES

"Asia Pacific" is a contested term, and, as Rob Wilson says, it needs to be "situated and unpacked from within distinct cultural-political trajectories to disclose what this signifier stands for in its present ambivalent implications."[5] Following Arif Dirlik, I adopt a world system approach to interpret the Asia Pacific as a regional formation, developed as a result of European and American capitalist expansion.[6] The Pacific region, as we have come to know it, was an invention of Europe. Christopher Columbus's original intention to go to India linked Asia with the "newly discovered" Pacific. Columbus thought that he had found the fabulous East, the earthly paradise, and its peoples were Asians—the "Indians."[7] The Pacific emerged in the European consciousness as an extension of the conquest of the Americas. The Pacific was called a Spanish lake during the sixteenth and seventeenth centuries and an English lake from the eighteenth to nineteenth centuries. With the rise of the U.S. in the late nineteenth century, it has been renamed an American lake. Although the peoples living in the region have their diverse cultures and ways of life, it was the Euro-American powers that invented the regional structure both economically and ideologically to serve their capitalist interests. Arif Dirlik calls it a dominantly Euro-American formation. He observes:

> Entering the Pacific from the west or the east, the Portuguese, the Spaniards, the Dutch, the Russians, and the English, as well as their colonists in the Americas, all contributed in turn to the creation of a regional structure, in which Asian and Pacific societies provided the building blocks and the globalized interests of Euro-American powers furnished the principles of organization.[8]

The domination of Western powers in the Asia Pacific has not been unchallenged. After the modernization of Japan, the Japanese government attempted to create a Greater East Asian Coprosperity Sphere in the early twentieth century through the colonization of Korea and Taiwan and brutal military aggression in other Asian countries. The U.S. reasserted its power by joining World War II after the attack on Pearl Harbor and remodeled Japan, including drafting the Japanese Constitution, in the postwar era under American tutelage. Since the 1970s, the rapid economic growth of the Asian dragons (South Korea, Taiwan, Hong Kong, and Singapore) and the cultural assertion of an Asian way to modernization have highlighted the Asian contributions in redefining the region as Asia Pacific. The Asia Pacific regional formation affects women's lives differently than those of men, and feminists have sought to disrupt a unified, seamless, and cooperative myth of coprosperity among Asian nations.

The discourse on the Asia Pacific in the academy and mass media has undergone several shifts since World War II, but the influences from the area studies model remain strong. During the Cold War, area studies were set up in American colleges and universities to provide information about the enemy countries and other strategic regions. Asia was divided into the subregions of East Asia, Southeast Asia, and South Asia, and the countries in the Pacific were left out of this purview. Although designated as subregions, the focus was on national entities. For example, "East Asia" means the study of Japan, Korea, and China. Scholars went into the field to observe and represent "native" culture, as if East Asia were a unified and bounded unit. This research produced a theory of knowledge of the non-Western world based on the authority and authenticity of indigenous experience and the asymmetrical relation between the researcher and the so-called native informants.[9]

Early feminist literary and theological writings presented images of the Asia Pacific that challenged fixed boundaries of nation and the homogeneity of culture. For example, Maxine Hong Kingston's *Woman Warrior* (1976)[10] created a genderized and racialized narrative of Chinese immigrants for whom crossing the Asia Pacific had become "a space of fractures, disjunctures, traumas, confusion, and disappointments."[11] In *Compassionate and Free* (1979), the first book on Asian feminist theology, Marianne Katoppo describes in detail the cultural, ethnic, and religious diversity in her country, Indonesia, and the ways women are situated as the Other in Christian, familial, and national narratives.[12] From the beginning, Asian American feminist theologians have also emphasized their multicultural context and their in-between social location.[13] These feminist writings disrupt homogeneous national tales by including race, ethnicity, gender, and class in their analysis of the female subject.

Since the mid-1970s when the newly industrialized Asian countries began their economic takeoffs, following Japan's phenomenal success, the discourse on the Pacific Rim caught public attention. Commentators and the media soon predicted that the twenty-first century would be a "Pacific" century. The success of the East and Southeast Asian countries was hailed as a model for the "underdeveloped" world, just as Asian Americans were held up as a "model minority." The Pacific Rim discourse had great appeal for the capitalist managers in North America who saw the benefit of Asia being successfully integrated into the capitalist economy.

In Asia, politicians and scholars also seized the opportunity to reassert their cultural identity and argued for a Pacific way of development. In particular, Neo-Confucianism was revived from Japan all the way to Singapore as the characteristic feature of this Asian way of modernization. The devastating 1997 Asian economic crisis, which brought several Asian countries to the brink of bankruptcy, sent a cautionary signal to any overheated and celebratory "Rimspeak."

While Asian politicians boasted about the prosperity of the Rim, Asian feminist theologians contested that the majority of Asian people were poor, and that economic development in Asia was grossly uneven. The so-called Asian miracle was built on the availability of cheap female labor, unsafe and unhealthy working conditions, and inadequate labor protection. I have articulated the ways Neo-Confucianism, patriarchy, and capitalism have formed an "unholy trinity" to oppress women.[14] While Asian women were increasingly absorbed into the labor force in the newly industrialized Asian countries, a growing number of Asian immigrant women arrived to work in the garment and other light industries in the U.S., following the change of the Immigration Act of 1965, which lifted the national quotas for Asians. Activists and scholars have paid attention to the struggles of Asian immigrant female workers whose work in the sweatshops and other low-paid jobs has bolstered the American economy.[15]

The economic development of some of the Southeast Asian countries depended also on the exploitation of the sexual labor of women. During the Vietnam War, Southeast Asia provided places of "rest and recreation" for American soldiers, and a growing sex industry developed around the military bases and large urban centers. The rape of Nicole reflects both the socialization of men to use sex for dominance and the subtext that Asian women's flesh is available for the taking.[16] The sex industry has been crucial to the economic development of countries such as the Philippines and Thailand, not only on their soil but also in the funds that women trafficked for sex work have sent home. Some of these trafficked women and children were brought to the U.S. through an international ring of organized criminal activities.

Since the end of the Cold War, discourses on the Asia Pacific have taken different directions. On the one hand, the forum of Asian Pacific Economic Cooperation, formed in Canberra in 1989, promotes an image of the Asia Pacific with open borders, regional coherence, shared direction, and transnational globalization. On the other hand, the rapid rise of the Chinese economy and the huge trade deficit between China and the U.S. have made Samuel P. Huntington's prediction of a "clash of civilizations" plausible to many people. Huntington has surmised that the conflict in the future would not be a clash of ideologies, but, rather, it would be a clash of civilizations. Not surprisingly, he predicts that a major fault line will be drawn between the Western and the Sinic worlds.[17] While many have criticized Huntington's concept of civilization as bound and essentialist (much based on the area studies model), I underscore how globalization has produced new discourses about the Asia Pacific, through a rehashing of old myths and the addition of new fantasies.

Globalization and transnationalism require feminists to use fresh conceptual frameworks and mental constructs to analyze the Asia Pacific. While transnational processes have occurred since the formation of nation-states, transnationalism as a contemporary phenomenon is largely associated with flexibility and globalization. Michael Chang refers to transnationalism as "the movement across national borders of human beings, capital, and the cultural and social ideas and practices that come with both people and money."[18] In the course of a constant transnational flow of capital, labor, and ideas, basic categories such as gender, race, ethnicity, nation, and citizenship are being rearticulated. For example, we can no more embark on the study of a nation without taking into consideration the phenomena of migrancy and diaspora. The large number of female migrant workers from the Philippines, Thailand, Indonesia, and Sri Lanka working overseas changes the shape of the international division of labor as well as gender relationships both in the home and the receiving countries.

Feminist theorists and theologians have grappled with the challenges of globalization in various ways. The anthropologist Aihwa Ong articulates the concept of flexible citizenship to describe how individuals and governments have developed a flexible notion of citizenship and sovereignty to accommodate capital accumulation and people's mobility.[19] Assimilation is no longer the only route open for immigrants who can maintain transnational loyalties and relations via travel and communication networks. Using a transnational methodology, Lowe studies immigration, nationhood, and the racialized feminization of labor.[20] In theological circles, Nami Kim challenges the use of the unifying category "Asia," argues that Asian feminist theology should go beyond speaking for or to "Asian" women, and tells us that, instead, it should be rearticulated as a critical global feminist theology.[21] Employing a postcolonial lens, I have suggested a diasporic imagination for interpreting the Bible and developing an intercultural feminist theological framework.[22]

A transnational analysis will help us see Asia and America not as two separate entities but as constantly influencing each other within the broader regional formation of the Asia Pacific. There are different existing models to help us conceptualize how "Asia" and "America" are mutually inscribed. Paul Gilroy's study of the so-called Black Atlantic comes easily to mind.[23] He uses the images of the ships and sea voyages crisscrossing the Atlantic to describe Black culture as multiply centered and diasporic in the Atlantic space, which transcends the narrow confines of ethnicity and nationality. In so doing, Gilroy transgresses the disciplinary boundaries of Black, American, Caribbean, and British studies, and also debunks the rigid notions of Afrocentrism and Eurocentrism. With an expansive imagination Gilroy describes Black Atlantic culture with multiple points of entries and polyrhythmic beats, following not a single linear pattern but constantly improvising. Gilroy's work stimulates us to think about the multiple linkages of the Asia Pacific in critically new ways, even though we might not want to call it a "yellow Pacific" because of the residual fear of the "yellow peril." In popular consciousness a "Black Atlantic" and a "Yellow Pacific" have drastically different connotations because unlike the Black people in the

Atlantic, Asian peoples have much more power to contest Euro-American economic and political power, and China is poised to become a major threat to
U.S. hegemony.

In postcolonial discourse Said has used the counterpoint in Western classical
music to develop his contrapuntal reading, which looks at metropolitan history
and histories of the colonies as overlapped and intertwined.[24] If we analyze the
history and cultures of any Asian nation, we will see how much they have been
restructured to fit into the model of U.S. hegemony in the region. Although Said
is not primarily interested in racial minority issues, we can utilize insights from his
contrapuntal reading to unpack racialized and genderized migration patterns in
the Americas and to understand how Asian Pacific peoples have contributed to the
shaping of the national cultures, although such contributions are often relegated to
the margins of metropolitan history or remain silenced and exempt from history.

DEVELOPING TRANSNATIONAL FEMINIST
THEOLOGIES IN THE ASIA PACIFIC

If we use transnationalism as a critical lens, we will see that Asian and Asian
American feminist theologians need to give more critical attention to the issues
of globalization. While we have done more work on how colonialism has
impacted the church and the lives of women, we have yet to develop substantial theological thinking on how globalization is reshaping the Asia Pacific. As
Michael Hardt and Antonio Negri have observed, the old form of colonialism,
based on the sovereignty of the nation-state, has given way to a new global form
called "the Empire." This Empire is composed of decentered and deterritorialized as well as complex and expansive networks of power with multiple centers
and margins. They write: "Empire manages hybrid identities, flexible hierar-
chies, and plural exchanges through modulating networks of command."[25]

The Asia Pacific region plays critical roles in the development of Empire in
terms of capital and technology transfer, sharing of managerial know-how, out-
sourcing of manufacturing and service industries, migrant workers across the
region, and so forth. No matter how differently we may assess the impact of
globalization, we have to realize that the "natives" are no longer on the outside,
as once imagined, but are "subjected to the same political-economic processes
and structures that all of us encounter in our everyday lives, everywhere and
anywhere."[26] Asians and Asian Americans are strategically located in the interstices of some of these immense transnational networks, whether they work in
the Silicon Valley or in the financial districts of Seoul, Hong Kong, or Tokyo. A
critical scrutiny of their experiences will help us look at Empire from many vantage points, not just through the lens of U.S. dominance but also with attention
to competition from China and Japan. In the following I will discuss three areas
to which feminist theology will need to attend: economic and social formation,
cultural difference, and power and resistance in the age of transnationalism.

Transnational feminist theology in the Asia Pacific has to pay more attention to economics and social formation and to the question that the anthropologist Arjun Appadurai has asked: "What is the hidden dowry of globalization?"[27] Although Appadurai may not have intended it this way, the genderized and sexualized nature of dowry brings into sharp relief the collateral that the majority of the world's women and their families must pay to the deregulation of the market, the unfettered chase for consumer goods, the commodification of sex and culture, the privatization of public services, and the structural adjustment that the international financial and monetary agencies impose. And we have to ask ourselves what roles religious and cultural ideologies have played in justifying this unequal burden on the vast number of women.

If Calvinistic ethics served as the religious backdrop for the rise of capitalism, as Max Weber claimed,[28] today's economic globalization is promoted by the Christian Right, made up of religious fundamentalists and evangelicals of various stripes. These televangelists, conservative pundits, and web-savvy leaders exert a huge influence in the Asia Pacific through megachurches, the mass media, and other transnational networks. They promote a gospel of prosperity, individual salvation, family values, and economic success as the sign of God's grace. A substantial number of Asian and Asian American professionals in the Asia Pacific, many of whom occupy key positions in economic globalization, are conjoined in their subscription to this gospel of upward social mobility. They can be found among those waking up at 5 a.m. to attend morning prayers in Seoul, speaking in tongues in charismatic worship in Singapore, or devoting time to organize cell groups of ethnic churches in the U.S. The Asian American ethnic churches are mostly conservative in their worldview, patriarchal in their leadership, and dedicated to providing services for displaced immigrants as opposed to challenging racism and the status quo.

Fundamentalist Christianity is not the only religion competing for hegemony in globalization. As we have seen, Neo-Confucianism has been revived in the Pacific Rim discourse. If Weber dismissed Chinese religion as stagnant and lacking progress in his comparative study of world cultures,[29] Asian scholars today proudly point to the fact that Confucianism provides religious motivation for economic growth equivalent to Calvinism in the West. They insist that Asian people have found their own way of development and need not adopt a wholesale Westernization in order to be modernized. Confucianism, they claim, is making a critical contribution to world civilization by offering an alternative model of modernization.[30] In the U.S. the argument that Asian peoples have strong family support and cultural values has also drawn from the Confucian background of East Asians, the largest group among Asian Americans.

If women do not fare well in fundamentalist Christianity, they are also discriminated against in Confucian ethics. In the discussion of "Asian values," the emphases have been on Confucian family relationships and on human relatedness. Asian communitarian ethics are seen as superior to Western individualism. The theologian Namsoon Kang cautions against such binary constructs

and points to patriarchal domination in the Confucian family and social relations. She articulates the contradiction that while South Korea marches forward
toward modernization, the Asian values discourse "freezes women in the patriarchal past, the traditional images, and the pre-modern reality."[31] And she has
discussed how Confucian familism has cast its huge influence on the construction of patriarchal Korean Christianity in its religious leadership, theology, and
theological education.

Fundamentalist Christianity and the Confucian revival have several things
in common. In the U.S., the Christian Right has exerted tremendous influence in politics and is part of the neoconservative forces supporting big business
and tax cuts for the rich. From Japan to Singapore, the so-called "Asian way of
modernization" developed under strong leadership (or intervention) from the
state and resulted in a small group of politicians and business leaders wielding
enormous power. Both fundamentalist Christianity and the Confucian revival
support modern globalization, yet they claim their moral authority by assuming
a countercultural and countermodern stance. To bolster their conservative political agenda, both appeal to a "traditional" patriarchal morality and condemn
feminism and homosexuality as antifamily ideologies. To various degrees, both
ideologies subscribe to the conservative moral worldview and, as George Lakoff
describes, both (1) promote strict father morality; (2) promote self-discipline,
responsibility, and self-reliance; (3) uphold the morality of reward and punishment; (4) protect moral people from external evils; and (5) uphold the existing
moral order.[32] It is evident that controlling women and their sexuality, which
consolidates patriarchal control in the public and private realms, is a central
component of the family values ideology. I would name this temporal lag, or
what Kang has sarcastically called "freez[ing] women in . . . the pre-modern reality," as the hidden dowry of globalization.

While Confucianism was rearticulated to serve the capitalist cause, other
religio-cultural elements in the Asia Pacific have been utilized to construct
counterhegemonic discourses. I compare here the work of Kathryn Tanner and
Aruna Gnanadason because both address economic and ecological consequences
of runaway capitalism. Tanner, a university professor in the U.S., notes that
several Western scholars have found gift exchange in non-Western societies,
especially in the Asia Pacific, as an alternative to the commodity exchange that
defines modern capitalism. I have observed that some of these writings tend to
romanticize the gift exchange and the human relatedness in Asia Pacific societies. After offering an assessment of gift exchange, Tanner proceeds to develop an
economy of grace based on the unconditional and universal giving of God. Out
of joyfulness and gratitude for God's free gifts, human beings also give to others.
She offers the image of a noncompetitive community of mutual benefit as an
alternative to cutthroat capitalist competition.[33]

With good intention, Tanner and the British theologian John Milbank
articulate an alternative social imaginary and look to the marginal spaces they
thought were less absorbed into the capitalist economy for inspiration.[34] Not

being experts in these marginal spaces and cultures, they rely on anthropological accounts, often without some serious questioning of the ways that scholars, such as Marcel Mauss and Bronislaw Malinowski, had represented the "primitive" societies in the Pacific. Just as anthropologists and social scientists draw raw data from the field to develop their grand theories (such as reciprocity and gift economies), theologians extract from these theories ideas and concepts (in this case, "gift exchange") to construct their grand ideas about God. From the localized idea of gift exchange, Tanner develops the doctrine of God as the perfect giver whose love is unconditional and universal and does not depend on human beings. In so doing, Tanner superimposes the Christian model of self-sacrifice onto a more generous and reciprocal model of gift exchange in non-Western societies.[35] This understanding of God and the sacrificial love on the cross can now be universalized, context free, ready to be adopted not only in the American churches but circled back to places in the Asia Pacific.

Aruna Gnanadason is from India and has served as the coordinator for Justice, Peace, and Creation of the World Council of Churches. Instead of focusing on gift exchange, she begins with elaborating on the traditions of "prudent care" of the earth; a practice found in several areas where indigenous peoples live in India. She highlights human beings' relationship with the earth and not just human relatedness through gift exchange. Instead, Gnanadason shifts the traditional understanding of grace coming purely from divine power to a relational power that motivates us to love the earth and work for justice.[36] She articulates the concept of brown grace, which stands for the traditions of prudent care—"of people who live in closest proximity to the earth and who give to the land its integrity."[37] Contrasted with Tanner's anthropomorphic God based on the cross, Gnanadason points to the metaphor of God as the self-giver who transforms the earth with grace, such as the earth as the body of God. Their different approaches can be attributed to their adherence to diverse theological frameworks: Tanner from a postliberal tradition and Gnanadason from an ecofeminist perspective. But I emphasize that both use Asia Pacific resources and, by staying close to the context, Gnanadason both respects peoples' stories and describes how theological ideas are contested, modified, and rearticulated through concrete struggles. By contrast, Tanner's theological economy of grace sounds too utopian, and her discussion of noncompetitive community is hard to put into practice in the face of grinding competitive economic forces.

The above discussion has already drawn us into the deep waters of identity, cultural difference, and cultural politics, issues that have been discussed widely in Asian and Asian American feminist theology. The Chinese cultural critic Rey Chow has coined the term "the difference revolution"[38] to describe the preoccupation with difference in critical theory, cultural studies, literary criticism, and cognate fields resulting from poststructuralism. She cautions that the self-referential discourse on difference, focusing on language and texts, could be academically avant-garde but politically conservative if the material and sociopolitical dimensions are foreclosed or overlooked.[39] As I have described above the articulation of so-called Asian values, based on neo-Confucianism, can create a competing cultural discourse while the notion is simultaneously used to serve conservative political and economic agendas.

How do we understand the terms "Asian" and "Asian American" at a time when some feminists have cautioned against "mapping politics and identities geographically or culturally"[40] because of the tendency to homogenize regions and cultures as bounded units? Why is it that Asian, African, Latin American, Black, Hispanic feminist, and womanist theologians have refused to drop these modifiers in order to differentiate their work from the "unmarked" feminist theology produced by some European and American white women? By using these cultural, racial, and geographical modifiers, these feminist and womanist theologians claim that they speak to the world from a particular social and cultural context, and they also specify their positionality in relation to other theological projects and discourses. These theologians contend that European and Euro-American feminist scholars also speak from particular vantage points though the latter tend to leave their positions unmarked as a tactic to universalize their experiences and theology.

In claiming their cultural difference, these marginalized and minoritized feminist and womanist theologians have learned to avoid a binary construction of the West and the Other, on the one hand, and essentializing Asian, Black, Latina, and so forth, on the other.[41] At the same time, they know from their involvements in social movements and struggles that the fine splitting of differences will not serve the political cause of mobilizing women to form coalitions. They criticize the postmodern play on the indetermination of meanings and difference and insist that the social and political must not be left out in the definition of culture and the theorization of cultural difference.[42] The historian Harry D. Harootunian articulates this clearly: "The politics of identity based on enunciation of cultural difference is not the same as political identity whose formation depends less on declarations of differences than on some recognition of equivalences."[43] These dynamics are evident when Asian Americans used the term "Asian American" during the civil rights era to denote a plurality of Asian peoples of diverse cultures, histories, and languages in the U.S.

In the globalized world we will need a new imagination to conceptualize geographies, cultures, and peoples. Appadurai suggests that we shift away from "trait" geographies, which are the legacy of the area studies model, to what he calls "process" geographies. He argues that area studies tended to

> mistake a particular configuration of apparent stabilities for permanent associations between space, territory, and cultural organization. These apparent stabilities are themselves largely artifacts of the specific trait-based idea of "culture" areas, a recent Western cartography of large civilizational landmasses associated with different relationships to "Europe" (itself a complex historical and cultural emergent), and a Cold War-based geography of fear and competition.[44]

His process geographies see human organization not as static but as always on the move, with action and interaction—trade, travel, warfare, colonization, proselytization, and the like.[45] While the trait model most often speaks from the center, from the male elite point of view, the process model allows room for feminists to imagine the margin, the migrant, and new social subjects that are being formed.

Additionally, this process model helps us to theorize authenticity, hybridity, and heterogeneity among Asians and Asian Americans in newly fashioned ways. Emerging in the late 1970s, Asian feminist theologians were concerned with finding out what is "unique" about Asia and what could be said of a distinctive Asian feminist methodology.[46] The use of Asian religio-cultural resources such as folklores, stories, legends, songs, and peoples' popular religions, was encouraged. As Wai Ching Angela Wong has commented: "This emphasis on the 'Asian-ness' of doing theology in Asia is echoed by what postcolonial discussion calls a 'fictional' return (of the colonized) to one's indigenous history and culture."[47] The search for "Asian-ness" can easily fall into the traps of the trait model of areas studies when theologians characterize the essential features of Asia as poverty and religious diversity.[48] But the search for the past need not be a self-Orientalizing exercise if it is consciously done as a process to suture a broken historical and cultural memory repressed and disrupted by colonialism; to point to the contradictions of historical trajectories of modernity and contest the "McDonaldization" of the world.

If Asian feminist theologians tend to return in time to find out what is "authentically Asian," their Asian American counterparts look to space to create their new fluidly global identities. Many use spatial metaphors to describe and elaborate their hyphenated and hybrid identities. These metaphors include: the in-between space, the third space, the interstices, the imaginary homeland, and a notion of deterritorialized pan-ethnicity.[49] The Japanese American theologian Rita Nakashima Brock has coined the term "interstitial integrity" to describe the need to balance multiple dimensions of the self in the fluid yet unsettling spaces. She writes: "Interstitial refers to the places in between, which are real places, like the strong connective tissues between organs in the body that link the parts. . . . Integrity is closely related to integration, to acts of connecting many disparate things by holding them together."[50] Because of racism, the margins and the in-between spaces become sites for Asian Americans to create cultural productions that both resist the white dominant culture and reinvent themselves.

It would be difficult to create a meaningful dialogue if Asian feminists emphasize their Asianness while Asian North American women claim their rights to be Americans and Canadians while downplaying their connection with Asia to avoid being labeled perpetual foreigners. But if we can see cultures, nations, and geographies not in terms of reified traits but as process, we will see that heterogeneity and competing positionalities are part and parcel of globalization. The need to return to what is "authentically Asian" is the result of a globalized culture in which one is made to feel alienated and diasporic even at home. While the global increasingly impinges on the local, hybridization is a phenomenon in North America as well as in many Asian cities. As Michael Chang says:

"Transnationalism has also brought an unprecedented hybridity within this global culture. . . . [G]lobal capitalism is digested at the 'local' level, imprinting it with a hybrid mix of Western and 'local' cultural practices and views."[51] In fact, Wong, writing from the cosmopolitan city of Hong Kong, proposes using the language of hybridity, instead of a binary opposition of "Asia and the West," as a new strategy of doing Asian feminist theology.[52]

The flexibility and innovation associated with the fluidly global can also be symptomatic of a highly adaptive global culture, which tends to commodify and aestheticize ethnic differences for commercial gain. In the name of diversity and multiculturalism, different cultural elements have been brought together superficially and selectively, disregarding context and history, as in a sprawling buffet of multiethnic food. To guard against such commodification of ethnic difference, one must go beyond a superficial embrace of hybridity and the in-between spaces to find out the ways in which the material history of racial dynamics is inscribed in such spaces. Lowe reminds us that the "difference" of Asian American cultural forms is not "a matter of mere technical innovation that we might find in aestheticist texts that are critical of traditional forms and of mass culture but reside in racial formation as *the material trace of history.*"[53]

Speaking within Asia and in between Asia and North America, feminist theologians of Asian descent occupy different positions—sometimes mutually reinforcing and other times contesting, in the vast flows of ideas, peoples, cultures, and histories of the transnational Asia Pacific. They will start from disparate points, plot various trajectories, and mold distinct shapes and spaces for their cultural matrices and theological interstices. Their feminist theologies are heterogeneous not only because of cultural difference but also because of material inequities and the historical and political vicissitudes in the Asia Pacific. Yet for more than three decades some of them have found one another and established dialogical relations within, between, and among cultures, ethnicities, and nations along the many shores of the ocean. These conversations are held despite some of their countries having been at war with one another and some having colonized others. Out of these mutual probings and learnings, as well as debates and criticism, they contribute to the theological discourse by offering a wide range of possibilities for imagining new social life, cultural forms, subject positions, and theological sensibilities while also contesting the overdetermination of global capital and consumerist culture. They also point to the heterogeneity of the construction of time and space and the changing multiple subject positions they occupy as they continuously renegotiate the meanings of "Asian" and "Asian American" in a world in flux.[54] Together they are creating feminist theologies that disrupt the dominant forms of theological discourses emerging from nationalist, imperialist, and Euro-American feminist traditions.[55]

I conclude by elaborating upon Appadurai's concept of grassroots globalization, or globalization from below,[56] in the Asia Pacific theological context. By "grassroots globalization" he refers to the work of nongovernmental organizations, transnational advocacy networks, public intellectuals, and socially concerned academics. In the theological context the challenge is to reconceptualize power, especially divine power, from below and not from above. Historically the images for divine power—such as father, warrior, and king—portray a God situated at the apex of power. Even the masculinist image of Jesus as the liberator portrays him as having the enormous power of intervening in history and liberating humankind from structural oppression. What would divine power look like if we speak of a theology from below and not a theology from above?

One of the images I suggest is a God of the interstices. The interstice is the space where different cultural currents, flows of people, and streams of ideas collide and coalesce. The feminist theologian Catherine Keller has raised the question of whether the interstitial will help to confront the imperial.[57] I posit that the imperial is not totalizing since it produces contradictions, disjunctures, and competing interests. Said has said, "Every situation also contains a contest between a powerful system of interests, on the one hand, and, on the other, less powerful interests threatened with frustration, silence, incorporation, or extinction by the powerful."[58] The interstice is where such kinds of competing interests and powers occur most clearly. The task of theologians as public intellectuals is to reveal and elucidate this contest. We can no longer focus our resistance as citizens of one nation against another as we did in the older form of nationalist struggles against colonialism. Rather, we have to look toward "those institutions, spaces, borders, and processes that are the interstitial sites of the social formation in which the national intersects with the international."[59] It is in these interstitial sites where cultural hybridity occurs and new social subjects are formed because the boundaries of the nation-state, citizenship, race, gender, and culture are being redrawn and rethought. If we imagine divine power in the form of a matrix rather than as hierarchical, unilateral, and unidirectional, then the interstices are the nodal power connections where something clever and creative can occur.

The young woman Nicole and her family courageously brought her case against the military of the greatest superpower the world has ever seen. Her story reminds us of other incidents of rape, sexual abuse, and torture of women committed by American servicemen in Okinawa and Iraq. Confronting the powers in Manila and Washington, D.C., Nicole is like a small David facing a gigantic Goliath. Yet she cannot be silenced because her case has been brought to the attention of the international civil society through the media, the Internet, grassroots organizations, and Christian women's networks.[60] In the mobilizing of transnational networks that stand in solidarity with her and with other victims of violence, war, and oppression, we see the grace of God—divine interstitial power at work. Such a power is energizing and enabling because it rejoices in creating "synergetic relations,"[61] readjusts and shifts to find new strength, and discovers hope in the densely woven web of life that sustains us all.

Chapter 7

The Hong Kong Protests and Civil Disobedience

No splitting, no severing of ties, and no snitching.
Slogan during the 2019 Hong Kong Protest

In November 2019, hundreds of black-clad protesters, many of them students, clashed with police on a bridge leading to the Chinese University of Hong Kong. The incident began when some protesters threw objects onto railway tracks near the university to stop traffic to support a general strike in Hong Kong. When the police wanted to stop the protest and enter the university to arrest people, protesters erected barricades to stop the police from doing so. The police fired rubber bullets and launched a heavy volley of tear gas. Protesters responded by hurling bricks and petrol bombs at the police and building massive bonfires.[1] At one point during the intense standoff, university vice chancellor Rocky Tuan tried to mediate between the police and protesters, but to no avail. It was surreal to see the serene campus turned into a smoking battlefield with the police stomping inside to arrest students.

The confrontation was part of the protests against an extradition law amendment bill, which would have allowed criminal suspects to be extradited to Communist China. Many Hong Kong people feared that the bill would erode civil liberties in Hong Kong because people might be extradited without due process. They could not trust that the legal system in China would offer people a fair trial. For two consecutive weekends in June 2019, millions took to the streets

123

to demand the bill's withdrawal. When the government refused to respond to the protesters' demands and instead used excessive force to suppress the people, the protests escalated into an anti-government struggle. Many felt that China would no longer honor the "one country, two systems" arrangement, stipulated when the British government returned Hong Kong, once a colonial outpost, to China in 1997. Under this arrangement, Hong Kong would be part of China while its freedoms, independent judiciary, and other forms of autonomy would be preserved for fifty years.

As a graduate of the Chinese University of Hong Kong in the 1970s, I was reminded by the clash at the university of an earlier era of student activism when student leaders confronted the police. In the late 1960s and 1970s, student activists protested against government corruption, social inequity, and colonial suppression. The slogan of the movement was "Know about the motherland and be concerned about society." Radical and left-leaning students wore dark blue Mao jackets and organized study groups to discuss Maoist and Leninist thought. One of the demands of the protests was to have Chinese as one of the official languages of the city. For, even though the majority of Hong Kong's population were Chinese, English was the only official language until 1971. During orientation week before the start of my first year in college, student leaders screened a documentary showing the president of the student union being arrested and shoved into a police van. In those stormy days of student protests, there were rumors that the police would come to the dormitories to arrest students, but the colonial government hesitated to do so for fear of public backlash.

Much has changed in the span of fifty years. In the 1970s, students protested a colonial government that was corrupt and oppressive. In 2019, the target was the Hong Kong government, which protesters saw as following the marching orders of China's leaders rather than listening to Hong Kong's people. During the protests in the 1960s and 1970s, leftist students looked to China and studied Maoist thought for inspiration to fight the colonial government. Today, more and more people assert their local identity as Hongkongers,[2] as being separate and distinct from Chinese. Around the time of the handover, there was a tiny minority of people who wanted Hong Kong to remain a British colony, but there was no push for Hong Kong's independence. In recent years, however, young activists have become so disillusioned by both the Hong Kong and Chinese governments that they have advocated for independence or self-determination for Hong Kong's future.

THE HONG KONG PROTESTS OF 2019

The protests in 2019 were the culmination of growing distrust and widespread discontent with Beijing's intervention in local affairs. In the years after the 1997 handover, Hong Kong people had hoped that the guarantee of "one country, two systems" would allow a high degree of autonomy. But in 2003, the introduction of the National Security Bill shook people's confidence as they feared that their freedom of expression would be curtailed. The bill had to be withdrawn after half a million people took to the streets in protest. Then in 2010, the government proposed to introduce moral and national education as a compulsory subject for the purpose of inculcating a strong sense of national identity. The proposal was met with strong criticism from teachers, parents, and students alike. High school students, such as Joshua Wong, a leader of the student activist group Scholarism, circulated leaflets and organized protests against the proposal. Under strong local opposition, the government withdrew it in 2012. Two years later, the Umbrella Movement fought for true universal suffrage, which was stipulated in the Basic Law, the mini-constitution of Hong Kong. The movement was so named because protesters used umbrellas for defense against the police's use of pepper spray and tear gas. Using some of the strategies of the Occupy Movement in other parts of the world, protesters occupied three busy commercial districts for seventy-nine days. Although the movement failed to bring about concrete political change, it succeeded in propagating the idea of civil disobedience and arousing the people's political consciousness, especially among the young.

The "one country, two systems" framework presented special problems for the development of postcolonial democracy and subjectivity; for unlike other postcolonial nations, Hong Kong did not become independent and fully autonomous after 1997. During the Sino-British negotiations over Hong Kong's future, there was no representation from the people of Hong Kong. Although about one-third of the committee members who drafted the Basic Law were from Hong Kong, they were handpicked by the Chinese government, and the majority of them were pro-Beijing loyalists. During the handover, neither the British nor the Chinese government wanted to dwell on their colonial pasts. The British seized the occasion to tout their accomplishments in turning Hong Kong from a fishing village into the Pearl of the Orient—a vibrant, prosperous city with a sound legal system. The Chinese used the reunification of Hong Kong with the motherland to promote a nationalist tale of pride and patriotism. China promised that, as a Special Administrative Region, Hong Kong's political and economic system would be unchanged for fifty years. This pledge meant that the colonial political system and power structure would be operational after 1997.

Because of this arrangement, some people wonder whether Hong Kong has truly become "postcolonial," since the city was passed from one colonial master to another. Ironically, maintaining the colonial system became a way to resist the encroachment of Communist China, from which many people in Hong Kong had fled. There was little room for debates about overhauling the colonial system or to discuss its mechanism of control and oppression. For these reasons, Wing-sang Law, a professor of cultural studies in Hong Kong, said that the handover represented an "indefinite deferral of decolonization," and that Hong Kong people were prevented from developing political subjectivity after colonialism.[3] The situation has greatly changed as successive waves of public protests have conscientized the people, who are no longer willing to remain silent in the face of escalating pressure from Beijing. A new civic and political community has been formed gradually as more and more people realize that they have to stand up together to protect their Hongkonger identity and values. This stance is especially strong among the younger generation, who are anti-establishment and want to work outside existing power structures and political parties. They have formed their own parties and have pursued more radical social activism. Young people served as the vanguards of the 2019 protests and made up a high percentage of people arrested. Therefore, Law observes that "the local consciousness and localist movement that emerged in recent years in Hong Kong can be seen as a 'return of the repressed,' a revenge of the fate of 'being returned to China' unwillingly. What is coming back is the Hong Kong cultural and political subjectivity that had long been suppressed; it demands the overdue 'recognition.'"[4]

A notable phenomenon of the protests has been highly visible involvement of Christian leaders, pastors, and the larger Christian community. Clergy and leaders of religious organizations have spoken at public forums and church events, visited protest sites, and mediated conflicts between protesters and police. They enjoyed high-profile coverage in mass media and social media. Some pastors held the cross and sang Christian hymns among the protesters, attempting to bear witness to God's presence in the demonstrations. Religious leaders and church workers provided guidance and pastoral support for parishioners, students, and others in need. A local church gathered parents, social workers, and lawyers to launch a campaign, "Protect Our Kids," in the protests. Parents and elderly people placed themselves between militarized riot police and young protesters as a buffer to reduce conflicts. Different Christian denominations also issued public statements urging the government to withdraw the extradition bill. Christians organized prayer meetings in churches, public spaces, and in front of government buildings. Unlike public protests, religious meetings enjoy more protection from interference from the police, and the organizers do not have to apply for a permit to gather in public. Christians sang hymns and offered prayers for the city and for government officials and elected representatives. The Christian hymn "Sing Hallelujah to the Lord" emerged as a unifying anthem during the early stage of the protests, sung by Christians and non-Christians alike. Some churches near the protest routes opened their doors and offered hospitality to protesters. But there were also Christians who believed in separation of church and state, and that Christians should obey the authorities. Many evangelical churches did not want to become politically involved and see evangelism as their priority. These divergent opinions have split local churches and denominations, with some members leaving their local churches because of their dissatisfaction with their churches' response to the protests.[5]

As protesters risked their lives and future careers to fight for Hong Kong's future, Christian leaders and theologians discussed the nature of Christian witness and the roles of the churches in turbulent times and in polarizing situations. Since the protests in the 1970s, some theological educators in Hong

Kong have spoken of the need to develop a contextual theology that responds to social upheavals of the time. To prepare for the 1997 handover, biblical scholars and theologians discussed the themes of diaspora and return in the Bible, Hong Kong identity and the church's mission, and a theology of reconciliation that would bring people of diverse ideologies and backgrounds together.[6] Hebrew Bible scholar Archie C. C. Lee used the return of Hong Kong to China as a social text to present a cross-textual reading of the Jewish return from exile in Isaiah 40–66.[7] Theologian Francis Ching-wah Yip studied the relationship between church and state in China, changing Chinese religious policies, and struggle for religious freedom.[8] After the handover, some have used insights from postcolonial theory to develop a feminist theology and a theology of resistance.[9] Scholars have also analyzed changing church and state relations in Hong Kong and the relationships between politics and different religions after 1997.[10] Biblical scholars, theologians, and activists offered astute theological analyses of the Umbrella Movement in 2014 in dialogue with liberation theology, feminist theology, and Catholic social teachings.[11]

The development of political theology in Hong Kong took place in the historical context of popular movements for democracy in Asia and the theological awakening and ferment among Asian theologians over the course of decades. As I have discussed previously in this book, *minjung* theology in Korea, Homeland theology in Taiwan, and Theology of Struggle were developed in the turbulent years of the 1970s and 1980s. As massive numbers of people took to the streets, students demonstrated and occupied campuses, and political prisoners went to jail, Asian theologians could not do theology as usual without addressing political changes sweeping across Asia. They had to develop contextual theologies that were relevant and responsive to the social and political concerns of their time. Since Hong Kong is a hub for ecumenical activities in Asia, Hong Kong theologians have had ample opportunity to engage in conversations with other Asian theologians and ecumenical leaders. This chapter will explore the protests in Hong Kong as a case study for developing postcolonial political theology under the shadow of empires.

DEMOCRACY AND POLITICAL THEOLOGY

As a former British colony situated in the interstices of several global powers, Hong Kong raises important questions in the context of protest for democracy and political theology. The "one country, two systems" policy tests the limits of China's sovereignty and power over Hong Kong. The 2019 protests began as resistance to an extradition law. In the past, there were several incidences in which the Hong Kong government requested the National People's Congress of China to interpret the laws in Hong Kong. These cases have challenged the judiciary's independence and the political rights of Hong Kong people.[12] In the absence of a democratically elected government, the judiciary plays a key

role in protecting and safeguarding the people's rights. The assumptions behind
the laws in China and those of the common law in Hong Kong introduced
by the British are very different. China's imposition of a national security law
for Hong Kong in July 2020 and its bypassing of Hong Kong's legislature has
caused an uproar domestically and internationally. Many are afraid that this law
curtails the city's civic liberties, including its traditions of free speech and an
independent judiciary. Pro-democracy leaders, such as Martin Lee, argued that
this would be a breach of the promise of "one country, two systems."[13] However, pro-Beijing politicians, business leaders, and others supported the national
security law as a means to restore law and order after a year's mass protests and
strikes. They underscored that Hong Kong is a part of China and that China has
sovereignty over Hong Kong.[14]

It is noteworthy that during the debate about the national security law, scholars in China have used the work of German conservative jurist Carl Schmitt,
who casts a long shadow in Western political theology. Schmitt's major works
were translated into Chinese in the 2000s, and his ideas have sparked much
discussion in the philosophy, political science, and law departments of Chinese
universities—a phenomenon that has been dubbed "Schmitt fever." Since President Xi Jinping came to power, a group of Chinese scholars has gained attention
because they advocate an expansive view of state authority and support the use
of heavy-handed measures to maintain national stability. This group of scholars
is called the "Statists." Schmitt appeals to these scholars because, writing after
World War I, Schmitt supported a strong German nation by arguing that the
sovereign has the power to make exceptions to the rule of law while also protecting the country from foreign enemies. Citing Schmitt, Chen Duanhong, a
law professor at Peking University, argues that when the stability and security
of the country is at stake, state leaders have the right to suspend constitutional
norms, especially provisions for civil rights. During debates on the imposition of
the national security law in 2020, several scholars argued that protests in Hong
Kong have posed grave danger to Hong Kong's stability and prosperity. On
their account, the state has the right to use whatever means necessary to bring
back law and order in order to protect Hong Kong from infiltration by foreign
forces. Because of this concern, they argued, Hong Kong was in no position to
discuss civil liberties.[15]

However, the more liberal scholars in China do not share the views of the
"Statists" and are critical of Schmitt's theories about politics and state. Some
charge that Schmitt's political theories contain dangerous elements of fascism
and that he was Hitler's "Crown Jurist" in addition to being a member of the
National Socialist Party. Others argue that Schmitt tended to overemphasize
extraordinary politics during emergency situations while failing to maintain a
balance between extraordinary politics and daily politics, which operate according to formal laws and procedures. Some Chinese scholars are particularly averse
to Schmitt's political philosophy because they find dangerous parallels in Mao
Zedong's thought, particularly in his sharp distinction between friend and foe.

During the revolutionary period, Mao told his cadres to join forces with friends to form a united front to attack their enemies. After the Communists took over China, the government spurred successive campaigns against landlords, the bourgeoisie, anti-revolutionaries, deviant party members, and others who were labeled enemies of the people. During the Cultural Revolution (1966–1976), the state completely controlled the whole society by intruding into people's private lives and reforming people's thoughts so as to eradicate the influence of enemy classes. Schmitt's idea that the sovereign can suspend constitutional order in a state of exception is deeply concerning because it reminds Chinese liberals of Mao's suspension of constitutional law during the Cultural Revolution.[16]

Working in a Communist country that promotes atheism, scholars in China do not dwell on Schmitt's Catholic background or his argument that "all significant concepts of the modern theory of the state are secularized theological concepts."[17] Schmitt argued that the sovereign's power to suspend juridical order is akin to God's sovereignty over the universe. From a comparative perspective, we can ask, "Are there religious underpinnings in Chinese understandings of sovereignty and the power of the state?" In Chinese tradition, people revere *Tian* (Heaven). The emperor was called *Tianzi* (the Son of Heaven) and ruled China with autocratic power. China's centuries-long monarchy was only abolished in 1911, when the last imperial dynasty was overthrown. But democracy was not developed. After the Chinese Communist Party rose to power, it mounted vigorous campaigns to purge traditional folk beliefs and what it saw as superstitions. Yet Communism functioned almost like a state religion. During the Cultural Revolution, Mao incited personal hero worship of himself, reminiscent of a religious cult in fervor. After turmoil and disturbance, Deng Xiaoping led the country toward reform and liberalization, to restore stability. Over the past several decades, the state saw its legitimacy as dependent not on any transcendental force, but on materialist things, such as the increase of income and the growth of China's GDP. The state whips up strong nationalistic fervor whenever it is criticized from the outside, especially during the Sino-American trade wars.

Many Western political leaders and pundits have hoped that, with liberalization and economic growth, China would become friendlier and move closer to Western democracy and allow more freedoms, including religious freedom. But their hopes remain distant, especially with the rise of President Xi Jinping, who is referred to as *Yi Zun* (one single authority) for his quick consolidation of power over the country. The struggle for democracy in China has been long and tortuous. The Hong Kong protests in 2019 took place on the centenary of China's May Fourth Movement. In 1919, students in Beijing demonstrated against foreign aggression. Reformers believed that traditional Confucian culture was responsible for the political backwardness of China. Radical leaders argued for the rejection of Confucian values and advocated for Western ideas of Mr. Science and Mr. Democracy. During the 2019 protests, some political leaders and commentators in Hong Kong referred to the May Fourth Movement and claimed that they were continuing the century-long pursuit of democracy that the Beijing students had begun.

In the West, the development of democracy came about because of many factors, such as the change of attitudes and values brought about by the Enlightenment, the rise of the middle class, and the availability of popular education. Christianity played a certain role because of its emphasis on the sinfulness of human nature. Such an understanding contributed to the development of checks and balances in democratic structures and values. Reinhold Niebuhr's realist assessment of sinful human nature led him to write, "Man's capacity for justice makes democracy possible; but man's inclination to injustice makes democracy necessary."[18]

On China's long road to democracy, scholars have debated whether or not Confucian tradition's optimism around human nature and its belief in moral education have hindered democratic development.[19] Instead of developing democratic checks and balances, this hope has been placed on "enlightened emperors," government officials, and on a hoped-for moral persuasion of ruling elites, specifically, in the event they should fail to take people's welfare to heart. But others have pointed to Confucian ideas, such as the emphases on people as the foundation of society and on human relationality, as building blocks of democratic thought. Sungmoon Kim has argued that Confucian tradition is not incompatible with democracy and that one should not assume Western models of democracy as normative. There are different models of democracy, he says, and a particular mode of Confucian democracy based on Confucian values and mores has developed in East Asia, as seen in South Korea and Taiwan.[20] Amid debates over democracy in non-Western societies, Hong Kong presents a special case to discuss the role of religion in the democratic struggle of a global city within an authoritarian state.

As a small city, Hong Kong is sandwiched between powerful nations and empires and occupies the "in-between" space that postcolonial theorists often discuss. The "in-between" space has been described as fluid, creative, and full of potentialities, yet it is also full of ambiguities and is difficult to navigate politically. Archie C. C. Lee observes, "Postcoloniality in the context of Hong Kong is then to be understood in terms of the conscious effort to combat marginalisation and to reaffirm the 'denied or allocated subjectivity' of Hong Kong against British colonisers before and the Chinese sovereign power at present."[21] As such, the construction of postcolonial identity in Hong Kong has been shaped by contesting narratives imposed by different colonizers, as well as by local narratives created by Hongkongers. The "in-between" status of Hong Kong is contingent upon changing geopolitics and uneven economic development between China and Western countries.[22] During the Cold War era, both China and Britain depended on Hong Kong to act as an intermediary. Hong Kong has served as a hub for China's import and export trade, and the bulk of foreign direct investment in China flows through Hong Kong. However, with China's phenomenal economic rise and keen competition from cities such as Shenzhen, often dubbed

China's Silicon Valley, Hong Kong's position as China's gateway to the world is no longer as important as before.[23] There is less incentive for China to maintain the in-betweenness of Hong Kong, and the Chinese government grips Hong Kong ever tighter.

This "in-between" status in Hong Kong challenges any easy and straightforward demarcation of "colonial" and "postcolonial" in political theology. Postcolonial subjectivity cannot be easily developed under the "one country, two systems" policy, though the policy is at stake due to increased Chinese control. Hong Kong's political structures, as well as its local culture, have been influenced by the colonial legacy with its values, institutions, and way of life. Hongkongers want to protect and maintain this way of life. Tensions between the local, the national, and the global in constructing political identity complicate the struggle for democracy. Hong Kong's local culture is defined as contrasting that of the mainland, and a populist-localist discourse has emerged amid growing conflicts with China. Yet most Hongkongers are Chinese, and speak Cantonese, and Chinese culture forms an important part of the city's culture. Many of the older generation of pro-democracy leaders and activists harbor a strong nationalist sentiment, regarding the struggle for democracy in Hong Kong as conducive to democracy in China. They have organized annual candlelight vigils for more than three decades to commemorate the bloody crackdown by Chinese troops at Tiananmen Square on June 4, 1989. But younger activists, who grew up after 1997, have experienced China's over-bearing postures and harbor no illusions about the "motherland." They want to fight for freedom and assert greater autonomy against Chinese rule. Both the Chinese and Hong Kong governments tout that Hong Kong is a global city—an international metropolis in a national sense within the Asian region. Sociologist Agnes Shuk-mei Ku has noted the colonial has been transfigured into the global, because colonial cities can be seen as forerunners of what capitalist world cities will eventually become. Globalization is built on the legacy of capitalist expansion because of colonialism and neocolonialism.[24] China wants to keep Hong Kong a vibrant and cosmopolitan city in service of China's capitalist development and economic growth. However, young protesters want to connect the local with the global to fight against nationalistic overtures. They argue that Hong Kong shares the universal values of democracy and human rights, in contrast to China's authoritarianism and suppression. Joshua Wong writes, "A new cold war is brewing between China and the rest of the democratic world, and Hong Kong is holding the line in one of its first battles."[25] He continues, "China's tightening grip on Hong Kong is part of a much broader threat to global democracy."[26] In this David-versus-Goliath struggle, protesters galvanized international support by running advertisements about the Hong Kong situation in major international newspapers and by sending representatives to lobby the United Nations, the U.S., Europe, and other countries.[27] They appealed to President Donald Trump and the U.S. government to take a hard stance against China. Dissidents from Hong Kong who have immigrated or sought asylum in other countries continue to galvanize overseas support on the international front. Ku summarizes the contentious relations between the local, the national, and the global succinctly: "the increased tensions between Chinese nationalism and global universalism, and between Chinese nationalisation and local autonomy, continue to underscore Hong Kong's uneasy relationship with the mainland."[28]

SOCIAL MOVEMENTS AND CIVIL DISOBEDIENCE

During the months that protests persisted in Hong Kong, demonstrations also broke out in Chile, Colombia, Sudan, Algeria, Lebanon, India, France, Spain, and other places.[29] Since the Great Recession, mass demonstrations and assemblies in public spaces have become dominant modes of protest used by grassroots movements to fight for economic justice, political change, racial equality, and queer people's rights. There were transnational elements in the Hong Kong protests, as people made connections between and drew inspiration from other social movements, both past and present. For example, demonstrators formed human chains across the city, an action reminiscent of large-scale anti-Soviet demonstration in the 1989 Baltic Way protest. The Baltic Way was a peaceful demonstration that took place on August 23, 1989, when approximately two million people from the Baltic countries of Estonia, Latvia, and Lithuania joined their hands, forming a 360-mile human chain to demand freedom from the Soviet Union.[30]

Some protesters and commentators in Hong Kong also linked the protests with the struggle for democracy and student uprisings in South Korea in the 1980s. During a protest in June 2019, a group of protesters sang an iconic Korean protest song "March for the Beloved," which was composed to commemorate those who died during the Gwangju Uprising in 1980.[31] Korean feminist scholar Nami Kim has noted the similarities between the pro-democracy demonstrations in Korea and Hong Kong, especially regarding state violence and police brutality. She characterizes the Hong Kong protests as a *minjung* event, because the demonstrations have formed a *minjung* community to stand up against China's imperial expansion. Korean *minjung* theologians have borne witness to *minjung* struggles, and Kim has called upon Hong Kong theologians to keep the counterimperial struggle and memory alive. She also emphasizes the need for transborder solidarity, stating, "Minjung events, as liberative events, are not limited to a few places or historical moments. . . . Witnessing to the ways in which people's struggles converge can help us to see how the *minjung* have risen up against the root causes of suffering that are undeniably interconnected."[32]

Social theorists and philosophers have commented on both mass demonstration and the use of technology and media in the protests. For example, Judith Butler expands her gender performative theory to the assembly of bodies in public protests. She argues that these protests challenge the reigning notion of the political and demand the recognition of the "right to appear" in public. The embodied way of coming together enacts a form of radical solidarity in opposition to political and economic forces that render bodies precarious.[33] Many of these movements were spearheaded by young people, who are adept at using the Internet and social media to organize and connect with one another. Social scientists have discussed the use of social media in protests and grassroots organizing. They have also discussed global networking in the digital age.[34] Through the use of social media and digital platforms, the Hong Kong protests have been made decentralized, fluid, spontaneous, and adaptable to the situation at hand. Political theology from Hong Kong can draw from these ideas of radical solidarity and social connectivity to discuss political subjectivity, community, and praxis.

The protests also present challenges to Christian social ethics, especially regarding the use of violent tactics in social movements. During the Umbrella Movement of 2014, conflicts arose between those who advocated nonviolence and more radical activists, who wanted to use more direct and confrontational protest actions. Benny Y. T. Tai, a Christian and one of the leaders of the movement, cites Martin Luther King Jr.'s "Letter from a Birmingham Jail" to support the principle of civil disobedience. Tai writes, "As King said, the objective of civil disobedience is to raise the concern of other people with the injustice in the existing laws and systems. Winning people's sympathy and support may cause them to join or even initiate subsequent actions to change the unjust laws and systems."[35] Tai favors indirect actions such as symbol wearing, street performance, exhibition, and community organizing. But as the movement failed to bring concrete political changes, some people, especially the youth, began to question the strategies used by the older generation. The protests in 2019 were peaceful in the beginning; but when police used excessive force to quell the protests, some began to throw bricks and Molotov cocktails, vandalize subway stations and pro-Beijing businesses, set fires, and engage in acts of vigilantism. These actions have created controversy within the Christian community and in wider society.

Christians who support nonviolence often cite the teachings and example of Jesus. They point out that Jesus' central message is love and that he taught us to love our enemies and turn the other cheek (Luke 6:27–29). Jesus did not resort to violence to rebel against the Roman Empire, they emphasize, though the Jewish people were under a Roman yoke. He was crucified on the cross, like a lamb led to slaughter, thereby reconciling human beings to God. Martin Luther King Jr., said, "love is creative and redemptive. Love builds up and unites; hate tears down and destroys. The aftermath of the 'fight fire with fire' method . . . is bitterness and chaos, the aftermath of the love method is reconciliation and the creation of the beloved community."[36] King urged seeking justice without violence out of the belief that the ultimate goal is not to defeat one's opponent, but to win the friendship of one's opponent.

During the Hong Kong protests, a majority of protestors, Christian or not, supported a "peaceful, rational, and nonviolent" strategy because they wanted to win popular support. This majority also knew that violent actions would be met with escalating police brutality and that those on the front lines would pay heavily. Furthermore, images of violence would also be used by pro-Beijing media to popularize the view that the protesters were a bunch of rioters, with no regard for law and order. In addition, Erica Chenoweth and Maria J. Stephen have studied violent and nonviolent resistance campaigns for regime change, against occupation, and for secession between 1900 and 2006. In their book *Why Civil Resistance Works: The Strategic Logic of Nonviolent Conflict*, they show that nonviolent resistance was nearly twice as likely to achieve full or partial success than their violent counterparts. They point to the decades-long anti-apartheid campaigns in South Africa and the People Power movement against the Marcos dictatorship in the 1980s as examples. They show that nonviolent campaigns attract more support from the public and more diverse membership.[37]

Those who support civil disobedience and nonviolent action often cite John Rawls' theory developed in his *A Theory of Justice* as reference.[38] For Rawls, civil disobedience is a conscientious, public, and nonviolent breach of law undertaken to persuade the majority to change a law or policy in a nearly just society. The use of nonviolence excludes coercion or activities that will inflict harm. Furthermore, Rawls suggests that agents of civil disobedience should accept or even seek out consequences of their actions to demonstrate their fidelity to the law. This is exactly what Benny Tai and other leaders of the Umbrella Movement did. They turned themselves in for violating Hong Kong laws around unlawful assembly, and some of them served prison terms.

But are there justifications for resistance that are more radical than what Rawls would have allowed? In *A Duty to Resist: When Disobedience Should Be Uncivil*, Candice Delmas points out the limitations of Rawls' theory.[39] First, she notes, the kind of civil disobedience that Rawls describes would work only in a nearly just society, in which people trust the legal system and law enforcement, but would not work under corrupt and/or authoritarian governments. Second, Rawls's theory is largely based on the civil rights movement in the U.S. Delmas argues that many have chosen to sanitize the movement and remember only the nonviolent actions by Martin Luther King Jr. But in fact, the movement was more complex and included the Black Panthers, Black nationalists, the Nation of Islam, and assorted Marxist liberation movements. Adherents of some of these groups resorted to violence to overthrow the racist and imperialist legal system in America.[40] Without these movements as foils, Delmas points out, King's movement would not look so moderate and acceptable to white liberals.

Delmas argues that we not only have the duty to obey the law, but we also have the duty to justice. On her account, the obligation to resist injustice demands principled disobedience, and such disobedience needs not always be civil. She writes, "the duty of justice demands resisting injustice, bettering institutions, and frustrating wrongs, and it supports principled disobedience in the process. Given our less-than-ideal polities, obeying the law is neither the sole, nor necessarily the most important, of our political obligations."[41] The Hong

Kong protests in 2019, she argues, challenge the common assumption that protests should always be civil and nonviolent because many think that "violence and incivility are morally wrong and strategically counterproductive."[42] During the protests, the frontline militants, called the "braves," were tasked with fighting the police to protect crowds of protesters. They erected roadblocks and barricades, threw Molotov cocktails, set up catapults, and slung arrows. Despite the fact that the protests disrupted people's lives and caused inconvenience, many people from all walks of life provided either direct support or indirect assistance to the protesters. According to a survey in December 2019, nearly one-fifth of Hongkongers supported violent action by protesters, including hurling bricks and petrol bombs at police.[43] Tactics such as wearing black clothes and covering their hair and faces with hats, masks, and googles lowered protesters' risk of being identified. Protesters helped each other avoid police brutality and criminal arrest. Delmas contends, "Hongkongers have continued to protest *en masse* not in spite of, but *thanks to* the movement's turn to uncivil disobedience."[44] In the Hong Kong situation, she says, "calling on protesters to remain nonviolent and passively absorb police brutality seems politically and morally obtuse. Perhaps Hongkongers' example will prompt social scientists to study the different effects of uncivil disobedience on mobilization and support"[45]

Whereas the Umbrella Movement was divided over the use of civil and uncivil tactics, Hong Kong protesters in 2019 showed a new respect for the variety of forms of resistance and the degree of risk that different people were willing to take. Popular slogans, such as "No splitting, no severing of ties, and no snitching," and "Peaceful and valiant resistance are inseparable" underscored the need for cooperation and solidarity. Many people, though supportive of nonviolence, were reticent in condemning the "braves." There were three major reasons for this. First, the Hong Kong protests did use nonviolent strategies, including millions taking to the streets and boycotting pro-China businesses. But the government turned a deaf ear to the people's demands and refused to budge. As one protester scrawled across the wall of the Legislative Council, after protesters stormed inside: "It was you who taught me that peaceful marches did not work." Second, many people pointed to institutional violence and disproportionate use of force by police. Third, folks understood that young people had sacrificed themselves for the future of Hong Kong, risking arrest and prison sentences. Among the more than 9,000 people who were arrested, many were young people, some under the age of eighteen. Lai Tsz-him, a doctoral student from Hong Kong studying Christian social ethics, comments, "Hong Kong protesters are similar to other resistance movements, defending their political rights 'by any means necessary.'. . . The coexistence of numerous means of resistance in Hong Kong underscores the limitations of the violent/nonviolent dichotomy, pointing out that achieving social change is not either peaceful or militant but can be both depending on the context."[46]

The above discussion prompts us to look at Jesus's teaching and model of political action from a different perspective. In *The Politics of Jesus*, John Howard

Yoder argues that Christian pacifism is the most faithful approach for the disciple of Christ.[47] Miguel De La Torre notes that Yoder, who was a Mennonite, "may have envisioned a nonviolent white Mennonite" when he wrote his
book.[48] De La Torre cautions, "Even white pacifists, with the best intentions,
remain complicit with oppression."[49] If we look at the Jesus movement through
the lens offered by Delmas, a more complex picture emerges. Jesus' teaching
of the Kingdom of God was subversive because it challenged Roman imperial
authority. He repeatedly denounced the Pharisees and Jewish leaders who acted
as agents of the empire. When the Pharisees accused him of breaking the Sabbath, he retorted, "it is lawful to do good on Sabbath" (Matt. 12:12) and "The
Sabbath was made for humankind, not humankind for the Sabbath" (Mark
2:27). Jesus frequently attracted a crowd around him, which could be considered a political and public assembly. His feeding of the five thousand was a case
of occupying public space to form an alternative community in which the needs
of the masses were taken care of (Matt. 14:13–21). Jesus entered Jerusalem on a
donkey in a procession, which was a public spectacle and performance to counteract military processions, which were used to demonstrate imperial might. His
cleansing of the temple and overturning of the tables (Mark 11:15–19) could be
comparable to guerilla theatre. Scholars have debated whether Jesus was a Zealot
because among his disciples was Simon the Zealot (Matt. 10:4; Mark 3:18; Luke
6:15). When Jesus sent his disciples out, he told them "the one who has no
sword must sell his cloak and buy one" (Luke 22:36). When Jesus was arrested
at the Garden of Gethsemane, Simon Peter carried a sword and used it to cut
the ear of the high priest's servant, and Jesus admonished him (John 18:10).[50]
Jesus incited crowds, subverted authority, and created trouble for religious and
political leaders. He was crucified as a political prisoner and made into a public
spectacle to deter others. Seen from this perspective, a middle-class way of looking at Jesus' movement is flattened and sanitized to such an extent that it fails
to present the complexity of a movement with many actors and diverse motives.
In the real world, in which multidimensional struggles necessitate multifaceted
political action to resist injustice, it is important for political theologians to
develop ethical guidelines for principled disobedience.

On the one-year anniversary of the protests on June 9, 2020, thousands of
Hongkongers responded to an online call to gather in local malls and neigh-
borhoods to chant pro-democracy slogans and sing "Glory to Hong Kong,"
a protest anthem that has become very popular. They continued to push for
democracy, an investigation into police brutality, and amnesty for the people
arrested.[51] But the COVID-19 pandemic made public assembly difficult, and
a draconian national security law went into effect on July 1, 2020. The law
criminalizes secession, subversion, terrorism, and collusion with foreign powers. People who are convicted of such crimes can face sentences of up to life
in prison. In early 2021, the government detained 47 pro-democracy activists
and charged them under the national security law with "conspiracy to commit
subversion," according to police.[52] With many leaders either arrested or in exile,

the protests entered a very difficult and challenging phase. Yet the protests of 2019 have written a new chapter in Hong Kong's history because a new political community has been forged. Hong Kong Christian social ethicist Kung Lap-yan writes, "Through participating in the demonstrations, protesters have established a sense of solidarity and a political subjectivity that binds them together in what has been called 'a community of common destiny.'"[53] Like suffering people throughout the world, he says, the crucified people in Hong Kong bear witness to sin in the world that tramples on human dignity and freedom. "Theologically, the crucified people are the actualization of the crucified Jesus because Jesus is there wherever suffering people are to be found (Matt. 25:31–46)."[54] He believes a new dawn will come because Jesus overcomes death, and his resurrection means justice prevails.

PART THREE
PRACTICES

Chapter 8

Teaching Theology from
a Global Perspective

As a classroom community, our capacity to generate excitement is deeply affected by our interest in one another, in hearing one another's voices, in recognizing one another's presence.

bell hooks[1]

I have routinely taught courses on theology that include perspectives from the Global South. The students were from theological schools in Boston and Atlanta, and they came from different parts of the world and from various social locations. Because of the subject matter, these classes drew students from diverse racial and ethnic backgrounds in the U.S., along with international students, especially from Asia and Africa. The dissimilar backgrounds of the students heightened our awareness of the different ways of learning and the unacknowledged assumptions we brought to the interpretation of theology.

Teaching these courses raised several pedagogical questions for me: What does it mean to teach theology from a global perspective? How should one organize the course materials—geographically according to different parts of the world, doctrinally according to theological themes, or socially according to issues pertaining to class, race, gender, sexuality, colonialism, and so forth? How does the teacher help students who have relatively little knowledge of the Global South to understand theology arising from these contexts? Would racial and ethnic minority students and international students have privileged knowledge in the subject matter because of their marginalization in society? How can we avoid treating students from marginalized communities as if they are "native informants," especially when there are only a few of them in the classroom? How can we help Euro-American students feel that they have something meaningful to share and not feel isolated or silenced?

As someone interested in postcolonial theory and theology, I am concerned not only with Eurocentrism in the production of knowledge, but also with our hidden teaching assumptions and choice of pedagogies. Among the scholars who have contributed to postcolonial theory, Gayatri Chakravorty Spivak stands out in paying much attention to the politics of teaching. She has criticized what she calls "sanctioned ignorance" in the U.S. educational system. In her essay, "How to Read a 'Culturally Different' Book," she argues that it is important for professors in the West to teach across gender, ethnic, and class divisions.[2] Her insight is highly relevant for theological educators because approximately 40 percent of students in member schools of The Association of Theological Schools in the United States and Canada belong to racial and ethnic minority communities. But theological schools have been slow to adapt to their changing demographics, as evidenced by their continued use of a predominantly Eurocentric curriculum. In *After Whiteness*, Willie James Jennings argues, "Theological education in the West was born in white hegemony and homogeneity, and it continues to baptize homogeneity, making it holy and right and efficient—when it is none of these things."[3] For too long, theology has been a highly specialized discipline drawn predominantly from the experiences of white churches and communities. Today, theology must be done more intentionally in the public square, to promote dialogue for the common good and to educate global citizens. Theology must address social and political issues that concern the public, engage critical thinkers of our time, and articulate the public relevance of religious faiths and beliefs.[4] In this chapter, I discuss the context of the globalization of theology, different approaches to conceptualizing global theology, and the challenges of teaching theology in a global world.

THE CONTEXT OF GLOBALIZATION OF THEOLOGY

Globalization is often used to describe the interconnections of our world based on the neoliberal economy, the Internet and social media, mass and consumerist culture, and "complex connectivity" as a result of rapidly developing networks.[5] In a so-called global village, what happens locally is affected by events occurring far away and vice versa because of the intensification of global social relations.[6] In fact, sociologist Roland Robertson has suggested replacing the term "globalization" with "glocalization," arguing that globalization is in actuality a local process and that the worldwide exchange or fusion of culture is done in local terms. For Robertson, the global and the local are not opposing, but rather interdependent, forces that mutually influence each other.[7]

But globalization is not a new phenomenon; its roots can be traced back several centuries. It began with the so-called "discovery" of the New World when trade routes between the Old World and the New World were connected and people from different parts of the world were forcibly brought into an orbit with Europe as the center. Developments in industrialization, transportation and telecommunication, and large multinational corporations each facilitated capitalist growth and the integration of the market. Today, the Internet and social media allow real-time interconnection and affordable, fast communication across the globe. Because of this, globalization has broken down national and territorial boundaries while also compressing time and space. It has brought convenience to social life and connection among peoples, but it has also made possible the creation of a transnational capitalist class that is able to amass and control great wealth. Economic disparities between rich and poor have widened, causing social unrest, large-scale migration, and even war and violence in some places. The protests across North Africa, the Middle East, Europe, and the U.S. in 2011 and the Occupy movement around the world all pointed to the unsustainability of the world's economic system.

This growing awareness of doing theology from a global perspective must be viewed against the backdrop of rapid social, economic, and political changes since the latter part of the twentieth century. In the Catholic Church, the Second Vatican Council (1962–65) was a watershed event, for it opened the church to the modern world and encouraged the use of local languages and expressions of faith. In evangelical circles, the 1974 International Congress on World Evangelization in Lausanne, Switzerland, and the resulting Lausanne movement, heightened awareness of both the global connection of Christians as well as local diversity. Some scholars have urged evangelical Christians to move beyond Western theology to rethink theology in light of global realities.[8] At the same time, the World Council of Churches, the Ecumenical Association of Third World Theologians, and other ecumenical networks have provided forums for theologians from different parts of the world to dialogue with one another.

Contextual theologies began to develop in the 1960s and 1970s in Latin America, Asia, and Africa, challenging the colonial paradigms and Eurocentric domination in theology. Latin American liberation theology attracted worldwide attention with its emphases on theology as a reflection of social praxis, the preferential option for the poor, and the new understanding of people as subjects of their own history.[9] Latin American and North American theologians gathered to discuss the implications of liberation theology at the Theology in the Americas Conference in Detroit in 1975.[10] In Asia and Africa, some theologians emphasized sociopolitical liberation and shared similar concerns with Latin American liberation theology, while others focused on religio-cultural aspects, striving for inculturation or indigenization of the gospel in their own soil. Robert J. Schreiter argues that the emergence of local theologies and an increasing sensitivity to history and culture created "an important shift in perspective of Christian self-awareness and theology, both among the churches in the southern hemisphere, and among churches of the North Atlantic communities."[11]

The proliferation of local theologies raises the question of the relationship between the universal and the particular. In the past, Western theology has been taken as the norm and the "universal," while all other theologies are relegated as "particular" or derivative. Today, we have become aware that *all* theologies are contextual because each arises from a particular worldview and addresses particular social and cultural situations. Yet, while theology is contextual, our contexts are increasingly interconnected so we cannot do theology limited to our local context. Stephen B. Bevans reminds us, "Theology today needs to be done in a dialogue with one's own contextual perspective and the broad and deep tradition of the Christian church, and in a dialogue as well with the results of this interaction and the perspectives of Christians from every part of our world."[12]

The shift of Christian demographics to the Global South prompted Christians to think of doing theology in a global way. Whereas in 1900, 83 percent of the world's Christians lived in Europe and North America,[13] today the majority of Christians live in the Global South. In 1900 Africa had only 10 million Christians, about 9 percent of the population. The number had increased to 360 million, roughly 46 percent of the population, by around 2000. By 2025, about one-half of the Christian population will live in Latin America and Africa, and another 17 percent in Asia.[14] At this rate, only one out of five of the world's Christians will be non-Hispanic whites by 2050. The phenomenal growth of the church in the Global South and the demographic shift has caused some scholars to argue that Christianity is becoming a non-Western religion. Lamin Sanneh, for example, has written, "Christianity as a truly world religion [is] increasingly defined by values and idioms of non-Western cultures and languages."[15] Sanneh, Kwame Bediako, Andrew Walls, Dana Robert, and others have urged scholars to pay attention to how Christianity in the Global South is reshaping the beliefs and practices of the Christian church. Sanneh's work, in particular, has focused on the vitality and agency of men and women on the ground, new ecclesial forms and practices, interactions between Christianity and Islam, and the reconception of an African Christianity free from European and imperial interests.

The study of world Christianity has made us more keenly aware of the plurality and diversity of the Christian tradition, both in the past and in the present. Instead of focusing on the history of European Christianity, scholars have shown the ways Asians, Africans, and people in what is called the Middle East today have contributed to the development of the Christian tradition. Sanneh differentiates between a "world Christianity," with its emphasis on the use of local idioms and indigenous responses and adaptations, and "global Christianity," which still places the center of gravity in Europe, as if the global church were built on replication of forms and patterns developed in Europe.[16] Although not everyone agrees with Sanneh, many have become more conscious of the shift of the center of gravity of Christianity, the interaction of global and local, and the need to go beyond European and North American frameworks in the study of Christianity.

As Christian demographics shift to the Global South, the religious landscape of Europe and North America is simultaneously becoming more and more religiously pluralistic because of immigration. New immigrants have brought religious traditions from their homelands, such as Islam, Buddhism, Hinduism,

Confucianism, and so forth. They have also made Christian communities more diverse in terms of race, ethnicity, and culture. In Europe, while church membership and attendance have been in steady decline, the face of the church has changed. Walter Hollenweger notes, "in many European cities there are more black, yellow and brown Christians coming together on a Sunday morning than white Christians."[17] In the U.S., Soong-Chan Rah argues that it is the immigrant, ethnic, and multiethnic churches that are flourishing, even while the white mainline churches are declining in membership. He laments, however, that American Christianity is still caught in Western cultural captivity and shows how individualism and materialism have influenced the megachurches and emergent churches.[18] Since there will not be a majority race in the U.S. by 2040, churches that fail to adapt will be ill-equipped to face the diverse population and the new racial and cultural reality.

Even though the religious landscape of Christianity has changed so much in the past decades, the teaching of theology in general has remained quite traditional. A review of some of the syllabi of courses in theology or systematic theology posted on the Wabash Center website shows that (1) there is little emphasis on the global nature of theology and the growing body of literature on the subject; (2) the majority of required texts are written by European and Euro-American male theologians; (3) only one required text, and often none, is by a theologian outside North America, usually from Latin America, such as Gustavo Gutiérrez; and (4) there is not enough acknowledgment of the contribution of the work of racial and ethnic minority scholars in the U.S.[19] The teaching of the theological discipline remains Eurocentric and, in terms of global sensitivity, lags behind the teaching of other fields, such as church history, world Christianity, missiology, and even biblical studies. The book *Teaching Global Theologies: Power and Praxis* offers important resources to remedy this and to reorient the teaching of the theological field.[20]

CONCEPTUALIZING GLOBAL THEOLOGY

Although we have a growing body of literature on "global theology," "theology in global dialogue," or "theology in a global context," there is no consensus on the scope of the subject matter, methodology, and evaluative criteria. I would like to discuss four approaches that have been used to conceptualize "global theology" in order to push the conversation further. These four approaches are selected to illustrate the diversity of opinion; they are not exhaustive. The first approach conceives of the "globe" primarily in a geographical or territorial sense. William A. Dyrness's edited volume *Emerging Voices in Global Theology*, published in 1994, includes contributions from Eastern Europe, Africa, Asia, and Latin America. Addressing a primarily evangelical readership, he stresses that theologies from non-Western settings have a lot to teach Western Christians and further argues, "any renewal that will come to western theology will come by interacting with voices from alternative traditions."[21] Dyrness notes that there is a great deal of diversity in terms of theological agendas in the non-Western contexts, and he takes care not to collapse the differences. The text serves the purpose of introducing readers to these newer and unfamiliar resources, but readers would need help to situate these emerging voices in the larger theological field. The separation of these voices from dominant theological discourses may also inadvertently marginalize these voices because only those who are already interested in theologies of the Global South may pick up a book like this.

Veli-Matti Kärkkäinen's several volumes on global discussions on the doctrines of Ecclesiology, Christology, God, and Trinity attempt to bridge the gap between the dominant and emerging voices.[22] These books are also organized according to a primarily geographical grid. Each volume begins with the classical traditions and historical development of the doctrine. The volumes on Ecclesiology and Christology move on to present contemporary formulations (mostly by Western European males), followed by contextual constructions (feminist, African, Asian, Latin American, and so forth). The volumes on the doctrine of God and Trinity are more explicit in their geographical framework, with sections divided into European, North American, and non-Western perspectives. The advantage of structuring the volumes in such a way is that both Western and non-Western authors are discussed in the same volume and readers can gain a comprehensive picture of the historical, ecumenical, and contextual approaches. The disadvantage is that a temporal order is imposed onto the geographical mapping, with the non-Western section consisting of newer, emergent voices placed at the end of the book. This section is usually the shortest, as if these voices are less important.

Hans Schwarz's *Theology in a Global Context: The Last Two Hundred Years* is an ambitious project. He presents a careful analysis of the development of modern European theology in its cultural, religious, and social contexts.[23] He then elucidates North American theology and Orthodox theology in different parts of the world before turning to the "emergence of new voices" from the Global South. The Eurocentric bias of the book is evident because the section on the "new voices" consists of only 78 pages out of a volume of 600 pages. The author assumes that his readers need to know European theology and its contexts in minute detail while the new voices receive a passing gloss.

Namsoon Kang articulates the danger of conceptualizing theology according to continents, as each of these scholars does, when she speaks about the Asian context. She warns against the tendency to construct theology of a particular continent in a geographically deterministic and culturally essentialist way without attending to the very broad range of experiences of Asian people.[24] In surveys of global theology, when only a small number of theological voices from Africa, Asia, or Latin America are singled out to be discussed, it is difficult to avoid over-generalization and simplification.

The second approach to global theology does not treat non-Western sources as "emergent" or "new" voices (with Europe as the norm),[25] since Christian theology has a long history of development outside the orbit of the Western world. This approach seeks to recover the multicultural and polycentric nature of the Christian tradition. The organizing principle is not "the West and the Rest," or center and margin, because there are multiple centers. As Tite Tiénou explains: "Polycentric Christianity is Christian faith with many cultural homes. The fact that Christianity is at home in a multiplicity of cultures, without being permanently wedded to any one of them, presents for Christians everywhere a unique opportunity for examining Christian identity and Christian theology."[26]

Just as scholars of world Christianity have emphasized that Christianity has been shaped by different cultures and histories from the beginning, theologians need to develop cross-cultural competency in the study of Christian doctrines. Andrew Walls notes, "A culture-sensitive reading of the history of Christian doctrine might reveal how the crossing of cultural frontiers develops and enlarges theology. This happens because entry into a new culture at any depth may both pose questions previously unconsidered and provide intellectual materials for pursuing those questions."[27] Walls argues that when the early church entered the Greek world, it began a long and arduous process of attempting to think in Greek in a Christian way by asking Greek questions and using indigenous categories and conventions. The words from the Nicene Creed—"God from God, Light from Light, Very God from Very God, begotten, not made, being of one substance with the Father"—came from interactions with the Greek world of thought and questions posed by it. Similarly, when Christianity came into contact with other cultural settings, the processes of translation and transposition also brought forth new questions and dimensions of Christian thought.

Let us look at Christianity in China as an example. Christianity arrived in China in the seventh century through the activities of Syrian missionaries from what was known as the Church of the East. These missionaries had to borrow Chinese expressions from Buddhism and Daoism to translate Christian ideas. In addition, they used the Buddhist symbol of the lotus to express this new faith to the Chinese audience. As the Christian tradition came into contact with the Chinese multireligious worldview and symbolic systems, new questions were raised by the Chinese cultural context. For example, the text on the stele erected by missionaries in Xian in 681 C.E. recounted the essentials of the Christian message, covering the Creation, the Trinity, the Incarnation, and baptism. But there was no mention of Christ's bloody sacrifice on the cross, probably because blood sacrifice as an act of redemption was difficult for the Chinese to understand.[28]

Contacts with Western Christianity began in the thirteenth century under the Mongol rulers, but these early efforts by Catholic missionaries did not take root. When Matteo Ricci (1552–1610) and other Jesuits arrived in the sixteenth century, they wanted to appeal to the Chinese literati by dressing in the attire of the scholarly class. Ricci studied the Chinese classics and found the ideas of *tian* (Heaven) and *zhu* (Lord) in the Chinese classics and combined them to translate the Christian term "God" as *Tianzhu* (Lord of Heaven). He saw no problem presenting Christianity in Chinese garb. Ricci also supported the Chinese practice of veneration of ancestors, which the Franciscans and Dominicans condemned as idolatry. The Rites Controversy, as the debate was called, led European intellectuals and theologians to learn about Confucian and other Chinese rituals. Chinese scholars also learned something about Christianity in order to defend their tradition. The Controversy thus led to the comparative study of Christianity and the Confucian tradition in both China and Europe.[29]

In the early nineteenth century, when Protestant missionaries arrived from England and the U.S., they worked among the lower classes and had to adapt to popular religious practices. They did not think the translation of the term "God" as *Tianzhu* appropriate and debated about the best Chinese translation. The British missionaries opted to use *shangdi* (the monarch above), while the Americans chose *shen* (spirit). Even today, there is no common consensus on how to translate the term "God" in the Chinese Christian community. Christian missionaries were allowed to preach in China because of the unequal treaties China was forced to sign with European countries with superior military power. As a result, many Chinese regarded Christianity as a foreign religion and associated it with imperialism. In response, Chinese theologians such as Wu Yaozong, Wu Leichuen, and Zhao Zichen had to reconstruct Christian theology in order to show that Christianity could contribute to resisting foreign aggression.[30]

The example of China shows that when Christianity crossed new cultural frontiers, questions such as the translation of Christian terms, the interpretation of Christ's sacrifice and redemption, the use of indigenous symbols, the role of Chinese rituals and practices, and the relation between religion and politics were raised. These issues were unavoidable when Christianity encountered a multireligious context in a colonial or semicolonial setting. Doing global theology from a Chinese perspective will be very different from that in the Western perspective.[31] Becoming aware of this difference expands our horizon and enables us to see the Christian theological tradition in a polycentric and multilayered way.

The third approach also recognizes the multiple cultural homes of Christianity and seeks to understand the relationship between the global and the local when there is a central teaching office, as in the Roman Catholic tradition. In *The New Catholicity: Theology between the Global and the Local*, Robert J. Schreiter addresses the changing contexts of the Roman Catholic Church.[32] He says globalization has made global capitalism a new reality, and the global hyperculture has created homogeneity on the one hand and provoked intensifications of the local on the other. In the face of this new reality, the church needs to develop a new catholicity, which he says,

> is marked by a wholeness of inclusion and fullness of faith in a pattern of intercultural exchange and communication. To the extent that this catholicity can be realized, it may provide a paradigm for what a universal theology may look like today, able to encompass both sameness and difference, rooted in an orthopraxis, providing *teloi* for a globalized society.[33]

This "universal" theology is not prescribed by the Vatican but rather shaped by dialogue and mutual understanding through intercultural hermeneutics.

Even though "local" or "contextual" theology might have emerged from a particular context, its implications and significance often far exceed its immediate context. Latin American liberation theology is an obvious example. Schreiter says that the global theological flows have been much shaped by the discourses of liberation, feminism, ecology, and human rights since the second half of the twentieth century. These theological discourses address the crises and contradictions of the global systems and can lay claim to the new universal theologies because they are ubiquitous and are highly influential in shaping contemporary theological consciousness.[34]

Schreiter's view is grounded in the classic doctrine of the church: one, holy, catholic, and apostolic. While some scholars in the postmodern and postcolonial era might shy away from using the term "universal," Schreiter does not avoid it. But unlike in the colonial era, when dominant Western culture was "universalized" to then be superimposed on other cultures, Schreiter's idea of global theological flows is grounded in a global consciousness that recognizes the flows of capital, resources, labor, and ideas in our interconnected world. Theological movements and currents do not flow only from the center out to the margin but can also travel in multiple directions across geographical and cultural boundaries. Published in 1997, Schrieter's book is inclusive and forward-looking, though the Vatican under Pope Benedict often harkened back to the old idea of catholicity and failed to acknowledge women's rights; the rights of lesbian, gay, bisexual, and transgender people; and the challenges of religious pluralism. Pope Francis has brought new hope and optimism to the Catholic Church, as he has addressed economic justice, ecological crisis, and war and violence, yet he remains adamant against women's ordination and does not support the blessing of same-sex unions.

Many Catholic scholars have urged the Catholic Church to address the Christian demographic shift since most of today's Catholics live either in the Global South or as members of racial and ethnic minority communities in the Global North. In *Idol and Grace: On Traditioning and Subversive Hope,* Orlando O. Espín argues against a Eurocentric Catholicism. He stresses that Western cultural tradition, as well as the Catholicism within it, is not monolithic but "the ambivalent mixture of the dominant and dominated, and neither side can claim to be the sole representative of this tradition."[35] In postcolonial parlance, colonized cultures have already been inscribed within the colonizers' cultures. In discussing the tradition of the church, he says, it is not sufficient to focus on the contents of tradition, authority, and related topics, without paying attention to the process of reception. The contents of tradition have often been taken as propositional doctrines, whose truth and authority are guaranteed by the popes and the bishops. But, in fact, the contents of tradition must be interpreted and received within particular contexts for them to be passed on from generation to generation. He proposes the term "traditioning" to shift the focus to the process and context. Traditioning, as a dynamic process, would counteract the idolatrizing tendencies that take some de-contextualized doctrinal propositions as a *depositum fidei.*[36]

The fourth approach offers transnational feminist perspectives to look at glo-balization and theology. Although the book *The Oxford Handbook of Feminist Theology* does not have the term "global" in its title, it is based on a gathering of feminist theologians from around the globe and its central theme is globaliza-tion. The editors of the volume, Mary McClintock Fulkerson and Sheila Briggs, explain that in addition to gender, race, ethnicity, class, and sexual orientation, which continue to be important in defining the contexts of feminism, globaliza-tion brings three more factors: deterritorialization, hyperdifferentiation (in that people have multiple identities and live in multiple realities), and hybridity of cultures.[37] The book opens with Serene Jones's discussion of global imagination and encourages the readers to move beyond a narrowly defined and essentialized identity politics to enter into a global conversation.

Even though deterritorialization is a defining character of globalization, the editors recognize that territorial geography still exists and devote almost half of the book to feminist theological issues by geographical regions. One of the reasons for doing so is to honor the diversity of women's experiences and their regional differences. The organization is different from that in the books I have discussed in the first approach above, in which the Global South is separated from the Global North or presented at the tail end. Here, Europe or North America are treated as one region among many and are not given any special status. In fact, priorities are given to the voices of women from the Global South and to racial and ethnic minority women (for example, there are three chapters on African women, two chapters on Native American and indigenous women, but only one chapter on European women). Although many of the contributors are North Americans or international scholars currently teaching in the U.S., the book has a wide range of voices and seeks to present an inclusive account of feminist theologies in the early twenty-first century.

Many contributors, both from former colonizing and colonized countries, are cognizant of the colonial legacy that is shaping the world and use postcolo-nial insights in their work. They articulate in various ways the negative impact of globalization on women in the world and the power imbalance between the Global North and Global South. For instance, postcolonial biblical critic Musa W. Dube from Botswana asks this critical question: In what ways does feminist theological discourse "reproduce and maintain the globalization power relations?"[38] She challenges that feminist theology cannot be a "one-way traffic" from the West with responses or counternarratives from the Global South. In other examples, Ellen T. Armour and Sharon Welch from the U.S. urge read-ers to eradicate colonial ideologies in feminist presuppositions and misconcep-tions about colonized and postcolonized others.[39] Welch especially draws from postcolonial theories to interrogate the construction of "religion" and religious difference and offers helpful alternative forms of interreligious engagement.

A distinctive feature of this volume is that people from non-Christian tradi-tions are not just talked about, as in many volumes on theology of religions and comparative theology, but are invited to join the global conversation. Feminist scholars from Jewish, Hindu, Native, and Muslim traditions, as well as scholars who are knowledgeable about African indigenous religions, are all part of the dialogue. They provide critical insights into how globalization has reshaped women's religious lives, especially with regard to the rise of fundamentalisms and gender violence, and how women's groups have critiqued capitalism and brought forth changes. Throughout the book, there is an urgent call to combine feminist scholarship with activism, to go beyond the 1990's preoccupation with "difference" to connect and engage, and to find new visions and imaginations to address the challenges of the globalized world.

These four different approaches show that there are both advantages and disadvantages in conceptualizing global theology in geographical and territorial terms. Even as globalization has heightened our sense of a deterritorialized world, the old cartography of the world in terms of continents and geographical regions remains strong in theological discourse. Gayatri Chakravorty Spivak's notion of a "critical regionalism," which attends to the plurality and diversity of any given region, might be a helpful reminder if we continue to use continental labels.[40] What is seen as global theology is contingent upon one's social location, history, and background. The discourse on global theology in China will be quite different from that in the U.S. The relation between global and contextual theologies is shaped by denominational histories, theological traditions, and institutional structures. Global theological flows are increasingly not a one-way traffic, since theology developed in one part of the world has implications for other parts. Furthermore, globalization has impacts on the configuration of gender, race, class, sexual orientation, religion, and so forth. Transnational feminist theology, transnational queer theology, and renewed theological engagements with race and class that address the global situation have much to contribute to global theology.

CHALLENGES OF TEACHING THEOLOGY IN A GLOBAL WORLD

Although the Association of Theological Schools in the United States and Canada has discussed globalization and theological education since the mid-1980s[41] and a growing body of literature on global theology is available, the theological curriculum in many schools is still very Eurocentric and Euro-American. There is a time lag between the field of theology and what is happening in other fields in the humanities and social sciences. For example, postcolonial theory was not introduced to the field of theology until almost twenty-five years after Edward Said published the foundational text *Orientalism*.[42] To many people, theology is a parochial discourse addressing only people in the church, with no significant import for the larger issues facing humanity and the planet. Even for those who are interested in theological questions, the field of theology seems quaint and outdated.

For theology to speak to our contemporary world, we must emphasize the public nature of doing theology and reimagine the scope, contents, and pedagogy of the field. We have to engage the church, academia, and the wider public to discuss what theological literacy and competence is in the twenty-first century. We need to interrogate the curriculum, contents, courses, paradigms, staff, and pedagogies of theological departments, seminaries, and divinity schools. Musa W. Dube warns against the danger of tokenism and paying only lip service to diversity. She says we should seek to

> establish whether the contents and structures of theological programs reproduce and maintain the globalization practices of one-way traffic and tokenist paradigms that maintain Eurocentrism. In the latter paradigm, theological programs admit Two-Thirds World staff, theological perspectives, theories, and methods in the non-threatening margins and ignore the ever-changing faces, accents, and foods of its neighborhood.[43]

Dube's comments point to three significant problems in theological programs that we would do well to avoid: (1) add a few courses on theologies from the Global South, usually as elective courses, while the core courses and the general ethos of the program remain largely Eurocentric; (2) include only perspectives and theologies from the Global South that do not present radical challenges and can be domesticated or appropriated; and (3) separate theological concerns from the Global South from those raised by racial and ethnic minority scholars closer to home, because it might be easier to discuss oppression in faraway places than in our own neighborhood.

Even if a teacher wishes to include theological sources from the Global South, it is not easy to find and have access to those materials. The number of titles on theologies from the Global South published in the U.S. and Europe has been in decline, with some of these books easily going out of print. Only a small number of theologians from the Global South have been included in the theological curriculum. This does not do justice to the plurality of voices. Those who do not write in one of the major colonial languages will remain obscure even if they have something important to say. To add to the complexity, most of the books on "global theology" or "theology in a global context," are written or edited by European and Euro-American scholars and filtered through their theological assumptions and epistemological frameworks. In order to overcome these challenges, the teacher and the school's librarian must be familiar with local and regional publishing programs and establish relationships with different theological networks.

The teaching of theologies from a global perspective is challenging in the U.S. because transnational literacy[44] is low and many students do not possess adequate knowledge of other parts of the world. For example, students may not know the history of Peru, the influences of Marxism among intellectuals in Latin America, or the culture of Latin American churches when they read Gustavo Gutiérrez's *A Theology of Liberation*.[45] If theology grows out from lived experience and a particular context, students have a lot of catching up to do in order to know the context before they can engage the theological material. Furthermore, students need to be aware of their own biases and presuppositions before they can enter the worldview of theologians speaking from a very different context. Rauna Kuokkanen notes that the epistemological foundations and practices of the academy are selective and exclusionary, influenced as they are by the Enlightenment, colonialism, modernity, and in particular, liberalism. She continues, "These traditions, discourses, and practices have very little awareness of other epistemologies and ontologies, and offer them heavily restricted space at best. Even in the academic spaces that consider themselves most open to 'changing the paradigm,' individuals are often unwilling to examine their own blind spots"[46]

William A. Dyrness gives an example of how this relates to the teaching and learning of theology. He says that much of Western Christianity is indelibly shaped by the "liberal self," which gives priority to the individual and separates him or her from society. But for most people outside the West, community and relationships are seen as primary, and actual relationships take precedence over dogmatic abstractions, whether these involve the veneration of the Virgin of Guadalupe in Mexico or the presence of spirits in Africa. While the Enlightenment has determined Western people's attitude toward truth or knowledge, this does not affect many other people.[47] It is challenging, therefore, for students in the U.S. to understand or engage in dialogue with African notions of gods and spirits.

In a traditional and Eurocentric theology class, the experiences of international students or racial and ethnic minorities do not count for much and they are not seen as capable of producing knowledge. But in a course on theology from a global perspective, these students are often put on the spot as "authentic" representatives or spokespersons of their cultures. As "native informants," their assigned role is to educate Euro-American students about their ignorance, an ignorance sanctioned by the larger society. In other classes, the accent or lack of linguistic skills of some of these students may be seen as a liability, but in a class on global perspective, their accent may suddenly become an asset as one of the marks of their "authenticity." The teacher should recognize there is an imbalance of knowledge among the students: international students and racial and ethnic minority students have to know the West because of Western hegemony, but the Euro-American students are not required to know about the rest of the world. It is the Euro-American students' responsibility to educate themselves and not rely on their darker-skinned classmates to educate them. In such cases it would be helpful for the teacher to discuss some of the power dynamics shaping the classroom and offer guidelines to deal with difference at the beginning of the class.

It is also important for the teacher to be aware of the range of emotions that the class may elicit, which contributes to diverse responses. I have had Euro-American female students crying in class because they felt that they were complicit in the oppression of women in the Global South. I have also had Korean students in their twenties who found Korean *minjung* theology perplexing, because they could not relate to a time when Korea was poor and under a dictatorship. Althea Spencer Miller notes that feminist and multicultural educators have categorized responses in the classroom as "resistance," "non-engagement," and "engagement."[48] Resistance is negative engagement that dissents against the liberatory impulse and philosophy. A student becomes non-engaged because the process is perceived as boring or irrelevant, or it is too alien to the student's more comfortable learning style. The student may also feel there is a lack of safe space. The desired response is engagement wherein the student actively participates in the classroom and takes responsibility for his or her own learning. Such engagement, Spencer Miller notes, may be marked "at a deeper level by self-assessing reflexivity, recognitions of connectedness, and the movement from personal experience to theorizing, a form of praxis."[49]

Although the challenges of teaching theology from a global perspective are immense, there is no turning back if we want our students to be global citizens and future leaders of faith communities in a transnational world.[50] Our students who belong to Generation Z, and the generations coming up swiftly behind them, have grown up in a world of the Internet, instant messaging, Facebook, Twitter, Instagram, and other social media. They are the most globally connected generations the world has ever seen. They are the "digital natives," who use mobile devices to access information on the go and to connect instantly with their friends, families, and colleagues across distances.[51] The field of theology will have a bright future if we can speak to the globalized world and capture the imagination of these upcoming generations.

Chapter 9

Postcolonial Preaching
in Intercultural Contexts

*We cannot continue to foster a preaching style so alien to our people that "if
you just close your eyes . . ." you may think that the preacher is a foreigner.*
Pablo A. Jiménez[1]

Over the past several decades, much has changed in discussions on the nature and
function of preaching, the role of the preacher, and the form and rhetoric of the
sermon in homiletical theory. The emphasis has shifted from the preacher as God's
messenger delivering divine truth to God's people, to one that celebrates mutuality
and solidarity between the preacher and the congregation.[2] At the same time, North
American societies have become more culturally and religiously pluralistic because
of immigration, travel, refugees, and diaspora. However, relatively little has been
written so far on how postcolonial studies might open up discussions in homiletics,[3]
though several volumes have offered postcolonial perspectives on worship.[4] This
chapter explores issues of postcolonial preaching in intercultural contexts, discussing preaching in the hybrid church, preaching and decolonizing worship, engaging
the performative in postcolonial biblical criticism, and preaching and heteroglossia.

POSTCOLONIAL PREACHING IN THE HYBRID CHURCH

Christian community can be intercultural in many ways. For example, since
global cities have become the crossroads of global migration, an urban church

155

in a metropolitan area may have parishioners coming from diverse racial and national backgrounds. Some Black and Hispanic/Latinx churches have members from a number of African and Latin American countries and must negotiate commonalities and differences in multiple ways. Even in a seemingly racially homogeneous church, such as a Korean American congregation, members of different generations may speak different languages and relate to the mainstream white culture in various ways. Both in our faith communities and in the wider society, more and more people are living in intercultural realities. As a result of colonialism and slavery in the past and globalization in the present, cultures are not isolated from but are intertwined with one another. I have defined "intercultural" as "the interaction and juxtaposition, as well as tension and resistance when two or more cultures are brought together sometimes organically and sometimes through violent means in the modern world."[5] This intercultural approach allows us to theorize identity, experience, agency, and justice through a cross-cultural lens.

An important contribution of postcolonial theory is its challenge to the myths of racial or national purity, homogeneity of identity, and monolithic culture. Homi Bhabha uses the term "hybridity" to describe the intermingling of cultures, particularly in a colonial context. For him, hybridity is different from multiculturalism or the diversity of cultures, which liberals embrace and celebrate. Hybridity focuses on "the 'inter'—the cutting edge of translation and negotiation, the *in-between* space—that carries the burden of the meaning of culture."[6] Bhabha has called this in-between space the Third Space, which transgresses binary logic and questions narrowly-defined identity politics. Postcolonial hybridity and the emergence of the Third Space challenge narratives of modernity based on colonialism, class, and patriarchy and any attempts to define the other based on race, gender, sexual orientation, and other indicators.[7]

Christopher Baker builds on Bhabha's theory to elucidate the characteristics of the hybrid church in the city. Studying emergent patterns of church-based communities that are involved in urban regeneration and civil renewal in England and the U.S., Baker noticed important themes and implications for what he calls Third Space ecclesiology.[8] These church-based communities each constructed a local performative theology that was keenly aware of how global forces impinge upon the histories, experiences, and memories of locality. For Baker it is "performative," which means it is pragmatic and committed to delivering outcomes. These communities hold the tension of local and global identities, which is an important form of hybridity in our global society. Instead of constructing rigid boundaries and narrow identities, these communities develop blurred identities to make room for all members, and to build coalitions with other faith groups and nongovernmental organizations. In terms of structure, these communities exist in the hybrid spaces between the solid church and the liquid church. The solid church is associated with institution, hierarchy, and formal procedures, whereas the liquid church is dynamic and adaptable, relying on networks and relationships. These communities also display a greater understanding of a spectrum of different types of hybridity—some do not challenge the status quo while others aim to subvert and destabilize the center. Baker recognizes that the Third Space is a difficult space to inhabit, with both potentialities and dangers. He writes, "This is the paradox of the Third Space; that just as it creates new potential identities and methodologies for all sections of society, but especially churches and other faith groups," it also "creates the climate of fear of encountering the Other, who is now more in our midst than ever before."[9]

Drawing from Baker's work, I would portray postcolonial preaching as a locally rooted and globally conscious performance that seeks to create a Third Space so that the faith community can imagine new ways of being in the world and encountering God's salvific action for the oppressed and marginalized. Traditional homiletical theory understands the purpose of preaching as persuasion or transmission of the sermon's truth and message to the congregation. This understanding presumes that there is a gap between the preacher and the congregation, and that "the preacher has some insight or belief that the congregation needs to understand and accept."[10] Preaching as performance does not concentrate on the preacher but calls for greater focus on context and the rich convergence of performer, situation, setting, audience, and society. As some speech act theorists, such as J. L. Austin, have pointed out, utterances are not mere words, for they perform actions and have outcomes.[11] Through speech act and gestures, the preacher as performer seeks to act or consummate an action, to construct new realities, and to perform or signal possible new identities.

As both globalization and localization intensify in our contemporary world, it is critical for the preacher as performer to understand multiple subjectivities and belongings among members of the congregation. She must avoid defining identity based on territorial essentialism (e.g. Asia or Africa), cultural essentialism (e.g. Confucian), or racial essentialism (e.g. Black), because identity is fluid, porous, and hybrid, and is constantly shifting. With migration, international travel, and diaspora, we have to speak of identity not only in terms of multiplicity, but also in terms of translocality. Eleazar S. Fernandez says, "The translocal is a self that is porous to the interweaving of the many localities in the self. This person is locally rooted and globally winged. A translocal is one who experiences the interweaving, the tension, and the possibilities of one world of many worlds."[12] Like a jazz player or a *bricoleur*, the preacher has to create or construct her performance from a diverse range of traditions and bring disparate elements together. Biblical scholar Tat-siong Benny Liew exhorts postcolonial critics to draw "resources available from various sites and transits liberally and flexibly, without pledging to any cultural, racial, or national canons or canonical standards, for the sake of justice making."[13]

Since the aim of postcolonial preaching is to create a subversive Third Space, the preacher must dislodge the audience from common sense (which usually serves the status quo) and challenge the legacy of colonialism and the logic of empire. Sarah Travis describes the tasks of decolonizing preaching as follows:

These include recognizing difference and diversity within the listening community and beyond, naming colonialism/imperialism as a past and present reality, speaking against the damaging and destructive patterns and discourses that have emerged within colonial/imperial projects, and coming to terms with the relationship between Church and empire.[14]

To accomplish these tasks, preachers can learn from some of the approaches used by postcolonial theologians, including questioning Eurocentrism in biblical studies and theology; changing signifying practices; creating oppositional readings; questioning ideologies shaping gender, race, and class; lifting up marginalized or subjugated voices; and committing to anticolonial and anti-globalization theory and praxis.

To create Third Space is to enable both preacher and listener to imagine new ways of being in the world and to discern God's grace for the victims of history and for the marginalized. The authority to speak and preach cannot reside in one person—as it usually does in the pastor—but should be shared among members of the community. The separation of the preacher from the community could reinforce clericalism and the notion that the expert knows best. Instead, the postcolonial approach is "multivoiced, dialogical, and polycentric," as theologian Christopher Duraisingh says.[15] The responsibility of preaching can be rotated among ordained and lay leaders, and others can and should be trained and equipped to take up the task. In a reversal of empire, those who are not given voice by society should be given the space and be empowered to share their stories of God's action in their midst.

Preaching as performance is political when it does not reinscribe power dynamics in the church and society but seeks, rather, to change and subvert them. As the work of Judith Butler has shown, the performative, including gestures and speech acts, produces results and constructs social reality. For her, identity is not something inborn or natural, but is acquired through repeated performances, which can be challenged and queered.[16] Butler has increasingly focused on the performative in the political and she has worked with her colleague Athena Athanasiou, a Greek feminist theorist. Commenting on mass protests such as the Occupy movement, Athanasiou says these public gatherings enable and enact a "performativity of embodied agency" for social and political changes.[17] While participation in these gatherings involves corporeal vulnerability to fatigue, weariness, and police repression, it also offers "a shared affective economy of motivation, endurance, changeability, and vitalization."[18] I have written elsewhere about how the church can learn from the Occupy movement.[19] The Christians I have interviewed who participated in the Occupy movement experienced the presence of God there in ways they have seldom experienced God in the traditional church. The liturgy, the songs, and the preaching are often so patterned and routine, they seldom stir people's imagination or touch their deepest feelings. It is little wonder that people in the pews are sometimes called "God's frozen people." For the church to be relevant and faithful to its prophetic calling, it needs to recover the "performativity of embodied agency" in preaching and worship.

PREACHING AND DECOLONIZING WORSHIP

Postcolonial preaching as performance does not take place in a vacuum, but in the matrix of Christian worship. Michael N. Jagessar and Stephen Burns have applied postcolonial inquiries to the study of worship, including liturgical texts, symbolic contexts, hymnody, the use of Scripture, and time and space. They aim to expose "the issues of ideology and colonial agenda of western Christianity," and to problematize "the issues of language, imageries, symbols and representation in our liturgical/worship texts and symbols."[20] For example, they point to the ubiquitous use of light/dark imagery in key texts and symbols in the classical Western liturgical tradition. Privileging light over dark can lead to the marginalization of dark-skinned people and the reinforcing of negative racial stereotypes. Their study also demonstrates that "much of European hymnody advances the cause of European colonialism." Victorian hymns were imperialistic, and many of them focused on empire and Christian militarism.[21] Many of these hymns, unfortunately, found their way into hymnody in many parts of the world and are still sung in translated versions. In the conclusion of their study, Jagessar and Burns call for more conscious reflection on liturgical rites and worship, with an openness to tradition—its authority and ambiguity—and a concomitant commitment to subject tradition to questions of colonial and postcolonial concerns.

Postcolonial preaching must take into consideration the totality of the worship experience and the communal environments in which the preaching occurs. The preacher needs to pay attention to the use of sacred space, liturgical texts, symbols, architectural design, and hymnody. A tall pulpit placed far and away from the congregation reinforces the authority of the preacher and her distance from members of the community. Also, the effects of liberative and subversive preaching are undermined by the singing of nineteenth-century triumphant, missionary hymns. The message of God's inclusive love for all is compromised by the repeated use of androcentric language and images, which marginalize women's experiences. A pale-skinned Jesus and disciples portrayed in stained glass windows, together with predominantly Western symbols and ambience in many churches, will also work against intercultural emphases in worship and preaching.

The preacher must be self-reflective about how her role, persona, rhetoric, style, and gestures might either hinder or further the cause of decolonizing worship. For example, in many traditions, the pastor or the preacher robes or puts on particular clothing or vestments.[22] Some, such as Presbyterian priest Jeffrey J. Meyers, argue that robing or putting on special clothing will emphasize the office of the pastor (or the preacher) and deemphasize the personality of the person in the pulpit. The preacher plays a symbolic role in worship, and the robe does not set him or her above the congregation; rather, it sets him or her apart because of the unique office the pastor or preacher plays in leading Sunday worship. Robing adds dignity and reverence to worship and makes the preacher look less like a CEO in formal business attire.[23] However, robing or wearing special clothing also has the danger of reinforcing a two-class system—clergy and laity—and a hierarchical structure. Moreover, in some traditions, the vestment or clothing reflects vestiges of empire and colonial authority. Glauco S. de Lima, Anglican bishop of Sao Paulo, Brazil, notes, "Beyond the very order and linguistic sources of our worship, even our clothing bears witness to a colonial origin. In the vestments and trimmings of the clergy, for example, on the bishop's surplice, the sleeves finish up at the cuffs in the same way as those of the noblemen in the British court."[24] Even though the majority of Anglicans now live in the Global South and more women are being ordained, with some even becoming bishops, vestments have not changed much. It is important for the preacher to remember that she assumes certain roles and projects a certain persona when she robes or wears special clothing, since there are both expectations of and projections from the gathered community. If she chooses to wear the robe or vestment, she must be clear in her mind on why she is doing so and on how such a gesture will facilitate or hinder her postcolonial preaching. She should also explain her reasons to the congregation.

Traditionally, preaching means delivering a sermon behind the pulpit. Many books on homiletics provide guidelines and hints for the development of sermon forms, narrative structures, and rhythm and cadence of delivery.[25] But preaching a sermon is monological and, as such, does not create a plurivocal and dialogical community.[26] Except in the case of gifted preaching, listening to a sermon can be monotonous and boring, especially for young people who have grown up with mixed media in a digital age. Preaching as performance emphasizes the act as an art form; hence, it can borrow from different creative styles, such as dialogue, storytelling, dramatized presentation, skit, street theater, call and response, and mixed media with images and music. In addition to using words, the preacher can evoke memories of the past and can inculcate new values and understanding through intentional movements, gestures, music, habits, and affects in the creation of new communal environments. Instead of delivering a lecture-style sermon taught in the academy, preachers can learn from creative forms used by common folk and in popular religiosity. Justo L. González writes, "Most Hispanics do not see the sermon as a text, but rather as an event."[27] An example is a sermon for Good Friday preached by Virgilio Elizondo and Patricia Elizondo in a dialogical form. The sermon included the voices of the narrator and the preacher, and between each section, a popular hymn in the Hispanic congregation was sung.[28] Virgilio Elizondo writes that this sermon "demonstrates that preaching is a lively way of doing 'teología en conjunto' [doing theology as a group]."[29]

Postcolonial preaching challenges Eurocentric styles of worship and preaching methods. Much has been written on how Black culture and preaching style are important for the vitality and empowerment of Black congregations. For example, Henry H. Mitchell focuses his study on the use of storytelling, role-play, spontaneous dramatization, imaginative elaboration of biblical stories, and preaching styles rooted in African American culture. He accentuates the idea of preaching as performance by discussing the use of mannerisms, musical tones or chanting, rhetorical flair, and slow delivery in preaching.[30] Evans E. Crawford turns his attention to a particular style of African American folk preaching: call and response. Rooted in West African tradition, the call and response style accounts for the musicality of speech in Black churches. In some churches, as the preacher speaks, the choir responds with a low rumbling hum to the musical intonations of the preacher. Crawford calls this "hum thoughts."[31] In other styles of call and response, members of the congregation respond with sounds and gestures, and unburden their hearts with a "Preach!" or "Have Mercy!" or "Truly!" Both the preacher and congregation are engaged in creating a multivocal and lively performance that transgresses the speaker-listener model seen in most white churches.[32] Black female scholars have also discussed the gifts of Black women preachers and their struggles to overcome institutional sexism and gender bias. Teresa Fry Brown traces the rich heritage of African American women proclaiming the Word of God and discusses Black female preachers' sermon preparation, contents, delivery and personhood.[33]

Besides Black preaching, other preaching styles in racial and ethnic minority churches have also been studied. For example, Eunjoo Mary Kim analyzes the use of silence and indirect communication in Asian American preaching. She points out that silence is an important form of communication, especially in Buddhism: "Silence does not mean an absence of meaning but a moment through which thoughts and feelings occur from emptiness."[34] While traditional Western style of speech patterns are generally very direct, Asian communication style pattern is indirect, which leaves room for intuition and imagination.[35] An example of using indirect communication is the spiral form of preaching. Instead of following a linear movement toward the conclusion, the spiral form turns "around and around the subject until it reaches the central point."[36] Her analyses remind us to pay attention to different communicative styles in diverse cultures because preaching is a performative practice. In *Postcolonial Preaching: Creating a Ripple Effect*, HyeRan Kim-Cragg engages homiletical theory and postcolonial studies and offers suggestions for better preaching and sermon examples.[37] The book shows the author's creativity as she uses RIPPLE as an organizing framework: rehearsal, imagination, place, pattern, language, and exegesis. Each chapter discusses the concept, drawing upon a wide range of scholars in postcolonial theory, preaching, biblical studies, gender studies, and critical race scholarship. The book is different from many preaching books, which tend to focus on congregational settings. Kim-Cragg stretches our imagination to include preaching for the world. She asks future preachers to pay attention to how global issues, such as migration and immigration, the rise of white nationalism, and the growing disparity between the rich and the poor, shape the local context. These different preaching styles and homiletical issues, however, are seldom analyzed in white, mainstream texts on preaching, which often focus on the preacher and the sermon, and less on the audience and the context.

ENGAGING THE PERFORMATIVE IN
POSTCOLONIAL BIBLICAL CRITICISM

Postcolonial biblical criticism has made significant contributions to the field of biblical studies. Postcolonial studies of the Bible offer new insights to examine the relationship between religion and empire both in the text and in the history of interpretation. Several scholars have discussed the implications of postcolonial biblical criticism for worship and preaching. Jagessar and Burns apply postcolonial criticism to the questioning of the assumptions and biases of lectionaries, while Travis offers examples of how postcolonial biblical criticism can be used in preaching.[38]

I want to explore the performative aspect of postcolonial biblical criticism to glean insights from it for postcolonial preaching as performance. Musa W. Dube, a Batswana biblical scholar and author of *Postcolonial Feminist Biblical Interpretation*,[39] has written a creative piece of work titled "The Unpublished Letters of Orpah to Ruth."[40] In the beginning of the piece, Dube creates a scene telling the readers how the narrator has found Orpah's letters. Several women were sitting outside around a fire at night, discussing the images of Africa on TV and in newspapers and books. A young woman named Lesedi was among them, and though she had been offered a scholarship to study anthropology elsewhere, she had just returned to Botswana. Lesedi was offended by the portrayal of non-Western and non-Christian people as savage, childish, lazy, and sexually immoral in the anthropological books she had read. All the women around the fire agreed they should tell their own stories and not let others define who they are. And even though the eldest grandmother had been telling stories about their intelligent ancestors all her life, no one had ever written or published them. Lesedi said she had returned to write their stories and spent day and night doing it, though she could find no publisher. The narrator of the story found the letters to Ruth in a box in Lesedi's room labeled "NO PUBLISHER."

By creating this imaginative scene, Dube lifts up several important themes in postcolonial criticism. Colonized peoples and people living in the Global South have been portrayed as inferior, immoral, and lazy in order to justify Western colonization and control. The production of knowledge is closely related to power, and native peoples do not have easy access to the means for publicizing their own ideas. This reinforces the colonial ideology that natives cannot represent themselves; therefore, the colonial West must represent them. In many cases, colonial knowledge about natives is taught to natives as "objective" scholarship, so that they will harbor and internalize a biased view about themselves. But natives are not passive, for they have constructed a counter-memory through their stories, told from generation to generation, with women playing a critical role in their remembrance.

In Dube's work, the four letters that Orpah sent to Ruth, the younger Moabite sister, speak about the origins of the Moabite people. Long ago after an earthquake in the land, Lot's children fled and sought refuge in Zoar, a small town at the southern end of the Dead Sea, and they multiplied into a people called Moabites. Because of a severe famine in Judah, Elimelech and Naomi came to Moab, and King Eglon offered them hospitality, so they settled there. Elimelech was very loyal to the king for this, and he was killed when he went to fight for the King's country during a war. The king vowed to bring up Mahlon and Chilion, the sons of Elimelech and Naomi, and betrothed his own daughters, Orpah and Ruth, to them. After King Eglon died, Balak, brother of Orpah and Ruth, succeeded him, but Mahlon and Chilion wanted to usurp the throne, so they murdered the king. Naomi became so distraught that she decided to return to her country with her daughters-in-law. Ruth had been close to Naomi since childhood and Orpah said it was right for Ruth to stay in Judah to take care of Naomi, an old childless widow. But Orpah followed Naomi's advice to return to Moab to take care of their widowed mother, and she later became the regent queen and priestess to her people. Orpah married a priest named Balaam, and they had a son named after Lot and a daughter named after Ruth, so that Ruth's name would not be forgotten in her own land. Orpah asked Ruth to tell her children about the stories of the Moabites, of their origins, of their hospitality, and of their struggles to survive.

In Orpah's letters, Dube uses the storytelling method to portray the history of the Moabites in a positive light, since the Hebrew Scripture often describes them negatively because Moab was often in conflict with its neighbor Israel. The letters tell the story from the side of Orpah, a minor and often forgotten character in the book of Ruth. Ruth's story is included in the canonical Bible, and she is remembered as an ancestress of Jesus in the genealogy in Matthew's Gospel (1:5). But Orpah, who returned to Moab, was forgotten, and she is never mentioned again in the Bible. The letters say Orpah and Ruth were princesses who lived in the royal court and were victims of the power struggles among their male kinsmen. After returning to Moab, Orpah became a leader of her people and officiated in religious duties, and she also bore two children. Even as Orpah's name was erased from Jewish memory, Orpah wanted Ruth's name to be remembered among her own people. Dube's storytelling demonstrates that the Bible can be interpreted from multiple perspectives, and she highlights the suffering of women and their children during war and political strife. By creatively imagining the history and voice of the subjugated Orpah, Dube contributes to a growing body of postcolonial biblical criticism that focuses on the stories of indigenous women and women living in the contact zone, women like Rahab, Ruth, Orpah, and the Syrophoenician woman.[41] Her storytelling offers a concrete example of postcolonial feminist criticism, which, she says, must resist "both patriarchal and imperial oppression in order to cultivate a space of liberating interdependence between nations, genders, races, ethnicities, the environment, and development."[42]

Another example of performative postcolonial criticism is my self-interview, "On Color-Coding Jesus: An Interview with Kwok Pui-lan," published in one of the early texts of postcolonial biblical criticism.[43] I decided to use the form of interview that many other postcolonial theorists such as Edward Said, Homi Bhabha, and Gayatri Chakravorty Spivak have used, which offers tremendous insights to their work and the background of their thinking.[44] In this self-interview, I playfully create a character "Quest" as the interviewer, since I want to discuss the contemporary interdisciplinary quest for the historical Jesus. The interview is conducted in a dialogical and colloquial manner:

> **Quest**: Why are you obsessed with Jesus?

> **Kwok**: I am not obsessed with Jesus, but I am obsessed with other people's obsession with Jesus.[45]

The mock interview discusses the work of the Jesus seminar, formed in 1985, to determine who Jesus really was and what he actually said. The participants cast colored balls to vote to determine which sayings are close to what Jesus actually said and which are less certain or were created by his followers. The interview proceeds to point out that the quest for the historical Jesus is a coded quest for origins. In the nineteenth century, the quest first took place in Europe, when Europe underwent tremendous changes as a result of its encounter with the colonized world. The current quest began in the U.S. around the 1980s and caught the attention of the mass media, and it was reported on National Public Radio, in *People* and *Time* magazines, and on TV.

> **Quest**: Then why do the Americans have to search for origins?

> **Kwok**: The straight white males in America have made a lot of noises saying that they have lost a lot of ground to women, minorities, and gays and lesbians. The mass media in the US has played up the angry white male syndrome. Whenever the white males are not certain about their identity, they search for Jesus.[46]

The self-interview discusses important topics, such as the changing contexts of the historical quests for Jesus, Orientalism in the study of the Bible and other sacred texts, and the treatment of the Bible as fetish and a museum object instead of a living tradition. It asks Christians from the Global South to liberate themselves from the European and Euro-American hallucinations, and to reimagine reading the Bible as diasporic adventure. Yet the interview is conducted with humor and satire, poking fun at the work of scholars engaged in the quests. The lightheartedness of performance is a great way to say that we cannot take the historical quest of Jesus seriously, as if anyone can really, truly offer us the "real Jesus."

Postcolonial biblical criticism has been done in creative and imaginative ways, especially by women. In these two examples using letter writing, storytelling, and interview, I have shown how preachers can learn from the ingenuity of postcolonial critics, and how they can use different methods to introduce postcolonial biblical criticism in lively and contextual ways. I have published dramatized Bible studies and sermons, which can provide additional resources and insights for preachers.[47]

POSTCOLONIAL PREACHING AND HETEROGLOSSIA

If the aim of postcolonial preaching is to create a multivocal and dialogical faith community committed to justice, we have to attend to the issue of language in intercultural contexts. In urban global cities, it is increasingly common to have church members speaking different mother tongues and immigrants who struggle with English or another colonial language. Many of them live in bicultural and bilingual worlds, speak the dominant language with an accent, and must negotiate and translate constantly between hybrid contexts. The Russian linguist Mikhail Bakhtin introduced the concept of heteroglossia, which refers to the co-existence of a diversity of voices, styles of discourses, or points of views in a literary work, particularly in a novel.[48] For Bakhtin, as Andrew Robinson notes, "Even within a single perspective, there are always multiple voices and perspectives, because the language which is used has been borrowed from others."[49] Bakhtin criticizes monoglossical language, which is closed off or deaf to voices of difference while also supporting centralized forces. Heteroglossia interrupts the dominant discourse with other voices and celebrates diversity, folk, and festive language. How might heteroglossia impact our ways of thinking about preaching and its cultural environment?

Acts 2 offers a powerful image of heteroglossia. On the day of Pentecost, the Spirit descends on the disciples. Biblical scholar Frank Yamada notes that "they do not break into a meta-language, a single tongue," but "divided tongues, as of fire, appeared among them, and a tongue rested on each of them. All of them were filled with the Holy Spirit and began to speak in other languages" (Acts 2:3–4).[50] The people who gathered in Jerusalem were quite diverse, for there were diasporic Jews and other proselytes scattered throughout the empire.

> Now there were devout Jews from every nation under heaven living in Jerusalem. . . [there were] Parthians, Medes, Elamites, and residents of Mesopotamia, Judea and Cappadocia, Pontus and Asia, Phrygia and Pamphylia, Egypt and the parts of Libya belonging to Cyrene, and visitors from Rome, both Jews and proselytes, Cretans and Arabs (Acts 2:5–11).

The crowd gathered was bewildered, "because each one heard them speaking in the native language of each" (v.6). Yamada says that this passage affirms that God "prefers the plural over the singular, languages over a single-tongue, [and] cultures over one defining culture."[51]

The diversity of the crowd speaking in different tongues in Jerusalem is not unlike what we can find in today's urban churches in global cities, where immigrants from different nations gather to worship together. Language continues to be an important issue in postcolonial studies. In *Not Like a Native Speaker*, cultural critic Rey Chow discusses racialization as an encounter with language. The colonized encounter with the colonizing language has racial overtones and is associated with severance from the mother tongue and with deprivation of linguistic autonomy and integrity. But Chow argues, such an encounter also "offers a privileged vantage point from which to view the postcolonial situation, for precisely the reason that this language has been imposed from without."[52] The use of Black English in preaching is a case in point.

Black English is the rich rendition of English spoken in the Black community, full of subtle shadings of sound, cadence, and color. For Henry H. Mitchell, a Black preacher must be able to preach in Black English in order "to touch the souls of black folk with soul language" and "to generate rapport with the congregation by means of an identity which is perceived as close."[53] The kind of closeness and emotional support is not available in white-language preaching. He asserts, "No Black person can truly identify with a God who speaks only the language of the White oppressor."[54] The use of Black language supports Black identity because it demonstrates that God's message can be expressed by the language of the people. Yet the use of Black language has received pushback from middle-class Blacks, who think that the preacher should not use Black language. Moreover, colleges and seminaries have trained Black clergy in standard white middle-class American English, with the assumption that "White is right." The Black-culture churches find it difficult to understand or relate to trained Black clergy persons "preaching Whitese to them." Mitchell's hope is that Black clergy can both preach Black English in Black-culture churches and use "standard" English when communicating with the larger community, so that Black churches will not be isolated. In this sense, the preacher serves as a cultural translator between the two communities.

Language is also an issue in Latinx congregations, as they are bicultural and bilingual to varying degrees: some are Spanish-dominant and some are English-dominant. There are also generational differences between the older and younger generations, with the older generation being less acculturated into the mainstream culture. González describes the various ways Latinx preachers adapt to the bilingual contexts:

> Many preachers preach in one language and summarize their sermon in the other. Some translate their own sermon as they go along. An increasing number are becoming adept at a style of preaching in which a few sentences are said in English, the next few in Spanish, and so on, and this is done in such a way that people who have very limited proficiency in one of the two languages can still follow the sermon.[55]

González says that we should not regard bilingualism as a problem to be overcome, because the church should look toward a future in which a great multitude will come from every nation, tribe, people, and language (Rev. 7:9). The church serves as a subversive sign of the future when it finds ways to worship and live in multicultural and multilingual ways.

The issue of language multiplies in a congregation with people who come from different nations and cultures. The Pentecost story says that when the Holy Spirit descended on the people, they began to speak in other tongues. They did not speak in their own languages; otherwise the crowd would not have been surprised. The Spirit empowered them to speak a language not their own. The challenge before us is, can we learn to speak the other tongue? Learning to speak the other tongue can be literal and figurative. It means entering another cultural world deep enough and long enough to begin to understand it. It means trying to see the world through the other's perspective and, by doing so, acquiring new insights with which to look at our own culture. Embracing multiculturalism is hard work. But we will be blessed to hear the voice of God speaking in many cultures and tongues. Let's not forget what missiologist Max Warren says: "It takes the whole world to know the whole Gospel."[56]

By entering into other cultural worlds, we will find that words, metaphors, and symbols are polyvalent and might mean different things in different cultures. The preacher needs to be sensitive when helping the congregation navigate cultural negotiation. For example, the symbol of the dragon represents the devil or something evil in the Bible and in the Christian tradition. The book of Revelation is replete with negative images of the dragon and slaying and throwing down the beast (12:9; 13:1–2; 16:13; 20:2–3). However, in Chinese culture, the dragon symbolizes power, strength, and good luck, and during the Chinese New Year, there is a dragon dance in many cities' Chinatowns. The preacher can avoid cross-cultural misunderstanding if he or she is alert to the cultural backgrounds of church members. Opportunities for different groups of church members to share their culture with the congregation will promote dialogue and inclusivity.

Heteroglossia can be a threat but also a promise. In traditional homiletical theory, language is seen as transparent and meaning as stable. The task of the preacher is to impart to listeners the claim of the scriptural text or a message from God. In postcolonial preaching, preaching is a communal event, with the congregation participating and responding. The preacher needs to respond to the congregation—with its diversity and heteroglossia. As Edward Farley notes, "the world of preaching is not the safe and efficient world of applying verses and passages but the more muddy, unsafe, and uncertain world of interpreting the mysteries of faith."[57] When different voices and discourses are brought to negotiate with one another on how best to accommodate diverse perspectives, heteroglossia is a promise. All are invited to encounter the liberating grace of God in fresh ways in this Third Space by examining the "inter" in our identities, languages, and cultures.

Chapter 10

Interreligious Solidarity and Peacebuilding

Living in society, we should share the sufferings of our fellow citizens and practice compassion and tolerance not only towards our loved ones but also towards our enemies.

The Dalai Lama[1]

Peace does not demand winners or losers, but rather brothers and sisters who, for all the misunderstandings and hurts of the past, are journeying from conflict to unity.

Pope Francis, speaking in Iraq[2]

I have only met the Dalai Lama once, almost twenty-five years ago at Madison Square Garden in New York. He came with a group of monks to discuss Tibetan Buddhism and to perform Buddhist rituals. Along with several thousands of other people, I listened to his teaching about kindness, compassion, and universal responsibility. A man in exile in a foreign country, he radiated a very special kind of happiness and had a great sense of humor. I did not know much about the rituals, but I remember the Dalai Lama's demeanor and the glow on his face. At the end of the ceremony, the Dalai Lama asked the monks to distribute packets of seeds and asked us to return home to sow love, kindness, and peace.

When we look around the world, we see persistent wars and conflicts in which religion plays a contributing factor—places such as Israel-Palestine, the Balkans, Nigeria, Myanmar, and South Asia. Palestinians have resisted the occupation of Jerusalem, West Bank, and Gaza for decades. This occupation has been justified by Zionism, and many rounds of peace talks have not resolved animosity between the peoples. President Trump added oil to the fire by recognizing Jerusalem as Israel's capital and relocating the U.S. embassy there in his attempt to appease U.S. evangelicals. In Nigeria, religious conflicts erupted between Christians and Muslims, causing riots that resulted in casualties of thousands on both sides. Today, Boko Haram insurgency, which aims to establish an Islamic State in Nigeria, has caused bloodshed, violence, and the kidnapping of innocent schoolgirls. In war-torn Southeast Asia and in South Asia, conflicts between different religious groups have torn communities and countries apart. The Muslim minority of about one million Rohingyas have lived in the majority Buddhist Myanmar for centuries but have not been recognized as full citizens. More than 650,000 Rohingyas had to leave the country when government troops ransacked their villages and committed mass killings and other human rights abuses. In the West, the attacks on September 11, 2001, and subsequent attacks in Paris, London, Brussels, and Berlin perpetuated by Muslim extremists have caused alarm and anti-immigrant reactions.

German theologian Hans Küng surmised that the "most fanatical and cruelest political struggles are those that have been colored, inspired, and legitimized by religion."[3] The relationship between religion, conflict, and peace has captured widespread interest, and a religious subfield has been developed on religion and peacebuilding. A postcolonial approach must begin with demystifying dominant myths about religion that impede productive discussion. Popularized by academics, pundits, and the media, these myths reflect Eurocentric and Euro-American biases that have deep roots in colonialism. Demystifying these myths will make it easier to engage in peacebuilding work across religious traditions.

DEMYSTIFYING MYTHS AGAINST PEACEBUILDING

The first myth is the "clash of civilizations" proposed by political scientist Samuel P. Huntington. Huntington suggested that future wars and conflicts will be fought not because of ideological differences, but because of clashes of religiously-based civilizations.[4] His hypothesis became widely popular because it asserted Western hegemony and provided an explanation of world politics in the post-Cold War era. However, his understanding of cultural and religious difference has deep connections to colonial discourse. In *Orientalism*, Edward Said points out how, in pursuit of colonization, the West created an image of the "Orient" as inferior, backward, and uncivilized for the purposes of control and domination.[5] Huntington reactivated this threat and the fear of colonial difference by treating civilizations as homogeneous and bounded entities with no civilizational interactions and crossovers. Said charges that Huntington has reductively defined Islamic civilization "as if what matters most about it is its supposed anti-Westernism."[6] In contrast, Scott Appleby's influential book *The Ambivalence of the Sacred* argues that religion can generate ambivalent responses. Terrorists and peacemakers may grow up in the same community and belong to the same religious tradition. He pays attention to the internal diversity and plurality of religious traditions and points to potential constructive roles for religion in peacebuilding.[7]

The second myth equates secularism as progress and regards religion as irrational, absolutist, divisive, and incompatible with modernity. Since the Enlightenment, this secularist view has been popular and dominant in Western societies. Proponents can easily point to religious groups and institutions for providing justifications or serving as an impetus for social conflict and even violence. This secularist paradigm treats religion as either irrelevant to or problematic for social life in general, and for conflict resolution in particular. In the field of social sciences and international affairs, the secularist position has been taken as normative until recent decades. But in his book *The Myth of Religious Violence*, William T. Cavanaugh counter-argues that ideologies like nationalism, Communism, and capitalism, which are normally considered secular, can wreak havoc just as often as religious ideologies and institutions.[8] From a cross-cultural perspective, scholars who study non-Western societies have contested Western biases in the secularist myth. Anthropologist Talal Asad argues that the secular cannot be viewed as a successor to religion or be seen as on the side of the rational. The secular has a multilayered history in different cultures.[9] The secularist paradigm creates problems for peacebuilding because it overemphasizes the roles of nation-states and economies while neglecting the roles of religious symbols, actors, and organizations. It also overlooks the fact that religious and secular organizations can collaborate and form alliances to further peace. Over the past decades, the roles of religious actors and faith-based communities in peacebuilding and reconciliation have been recognized by government agencies, international organizations, and nongovernmental organizations.

The third myth is dangerous and Islamophobic, for it proposes that some religions, such as Christianity, are inherently peaceful, while Islam is militant and condones violence and Jihadism. On YouTube, one can find many videos debating whether or not Islam is a religion of peace. This singling out of Islam is simplistic and ahistorical, for it overlooks the Crusades, Christianity's complicity in genocide and colonialism, and the internal rivalries within Christian traditions. It is also misleading and dangerous, because it can lead to false stereotyping and the scapegoating of whole populations. Mohammad Yaseen Gada writes, "Muslims are depicted as a collective body that is responsible for the violent acts committed by some individuals or groups who have interpreted and transformed the Islamic faith into an ideology."[10] He says that Islamophobia has long historical roots traceable to the Crusades in the medieval time and to wars and conflicts during the colonization of Muslim countries in modernity. The association of Islam with religious violence and the language of "religious insurgence" as threatening shows strong Orientalist biases. Muslims have very different understandings of their traditions and strongly object to these politically charged and dangerous representations by commentators, scholars, and pundits. Gada argues that Islamophobia serves the U.S. and its allies politically and economically in the same way as the Crusades in medieval Christian Europe did against the Muslim world.[11] President Trump issued a travel ban against seven Muslim-majority countries and regarded radical Islamic terrorism as a global existential threat. Islamophobia has resulted in an increase of the number of hate crimes against Muslims in the U.S., as well as in the United Kingdom in recent years.[12]

Postcolonial criticism can help demystify these myths by shedding light on the problems in the construction of "religion" and religious identities and boundaries. Postcolonial critics point out that "religion" is a problematic category, and the study of religion in the modern West has often been linked to racism and construction of the Other. In the nineteenth century, Christianity was taken to be the reference point when compared to the "mythic" religions of the East and the "primitive" religions of Africa. As religion emerged as a field of study in academia, there was a tendency to treat "religion" as *sui generis* and separate from other cultural, social, and political aspects. This reductionist and simplistic approach continues to be seen in some introductory "World Religions" course syllabi and texts. Here, different religious traditions are reduced to certain belief systems, creeds, heroes, and a few key practices selected and told mostly for white curiosity and intended for white consumption. Scholars have argued that the promotion of "religious literacy" is important to understand religious influences in social and cultural life and in political policies and debates.[13] But the question about representation looms large: "Who decides what is religious literacy for a particular tradition?" If, in the name of religious literacy, a very truncated form of knowledge is introduced, this will only sharpen the differences of diverse traditions and reinforce biases students already held. Just how can a tradition as long and complex as Buddhism be summarized in one chapter in an introductory text to "World Religions"? Is there any space or attempt to discuss multidimensional and complex interactions and cross-fertilization of religious traditions, including songs and dances, in a brief survey? If not taught well, introductory courses in "World Religions" will not promote dialogue and peacebuilding but end up reinforcing colonial and Orientalist myths.

Postcolonial criticism also focuses on the ways that colonial practices have contributed to or exacerbated religious rivalry and the hardening of cultural and religious boundaries. For example, in India, while there was a clear sense of differences between Hindu and Muslim communities before the British arrived, colonial management heightened the awareness of religious identities and boundaries through mechanisms such as the first scientific census of 1871 and the introduction of separate Hindu and Muslim electorates. The British "divide-and-rule" policy drove religious communities apart and contributed to the violence between them.[14] In Africa, the arbitrariness of the boundaries initially drawn up by European colonial powers have caused substantial intrastate violence. These arbitrary boundaries worsened long-standing enmity between African territories. Interethnic conflicts and violence break out when religious, racial, cultural, and linguistic differences are politicized.[15] In the Middle East, colonial powers came to the region and encompassed territories with a patchwork of ethnic and religious communities. The political choices of colonial powers have led inexorably to inter-communal conflicts because modern boundaries were more or less artificially created as the result of war or by the pencils of colonial mapmakers.[16]

Since religion is always emmeshed in the larger cultural, social, economic, and political dynamics in society, it is simplistic to reduce complex conflicts and violence to religious factors alone. It is, therefore, overly simplistic to look at wars and conflicts as if religion is the sole or the most important cause and to blame religion for causing violence and bloodshed. Rabbi Alan Lurie points out that wars in the ancient world were for "territorial conquest, to control borders, secure trade routes, or respond to an internal challenge to political authority" and rarely based on religion. Most modern wars, such as the Napolean campaigns, the American Revolution, World Wars I and II, and the wars in Korean and Vietnam were nationalistic and ethnic in origin, not religious. He recognizes that religion has been a cause for conflict and will continue to be, and urges us to be vigilant about those who commit horrendous acts based on religious zeal and fanaticism. But he helpfully reminds us that in a world with billions of people who profess they are religious, those who commit acts of violence and murder innocents as if this is God's will belong to a tiny minority. The acts of a small minority should not lead people to believe that religious people are always anti-science and that faith is incompatible with reason.[17] In fact, as I will discuss below, many religious actors and organizations have worked tirelessly for justice and have sown seeds of peace in the world's hot spots of religious conflicts.

INTERRELIGIOUS LEARNING AND SOLIDARITY

The emerging field studying religion and peacebuilding focuses on the themes of interreligious dialogue and learning, the retrieval of religious resources for peacebuilding from various traditions, and the instrumental roles that religious actors and networks play in the dynamics of conflict and peacebuilding. Interreligious dialogue brings people of different traditions together, and it is not an academic exercise or the use of words alone. According to Leonard Swidler, it operates in three areas: "the practical, where we collaborate to help humanity; the depth or 'spiritual' dimension, where we attempt to experience the partner's religion or ideology 'from within'; the cognitive, where we seek understanding [of] the truth."[18] Interreligious dialogue has taken place in various forms and served different purposes, including dialogue among high-level religious leaders, scholars in academia, interreligious bodies, and grassroots communities. Dialogue can also happen when conflict is ongoing as a step toward peace and reconciliation. In recent years, training in conflict resolution for interreligious groups also serves as a vehicle for dialogue. A postcolonial approach to this dialogue is especially valuable because it highlights that conflicts between different religious communities often have deeper historical roots in colonialism and postcolonial nation building.

As David Smoch, editor of *Interfaith Dialogue and Peacebuilding*, points out, interreligious dialogue is difficult to carry out in situations of serious conflict. Participants may bring prejudices and preconceptions of the beliefs and practices of the other religious community to the dialogue. When two religious groups have been on opposite sides of armed conflicts, even when religion is not a principal cause of conflict, participants may harbor hostility, mistrust, anger, and guilt that would complicate the dialogue process.[19] For meaningful dialogue to happen, discussions must be designed to provide measures of trust and safety for participants to discover one another's commonalities and differences. Participants have to take a certain degree of risk to enter into other religious worldviews and to abandon or suspend their preconceived knowledge or existing attitudes toward the other. Sometimes, it is necessary for participants to acknowledge the loss and victimization of people who belong to other religious groups, and to recognize shared pain as a result of the divide-and-rule tactics of former colonizers and the exploitation of neocolonial forces in the present.

To foster interreligious solidarity, we cannot wait until conflict or violence has occurred before we commit ourselves to dialogue and mutual understanding. Peace studies distinguishes between negative peace, when there is an absence of conflict, and positive peace, which involves "the establishment of institutional mechanisms through which to realize social justice and its associated values: equity, cooperation, empathy and harmony."[20] Interreligious learning and solidarity—in schools, churches, faith communities, and civic groups—can contribute to positive peace and the development of strategies to combat hatred, discrimination, and violence. A barrier to interreligious solidarity in the U.S. is the unacknowledged Christian privilege and hegemony in mainstream society. According to the Pew Research Center, the U.S. remains home to more Christians than any other countries in the world, with about 70 percent of the population identifying with some branch of the Christian faith.[21] Even with increasing religious diversity in the U.S., many Christians still harbor elements of cultural superiority and treat other religions with suspicion and discontent. The Christian Right has promoted white nationalism and influenced political discourse and policies for decades, contributing to the authoritarian and imperialistic impulses of the country. Scholars have challenged the construction of white Christianity and its grips on the national imagination. In *White Christian Privilege: The Illusion of Religious Equality in America*, Khyati Y. Joshi demonstrates that "white privilege in the U.S. has always been entangled with notions of White Supremacy."[22] Her work shows that the co-constitution of religion, race, and national origin has privileged those who are Christian, English, free, and white and led to the discrimination of those who belong to other religious traditions.

White Christian theologians and scholars have responded to the critique and challenge of white Christian hegemony. For example, Catholic theologian Jeannine Hill Fletcher has investigated the connections between Christian hegemony and ideologies of racial supremacy and challenged white Christians to dismantle racism and accept responsibility for structural oppression in America.[23] Practical theologian Sheryl Kujawa-Holbrook has explored postcolonial implications for interreligious learning and provides several helpful guidelines for interreligious dialogue and learning that challenge Christian hegemony. An Episcopal priest, her work has engaged postcolonial theory and is based on her experience of helping churches address anti-racism and multiculturalism over several decades. She suggests the following guidelines for interreligious engagement that recognizes cultural and religious difference:

1. Recognize your tradition's participation in prejudices and oppression against peoples of other faith traditions. Interreligious understanding and solidarity require each person and each faith community to develop an understanding about how they impact persons and faith communities from different religious traditions.
2. Know the difference between religion, race, ethnicity, and culture, and apply this knowledge to local and global contexts. Religion is only one factor shaping the social identities of people, and it intersects with other markers such as race, gender, class, and sexuality. We need to know how colonialism shapes religious identities and how Christian hegemony impacts other religious groups.
3. Challenge the myth that all religions are the same and uphold their particularities in relationship. While there are commonalities in religious traditions, differences cannot be overlooked or elided if we want to form genuine interreligious communities.
4. Recognize that there are multiple centers of truth, the legitimacy of which is determined by power dynamics in each given context. It is important to provide space for sharing histories and traditions of less-recognized groups.
5. Acknowledge that postcolonial interreligious learning requires long-term commitment. Genuine interreligious learning and solidarity is a slow process, for it needs to take time to go beyond superficial niceties before critical engagement of differences can occur.[24]

From another perspective, Najeeba Syeed, a Muslim scholar and an award-winning leader in peacebuilding, cautions us that interfaith spaces in the U.S. have long been dominated by Christian-based institutions that are largely white, and the majority of books on interreligious dialogue have been written by white scholars. She urges us to use an intersectional approach in interreligious learning: "Interfaith or interreligious education needs to take into consideration not only religious differences but also differences in language, ethnicity, race, and varying degrees of admission into the literal and figurative citizenry of this country."[25] Interreligious learning cannot stay at the abstract, intellectual level, but must involve the whole person. To cultivate understanding and empathy, we need to treat religious boundaries as porous, instead of rigid, and recognize that there has been a long history of cross-fertilization and hybridity between traditions. We have to move beyond polite, appreciative inquiry, she says, to attend to issues such as the harm done in the name of religion, the trauma of forging a new religious identity because of migration, and the pain and alienation one feels in one's own tradition because of gender, sexuality, or political commitment. Syeed's goal is to move interreligious learning to a deeper level so that students "become not only religiously literate of another tradition but they become readers of other communities and contexts. They become translator of one tradition to another, of one culture to another."[26] While some interfaith educators want to avoid political discussion for fear that it will lead to division and tension, Syeed recognizes the need to acknowledge the lived political realities of students. The educator can help students build new narratives drawing upon resources of transformative justice from different religious traditions. In her work, she describes "this process as 'remythologizing' the narrative of communal histories to highlight the times when cooperative relationships existed in order to develop interreligious solidarity on jointly defined socio-political issues."[27] In this way, interreligious learning can be a springboard for coalition-building and faith-based organizing.

RECLAIMING TRADITIONS IN PEACEBUILDING

Scholars in various religious traditions have retrieved and cultivated religious ideas, motifs, and practices that are conducive to bringing peace. Given Christianity's complicity with colonialism and cultural imperialism, Christians especially need to learn from other traditions if we want to embrace our religious neighbors and work with them in solidarity. In Buddhism, the Zen Buddhist Master Thich Nhat Hanh developed "engaged Buddhism" in the aftermath of the Vietnam War and has taught mindfulness, compassion, and peace throughout the world. In the U.S., he has worked with Vietnam War veterans who suffered from trauma from the war. For him, nonviolence is a natural and necessary part of the Buddhist tradition. He teaches that all phenomena are interdependent, interconnected, and interwoven, and he calls it the principle of "interbeing." Meditation and mindfulness enable us to see into the nature of things and to discover the true nature of interbeing. His engaged Buddhism brings social consciousness and involvement to Buddhism.

In teaching Thich Nhat Hanh's thought, I have found that the most difficult thing for American students to grasp is the principle of non-duality. My students tend to view the world as being made up of separate and isolated entities, with the individual self being autonomous and having clear boundaries. Non-duality means "not-two" and "non-separation," and goes against binary and dualistic thinking. Thich Nhat Hanh uses the principle of non-duality to challenge the construction of self and the other, and of "us" versus "them." He teaches that every person is made up of all the elements that are not themselves. We are capable of doing good and committing evil. In his poem "Please Call

Me by My True Names," he describes the tragedy of the boat people fleeing Vietnam after the war:

I am the twelve-year-old girl,
refugee on a small boat,
who throws herself into the ocean
after being raped by a sea pirate.
And I am the pirate,
my heart not yet capable
of seeing and loving.[28]

Thich Nhat Hanh has said that it is easy to take side of the girl raped by the pirate. But on meditation, he says, "I saw that if I had been born in the village of the pirate and raised in the same conditions as he was, I would now be the pirate. There is a great likelihood that I would become a pirate. I can't condemn myself so easily."[29] My students find this compassion for the pirate very hard to imagine, for they want to distinguish the good guy from the bad guy. But Thich Nhat Hanh reminds us that all those who are victims of injustice, and the perpetrators of injustice, are within each of us. Given certain circumstances, we have the potential to commit evil and inflict pain and suffering, just as the bad guys do. Such an awareness enlarges our moral imagination by focusing not only on an individual act, but also the social and historical conditions that cause it. We develop compassion for ourselves and others, knowing that we are also fallible and can succumb to temptations to commit violence. We are challenged to take responsibility for and work to change the social conditions that create social evil.

In the Islamic tradition, Mohammed Abu-Nimer, a professor at the American University School of International Service in International Peace and Conflict Resolution in Washington, D.C., is noted for his contribution to the study of Islam and peacebuilding. He has conducted peacebuilding workshops in Gaza, Cairo, Amman, Sarajevo, Mindanao, Washington, D.C., and many other American cities. He laments that there is a widespread assumption that Islam is inimical to the principles of peacebuilding and conflict resolution, offering many reasons for this assumption. Among them are selective and biased reporting in the media, the lack of academic research on positive and nonviolent traditions in Islamic society, the colonial legacy of the West, ignorance of cultural differences, the Arab-Israeli conflict, and the failure of Muslims to convey their message.[30] To counteract this one-sided impression, Muslim scholars have shown that Islam is compatible with democracy and that there are resources in the Islamic tradition for nonviolence and peace.

Abu-Nimer's book *Nonviolence and Peacebuilding in Islam* explores the principles and values of Qur'an, Hadith (the sayings of Prophet Muhammad), and Islamic tradition that support peacebuilding strategies in resolving conflicts. He underscores the core Islamic values of justice, benevolence, patience, and forgiveness, and argues that the spirit of these key concepts is inimical to violence. There are innumerable verses in the Qur'an that command believers to be righteous and to seek peace, kindness, and mercy. Two examples of this are "God commands you to treat (everyone) justly, generously, and with kindness" (16:90) and "Whenever they kindle the fire of war, God extinguishes it. They strive to create disorder on earth and God loves not those who create disorder" (5:64). Furthermore, the quest for peace can be seen in the Prophet's life and tradition. The Hadith supports the shunning of violence and calls for restraint. During the Mecca period, the Prophet waged nonviolent campaigns for resistance and showed no inclination toward the use of force of any kind. Instead, he relied on spiritual teaching when he was faced with opposition and confrontation. When someone asked the Prophet, "Who is the best Muslim?" he replied, "the one whose hand and tongue leave other Muslims in peace." The Prophet's tradition highlights the importance of peacemaking and reconciliation of differences. The Islamic teachings of mutual consultation, independent judgment, and mutual consensus can be readily applied to the study of conflict resolution and nonviolence in Islam.

Abu-Nimer notes that Islam is a pluralistic and multilayered tradition, and one that changes over time. There are those who argue that Islamic tradition justifies the use of violence under certain limited conditions. Those who support war often point to a particular verse in the Qur'an: "Fight in the cause of Allah those who fight you, but do not transgress limits; for Allah does not love transgressors" (2:190). Muslim scholars determine whether war is just or unjust based on whether it serves the interest of the ruler or promoted the interests of the people. *Jihad* is a term cited frequently in the media and is subjected to many misinterpretations. The word *Jihad* in classical Arabic and in the Qur'an means "to do one's most, to make efforts, to strive, to exert, to employ one's self diligently" and does not mean fighting or warfare. It was only later applied to religious war but was not used in such a sense in the Qur'an. While the Qur'an contains passages that seem to provide justification for the use of war to subdue unbelievers, the Qur'an also says: "Let there be no compulsion in religion." Some scholars argue that "the Qur'an seeks to effect more restrictions on the use of force, permitting its expression only defensively and within the context of interpersonal human conduct."[31] Thus, Abu-Nimer argues that any *jihad* that leads to senseless killing and ignores the concerns for peace and justice is not following the Qur'an and Islamic teaching. But in popular media, the term *jihad* is used in a way that portrays Islam as a religion that condones violence.

The Jewish tradition has important religious and ritualistic resources for peacebuilding. The Hebrew word for peace, *shalom*, has the rich meanings of wholeness, tranquility, prosperity, and completeness. One of the most quoted passages in the Hebrew Scriptures for peace is: "they shall beat their swords into plowshares, and their spears into pruning hooks; nation shall not lift up sword against nation, neither shall they learn war any more." (Isa. 2:4 and Mic. 4:3). In the midst of the Israeli-Palestinian conflict, Jewish scholars have reached into their tradition to find resources and strength for justice and peacebuilding. Marc Ellis argues that a distinctive gift of Jewish culture to the world is the prophetic tradition. For years, Jews of Conscience and Ellis have argued that the Jewish prophetic tradition demands Jews to live in solidarity with the oppressed. Yet, to justify the dispossession of Palestinians, Zionists have drawn upon the notion that God made a covenant with the Jewish people and gave them the promised land. For Ellis, the covenant with Jewish people does not mean privilege but a special calling and responsibility to live out and embody the prophetic tradition. He writes, "Chosenness is a religious marker for Jews; it cannot be used to justify a political program."[32] Seen from this perspective, the occupation and oppression of Palestinians does not fulfill God's promise but inflicts suffering and endangers peace in the Middle East. Ellis argues that the painful memory of the Holocaust and the long suffering of Jewish people should never be used as justification for the occupation and dispossession of Palestinians.

In addition to Ellis, Jewish scholar Regina Schwartz tackles religion and violence head on by offering a provocative interpretation of Hebrew Scriptures. She begins her book *The Curse of Cain: The Violent Legacy of Monotheism* with the question, "What about the Canaanites?"[33] Schwartz argues that the exclusive principle of one God, one nation, and one land has caused much violence and bloodshed. For her, monotheism provides a religiously sanctioned worldview in which violence of "us" against "them" is legitimated. She warns against reading the Exodus story, so central to Jewish identity formation, as invariably linked with conquest and dispossession of land. Instead of reading Scripture with what she calls a scarcity principle, she points to the principle of plentitude, which includes hospitality to strangers and aliens. She envisions "an alternative Bible that subverts the dominant vision of violence and scarcity with an ideal of plenitude and its corollary ethical imperative of generosity."[34] Schwartz hopes that more inclusive and fluid identities, respect for multiplicity and difference, and plenitude and generosity based on divine plurality will open new opportunities for struggling against violence.

Another Jewish scholar, Marc Gopin, has written on Judaism and peacebuilding and has been involved in training people in conflict resolution in Israel-Palestine, Ireland, India, and other places. Gopin argues that "the deadliest combinations in the history of religion are modern and highly politicized ethnonationalist aspirations that merge in new ways with old traditions, rituals, and meaning systems."[35] For example, *jihad* has been completely redefined and combined with modern methods of terror, and the old Jewish attachments to the land of Israel and the accompanying commandments have been reworked to justify oppression of local populations. Therefore, Gopin argues that it is important to draw from rabbinic literature and ritualistic resources to change worldviews and create new narratives and experiences. He offers many examples from Jewish literature for conflict resolution and taps into Jewish symbolic resources and rituals for peacebuilding, such as helping each group to mourn its losses, joint fasting on religious festivals such as during the Ramadan, chanting Shalom and Sala'am simultaneously on Fridays, and memorials at the site of wars, mass graves, and past horrors.[36]

Christianity has had an ambivalent and checkered relationship with violence, war, and conflict in its history. In the Gospels, Jesus confronts the power of the Roman Empire and the religious elites of his time. He proclaims the coming of the Kingdom of God as a counter-narrative to the imperial rule of Caesar. Instead of glorifying military might and the fanfare of war and violence, Jesus says, "Blessed are the peacemakers, for they shall be called sons of God" (Matt. 5:9). He was tortured and died a political prisoner on the cross, an instrument to instill suffering and fear for anyone who dared challenge imperial rule.

But, after the conversion of Constantine, a kind of Constantinian Christianity developed and became closely allied with the powerful elites and Empire. Just war theory was developed and institutionalized during the time of the Crusades, justifying warfare and providing spiritual rewards for those who fought against Muslims. In later centuries, Christian doctrines and beliefs have been misused and misappropriated to justify the conquest of the Americas, slavery, and the colonization of the majority of the world's land and population. Today, the Christian Right has propagated a muscular Christianity and supported policies that reinforce white hegemony, xenophobia, and anti-immigrant sentiment.

One source of hope is the increasing awareness among progressive Christians of the need to dislodge the Christian tradition from its colonial and imperial syndrome and practices and to recover the rich traditions of peace and reconciliation. A postcolonial approach is helpful in this process, for the pursuit of peace requires nothing less than a collective *metanoia* (repentance) of complicity in supporting unjust systems, state violence, and remaining silent when injustice occurs. It also requires a spirituality of generosity and a radical commitment to nonviolent action. Facing police brutality and white retaliation in the Civil Rights Movement, Martin Luther King Jr. courageously said, "our aim is not to defeat the white community, not to humiliate the white community, but to win the friendship of all of the persons who had perpetrated this system in the past. The end of violence or the aftermath of violence is bitterness. The aftermath of nonviolence is reconciliation and the creation of a beloved community."[37] King's vision of a beloved community is even more relevant in today's fragmented and broken world.

King's nonviolent approach has influenced Palestinian theologian Naim Stifan Ateek. In *A Palestinian Cry for Reconciliation*, Ateek pleads for the use of nonviolence in conflict resolution. He recalls that Jesus was immersed in the political situation of his time but that he rejected the revolutionaries' strategies because he was keenly aware of the power of the Roman Empire and did not think that it would be toppled by armed revolutionaries. He told his disciples if people force them to go one mile, also go the second mile (Matt. 5:41) because he believed that evil can be resisted without violence. Violence only brings misery and disaster. For Ateek, there cannot be peace without justice. The prophet Micah exhorts us to do justice, to love mercy, and to walk humbly before God (Mic. 6:8). Yet many prefer to be "involved in acts of mercy, but they hold back from the direct work of doing justice. They love justice from afar. However, the prophetic formula is clear: we must do justice."[38] In the Israeli-Palestinian conflict, Ateek says that justice requires the admission of the government of Israel of injustice done to the Palestinians in the confiscation of Palestinian land, the violation of human rights, and its system of oppression. Accepting responsibility, repentance, and restoration can lead to forgiveness and reconciliation. Ateek draws from the New Testament, especially Pauline writings, to develop his idea of revolutionary forgiveness as grace, a free gift. Paul has said we forgive each other because God has forgiven us (Col. 3:13). Ateek thinks that this is revolutionary and the essence of the gospel because it is not earned or achieved. As all is from God and we are reconciled to God through Christ, we are given the ministry of reconciliation (2 Cor. 5:18–19), for God's abiding and unceasing love is for all.[39]

The commitment to peace and interreligious solidarity requires us to reclaim traditions of peace, create new symbolic universes, and tell new stories. This will require us to speak of divine power in radically new ways, for Christian images of God are commonly shaped by dominant images of power and might. In the past, God was often envisioned as a heavenly patriarch or monarch. Divine power, understood as hierarchical, patriarchal, and one-sided, has been used to reinforce the powers and principalities on earth. The pursuit of peace requires us to see divine power in relations, in the interstices, in the spaces between us. A postcolonial approach emphasizes that the aim in interreligious dialogue and engagement is to build relations and avoid drawing a hard and fast line between "us" and "them," or between "Christians" and "non-Christians." The issue at hand is not whether people profess belief in God or not: the question is what kind of ultimate reality and what kind of power people affirm. Those who affirm power as a top-down process and those who see God or ultimate reality upholding that power are closer to each other, regardless of whether they are Christian or not, than those who affirm alternative forms of power that move from the bottom up.

GLOBAL AND LOCAL PEACE EFFORTS

Over the past decades, governmental and nongovernmental agencies, journalists, diplomats, and funding bodies have increasingly paid attention to the contribution of religious actors, organizations, and networks in peacekeeping. At an ecumenical and transnational level, the International Committee for Peace Council and the World Conference on Religion and Peace have held summits for religious leaders to discuss interreligious cooperation and share strategies for conflict resolution and transformation. Other networks active in religious peacebuilding include the Gulen movement, Buddhist Peace Fellowship, Christian Peacemaker Team, and various Mennonite networks. Some peacebuilding efforts by religious actors and bodies have produced tangible results, including the mediation by the Catholic lay group Sant'Egidio to end the civil war in Mozambique; the participation of religious leaders, such as Archbishop Desmond Tutu, in South Africa's Truth and Reconciliation efforts; and the intervention of Muslim and Christian leaders in Nigeria to mitigate Christian-Muslim violence.

Local religious leaders and communities have expressed communal and radical solidarity in what Miguel De La Torre calls *acompañamiento*, which means accompanying the oppressed and walking alongside the least. He cites the example of hundreds of Egyptian Muslims, who during a time of religious strife in 2011, showed up for Coptic Christmas Eve mass and offered their bodies as human shields, so that the Coptic Christians who were fearful for their security could worship in peace.[40] A more recent example of *acompañamiento* was the solidarity shown by Pittsburgh's Muslim community in 2018 after a hideous attack during sabbath services at the Tree of Life Synagogue that took eleven lives. The local Muslim community raised funds to pay for the funeral services of the victims and offered to stand guard at the doors of local synagogues, if needed, and accompany the Jews if they felt unsafe running daily errands. Five months later, when mosques in Christchurch, New Zealand, were attacked by a gunman that killed fifty-one people and injured forty, it was Tree of Life Synagogue's turn to reach out to offer support for the Islamic community in Christchurch.[41]

The religious peacebuilding field has tended to focus on the work of male academics, educated elites, and prominent religious leaders. As I have already discussed previously, Gayatri Chakravorty Spivak asked this question more than thirty years ago, "Can the subaltern speak?"[42] Her question raised issues concerning the politics of representation and the importance of creating infrastructures so that subaltern voices, such as those of tribal women and migrants, could be heard and understood. In the study of religion and peacebuilding, it is crucial to pay attention to subaltern religious consciousness and grassroots efforts in promoting peace.

Women's participation in peacebuilding also needs to be highlighted. The book *Women, Religion, and Peacebuilding* discusses the obstacles and opportunities women religious peacebuilders face because patriarchal practices have often prevented them from assuming authority in religious organizations and leadership in peace efforts. Some women seek to work through religious institutions or find other spaces to promote peace and exert their influence. The book includes case studies of women peacebuilders and discusses how their faith has motivated their work, their relationship with religious institutions, their accomplishments, and the challenges they face.[43] Jewish women in Israel have formed the Women in Black movement and organized silent vigils on Fridays in key sites in different cities while dressing in black to protest the occupation and the brutality of the Israeli military. The movement has spread to other countries protesting the culture of war and violence against women. In the Global South, some of the women peacebuilders include the late Dekha Ibrahim Abdi of Kenya, a devout Muslim, who served as a trustee of Coalition for Peace in Africa and received several international awards for her peacebuilding efforts.[44] Buddhist nun Mae Chee Sansanee from Thailand led a peace walk and reached out to Muslim women when conflicts broke out between Buddhists and Muslims in southern Thailand. As the co-chair for the Global Peace Initiative of Women, she has traveled extensively across the globe promoting international peace and cultural understanding.[45] Catholic sister Marie-Bernard Alima of Congo formed a network called the Coordination of Women for Democracy and Peace to educate and train women to provide leadership in human rights, political movements, and efforts to prevent sexual and gender-based violence.[46]

Christian ethicist Wonchul Shin has done research on women's interfaith efforts in peacebuilding and seeking restorative justice during the civil wars in Liberia. During the second civil war there from 1999 to 2003, about 250,000 people were killed and more than a half million out of a total population of 3.3 million were driven into exile. In this tragic situation of bloodshed, loss of lives, and suffering, women's groups consisting of both Muslims and Christians organized themselves for peace in a torn country. One such group was the Women in Peace Building Network, which organized the Liberian Mass Action for Peace. The group put an emphasis on grassroots women: market women, displaced women from camps, and other marginalized women. It organized protests, sang, prayed, shouted, and pressured the government to enter peace talks with rebellious factions. After peace negotiations, these women participated in the process of disarmament, demilitarization, and reintegration, and played critical roles especially in helping the child soldiers. They continued to serve as mediators in their homes and communities. According to Shin, these women actively pursued restorative justice, through enabling "victims, offenders, and communities to work together for achieving the ultimate goal of restoration, specifically restoring humanity of all parties."[47]

One of the tragedies of war and violence is that children and young people are being recruited as soldiers and perpetrators of violence. Therefore, the participation of young people in peacebuilding is important, since terrorist groups often target and recruit disenfranchised young people, in poor countries and in the West, to carry out violent actions. These young people often feel alienation and anger because of their lack of education, employment, and opportunities. The affiliation with a terrorist group offers these youth new identities and a sense of belonging. Therefore, peace efforts among youth must address structural issues such as education, jobs, economic inequity, and violence. Interreligious dialogue among youth can promote mutual understanding and commitment to building relationships and finding solutions together.

We will need a new imagination for our collective social life in order to have sustained peace. By challenging old religious scripts and reclaiming subaltern voices, postcolonial theology can contribute to this new imagination. Pope Francis often asks us to pray and work for peace and remember the plight of refugees and migrants. He encourages peace talks between Israelis and Palestinians and urges an end to the bloodshed in Iraq and Syria. On the World Day of Peace in 2017, the Pope said, "When victims of violence are able to resist the temptation to retaliate, they become the most credible promoters of nonviolent peacemaking."[48] Some thirty years ago, I first met the Quaker peace activist Jean Zaru who lived in Ramallah in Palestine. She shared with me the tensions and hardships of living in an occupied territory. Today, thirty years later, she is still working and praying for peace. It has not been easy. Sometimes she wondered, "How can I have peace within when others call my people terrorists and justify our oppression by quoting the Bible?"[49] How can she teach pacifism to her children and students when they have all been victims of violence? At times like this, she turns to her faith and spirituality. She says, "I have managed to find peace from within—without having to embrace with approval the violence around me. Love one's enemies forces me to recognize that my enemy, too, is a child of God. It is really only in the light of love that I am liberated to work for peace and freedom."[50] She reaches out to Jews and Muslims devoted to peacebuilding in the Middle East. Her example motivates and challenges us to never lose hope and to reach across barriers to work for justice and peace.

Chapter 11

Christian Mission
and Planetary Politics

*An Earth-centric framing for planetary solidarity is a different pathway of
perceiving, interpreting, and living. It could provide an alternative theological framing.*

Heather Eaton[1]

A nineteen-year-old American man visited Ceylon (present-day Sri Lanka) and
encountered something of interest to him. He recalled years later:

> It was 1926, and I was in Ceylon. British colonial officials were making new
> roads in the jungles so that the crop of the great tea plantations could go to
> market more efficiently. In the red cuts slashed through the dark green vegeta-
> tion I saw cones of earth left standing and asked what they were for. "Those are
> the snakes' nests," I was told. They were spared not because the workmen were
> afraid of snakes . . . but because of a feeling by the workers that the snake had
> a right to its house as long as it wanted to stay there. Ceylon's is a Hinayana
> Buddhist culture believing in metempsychosis, and any given snake may well
> be one's late great uncle. With all the noise and activity of road building, the
> snake would soon decide to move to a more desirable neighborhood. After that
> the cone of earth would be removed. There was no particular hurry, and the
> officials let the diggers handle the digging in their own way.
> Many of the officials seemed to be Scots, and it occurred to me that if
> the men with the shovels in their hands likewise had been Presbyterians the
> snakes would have fared less well.[2]

This story is fascinating because it took place in a colonial setting, where
the young man had his consciousness raised after meeting Buddhist workmen,

185

whose views about human beings, animals, and nature were very different from his own. Some forty years later, in 1967, this man, Lynn White Jr., would write his watershed essay, which unleashed debates on religion and the environment. His essay, "The Historical Roots of Our Ecological Crisis," published in *Science*, has been widely discussed and has stimulated the study of environmental history and ecological theology.[3] His essay argues that the modern ecological crisis grew out of Western technological and scientific advances made since the medieval period. These advances have occurred in a social and cultural context informed by the Western Christian tradition. After comparing the Western tradition with Asian and indigenous traditions, he asserts that Western Christianity is "the most anthropocentric religion the world has seen."[4] Such a religion gives humans license to exploit nature, for within Western Christian theology, "nature has no reason for existence save to serve [humans]."[5] Therefore, White argues, Western Christianity bears the burden of guilt for our environmental crisis. His article has prompted debates, rebuttals, and serious reflections on creation and on the relation between God, human beings, and the earth among biblical scholars and theologians.[6]

Lynn White Jr.'s story clearly demonstrates that colonialism impacts not only human society, but also the physical environment. British officials slashed through thick green vegetation to build roads so that tea companies could bring Ceylon tea to town, and, eventually, to market in England. The East India Company was the first to experiment with growing tea in Ceylon. Since the 1860s, tea plantations, mostly owned by the British, were established in the colony. Tea production increased dramatically in the 1880s, and the area under cultivation grew to 400,000 acres by 1899. Ceylon's natural environment provided ideal climatic conditions for producing fine blends and flavors of tea, which netted high prices at London tea auctions. Tea exports became a very profitable business and the mainstay of the colonial economy.[7] The growth of Ceylon tea transformed the local economy and natural habitat to produce cash crops catering to middle-class consumers in richer countries. While tea plantation workers, mostly female, earned meager money, tea companies reaped exponential funds from their cheap labor. Colonial structures allowed the exploitation of land and labor for corporate profits without much say from local inhabitants. Given globalization and the neoliberal market, capitalist greed today reaches to the farthest corners of the world, resulting in deforestation, pollution, water shortages, global warming, and other environmental challenges.

At the United Nations Climate Summit in 2014, President Barack Obama declared that the "urgent and growing threat of climate change" will "define the contours of this century more dramatically than any other" issue.[8] He was clearly right because the decade 2010–2020 was the warmest decade in human history, with 2020 being the warmest year on record. In several cities in Asia and the Middle East, the temperature reached 130 degree in the summer. The year 2020 also saw a record breaking thirty named storms, with twelve of them making landfall in the U.S. The U.S. spent over $100 billion recovering from natural disasters in 2020 alone.[9] The wildfires in North California that same year burned more than two million acres, destroying homes, claiming lives, and charring woodlands, forests, and vineyards. On some days, smoke from the wildfires were so severe that the skies in San Francisco, Oakland, and other cities turned blood orange, as if from a scene in an apocalyptic movie.[10]

The severe weather occurred simultaneously with the rampage of COVID-19, a once-a-century pandemic that claimed more than 4.8 million lives worldwide by October 2021. John Kerry, the American special envoy for climate, said in an interview, "Climate will augment potential for more pandemics. Climate changes the cycle of nature, and when that cycle changes, certain diseases can spread more easily. So I think the pandemic has woken people up to the fragility of life itself, and the interconnectedness of nations in ways that just underscore we're all in this together."[11] At a critical time when climate change and other environmental crises threaten the survival of life on the planet, how should churches respond, and what should future Christian mission look like? I begin by discussing postcolonial criticism's contribution to environmental studies before moving on to Christian mission in our ecological age.

POSTCOLONIAL STUDIES AND PLANETARY POLITICS

In the past several decades, there has been a burgeoning alliance between postcolonial and environmental studies. Scholars have coined the term "green postcolonialism" and a subfield, "postcolonial ecocriticism," has gradually developed. Pablo Mukherjee discusses the connections between the two fields:

> Surely, any field purporting to theorise the global conditions of colonialism and imperialism (let us call it postcolonial studies) cannot but consider the complex interplay of environmental categories such as water, land, energy, habitat, migration with political or cultural categories such as state, society, conflict, literature, theatre, visual arts. Equally, any field purporting to attach interpretative importance to environment (let us call it eco/environmental studies) must be able to trace the social, historical and material co-ordinates of categories such as forests, rivers, bio-regions and species.[12]

Postcolonial ecocritics are interested in how colonialism and imperialism have affected environmental practices in colonizing and colonized societies both past and present. They follow the lead of environmental historian Alfred Crosby, who has coined the term "ecological imperialism."[13] For Crosby, colonization is both a historical and biological process, since colonizers brought permanent changes to the flora, fauna, and natural habitats of the New World, and elsewhere. Ecological imperialism refers to the dispossession of indigenous lands and the spread of germs and diseases that lead to the genocide of indigenous populations. It also included ill-conceived introductions of foreign livestock and plants, as well as European agricultural practices for profit-making. The results have been the biological expansion of Europe, the displacement of native populations, and European control of the most important agricultural lands in the world.

Another form of ecological imperialism goes by the name "biocolonization," which includes the privatization of the necessities of life, such as water, and the patent and control of life forms. Corporations compete to monopolize seeds, plants, and other life forms through patents, licenses, genetic engineering, and other biotechnological methods. Biopiracy occurs when researchers and companies take biological resources or use indigenous knowledge, without official sanction, for their own gain. For example, French researchers have conducted interviews in French Guiana about local antimalarial remedies and learned about the plant *Quassia amara,* which can fight malaria. Later, they patented a new compound from the plant based on knowledge gained from locals. As climate change threatens, many agribusinesses and scientists have begun to patent heat-resistant and drought-resistant genes from plants for future crops.[14]

A third form of ecological imperialism is environmental racism, which takes many guises.[15] In a poignant essay "Whose Earth Is It, Anyway?" Black theologian James Cone points out, "The logic that led to slavery and segregation in the Americas, colonization and apartheid in Africa, and the rule of white supremacy throughout the world is the same one that leads to the exploitation of animals and the ravaging of nature."[16] Examples of environmental racism include the dumping of toxic waste landfills in Black communities and the concentration of hazardous waste facilities in Black and Hispanic communities. In the South Pacific, the U.S., Britain, and France conducted nuclear testing programs in the second half of the twentieth century, which threatened the livelihood and environment of Pacific Islanders. Although these nuclear tests have stopped, the health and environmental impacts live on, with some islands still unsafe for human habitation.

Given the history of ecological imperialism, postcolonial politics cannot separate social history from environmental history and must situate humans in the wider schema of the planetary. Gayatri Chakravorty Spivak distinguishes between the global and the planet: "The globe is on our computer: No one lives there. It allows us to think that we can aim to control it. The planet is in the species of alterity, belonging to another system; and yet we inhabit it, on loan."[17] She develops the concept of "planetarity" in response to global neocolonialism, such as the domination of global economics by the International Monetary Fund and the World Bank. Since current imperial designs do not follow national and geographical boundaries, a new imaginary is necessary to nurture resistance. Whereas the globe is created by human institutions and technology, the planet signifies an alterity that is beyond us that we cannot control. As I have noted elsewhere, the concept of "planetarity" allows Spivak to "move beyond the discourses of the nation, gender, class, culture, and colonialism to edge toward species talk. . . . She invites us to imagine the complexity and pluralization of planetary systems, and not be confined by narrow identity politics or superficial binary thinking."[18]

Planetary politics requires us to gesture toward this alterity through a capacious intuition of space and time. The term *politics* comes from the Greek word *polis*, which means a city-state. Today, we must expand our references beyond the city, nation, earth, and solar system to include the vast cosmos with its numerous galaxies, planets, exoplanets, and stars. Since I grew up in Chinese culture, I have always admired the cosmological awareness shown in traditional Chinese landscape paintings. Many Chinese artists have been influenced by Daoist philosophy, which stresses that human beings are but tiny specks within the great cosmos. I also find Glynn Gorick's artwork insightful in cultivating our planetary consciousness and stretching our imagination. Gorick is known for his depiction of the complexity of ecosystems in his art through variations in scale. In his piece titled "Earth-centered World," he portrays the image of the universe through layers of concentric circles. At the center is the dark space inside of an atom and a lattice of silicon atoms forming quartz.

> Outside this flows the water cycle that erodes rock and sustains plant life gaining a foothold in the barren landscape. Earth is surrounded by the Milky Way galaxy containing the sun and its planetary system. This is framed by other galaxies of varying structures and histories stretching out to those at the four corners whose light, emitted billions of years ago, is now just visible to us through powerful telescopes.[19]

Gorick's artwork reminds us that if we were to understand spatial relationships in planetary scales, we must modify the timescales as well ("billions of years ago!"). Using evocative language, Catherine Keller describes the different timescales that coexist: "[The earth] pulses with the polyrhythmic temporalities of a planet embedded in a cosmos itself multiple and vibrant beyond our imagining."[20] But it is precisely because of the difficulty in grasping different timescales simultaneously that makes climate change such a mind-boggling issue to tackle, notes historian Dipesh Chakrabarty. He points out that we are at the conjuncture of three different histories "whose events are defined by very different timescales: the history of the planet, the history of life on the planet, and the history of the globe made by the logics of empires, capital, and technology."[21] He says that the problem is that the million-year timescale of the planet's carbon cycle may not be relevant for policy makers who think in terms of years, decades, and at most centuries, and politicians in democratic societies in terms of election cycles.[22] Though we might be able to draw from human experiences to tackle problems we face in a familiar scale of time, we are much less prepared to come to grips with the vastness of non- or inhuman scale, such as the carbon cycle. Our social institutions and international agencies and protocols are being tested to the limits to meet with planetary crises in a scale incomprehensible to most people without training on the subject.

Scientists have proposed to use the term Anthropocene to designate our epoch in which human activities have had significant impacts on the earth's climate and ecosystems. Although scientists debate when this epoch began—some trace this to the beginning of the industrial revolution, while others date it much earlier—many people have become aware of the detrimental effects human beings have brought to our planet. We spew each year "more than 100 times as much CO_2 into the air as volcanoes do, and we're currently overseeing the biggest disruption to the planet's nitrogen cycle in 2.5 billion years."[23] As a response, theologians and church leaders have issued clarion calls for Christian communities to respond to climate change and other ecological crises and push back against our colonialist and imperialist attitudes toward the planet. In his encyclical *Laudato Si'*, Pope Francis builds on twenty-five years of papal attention to ecology and climate change as moral issues. The Pontiff appeals for "a new dialogue about how we are shaping the future of our planet," and says, "We need a conversation which includes everyone, since the environmental challenge we are undergoing, and its human roots, concern and affect us all."[24] He especially calls upon the church to address climate crisis in dialogue with climate scientists who have pointed out the gravity of our present situation. The Ecumenical Patriarch Bartholomew, spiritual leader of the Eastern Orthodox Church and popularly known as the "green patriarch," has often spoken about environmental degradation as a crime against the natural world and about the spiritual roots of environmental problems. He invited Christians to "accept the world as a sacrament of communion, as a way of sharing with God and our neighbours on a global scale. It is our humble conviction that the divine and the human meet in the slightest detail in the seamless garment of God's creation, in the last speck of dust of our planet."[25] In June 2015, the Patriarch and Archbishop of Canterbury Justin Welby jointly wrote, "our response to climate change—both in terms of mitigation and adaptation—will reduce human suffering, while preserving the diversity and beauty of God's creation for our children."[26]

CHRISTIAN MISSION IN THE ANTHROPOCENE

The relationship between Christian mission and the natural environment has been complex and has changed over time, depending on our knowledge about nature and political situations. The modern Christian missionary movement has been criticized as colluding with colonialism and therefore being complicit with the usurping of land and resources and the exploitation of people.[27] But as Dana Robert has pointed out, some missionaries have also helped to observe, classify, and preserve species, introduced crop rotation and reforestation projects, led famine relief, and protected the land rights of indigenous peoples against European colonists.[28] As we think about mission practices in the Anthropocene era, we need to avoid past mistakes and shortcomings. Kapya John Kaoma, a Zambian theologian and human rights activist, notes that Christian mission has often been conceived of as spiritual transformation of individuals and new inter-human relations based on salvation brought by Jesus Christ. As such, Christian mission has been preoccupied with God's interaction with humanity. Concern for the environment has been rendered secondary or absent. Yet environmental crises challenge us to see God's missionary purpose as integrated with environmental concerns and responsibilities. He reminds us that "the God who acts in Jesus Christ to bring salvation is the same triune God who is the creator of the heavens and the earth."[29] This means that we need to radically expand our understanding of Christian mission—from an anthropocentric to a cosmological focus.

The modern missionary movement has been influenced by Enlightenment ideas of progress and assumed the superiority of Western ideals, values, education, and customs. It treated non-Western and indigenous peoples as objects of its "civilizing mission" and contributed to the destruction or suppression of deep reservoirs of wisdom of living in harmony with nature. As George E. Tinker, a member of the Native American Osage nation in the U.S., has documented, the missionary conquest of the Americas attempted to change the attitudes, values, and worldviews of native peoples through cultural genocide.[30] Today, many Native peoples live in poverty and suffer from depression and alcoholism because they are torn from their cultural and spiritual roots, have lost the ability to speak their native language, and feel alienated from the dominant culture. Tinker notes that, while Christianity emphasizes the time dimension, Native cultures attach more importance to space and place. The destruction of native lands and environments affects Native peoples not only physically, but also spiritually and emotionally. A genuine Christian mission to the Native peoples must respect their cultures and support their struggles for land, sovereignty, and social and cultural empowerment.

Christian mission also introduced what Catherine Keller has called a "theologically sanctioned anthropic exceptionalism"[31] that is quite foreign to Asian and indigenous traditions. In *Political Theology of the Earth*, Keller engages Carl Schmitt's political theory, especially his notion of sovereignty as having the power to decide on the exception.[32] She charges that Christianity often teaches that human beings are superior and distinct from all creation. Anthropocentrism sets humans as exception to all other species. The proof text for such a claim is Genesis 1:26, which says that human beings are created in the image of God and that they have dominion over all creatures. The idea of "dominion" has given license for human beings to plunder the earth, drive species to extinction, and poison entire ecosystems, to our own detriment. Keller offers a counternarrative to interpret this problematic verse. She argues that we should read the Genesis story with a postcolonial lens, for the text was written when the Hebrew people were in exile under Babylonian imperial sovereignty. In contrast to the Babylonian *Enuma Elish*, which mentions that humans are created as slaves to God, the Genesis account says all humans, without exception, reflect God's divinity on earth. Genesis says that both male and female share *imago Dei*, in contrast to the demonizing of the goddess Tiamat in the Babylonian story. Furthermore, in the Genesis account, the earth and water are not passive, for they participate in the creative process ("Let the earth bring forth," etc.). Both humans and animals are to share the same foods, which are plants, fruits, and seeds (Gen. 1:29–30).[33] Keller surmises that "the biblical narratives inaugurate no zero-sum game of Man versus Earth."[34]

Like Keller, many eco-conscious Christians are aware that an anthropocentric, hierarchical, and patriarchal religious system is part of the problem and not part of the solution. In much of traditional theology, the relation between God and human beings and creation is imagined in a hierarchical way with an emphasis on divine sovereignty. Human beings share God's image and therefore have sovereignty over the rest of creation. The image that best describes such a relation is a triangle. Such an understanding of God and creation needs to go through a recycling process so that it can be reused and reappropriated for the age of Anthropocene. A hierarchical model establishes a dualistic worldview separating mind from body, male from female, and humans from the non-human world. The worth of an individual or a natural object depends on one's position in the hierarchy instead of one's intrinsic value and worth.

An ecological model with postcolonial sensitivity does not project God above everything else. God, human beings, and creation are interdependent and interrelated, just like the three interconnected arrows of the sign for recycling. Instead of placing human beings at the center of the universe, many mystics have spoken of the integrated universe and God's love for what God has created. Hildegard of Bingen, in the twelfth century, spoke of the world as the "cosmic egg," and she was famous for describing the greening power (*viriditas*) in all life. In her *Book of Divine Works*, she says: "I awaken everything to life. The air lives by turning green and being in bloom. The waters flow as if they were alive. The sun lives in its light, and the moon is enkindled, after its disappearance, once again by the light of the sun so that the moon is again revived. The stars, too, give a clear light with their beaming."[35] In our own time, Thomas Berry also speaks of the close relationship between human beings and the environment: "There is no such thing as 'human community' without the earth and the soil, and the air and the water and all living forms. Without these humans do not exist. There is, therefore, no separate human community. Humans are woven into this larger community. The larger community is the sacred community."[36]

Western anthropocentrism thinks of God in terms of images of human beings: God as king, father, judge, warrior, etc. God is the Lord of history, intervening in human events. Much of the classic Latin American liberation theology portrays God as active and exercising control over history. In contrast, Asian and indigenous peoples who are tied to the soil imagine the divine, the Dao, or the great spirit as living, embracing, but nonintrusive. They speak of the earth with respect and reverence as the mother who is sustaining and life-affirming. A shift from anthropocentrism to biocentrism necessitates a change in our way of thinking about God and the *missio Dei*. A postcolonial approach does not think that humans should colonize other species and opens us to new publics—the billions of species that have claims on us—in thinking about our responsibilities toward God's magnificent creation.

A NEW CLIMATE FOR CHRISTIAN MISSION

Laudato Si' elicited much discussion in the Catholic Church, Protestant Christian communities, and also the wider public. The Encyclical includes concrete actions such as the development of a new lifestyle to curb consumerism, environmental education aimed at creating an "ecological citizenship," a Christian spirituality of humility and gratuity, and civic and political actions to promote the common good and defend the environment. Many Catholics have responded to the Pope's call for "ecological conversion" and have been involved in local and global efforts to respond to our current crisis. In the U.S., some Catholic churches have turned to use solar energy, and hundreds of parishes have formed Creation Care Teams to work together to reduce local waste and energy consumption. Many parishes, schools, and agencies organized educational events in celebration of the Feast of St. Francis and Earth Day.[37]

In Protestant circles, in Edinburgh in 2010, a gathering to commemorate the centenary of the 1910 World Missionary Conference highlighted concern for the environment and our responsibilities as humans. Whereas Edinburgh 1910 was motivated by evangelizing zeal for converting "heathens," the mood a hundred years later was far less paternalistic and triumphant. Daryl Balia and Kirsteen Kim note that there was "a deepening awareness of processes of globalization, of the fragility of the earth which we share, and of the interpenetration of religions and cultures as populations grow and move."[38] The study process set up prior to the conference included "Ecological Perspectives on Mission" as one of the seven important transversal topics. Edinburgh 2010 issued a document known as the "Common Call," which concludes with "we invite all to join with us as we participate in God's transforming and reconciling mission of love to the whole creation."[39] In this new climate of Christian mission, I discuss several areas for further conversation and action in the Christian community. I want to show that the values that postcolonial theology espouses, such as humility, mutuality, hospitality, and care for the environment and planetary community, will be important in reorientating the church toward actions that are justice seeking and spiritually grounded.

From Soul Care to Earth Care

From a narrow focus on salvation of human beings, we must extend our care and concern to the whole earth community. Christian mission that focuses on salvation of the soul is individualistic, disembodied, and serves the status quo, and it will not be able to meet ecological challenges on a planetary scale. Care for creation requires Christians to develop planetary consciousness and solidarity.

Ecofeminist theologian Heather Eaton argues that attention to our embedded-ness in the planetary processes, the evolution of the origins of life, our kinship with other animals, and our dependence on innumerable organisms for basic survival expands our customary reference points.[40] Human beings are not at the apex of creation, and quite to the contrary, evolution points to planetary processes that do not involve us. Eaton writes, "*Planetary* cannot mean simply international, worldwide, new cosmopolitanism, or global citizens. . . . To take seriously *planetary* is to integrate an evolutionary framework, to be ecologically literate, to see humans as one species among many, and to appreciate the other life forms in the Earth community."[41]

Planetary consciousness challenges us to think about the gospel with differ-ent scales of space and time. Influenced by Greek philosophy, Christianity has focused on the ascent of the soul from the physicality of this world and on the promise of eternal life, which overcomes mortality and finitude. This Christian narrative was based on a worldview and knowledge about nature available at the time. In our Anthropocene era, we need to retell the Christian story based on what we know about the planetary processes and human beings' roles in it. One of the key notions the global community has come up with to address the eco-logical challenges is *sustainability*. In the latter part of the twentieth century, the United Nations and many organizations promoted sustainable development, and many people have placed their hope in a kind of "techno-messianism"[42] and green capitalism. They do not want to shake up existing power dynamics of the world but only wish to make change around the edges. But Chakrabarty con-tends that sustainability still reflects anthropocentrism, because it foregrounds human activities vis-à-vis the environment, while relegating earthly processes to a mute background. To counterpose sustainability in global thinking, Chakrab-arty suggests *habitability*: "Habitability does not reference humans. Its central concern is life—complex, multicellular life, in general—and what makes *that*, not humans alone, sustainable."[43] He differentiates the problem of habitability from the concerns of biopolitics, a term popularized by Foucault. Biopolitics as it has been used connects life to the questions of state, capitalism, disciplin-ary power, and so forth. Chakrabarty writes, "The question at the center of the habitability problem is *not* what life is or how it is managed in the interest of power but rather what makes a planet friendly to the continuous existence of complex life."[44]

Theologians interested in ecology, the evolutionary process, and planetary consciousness have come up with different approaches to retell the Christian story. In *Sacred Gaia*, Irish theologian Anne Primavesi engages James Lovelock's Gaia theory and takes evolutionary theory seriously. She presents a theology based on the coevolutionary process of humans and the natural environment and uses this framework to reinterpret God, Jesus, life, and grace.[45] Brazilian theologian Ivone Gabara waxes poetic in reimaging the doctrine of trinity as the symbolic expression of interrelatedness, reciprocity, and communion of all life in a continuous and dynamic process of creativity. She says in the cosmos, trinity manifests as the multiplicity and complexity of the stars and galaxies. On earth, it is shown in the unfolding processes of creation and the interrelatedness of all things. In human relationships, trinity manifests in the mystery of the egalitarian I-Thou relationship. In every person, trinity can be seen in the multiplicity of the person, who is part of the evolutionary process, and part of the earth and the cosmos.[46]

Planetary habitability requires us to shift our thinking of salvation from anthropocentric to earth-centric terms. Instead of salvation of the soul through the redemption of Christ, we need to emphasize the Pauline depiction of salvation of the whole cosmos. Feminist theologian Carter Heyward writes, "The spiritual trivialization of creatures and creation is steeped in the long-standing Christian assumption that only human beings have souls—intrinsic spiritual value, a 'meeting place' with the divine, a dimension of creaturely being that seeks and can receive salvation."[47] In other words, we can no longer think of humans as "God Species,"[48] with we alone sharing special divine image and glory. As Paul says in Romans, salvation of the children of God cannot be separated from salvation of creation. The whole creation has been groaning in labor pains and longs for its freedom from bondage and for redemption (8:19–23).

As a part of creation, salvation will be utterly impossible without planetary solidarity. Knowledge gleaned from the earth sciences humbles us, for we can never fully know the intricacies of the immensely vast and complex planetary processes. Care for the earth does not mean control or management but signifies an acknowledgment that our collective human activities have caused harm to the environment. Postcolonial theology challenges us to reflect on our arrogance and presumption that we are the lords of the universe. With humility and new awareness, we have to commit to becoming ecologically literate and living and acting as one of the species in the whole planetary system. As Eaton writes, planetary solidarity "has to be more than a global solidarity of human communities, with a perfunctory mention of 'the environment.' It must be a form of solidarity wherein human communities are intimately intertwined with one another, within larger communities of life, and within the natural systems of the planet."[49]

Ecojustice and Christian Mission

The disruption and breaking down of planetary cycles, global warming, rising sea levels, and the loss of biodiversity demonstrate that we cannot continue to appeal to human rights, property rights, and social justice in the usual sense, without considering the environment. Ecojustice demands that we include the natural environment in our ethical and moral reflection of justice and consider the inherent value of other living things, whenever human actions impact them. Our current way of life is not sustainable—the U.S., with only 5 percent of the world's population, consumes nearly 30 percent of the world's resources. Yet more than 2.5 billion people live on less than two U.S. dollars a day. Many churches in the U.S. have responded by urging their parishioners to adopt a simpler lifestyle by recycling, reducing energy consumption and their carbon footprints, insulating their homes, creating community gardens, growing vegetables, and eating local foods. Different denominations have ecological networks and programs on earth care and environmental advocacy. For example, the United Church of Christ congregations have pledged to consume less energy, take part in an annual "Lenten Carbon Fast," and push local and national politicians to address climate change.[50] The Interfaith Power and Light project is a national initiative that aims to reduce greenhouse emissions to address global warming. The project encourages participating churches and faith communities to buy electricity from nonpolluting, renewable sources and to create emission-free churches and houses of worship and energy-conscious parishioners who will practice energy efficiency in their homes.[51]

While it is important for denominations and churches to reduce their carbon footprint and to educate their parishioners on consuming less energy, it is also important for Christian mission to address economic justice and the macroeconomic systems that privilege the rich and create an inhospitable environment for all. Many of our current global economic structures and systems have been formed as continuations of colonial appropriation of resources and dispossession, though expressed in other forms. The global protests that started from Tunisia, Egypt, Algeria, Yemen, and Jordan in 2011 had much to do with rising food prices resulting from water shortages and climate change in the region, as well as unjust social and economic policies.[52] The Occupy Movement that began in the fall of 2011 was part of worldwide protests against corporate greed, economic injustice, food insecurity, and political disenfranchisement. The dichotomy between the 1 percent and the 99 percent has widened, and economic inequality increased in 2020 amid a coronavirus pandemic, which disproportionately affected low-wage workers and racial and ethnic minorities in the U.S. In 2020, while many suffered from economic insecurity and food scarcity because of the shutdown, several global billionaires saw their wealth skyrocket at an unprecedented rate. The top 1 percent of U.S. households held fifteen times more wealth ($34.2 trillion) than the bottom 50 percent combined ($2.1 trillion).[53] Even though churches may be involved in feeding the homeless and providing temporary relief for needy families, the question of class is seldom discussed for fear of inciting "class conflict" or "class warfare." For churches to be prophetic, they must address structural issues of late capitalism and the culture of poverty.

Economic globalization and drive for profits have wreaked havoc on the world's ecosystems and destroyed natural habitats of people, affecting disproportionately women and children. Feminist theologian Gabriele Dietrich, who has lived and worked among women in India for many years, writes that ecology is concerned with "setting ourselves in relationship with one another in the day-to-day survival struggles for water, a piece of land to dwell on, a patch of beach to dry the fish on, the sea as a source of bounty. All this is mediated by women's work, both in the household and in wider production processes."[54] Deforestation, the large-scale building of dams, biotechnology, pollution of land and water, and the patent of seeds have threatened the very livelihood of women living in poverty-stricken communities across the globe. Yet women are not merely victims, as Indian environmental activist Vandana Shiva notes that women in the poor countries in the Global South have participated actively in managing sustenance economy and water resources, trying hard to feed their families and children.[55] Edinburgh 2010 paid attention to women's issues and women's roles in carrying out God's mission. In many societies, women are still excluded in leadership and decision-making processes in their churches and communities. To develop a wholistic understanding of mission and to build livable communities, women's voices and visions must be included. Through contextual Bible studies, education, and conscientization, Christian women must be empowered to take part in the struggle for a transformed community, which embraces equality, reciprocity, interconnectedness, and interdependence. From an ecofeminist perspective, this transformation must include the acknowledgment of the intrinsic connectedness between sexuality and spirituality, especially in women's experiences as gendered and embodied beings.[56]

Some Asian Catholic theologians have criticized *Laudato Si'* for its failure to include gender justice in the discussion of humans in creation. Malaysian Catholic scholar Sharon A. Bong points out that there is "the lack of a gendered analysis of the ecological crisis except to reinforce heterosexism and denounce certain reproductive health policies aimed at addressing the population crisis—which [*Laudato Si'*] remains silent on—that compounds the ecological crisis."[57] She argues that we need to further decenter the human in our theological framework and suggests the figure of the cyborg, which is boundary crossing and cannot be easily categorized. The cyborg figure breaks down the boundaries of human and animal, organism and machine, and physical and nonphysical. In addition, she invites us to de-essentialize our understanding of gender and sexuality to recognize the broad range of human sexual experiences. Queer ecofeminism has the potential to challenge androcentric and heteronormative constructions of *Homo sapiens* and thus "opens up the possibility of a radical pluralism for the human species."[58] As we protect ecological biodiversity, we need to stand in solidarity with people with a wider range of gender identities and sexual differences.

Planetary Solidarity and Interreligious Collaboration

Edinburgh 1910 was concerned about bringing the heathens and non-believers into the Christian fold. John R. Mott's best-known work, *The Evangelization of the World in This Generation*, became a missionary slogan in the early twentieth century.[59] It was only after nations in Africa and Asia regained their political independence that "dialogue" became a catch phrase in ecumenical circles. In the late 1960s, the World Council of Churches began to discuss dialogue with people of other faiths and to develop programs to cultivate mutual understanding. The Second Vatican Council opened the Catholic Church to encounter, dialogue, and engage with people of other religious traditions. Since then, the field of interreligious dialogue has grown and, more and more, Christians recognize the need to live in harmonious relation with their religious neighbors in an increasingly religiously pluralistic and interconnected world.

Today, we must add planetary solidarity as a major theme for interreligious dialogue and collaboration. Mary Evelyn Tucker, who has facilitated many conversations on ecology and religion, writes, "The environmental crisis calls the religions of the world to respond by finding their voice within the larger Earth community. In so doing the religions are entering their ecological phase and finding their planetary expression."[60] This requires a deeper ecological awakening—scriptural, symbolic, ritual, and ethical—of the spiritual resources within one's own tradition as well as learning from others. Through creative transformation of traditional resources and adopting new ones, we can develop viable forms of religious life beneficial to humans and other species. Tucker notes that there is growing interest in the emerging dialogue of ecology and religion, and many grassroots environmental movements have been inspired by religion. Religious traditions continue to shape many people's worldviews and their values and can be positive forces for change. Interfaith collaboration, informed by postcolonial sensitivities of humility and hospitality, can break down social and religious barriers and provide the impetus for working across differences to promote social transformation and planetary awareness.

Christians can collaborate with people of other faiths in grassroots environmental movements. For example, the Zen Buddhist master Thich Nhat Hanh has taught simplicity of life, interbeing, and living harmoniously with nature for many decades. His followers around the world have formed communities and led workshops and retreats to promote compassion, mindfulness, and healthy living. In Taiwan, under the leadership of Master Zhengyan, a Buddhist nun, a vibrant grassroots environmental movement has developed. Through recycling programs, publications, community education, and family activities, her Buddhist Compassion Relief *Ciji* Foundation raises people's awareness about environmental concerns and conservation of life. Christians in Taiwan, with Buddhist and other religious groups, and nonreligious environmental protection organizations, have developed eco-rituals to draw people into activism and spiritual commitment. They have also worked together to push the government to preserve primal forests.[61] Christian churches can learn from these interreligious grassroots efforts and form interfaith coalition in the process of building planetary solidarity.

Wholistic Spirituality

Lynn White Jr. emphasizes, "we shall not cope with our ecological crisis until scores of millions of us learn to understand more clearly what our real values are and determine to change our priorities."[62] This means more than just rethinking and reformulating our economic and political systems; finding new, renewable energy; and reducing consumption and pollution. This requires us to examine our orientations in life and our relations with God and other species in a much deeper sense, and touches on the spiritual dimensions of our being. Sandra Schneiders defines spirituality as "that dimension of the human subject in virtue of which the person is capable of self-transcending integration in relation to the Ultimate, whatever this Ultimate is for the person in question. In this sense, every human being has a capacity for spirituality or is a spiritual being."[63]

Today many people, especially the younger generation, say that they are "spiritual, but not religious." This means that they are discontented and dissatisfied with the dogmas, rituals, and rigid, hierarchal structures of organized religion, but they are concerned with the larger questions of the meaning of human life and humanity's place in the world. Ursula King, for example, seeks to explore spirituality and society in this context. For her, spirituality "also means to seek something greater outside and beyond the narrow confines of oneself, something or someone who transcends the narrow boundaries of our individual experience and makes us feel linked with a community of others, with a much larger web of life—in fact, the whole cosmos of which we are all a tiny part."[64] Facing the alienation of mass society and the bombardment of advertisements and consumerism, many people long for a sense of belonging and connectedness and a place to call home.

It is important for Christian mission to explore and nurture a spirituality that promotes a deeper sense of our place in the planet home: a spirituality that celebrates the indwelling of the spirit in the cosmos, connects social justice with ecojustice, and unites human beings with the rest of creation. Victoria Tauli-Corpuz, a Christian Igorot woman from an indigenous tribe living in the mountains of northern Luzon in the Philippines, urges Christians to learn from those who practice earth-based spirituality. The Igorots believe that the universe is a living thing, and everything has a spirit. Their rituals and lifestyles reflect the integral relationship between the spirit and nature and between human beings and the earth. She writes, "The effort of oppressed and marginalized peoples to sustain their struggles to transform an increasingly dehumanized society is pushing us to reclaim this earth-based spirituality."[65] The global environmental crisis has motivated Christians to pay attention to and learn from indigenous spiritualities and practices.

In the U.S., Sister Miriam Therese MacGillis, founder of the Genesis Farm in New Jersey, has inspired many Dominican and other women's religious order-established communities to form a loose network called Sisters of the Earth. These communities are ecumenical in their nature and often interfaith in practice. They are committed to living lightly, to living sustainably, and to living within the principles of ecology.[66] She has promoted an ecological spirituality, based on the work of Thomas Berry, which emphasizes the inherent spirituality of the universe, the role of the natural world as an assist to human beings to imagine and become like God, the centrality of community, the importance as well as the limitation of religious traditions, the awareness of agriculture as a priestly activity, the importance of attuning to the cycles, seasons, weather, and nature, and the eating of grains and vegetables instead of meat.[67] The development of spirituality is important to sustain our struggle for ecojustice and social equality in the long run, and to develop personal and communal resources to overcome frustration and despair.

The Christian church must carry out its mission in the context of global warming and other planetary emergencies and in the ecological turn of theology. Postcolonial theology can facilitate this turn by challenging anthropic exceptionalism, decentering the colonial mind, and espousing mutuality between humans and other species. The late theologian Sallie McFague produced many books on ecology and theology. In *A New Climate for Theology*, she writes, "theology must deal with global warming because one of the basic marks of the church is its ecological catholicity, which must be lived out in a political context. In other words, Christian faith is concerned with a just and sustainable existence for all of God's creation."[68] Earth care and planetary habitability must be an integral part of God's mission in the twenty-first century. Through working for ecojustice and interfaith collaboration, Christian churches can develop a new spirituality for the flourishing and fecundity of all God's creation.

Perhaps the Buddhist workmen in Ceylon in Lynn White Jr.'s story has something to teach us after all. The workmen believed that "the snake had a right to its house as long as it wanted to stay there" and did not kill them but waited until they moved out to another location. In some South Asian traditions and popular devotion, snakes are venerated, and their abodes and nests are sites of sacred importance. The workmen did not regard humans and animals as dichotomous: the snakes might be their ancestors or relatives in another life. They contested the colonial authority's disregard for the symbiotic relationships in the natural environment. Expressing solidarity with the snakes, they slowed down their work, perhaps took some rest amid exploitative, hard labor under capitalism. These workmen conscientized Lynn White Jr. and might also have valuable lessons for us in our Anthropocene age.

Epilogue

As I complete this book at the end of April 2021, the coronavirus has wreaked havoc in India, the daily infection tally shattering global records and crossing the 360,000 mark. The new daily number of deaths as a result of COVID-19 has passed the 3,200 mark, pushing the number of Indians who have died of the disease to more than 200,000.[1] The country has suffered from a crippling shortage of medical amenities, including essential supplies, like oxygen. While the coronavirus has magnified economic inequity and social injustice around the world, many countries have become increasingly nationalistic, trying to protect their own citizens and ward off the disease from their borders. Of the nearly 890 million vaccine doses that have been administered worldwide as of this writing, more than 81 percent has been given in high- and upper-middle-income countries. Low-income countries have received only 0.3 percent.[2] These countries are facing unconscionable shortage of vaccines, while richer countries, such as the U.S., enjoyed vaccine abundance. For as soon as the vaccines entered clinical trials, the wealthier countries began hoarding doses to protect their residents. As a result, the richest countries accounted for 16 percent of the world's population but held 53 percent of all purchased vaccines.[3] By the end of April 2021, 43 percent of the U.S. population has received one dose of the vaccine and 30 percent has received both doses, while only 10 percent of Indians has received one dose of the vaccine, and just 1.5 percent has received both doses.[4]

It was gut-wrenching to see photos of the bodies of COVID victims, lying burning in funeral pyres, and cramming New Delhi's sidewalks and car parks or mass burial sites in Brazil amid an explosion of new infections and deaths. More than 3 million people have died of COVID globally. Each one of them has family and friends and is not just a statistic. At a time like this, I am reminded of what Judith Butler has written about the precariousness and grievability of life. What Butler asks about war is equally valid for the coronavirus pandemic:

"whose lives are considered valuable, whose lives are mourned, and whose lives are considered ungrievable[?] . . . An ungrievable life is one that cannot be mourned because it has never lived, that is, it has never counted as a life at all."[5] What are the mechanisms that render a life as not counted as a life at all?

There are many people who, during the pandemic, have expressed a longing to go back to normal as soon as possible. But what if "normal" is not a dream but a nightmare for many people? The combination of illnesses and deaths, the global reckoning with racial injustice seen in rallies in support of Black Lives Matter, and the sharpening disparity between the rich and the poor point to the fact that the world we have created and are inhabiting is not sustainable. The international health organizations, whose roots can be traced to colonial medical institutions, were ill prepared to respond to the magnitude of the coronavirus pandemic. If we do not learn from the lessons of the coronavirus crisis, we have much less hope of effectively facing the looming larger crisis of climate change.

In this book, I have argued that the colonial legacy continues to shape global relations and politics. This includes the realignment of powers in response to COVID. Cold War rhetoric has been revived, as the U.S. and China have fought to exert their global hegemony. Instead of working as a human community, as equal partners to face a deadly virus, a convoluted patronage system has been created, with richer and more resourceful countries sending medical supplies and vaccines to their allies and strategic partners. Poorer countries have been caught between the mighty powers, forced to choose between which master to align with and to seek protection from, a decision that might mean life or death in the current situation.

Given the uncertainty and the unknown future that will emerge in the post-pandemic world, what are theological resources for hope? How might a postcolonial theologian imagine what hope can be? My hope lies in remembering that in the long history of anticolonial and postcolonial struggles for justice, there are Christians and people of faith who have stood up from the margins, and that the subaltern cannot be easily silenced. They are like a great cloud of witnesses surrounding us (Heb. 12:1). Even in the darkest days, they dare to work and hope for a better future. During a time when the military seized power in a coup in Myanmar and detained government leaders, a young theologian Lama Htoi San Lu from Myanmar said that "survival is not new for people on the margin. Survival is a daily praxis for persons and communities of color at work, at school, in the public, and private places." Facing the pandemic, racial reckoning, anti-Asian hatred, and other challenges, she urged us to practice "embodied solidarity and collective care" for one another and for our communities.[6]

Postcolonial hope is not a dream but a praxis. It is not passive waiting but an active pursuit of justice. The author of Hebrews summons us, surrounded by this great cloud of witnesses, to "run with perseverance the race that is set before us, looking to Jesus the pioneer and perfector of our faith" (Heb. 12:1). As Jesus resisted the Roman Empire in his time, so too must we refuse to be pawns of mighty empires, standing up to state violence and police brutality, challenging myths and lies, and making grieving a revolutionary practice. During the 2019 Hong Kong protests, the anthem "Glory to Hong Kong" became widely popular:

> Stars may fade, as darkness fills the air,
> Through the mist a solitary trumpet flares from afar:
> "Now, come on! For freedom we fight, with all might we strive!
> With valour, wisdom, that will ever last."[7]

Christians have often put their hope in the *eschaton*—the end time. But postcolonial hope is much more like a process, for we cannot defer hope till eternity. African American social ethicist Traci West describes hope in this way, as a process, writing, "Defiant spirituality gives birth to hope. . . . When we begin to recognize the ways in which defiant spirituality makes antiviolence creativity more possible, evident, and sustainable, hope surges outward."[8] Hope as a process means that we cannot rely on an individual or a hero to save us out of the blue; hope must be embodied and practiced in community in order to develop resilience for the long haul. As empire seeks to instill fear, helplessness, and fatalism, defiant communities must teach each other and the young how to nurture hopefulness as a daily ritual—as a practice.

The book of Revelation has important lessons for us today. When the author John was exiled to Patmos, a small island in the Aegean Sea, he allowed his imagination to run wild and wrote this extraordinary book. He demonstrated hope as a process by daring to imagine what was not seen and seemingly impossible. He committed to the ritual of writing, capturing visions, symbols, and allegory, especially in connection with future events. He offered us the image of "a new heaven and a new earth" (Rev. 21:1) as a symbol of this hope—a place of infinite beauty and glory, and a place full of God's presence. The central revelation of the book is that revolutionary hopefulness under mighty Rome was possible because Caesar did not have the final word—God does. The inbreaking of a new heaven and a new earth is always a possibility, even though partial, if we do not lose faith but, in defiance of the threats of empire, seize the opportunity and charge on.

Notes

Introduction

1. Vincent W. Lloyd, "Introduction," in *Race and Political Theology*, ed. Vincent W. Lloyd (Stanford, CA: Stanford University Press, 2012), 17.
2. Namsoon Kang, *Diasporic Feminist Theology: Asia and Theopoetic Imagination* (Minneapolis: Fortress Press, 2014); Nami Kim and Wonhee Anne Joh, eds., *Critical Theology against U.S. Militarism in Asia: Decolonization and Deimperialization* (New York: Palgrave Macmillan, 2016); and Jonathan Tran, *The Vietnam War and Theologies of Memory: Time and Eternity in the Far Country* (Malden, MA: Wiley-Blackwell, 2010).
3. Carl Schmitt, *Political Theology: Four Chapters on the Concept of Sovereignty*, trans. George Schwab (Cambridge, MA: MIT Press, 2005).
4. Stephen D. Moore, "Hong Kong and Ireland: Protests and Post/colonies," in *The Hong Kong Protests and Political Theology*, ed. Kwok Pui-lan and Francis Ching-wah Yip (Landham, MD: Rowman and Littlefield, 2021), 207–15.
5. Diana L. Eck, *A New Religious America: How a "Christian Country" Has Now Become the World's Most Religiously Diverse Nation* (San Francisco: HarperSanFrancisco, 2001).
6. Edward W. Said, "The Claims of Individuality," in *The Edward Said Reader*, ed. Moustafa Bayoumi and Andrew Rubin (New York: Vintage Books, 2000), 5–6. Said reminds his readers of this claim by Cardinal John Henry Newman in *Apologia Pro Via Sua*.
7. Kwok Pui-lan, "Reading Gutiérrez among the 'Pandas,'" in *Caught Reading Again: Scholars and Their Books*, ed. R. S. Sugirtharajah (London: SCM, 2009), 129–42.
8. Shoki Coe, "In Search of Renewal in Theological Education," *Theological Education* 9, no. 4 (1973): 243.
9. C. S. Song, *The Compassionate God* (Maryknoll, NY: Orbis Books, 1982), 7.
10. Song, *The Compassionate God*, 9.
11. Kwok Pui-lan, "God Weeps with Our Pain," *East Asia Journal of Theology* 2, no. 2 (1984): 228–32.
12. For example, Simon Shui-man Kwan, *Postcolonial Resistance and Asian Theology* (New York: Routledge, 2013).

13. Aloysius Pieris, *An Asian Theology of Liberation* (Maryknoll, NY: Orbis Books, 1988), 51. Emphasis his.
14. Pieris, *An Asian Theology of Liberation*, 89.
15. Pieris, *An Asian Theology of Liberation*, 56. To Aloysius's credit, he does say the agapeic and the gnostic are mutually exclusive.
16. See Richard King, *Orientalism and Religion: Postcolonial Theory, India and the "Mythic East"* (London: Routledge, 1999).
17. Kwok Pui-lan, ed., *1997 yu Xianggang shenxue* (1997 and Hong Kong theology) (Hong Kong: Chung Chi College Theology Division, 1983).
18. For example, C. S. Song, *The Tears of Lady Meng: A Parable of People's Political Theology* (Geneva: World Council of Churches, 1981).
19. Mary John Mananzan, "Sexual Exploitation of Women in Third World Setting," in *Essays on Women*, ed. Mary John Mananzan (Manila, Philippines: St. Scholastica's College, 1987), 97–105.
20. Kwok Pui-lan, "The Emergence of Asian Feminist Consciousness of Culture and Theology," in *We Dare to Dream: Doing Theology as Asian Women*, ed. Virginia Fabella and Sun Ai Lee Park (Maryknoll, NY: Orbis Books, 1989), 98.
21. Virginia Fabella, "A Common Methodology for Diverse Christologies?" in *With Passion and Compassion: Third World Women Doing Theology*, ed. Virginia Fabella and Mercy Amba Oduyoye (Maryknoll, NY: Orbis Books, 1988), 115.
22. Kwok Pui-lan, *Discovering the Bible in the Non-Biblical World* (Maryknoll, NY: Orbis Books, 1995).
23. Kwok Pui-lan, "Unbinding Our Feet: Saving Brown Women and Feminist Religious Discourse," in *Postcolonialism, Feminism, and Religious Discourse*, ed. Laura E. Donaldson and Kwok Pui-lan (New York: Routledge, 2002), 62–81.
24. Elisabeth Schüssler Fiorenza, *In Memory of Her: A Feminist Reconstruction of Christian Origins* (New York: Crossroad, 1983). See my response to her work in "The Feminist Hermeneutics of Elisabeth Schüssler Fiorenza: An Asian Feminist Response," *East Asia Journal of Theology* 3, no. 2 (1985): 147–53.
25. See the network's website, www.panaawtm.org, and Kwok Pui-lan and Rachel A. R. Bundang, "PANAAWTM Lives!" *Journal of Feminist Studies in Religion* 21, no. 2 (2005): 147–58.
26. Kwok Pui-lan, "Diversity within Us: The Challenge of Community of Asian and Asian-American Women," *In God's Image* 15, no. 1 (1996): 51–53; and chapter 6 in this volume.
27. Rita Nakashima Brock et al., eds., *Off the Menu: Asian and Asian North American Women's Religion and Theology* (Louisville, KY: Westminster John Knox Press, 2007); Su Yon Pak and Jung Ha Kim, eds., *Leading Wisdom: Asian and Asian North American Women Leaders* (Louisville, KY: Westminster John Knox Press, 2017); and Kwok Pui-lan, ed., *Asian and Asian American Women in Theology and Religion: Embodying Knowledge* (Cham, Switzerland: Palgrave Macmillan, 2020).
28. Katie G. Cannon, Alison P. Gise Johnson, and Angela D. Sims, "Womanist Works in Word," *Journal of Feminist Studies in Religion* 21, no. 2 (2005): 135–46.
29. Kwok Pui-lan, *Postcolonial Imagination and Feminist Theology* (Louisville, KY: Westminster John Knox Press, 2005), 2–3.
30. R. S. Sugirtharajah, *Postcolonial Criticism and Biblical Interpretation* (Oxford: Oxford University Press, 2002), 25.
31. Fernando F. Segovia discusses these themes in the Gospel of John: see "Johannine Studies and Geopolitical: Reflections upon Absence and Irruption," in *What We Have Heard from the Beginning: The Past, Present, and Future of*

Johannine Studies, ed. Tom Thatcher (Waco, TX: Baylor University Press, 2007), 281–306. These themes can also be found in other parts of the Bible.

32. Kwok Pui-lan, "Woman, Dogs, and Crumbs: Constructing a Postcolonial Discourse," in *Discovering the Bible*, 71–83.

33. Kwok Pui-lan, "On Color-coding Jesus: An Interview with Kwok Pui-lan," in *The Postcolonial Bible*, ed. R. S. Sugirtharajah (Sheffield, UK: Sheffield Academic Press, 1998), 176–88.

34. The steering committee of the consultation included Laura E. Donaldson, Stephen D. Moore, Fernando F. Segovia, R. S. Sugirtharajah, and me. For the history of the consultation, see Stephen D. Moore and Fernando F. Segovia, "Postcolonial Biblical Criticism: Beginnings, Trajectories, Intersections," in *Postcolonial Biblical Criticism: Interdisciplinary Intersections*, ed. Stephen D. Moore and Fernando F. Segovia (London: T. and T. Clark International, 2005), 1–10.

35. Donaldson and Kwok, eds., *Postcolonialism, Feminism, and Religious Discourse*.

36. Catherine Keller, Joerg Rieger, and I presented. Some of the papers were collected in Catherine Keller, Michael Nausner, and Mayra Rivera, eds., *Postcolonial Theologies: Divinity and Empire* (St. Louis: Chalice Press, 2004). My paper was not included because it was committed elsewhere.

37. Catherine Keller, *God and Power: Counter-Apocalyptic Journeys* (Minneapolis: Fortress Press, 2005), 114.

38. Kwok, *Postcolonial Imagination and Feminist Theology*.

39. Kwok Pui-lan, "Feminist Theology as Intercultural Discourse," in *The Cambridge Companion to Feminist Theology*, ed. Susan Frank Parsons (Cambridge: Cambridge University Press, 2002), 25.

40. Stephen D. Moore and Mayra Rivera, eds., *Planetary Loves: Spivak, Postcoloniality, and Theology* (New York: Fordham University Press, 2010).

41. Gayatri Chakravorty Spivak, "Foreword," in *Other Asias* (Malden, MA: Blackwell, 2008), 4.

42. Gayatri Chakravorty Spivak, *Death of a Discipline* (New York: Columbia University Press, 2003), 85.

43. See, for example, Ania Loomba et al., eds., *Postcolonial Studies and Beyond* (Durham, NC: Duke University Press, 2005); Revathi Krishnaswamy and John C. Hawley, eds., *The Postcolonial and the Global* (Minneapolis: University of Minnesota Press, 2008); Jane Pollard, Cheryl McEwan, and Alex Hughes, eds., *Postcolonial Economies* (London: Zed Books, 2011); Sandra Harding, ed., *The Postcolonial Science and Technology Studies Reader* (Durham, NC: Duke University Press, 2011); John C. Hawley, ed., *Postcolonial, Queer: Theoretical Intersections* (Albany: State University of New York Press, 2001); and Sandra Ponzanesi and Marguerite Waller, eds., *Postcolonial Cinema Studies* (New York: Routledge, 2012).

44. The term *imaginary* has been widely used in psychoanalysis, sociology, anthropology, philosophy, and other fields. Charles Taylor defines *social imaginary* as "the ways we are able to think or imagine the whole of society"; see his *A Secular Age* (Cambridge, MA: Harvard University Press, 2007), 156. Imaginary is the collective understanding of what the world should be and how we should live in it.

45. Edward W. Said, *The World, the Text, and the Critic* (Cambridge, MA: Harvard University Press, 1983).

46. See Joerg Rieger, *Christ and Empire: From Paul to Postcolonial Times* (Minneapolis: Fortress Press, 2007); and Kwok Pui-lan, Don H. Compier, and Joerg Rieger, eds., *Empire and the Christian Tradition: New Readings of Classical*

Theologians (Minneapolis: Fortress Press, 2007). Although the authors of the latter book may not explicitly use postcolonial theory, many share concerns with those of postcolonial theologians.

47. Marcella Althaus-Reid, *Indecent Theology: Theological Perversions in Sex, Gender and Politics* (London: Routledge, 2001).

48. Creston Davis, "Introduction: Holy Saturday or Resurrection Sunday? Staging an Unlikely Debate," in *The Monstrosity of Christ: Paradox or Dialectic?* ed. Creston Davis (Cambridge, MA: MIT Press, 2009), 3.

49. Kwok Pui-lan and Stephen Burns, eds., *Postcolonial Practice of Ministry: Leadership, Liturgy, and Interfaith Engagement* (Lanham, MD: Lexington Books, 2016).

50. Arjun Appadurai, "Grassroots Globalization and the Research Imagination," in *Globalization*, ed. Arjun Appadurai (Durham, NC: Duke University Press, 2001), 6.

51. Gayatri Chakravorty Spivak, *An Aesthetic Education in the Age of Globalization* (Cambridge, MA: Harvard University Press, 2012).

1: Toward a Political Theology of Postcoloniality

1. Achille Mbembe, "Religion, Politics, Theology: A Conversation with Achille Mbembe," *boundary 2* 34, no. 2 (2007): 153.

2. For the call for papers for the conference, see https://politicaltheology.com/cfp-deprovincializing-political-theology/. For the program and participants, see https://www.religionswissenschaft.uni-muenchen.de/download_sammlung/plakate/2019_pt.pdf. The idea of "provincializing" comes from Dipesh Chakrabarty, *Provincializing Europe: Postcolonial Thought and Historical Difference*, rev. ed. (Princeton, NJ: Princeton University Press, 2007).

3. Scholarly conferences on political theology were held in 2017 in Atlanta and in 2019 in New York. There is also the Political Theology Network, https://politicaltheology.com/.

4. Claude Lefort, "The Permanence of the Theologico-Political," in *Political Theologies: Public Religion in a Post-Secular World*, ed. Hent de Vries and Lawrence E. Sullivan (New York: Fordham University Press, 2006), 148–87.

5. For example, Timothy Snyder, *On Tyranny: Twenty Lessons from the Twentieth Century* (New York: Tim Duggan Books, 2017); Madeleine K. Albright, *Fascism: A Warning* (New York: Harper, 2018); and David D. Roberts, *Totalitarianism* (Cambridge: Polity Press, 2020).

6. Corey D. B. Walker, "Theology and Democratic Futures," *Political Theology* 10, no. 2 (2009): 200.

7. Walker, "Theology and Democratic Futures," 200.

8. Walker, "Theology and Democratic Futures," 200.

9. William T. Cavanaugh and Peter Manley Scott, "Introduction to the Second Edition," in *Wiley Blackwell Companion to Political Theology*, 2nd ed., ed. William T. Cavanaugh and Peter Manley Scott (Hoboken, NJ: John Wiley & Sons, 2019), 3.

10. Tatha Wiley, "Paul and Early Christianity," in *Empire and the Christian Tradition*, ed. Kwok Pui-lan, Don H. Compier, and Joerg Rieger (Minneapolis: Fortress Press, 2007), 47–61. For a fuller discussion of Paul, see Christopher D. Stanley, ed. *The Colonized Apostle: Paul through Postcolonial Eyes* (Minneapolis: Fortress Press, 2011).

11. Augustine, *The City of God*, trans. Marcus Dods (New York: Modern Library, 1993).

12. Max Weber, "Science as a Vocation," in *From Max Weber: Essays in Sociology*, ed. and trans. H. H. Gerth and C. Wright Mills (New York: Routledge, 2009), 155.
13. Carl Schmitt, *Political Theology: Four Chapters on the Concept of Sovereignty*, trans. George Schwab (Cambridge, MA: MIT Press, 2005).
14. Elizabeth Philips, *Political Theology: A Guide for the Perplexed* (London: T. & T. Clark International, 2012).
15. Saul Newman, *Political Theology: A Critical Introduction* (Cambridge: Polity Press, 2019).
16. Newman, *Political Theology*, 19. Emphasis his.
17. Cavanaugh and Scott, "Introduction to the Second Edition," 1.
18. Craig Hovey and Elizabeth Philips, eds., *The Cambridge Companion to Christian Political Theology* (Cambridge: Cambridge University Press, 2015).
19. Edward W. Said, *Culture and Imperialism* (New York: Knopf, 1994), 18.
20. Y. T. Wu (Wu Yaozong), "China's Challenges to Christianity," *Chinese Recorder* 65 (1934): 10.
21. Y. T. Wu, "Christianity and China's Reconstruction," *Chinese Recorder* 67 (1936): 212.
22. M. M. Thomas, *Christian Participation in Nation-Building* (Bangalore: National Christian Council of India, 1960); and *The Christian Response to the Asian Revolution* (London: SCM Press, 1966).
23. See the discussion in Sathianathan Clarke, "M. M. Thomas," in *Empire and the Christian Tradition*, ed. Kwok, Compier, and Rieger, 430.
24. Eleazar S. Fernandez, *Toward a Theology of Struggle* (Maryknoll, NY: Orbis Books, 1994).
25. One of the first essays on Dalit theology was Arvind P. Nirmal, "Toward a Christian Dalit Theology," *Asia Journal of Theology* 6, no. 2 (1992): 297–310.
26. Robert J. C. Young, *Postcolonialism: An Historical Introduction* (Oxford: Blackwell, 2001), 4.
27. Edward Said, "East Isn't East," *Times Literary Supplement* 4792 (1995): 5.
28. Ella Shohat, "Notes on the 'Post-Colonial,'" *Social Text* 31/32 (1992): 99–113; and Arif Dirlik, *The Postcolonial Aura: Third World Criticism in the Age of Global Capitalism* (New York: Routledge, 1998).
29. Aijaz Ahmad, *In Theory: Classes, Nations, Literatures* (London: Verso, 1992).
30. Benita Parry, "The Postcolonial: Conceptual Category or Chimera?" *The Yearbook of English Studies* 27 (1997): 12. See also her *Postcolonial Studies: A Materialist Critique* (New York: Routledge, 2004).
31. Neil Lazarus, *The Postcolonial Unconscious* (Cambridge: Cambridge University Press, 2011), 14. Fredric Jameson, *The Political Unconscious: Narrative as a Socially Symbolic Act* (Ithaca, NY: Cornell University Press, 1981).
32. Fanon's plays have been translated into English, see Frantz Fanon, *The Plays from Alienation and Freedom*, ed. Jean Khalfa and Robert J. C. Young, trans. Steven Corcoran (London: Bloomsbury Academic Press, 2020).
33. Young, *Postcolonialism*, 7.
34. Edward W. Said, *Orientalism* (New York: Vantage Books, 1979).
35. Homi K. Bhabha, *The Location of Culture* (London: Routledge, 1994), 171, 173.
36. Bhabha, *The Location of Culture*.
37. Ranajit Guha, *Selected Subaltern Studies* (New York: Oxford University Press, 1988).
38. Colin MacCabe, "Foreword" to Gayatri Chakravorty Spivak, *In Other Worlds: Essays in Cultural Politics* (New York: Routledge, 1987), ix.
39. Gayatri Chakravorty Spivak et al., "Love: A Conversation," in *Planetary Loves: Spivak, Postcoloniality, and Theology*, ed. Stephen D. Moore and Mayra Rivera (New York: Fordham University Press, 2011), 63–64.

40. Gayatri Chakravorty Spivak, "Scattered Speculations on the Question of Value," in *In Other Worlds*, 154–75; and *Critique of Postcolonial Reason: Toward a History of the Vanishing Present* (Cambridge, MA: Harvard University Press, 1999), 67–111.
41. Young, *Postcolonialism*, 7.
42. Olivia U. Rutazibwa and Robbie Shilliam, "Postcolonial Politics: An Introduction," in *Routledge Handbook of Postcolonial Politics*, ed. Olivia U. Rutazibwa and Robbie Shilliam (New York: Routledge, 2018), 1.
43. See the description of the book series in the Routledge Press website, https://www.routledge.com/Postcolonial-Politics/book-series/PP.
44. Partha Chatterjee, *Lineages of Political Society: Studies in Postcolonial Democracy* (New York: Columbia University Press, 2011), 9.
45. Timothy Willem Jones, "The Missionaries' Position: Polygamy and Divorce in the Anglican Communion, 1888–1988," *Journal of Religious History* 35, no. 3 (2011): 393–408.
46. Chatterjee, *Lineages of Political Society*, xii.
47. Chatterjee, *Lineages of Political Society*, 13–14.
48. Immanuel Wallerstein, "The Modern World System as a Capitalist World-Economy," in *The Globalization Reader*, 3rd ed., ed. Frank J. Lecher and John Boli (Malden, MA: Blackwell, 2008), 55–61; Walter D. Mignolo, *Local History/Global Designs: Coloniality, Subaltern Knowledges, and Border Thinking* (Princeton, NJ: Princeton University Press, 2000).
49. Anibal Quijano, "Coloniality and Modernity/Rationality," *Cultural Studies* 21, no. 2–3 (2000): 168.
50. Anibal Quijano, "Coloniality of Power, Eurocentrism, and Latin America," *Nepantla* 1, no. 3 (2000): 533–80.
51. Mignolo, *Local Histories/Global Designs*.
52. Walter D. Mignolo, "The Geopolitics of Knowledge and the Colonial Difference," *South Atlantic Quarterly* 101, no. 1 (2000): 57–96; and "Delinking: The Rhetoric of Modernity, the Logic of Coloniality and the Grammar of Decoloniality," *Cultural Studies* 21, no. 2 (2007): 449–514.
53. Gurminder K. Bhambra, *Connected Sociologies* (London: Bloomsbury Academic Press, 2014), 145.
54. María Lugones, "Toward a Decolonial Feminism," *Hypatia* 25, no. 4 (2011): 742–59.
55. Gayatri Chakravorty Spivak, *Nationalism and the Imagination* (London: Seagull Books, 2010), 42–43.
56. Michael Jon Kessler, ed., *Political Theology for a Plural Age* (New York: Oxford University Press, 2013).
57. Michael Jon Kessler, "Introduction," in *Political Theology for a Plural Age*, ed. Kessler, 4.
58. Michael Jon Kessler, "Difference, Resemblance, Dialogue: Some Goals for Comparative Political Theology in a Plural Age," in *Political Theology for a Plural Age*, ed. Kessler, 134.
59. Richard King, *Orientalism and Religion: Post-Colonial Theory, India and "The Mythic East"* (London: Routledge, 1999), 35–61; and Reid B. Locklin and Hugh Nicholson, "The Return of Comparative Theology," *Journal of the American Academy of Religion* 78, no. 2 (2010): 477–79.
60. John Thatamanil, *Circling the Elephant: A Comparative Theology of Religious Diversity* (New York: Fordham University Press, 2020), 109.
61. Thatamanil, *Circling the Elephant*, 111.

62. John Thatamanil refers to Paulo Gonçalves's work, see his chapter "Comparative Theology after 'Religion,'" in *Planetary Loves*, ed. Moore and Rivera, 252.
63. Thatamanil, *Circling the Elephant*, 121. Italics in original.
64. Francis X. Clooney, "Comparative Theology: A Review of Recent Books (1989–1995)," *Theological Studies* 56 (1995): 522.
65. Peter van der Veer, *Imperial Encounters: Religion and Modernity in India and Britain* (Princeton, NJ: Princeton University Press, 2001), 14.
66. Edward W. Said, "Zionism from the Standpoint of Its Victims," in *The Edward Said Reader*, ed. Moustafa Bayoumi and Andrew Rubin (New York: Vintage Books, 2000), 114–68.
67. For a discussion of Said's secularism, see Bruce Robbins, "Is the Postcolonial Also Postsecular," *boundary 2* 40, no. 1 (2013): 249–52.
68. Spivak, *A Critique of Postcolonial Reason*, 382–83.
69. Talal Asad, *Formations of the Secular: Christianity, Islam, Modernity* (Stanford: Stanford University Press, 2003).
70. Wilfred Cantwell Smith, *The Meaning and End of Religion: A Revolutionary Approach to the Religious Traditions of Mankind* (New York: Macmillan, 1962), 60–61.
71. Lionel M. Jensen, *Manufacturing Confucianism: Chinese Tradition and Universal Civilization* (Durham, NC: Duke University Press, 1997), 8.
72. Anna Sun, *Confucianism as a World Religion: Contested Histories and Contemporary Realities* (Princeton, NJ: Princeton University Press, 2013), 45–76.
73. Sun, *Confucianism as a World Religion*, 23–24.
74. Sun, *Confucianism as a World Religion*, 21–24.
75. Sun, *Confucianism as a World Religion*, 77–93.
76. Schmitt, *Political Theology*, 5.
77. Carl Schmitt, *The Concept of the Political*, trans. George Schwab (New Brunswick, NJ: Rutgers University Press, 1976).
78. Mark Lilla, "Reading Strauss in Beijing," *The New Republic*, December 17, 2010, https://newrepublic.com/article/79747/reading-leo-strauss-in-beijing-china-marx.
79. Schmitt, *Political Theology*, 36.
80. SherAli Tareen, "Muslim Political Theology Before and After Empire: Shāh Muḥammad Ismāʿīl's Station of Leadership (*Manṣab-i Imāmat*)," *Political Theology* 21, no. 1–2 (2020): 105.
81. Tareen, "Muslim Political Theology," 124.
82. Devin Singh, *Divine Currency: The Theological Power of Money in the West* (Stanford: Stanford University Press, 2018), 15.
83. Michel Foucault, *Security, Territory, Population: Lectures at the College de France, 1977–1978*, ed. Michael Senellart (New York: Palgrave Macmillan, 2007), 147–48.
84. Peter Pels, "The Anthropology of Colonialism: Culture, History and the Emergence of Western Governmentality," *Annual Review of Anthropology* 26, no. 1 (1997): 177.
85. Patrice Ladwig, "Thinking with Foucault Beyond Christianity and the Secular: Notes on Religious Governmentality and Buddhist Monasticism," *Political Theology*, January 2021, https://doi.org/10.1080/1462317X.2020.1866809.
86. Patrice Ladwig, "The Religious Foundations of Colonial Governmentality: Buddhism and Colonial Rule in Laos and French Indochina (1893–1953)" (paper presented at the conference on "De-provincializing Political Theology: Postcolonial and Comparative Approaches," Ludwig Maximilian University of Munich, Germany, October 26–27, 2019), 11–12. Used by permission.

87. Ladwig, "The Religious Foundations of Colonial Governmentality," 15.
88. Ladwig, "Thinking with Foucault," 6.

2: Empire and the Study of Religion

1. David Chidester, *Empire of Religion: Imperialism and Comparative Religion* (Chicago: University of Chicago Press, 2014), 23.
2. Kwok Pui-lan, "Gender, Colonialism, and the Study of Religion," in *Postcolonialism, Feminism, and Religious Discourse*, ed. Laura E. Donaldson and Kwok Pui-lan (New York: Routledge, 2002), 16–19.
3. For example, Talal Asad, *Genealogies of Religion: Discipline and Reasons of Power in Christianity and Islam* (Baltimore, MD: Johns Hopkins University Press, 1993); Timothy Fitzgerald, *The Ideology of Religious Studies* (New York: Oxford University Press, 2000); Thomas A. Idinopulos and Brian C. Wilson, eds., *What Is Religion? Origins, Definitions, and Explanations* (Leiden: Brill, 1998); Tomoko Masuzawa, "The Production of 'Religion' and the Task of the Scholar," *Culture and Religion* 1, no. 1 (2000): 123–30; Russell T. McCutcheon, *The Discipline of Religion: Structure, Meaning, Rhetoric* (London: Routledge, 2003); and Jonathan Z. Smith, "Religion, Religions, Religious," in *Critical Terms for Religious Studies*, ed. Mark C. Taylor (Chicago: University of Chicago Press, 1998), 269–84.
4. Asad, *Genealogies of Religion*; Richard King, *Orientalism and Religion: Postcolonial Theory, India and the "Mythic East"* (London: Routledge, 1999); Donald Lopez Jr., ed., *Curators of the Buddha: The Study of Buddhism under Colonialism* (Chicago: University of Chicago Press, 1995); R. S. Sugirtharajah, *Postcolonial Criticism and Biblical Interpretation* (Oxford: Oxford University Press, 2002); Kwok Pui-lan, *Postcolonial Imagination and Feminist Theology* (Louisville, KY: Westminster John Knox Press, 2005); and Laura E. Donaldson, "The Breasts of Columbus: A Political Anatomy of Postcolonialism and Feminist Religious Discourse," in *Postcolonialism, Feminism, and Religious Discourse*, ed. Donaldson and Kwok, 41–61.
5. The Board of Directors of the American Academy of Religion issued a statement on "The Academy of Religion Is Crucial to Higher Education," American Academy of Religion website, December 16, 2020, https://aarweb.org/AARMBR/About-AAR-/Board-of-Directors-/Board-Statements-/Academic-Study-of-Religion.aspx.
6. Edward W. Said, *Culture and Imperialism* (New York: Knopf, 1994).
7. Kuan-hsing Chen, *Asia as Method: Toward Deimperialization* (Durham, NC: Duke University Press, 2010), 111.
8. Chen, *Asia as Method*, 108.
9. Daniel Dubuisson, *The Western Construction of Religion: Myths, Knowledge, and Ideology* (Baltimore, MD: Johns Hopkins University Press, 2003), 39.
10. For a review of Dubuisson's book, see Steven Engler and Dean Miller, "Review Symposium: Daniel Dubuisson, *The Western Construction of Religion*," *Religion* 36 (2006): 119–78.
11. Dubuisson, *Western Construction of Religion*, 23.
12. Wilfred Cantwell Smith, *The Meaning and End of Religion: A New Approach to the Religious Studies of Mankind* (New York: Macmillan, 1962).
13. Guy S. Stroumsa, *A New Science: The Discovery of Religion in the Age of Reason* (Cambridge, MA: Harvard University Press, 2010).
14. Stroumsa, *A New Science*, 15.
15. Lionel M. Jensen, *Manufacturing Confucianism: Chinese Tradition and Universal Civilization* (Durham, NC: Duke University Press, 1997).

16. Stroumsa, *A New Science*, 25.
17. Jean-Pierre Charbonnier, *Christians in China: A.D. 600 to 2000* (San Francisco: Ignatius Press, 2007), 262.
18. Zhuo Xinping, *Shijie zongjiao yu zongjiao xue* (World religions and religious studies) (Beijing: Shehui kexue wenxian chubanshe, 1992), 191–92.
19. Stroumsa, *A New Science*, 149.
20. Jensen, *Manufacturing Confucianism*, 8.
21. Jensen, *Manufacturing Confucianism*, 8.
22. Stroumsa, *A New Science*, 27.
23. Peter Beyer, *Religions in Global Society* (London: Routledge, 2006), 71.
24. J. J. Clarke, *Oriental Enlightenment: The Encounter between Asian and Western Thought* (London: Routledge, 1997), 54.
25. Kwok, "Gender, Colonialism, and the Study of Religion," 18.
26. Ernest Renan, *The Life of Jesus* (New York: Peter Eckler Publishing Co., 1925).
27. "Luke 2:41–52: A Twelve-Year-Old Jewish Boy," Art&Faith Matters, December 20, 2015, https://artandfaithmatters.blogspot.com/2015/12/art-lectionary-jesus-twelve.html.
28. Suzannah Heschel, *Abraham Geiger and the Jewish Jesus* (Chicago: University of Chicago Press, 1998), 125.
29. Walter D. Mignolo, *The Darker Side of Modernity: Global Futures, Decolonial Options* (Durham, NC: Duke University Press, 2011), 153.
30. Vernon A. Rosario, *The Erotic Imagination: French Histories of Perversity* (New York: Oxford University Press, 1997), 88.
31. Kwok Pui-lan, "Touching the Taboo: On the Sexuality of Jesus," in *Sexuality and the Sacred*, 2nd ed., ed. Marvin E. Ellison and Kelly Brown Douglas (Louisville, KY: Westminster John Knox Press, 2010), 132.
32. David Chidester, *Savage Systems: Colonialism and Comparative Religion in Southern Africa* (Charlottesville: University Press of Virginia, 1996).
33. Chidester, *Empire of Religion*.
34. Ann Taves, "'Religion' in the Humanities and the Humanities in the University," *Journal of the American Academy of Religion* 79, no. 2 (2011): 299.
35. McCutcheon, *Discipline of Religion*, 42.
36. D. G. Hart, *The University Gets Religion: Religious Studies in American Higher Education* (Baltimore, MD: Johns Hopkins University Press, 1999), 243.
37. Lyman H. Legters, "The Place of Religion in Foreign Area Studies," *Journal of the American Academy of Religion* 35, no. 2 (1967): 164.
38. Taves, "'Religion' in the Humanities," 300.
39. Étienne Balibar, "Is there a 'Neo-Racism'?" in *Race, Nation, Class: Ambiguous Identities*, by Étienne Balibar and Immanuel Wallerstein (New York: Verso, 1991), 17–28.
40. Clifford Geertz, "Religion as a Cultural System," in *Anthropological Approaches to the Study of Religion*, ed. Michael Banton (London: Tavistock, 1966), 1–46.
41. Asad, *Genealogies of Religion*, 27–54.
42. Bruce J. Malina, *The New Testament World: Insights from Cultural Anthropology* (Atlanta, GA: John Knox Press, 1981).
43. James G. Crossley, *Jesus in an Age of Terror: Scholarly Projects for a New American Century* (London: Equinox, 2008), 101–42.
44. Geza Vermes, *Jesus and the World of Judaism* (Philadelphia, PA: Fortress Press, 1983); Richard A. Horsley, *Jesus and the Spirit of Violence* (San Francisco: Harper and Row, 1987); John Dominic Crossan, *The Historical Jesus: The Life of a Mediterranean Jewish Peasant* (San Francisco: Harper, 1991); Marcus J. Borg, *Jesus in Contemporary Scholarship* (Valley Forge, PA: Trinity Press

International, 1994); and Gerd Theissen and Annette Merz, *The Historical Jesus: A Comprehensive Guide* (Minneapolis: Fortress Press, 1996).

45. Bernard Lewis, *What Went Wrong? The Clash between Islam and Modernity in the Middle East* (New York: Oxford University Press, 2002); and Lewis, *The Crisis of Islam: Holy War and Unholy Terror* (New York: Modern Library, 2003).

46. John L. Esposito, *Unholy War: Terror in the Name of Islam* (New York: Oxford University Press, 2002); and Tazim Kassam, "On Being a Scholar of Islam: Risks and Responsibilities," in *Progressive Muslims: On Justice, Gender, and Pluralism*, ed. Omid Safi (Oxford: Oneworld, 2003), 128–44.

47. Hent De Vries and Lawrence Sullivan, eds., *Political Theologies: Public Religion in a Post-Secular World* (New York: Fordham University Press, 2006); and Mark Lewis Taylor, *The Theological and the Political: On the Weight of the World* (Minneapolis: Fortress Press, 2011).

48. Dubuisson, *Western Construction of Religion*, 159.

49. "List of Current Units," American Academy of Religion website, https://www.aarweb.org/AARMBR/Events-and-Networking-/Program-Units-/List-of-Program-Units.aspx.

50. Geraldine Heng, *The Invention of Race in the European Middle Ages* (Cambridge: Cambridge University Press, 2018).

51. See the Global Middle Ages website, http://globalmiddleages.org.

52. J. Lorand Matory, *The Fetish Revisited: Marx, Freud, and the Gods Black People Make* (Durham, NC: Duke University Press, 2018).

53. See The Sacred Arts of the Black Atlantic website, https://sacredart.caaar.duke.edu.

54. Michael Hardt and Antonio Negri, *Empire* (Cambridge, MA: Harvard University Press, 2000), xii.

55. Hussein Askari, Zamir Iqbal, and Abbas Mirakhor, *Introduction to Islamic Economics: Theory and Application* (Malden, MA: Wiley, 2015), 21–22.

56. Abbas Mirakhor and Hussein Askari, *Ideal Islamic Economy: An Introduction* (Cham, Switzerland: Palgrave Macmillan, 2017); and Obiyathulla Ismath Bacha and Abbas Mirakhor, *Islamic Capital Markets: A Comparative Approach*, 2nd ed. (Singapore: World Scientific Publishing Company, 2019).

57. Askari, Iqbal, and Mirakhor, *Introduction to Islamic Economics*, 10.

58. Hussein Askari and Abbas Mirakhor, *Conceptions of Justice from Islam to the Present* (Cham, Switzerland: Palgrave Macmillan, 2019).

59. Devin Singh, *Divine Currency: The Theological Power of Money in the West* (Stanford: Stanford University Press, 2018), 2.

60. Kathyrn Tanner, *Christianity and the New Spirit of Capitalism* (New Haven, CT: Yale University Press, 2019).

61. Joerg Rieger and Rosemarie Henkel-Rieger, *United We Are a Force: How Faith and Labor Can Overcome America's Inequalities* (St. Louis: Chalice Press, 2016), 59–60.

62. Rieger and Henkel-Rieger, *United We Are a Force*, 65–67.

63. Yen-zen Tsai, "The Current Development of Religious Studies in the Chinese Intellectual World," *Sino-Christian Studies: An International Journal of Bible, Theology and Philosophy* 8 (2008): 87–132.

64. Naomi Thurston, "Reading Religion in China Today: Interviews with Chinese Christianity Researchers," *Review of Religion and Chinese Society* 4 (2017): 5–31.

65. Zhuo Xinping, "Research on Religions in the People's Republic of China," *Social Compass* 50 (2003): 445.

66. Corydon Ireland, "Bhabha, Matchmaker of Disciplines," *Harvard Gazette*, June 6, 2008, http://news.harvard.edu/gazette/story/2008/06/bhabha-matchmaker-of-disciplines.

3: Race, Colonial Desire, and Sexual Theology

1. Marcella Althaus-Reid, *The Queer God* (London: Routledge, 2003), 4.
2. Timothy Willem Jones, "'The Missionaries' Position: Polygamy and Divorce in the Anglican Communion, 1888–1988," *Journal of Religious History* 35, no. 3 (2011): 393–408.
3. Philip Jenkins, *The Next Christendom: The Coming of Global Christianity*, rev. ed. (New York: Oxford University Press, 2007).
4. For example, Peter C. Phan, "A New Christianity, But What Kind?" *Mission Studies* 21, no. 1 (2005): 59–83.
5. Havelock Ellis and John Addington Symonds, *Sexual Inversion* (1897, reprint; New York: Arno Press, 1975), 4.
6. Ellis and Symonds, *Sexual Inversion*, 7.
7. Ernest Renan, *The Life of Jesus* (New York: Peter Eckler Publishing Company, 1925), 67–68.
8. Renan, *The Life of Jesus*, 118.
9. Renan, *The Life of Jesus*, 112.
10. Karl Barth, *Protestant Thought: From Rousseau to Ritschl* (New York: Harper and Row, 1959), 392.
11. Albrecht Ritschl, *The Christian Doctrine of Justification and Reconciliation* (Clifton, NJ: Reference Book Publisher, 1966), 3:13, quoted in Gerald W. McCulloh, *Christ's Person and Life-Work in the Theology of Albrecht Ritschl with Special Attention to Munus Triplex* (Lanham, MD: University Press of America, 1990), 34.
12. Albrecht Ritschl, "Instruction in the Christian Religion," in *Three Essays*, trans. Philip Hefner (Philadelphia, PA: Fortress Press, 1972), 240–54.
13. Albrecht Ritschl, "'Prolegomena' to The History of Pietism," in *Three Essays*, 105.
14. J. R. Seeley, *Ecce Homo: Life and Work of Jesus Christ* (1865, reprint; New York: E. P. Dutton, 1908), 56–57.
15. J. R. Seeley, *The Expansion of England* (Boston: Little, Brown, and Company, 1905), 226–27.
16. Seeley, *Ecce Homo*, 37.
17. Seeley, *Ecce Homo*, 86.
18. Seeley, *Ecce Homo*, 94–95.
19. Arthur Michael Ramsey, *An Era in Anglican Theology: From Gore to Temple* (New York: Charles Scribner's Sons, 1960), 18.
20. Charles Gore, *The Incarnation of the Son of God* (New York: Charles Scribner's Sons, 1891), 176.
21. Gore, *The Incarnation of the Son of God*, 185.
22. Gore, *The Incarnation of the Son of God*, 240, see also 179–80.
23. Marcella Althaus-Reid, *Indecent Theology: Theological Perversions on Sex, Gender and Politics* (London: Routledge, 2001), 25.
24. Gayatri Chakravorty Spivak, "Can the Subaltern Speak?" in *Marxism and the Interpretation of Culture*, ed. Cary Nelson and Lawrence Grossberg (Urbana: University of Illinois Press, 1988), 271–313.
25. Gayatri Chakravorty Spivak, *A Critique of Postcolonial Reason: Toward a History of the Vanishing Present* (Cambridge, MA: Harvard University Press, 1999), 308–11.
26. Spivak, *A Critique of Postcolonial Reason*, 307.
27. Althaus-Reid, *The Queer God*, 171.
28. Virginia Fabella, *Beyond Bonding: A Third World Women's Theological Journey* (Manila, Philippines: Ecumenical Association of Third World Theologians, 1993), 93.

29. Marcella Althaus-Reid, "On Queer Theory and Liberation Theology: The Irruption of the Sexual Subject in Theology," in *Homosexualities*, ed. Marcella Althaus-Reid et al. (London: SCM Press, 2008), 87.

30. Althaus-Reid, "On Queer Theory," 88.

31. Althaus-Reid, *The Queer God*, 123.

32. Rose Wu, "A Story of Its Own Name: Hong Kong's *Tongzhi* Culture and Movement," in *Off the Menu: Asian and Asian North American Women's Religion and Theology*, ed. Rita Nakashima Brock et al. (Louisville, KY: Westminster John Knox Press, 2007), 278–79.

33. Chou Wah-shan, *Tongzhi: Politics of Same-sex Eroticism in Chinese Societies* (New York: Haworth Press, 2000), 2–5.

34. Rose Wu, *Liberating the Church from Fear: The Story of Hong Kong's Sexual Minorities* (Hong Kong: Hong Kong Women Christian Council, 2007), 280–81.

35. Bret Hinsch, *Passions of the Cut Sleeve: The Male Homosexual Tradition in China* (Berkeley: University of California Press, 1990), and Chou, *Tongzhi*.

36. Hinsch, *Passions of the Cut Sleeve*, 2.

37. Ruan Fangfu, *Sex in China: Studies in Sexology in Chinese Culture* (New York: Plenum Press, 1991).

38. Chou, *Tongzhi*, 22–23.

39. Charlotte Furth, "Rethinking Van Gulik: Sexuality and Reproduction in Traditional Chinese Medicine," in *Engendering China: Women, Culture, and the State*, ed. Christiana K. Gilmartin et al. (Cambridge, MA: Harvard University Press, 1994), 131.

40. Tze-lan Deborah Sang, *The Emerging Lesbian: Female Same-Sex Desire in Modern China* (Chicago: University of Chicago Press, 2003); Elisabeth L. Engebretsen, *Queer Women in Urban China: An Ethnography* (New York: Routledge, 2014); and Hongwei Bao, *Queer China: Lesbian and Gay Literature and Visual Culture under Postsocialism* (New York: Routledge, 2020).

41. Achille Mbembe, *On the Postcolony* (Berkeley: University of California Press, 2001), 212–13.

42. Althaus-Reid, *Indecent Theology*, 63–71.

43. Miguel A. De La Torre, *Decolonizing Christianity: Becoming Badass Believers* (Grand Rapids: Eerdmans, 2021), 87–88.

44. Frantz Fanon, *Black Skin, White Masks*, trans. Charles Lam Markmann (New York: Grove Press, 1967), 41–62.

45. For example, Rey Chow, *The Protestant Ethnic and the Spirit of Capitalism* (New York: Columbia University Press, 2002), 183–85.

46. Robert E. Goss, *Queering Christ: Beyond Jesus Acted Up* (Cleveland: Pilgrim Press, 2002), 138.

47. Tat-siong Benny Liew, "Queering Closets and Perverting Desires: Cross-Examining John's Engendering and Transgendering Word across Different Worlds," in *They Were All Together in One Place? Toward Minority Biblical Criticism*, ed. Randall C. Bailey, Tai-siong Benny Liew, and Fernando F. Segovia (Atlanta, GA: Society of Biblical Literature, 2009), 266.

48. Rita Nakashima Brock and Rebecca Ann Parker, *Proverbs of Ashes: Violence, Redemptive Suffering, and the Search for What Saves Us* (Boston: Beacon Press, 2001).

49. Mbembe, *On the Postcolony*, 222. Emphasis his.

50. Leo Steinberg, *The Sexuality of Christ in Renaissance Art and in Modern Oblivion*, 2nd ed. (Chicago: University of Chicago Press, 1996).

51. Mark D. Jordan, *The Silence of Sodom: Homosexuality in Modern Catholicism* (Chicago: University of Chicago Press, 2000), 8.

52. Trinh T. Minh-Ha, "L' Innécriture: Un-writing/Inmost Writing," in *When the Moon Waxes Red: Representation, Gender, and Cultural Politics* (New York: Routledge, 1991), 135.

53. Althaus-Reid, *The Queer God*, 15.

54. Chou Wah-shan, *Tongshi shenxue* (Tongzhi theology) (Hong Kong: Ci wenhua tang, 1994); Rose Wu, "A Story of Its Own Name"; and Agnes M. Brazal, and Andrea Lizares Si, eds., *Body and Sexuality* (Quezon City, Philippines: Ateneo de Manila University Press, 2007).

55. Pushpa Joseph, "Revisioning Eros for Asian Feminist Theologizing: Some Pointers from Tantric Philosophy," in *Body and Sexuality*, ed. Brazal and Si, 34–57.

56. Sharon A. Bong, "Queer Revisions of Christianity," in *Body and Sexuality*, ed. Brazal and Si, 234–49.

57. Sharon A. Bong, *Becoming Queer and Religious in Malaysia and Singapore* (London: Bloomsbury Academic, 2020).

58. Kelly Brown Douglas, *Sexuality and the Black Church: A Womanist Perspective* (Maryknoll, NY: Orbis Books, 1999).

59. La Ronda Barnes, "Embracing a Female Christ through the Visual Arts," unpublished paper, 1. Used by permission.

60. These art works include Angela Yarber's "Sophia," Megan Clay's "Black Christa" and "Cosmic Christa," and Janet McKenzie's "Christ of the People."

61. David Hayward, "Neither," https://twitter.com/nakedpastor/status/5769206 72334704640/photo/1.

62. Barnes, "Embracing a Female Christ," 2

63. Althaus-Reid, *The Queer God*, 4.

64. I owe this insight to my former student Jane D. Nichols, who wrote a paper titled "Liberation and the Sexed Body" for my class "Feminist Theology from the Global South," and has completed a thesis, "The Indecent and the Queer: Identity in Althaus-Reid and Queer Theology" (Master's thesis, Emory University, 2019).

65. Patrick S. Cheng, *From Sin to Amazing Grace: Discovering the Queer Christ* (New York: Church Publishing, 2012).

66. Mario Costa, Catherine Keller, and Anna Mercedes, "Love in Times of Empire: Theopolitics Today," in *Evangelicals and Empire: Christian Alternatives to the Political Status Quo*, ed. Bruce Ellis Benson and Peter Goodwin Heltzel (Grand Rapids: Brazos Press, 2008), 203.

67. Mary Grey, *The Wisdom of Fools? Seeking Revelation Today* (London: SPCK, 1993), 84.

4: American Empire and Christianity

1. Reinhold Niebuhr, *The Structure of Nations and Empires* (New York: Charles Scribner's Sons, 1959), 89.

2. Emilie M. Townes, "Colored Orneriness as Critical Companion in U.S. Democracy," Anna Julia Cooper Lecture, Candler School of Theology at Emory University, September 17, 2020.

3. "United States GDP," Trading Economics, https://tradingeconomics.com /united-states/gdp.

4. Adam Taylor and Laris Karklis, "This Remarkable Chart Shows How U.S. Defense Spending Dwarfs the Rest of the World," *Washington Post*, February 9, 2016, https://www.washingtonpost.com/news/worldviews/wp/2016/02/09/this-remarkable -chart-shows-how-u-s-defense-spending-dwarfs-the-rest-of-the-world/.

5. Harriet Sherwood, "White Evangelical Christians Stick by Trump Again, Exit Polls Show," *The Guardian*, November 6, 2020, https://www.theguardian.com /us-news/2020/nov/06/white-evangelical-christians-supported-trump.

6. For example, Richard A. Horsley, *Jesus and Empire: The Kingdom of God and the New World Order* (Minneapolis: Fortress Press, 2003); and Joerg Rieger, *Jesus vs. Caesar: For People Tired of Serving the Wrong God* (Nashville: Abingdon Press, 2018).

7. For example, Mark Lewis Taylor, *Religion, Politics, and the Christian Right: Post-9/11 Powers and American Empire* (Minneapolis: Fortress Press, 2005); and Daniel K. Williams, *God's Own Party: The Making of the Christian Right* (New York: Oxford University Press, 2010).

8. Joerg Rieger, "Christian Theology and Empires," in *Empire and the Christian Tradition: New Readings of Classical Theologians*, ed. Kwok Pui-lan, Don H. Compier, and Joerg Rieger (Minneapolis: Fortress Press, 2007), 1.

9. Horsley, *Jesus and Empire*, 6.

10. Horsley, *Jesus and Empire*, 7.

11. Kwok, Compier, and Rieger, eds., *Empire and the Christian Tradition*.

12. Rieger, "Christian Theology and Empires," 2.

13. Reinhold Niebuhr, "Awkward Imperialists," *Atlantic Monthly* 145 (May 1930): 672–73.

14. Niebuhr, "Awkward Imperialists," 675.

15. Russell Bank, *Dreaming Up America* (New York: Seven Stories Press, 2008), 43, 44.

16. Quoted in James Hudnut-Beumler, "Shock and Awe: Life in Mr. Rumsfeld's Neighborhood," in *Anxious about Empire: Theological Essays on the New Global Realities*, ed. Wes Avram (Grand Rapids: Brazos Press, 2004), 53–54.

17. Rosemary Radford Ruether, *America, Amerikkka: Elect Nation and Imperial Violence* (London: Equinox, 2007), 70–72.

18. Jace Weaver, "From I-Hermeneutics to We-Hermeneutics: Native Americans and the Post-Colonial," *Semeia* 75 (1996): 165.

19. Weaver, "From I-Hermeneutics to We-Hermeneutics," 166.

20. Andrea Smith, *Conquest: Sexual Violence and American Indian Genocide* (Cambridge, MA: South End Press, 2005), 26.

21. George E. Tinker, *Missionary Conquest: The Gospel and Native American Cultural Genocide* (Minneapolis: Fortress Press, 1993), 4.

22. Smith, *Conquest*, 10.

23. Smith, *Conquest*, 15.

24. Laura E. Donaldson, "On Medicine Women and White Shame-ans: New Age Native Americanism and Commodity Fetishism as Pop Culture Feminism," *Signs* 24 (1999): 677–78.

25. Willie James Jennings, *The Christian Imagination: Theology and the Origins of Race* (New Haven, CT: Yale University Press, 2010).

26. Dwight N. Hopkins, *Shoes That Fit Our Feet: Sources for a Constructive Black Theology* (Maryknoll, NY: Orbis Books, 1993).

27. Roberto S. Goizueta, "Preface," in *We Are a People: Initiatives in Hispanic American Theology*, ed. Roberto S. Goizueta (Minneapolis: Fortress Press, 1992), vii.

28. Michael J. O'Loughlin, "The U.S. Catholic Experience Is Increasingly Hispanic and Southwestern," *America: The Jesuit Review*, September 6, 2017, https:// www.americamagazine.org/politics-society/2017/09/06/us-catholic-experience -increasingly-hispanic-and-southwestern.

29. From the title of Ronald Takaki's book, *Strangers from A Different Shore: A History of Asian Americans*, rev. ed. (New York: Little, Brown and Co., 1998).
30. Meghana V. Nayak and Christopher Malone, "American Orientalism and American Exceptionalism: A Critical Rethinking of US Hegemony," *International Studies Review* 11, no. 2 (2009): 253–76.
31. Khyati Y. Joshi, *White Christian Privilege: The Illusion of Religious Equality in America* (New York: New York University Press, 2020), 1.
32. Horsley, *Jesus and Empire*; Richard A. Horsley, ed., *Paul and the Roman Imperial Order* (Harrisburg, PA: Trinity Press International, 2004); John Dominic Crossan, *God and Empire: Jesus against Rome, Then and Now* (San Francisco: HarperSanFrancisco, 2007); Warren Carter, *Matthew and Empire: Initial Explorations* (Harrisburg, PA: Trinity Press International, 2001); and Stephen D. Moore, *Empire and Apocalypse: Postcolonialism and the New Testament* (Sheffield, UK: Sheffield Phoenix Press, 2006).
33. Horsley, *Jesus and Empire*, 20–34.
34. Richard A. Horsley, "Submerged Biblical Histories and Imperial Biblical Studies," in *The Postcolonial Bible*, ed. R. S. Sugirtharajah (Sheffield, UK: Sheffield Academic Press, 1998), 162.
35. See the discussion in Moore, *Empire and Apocalypse*, 12.
36. Fernando F. Segovia, *Decolonizing Biblical Studies: A View from the Margins* (Maryknoll, NY: Orbis Books, 2000).
37. Mark Lewis Taylor, "Spirit and Liberation: Achieving Postcolonial Theology in the United States," in *Postcolonial Theologies: Divinity and Empire*, ed. Catherine Keller, Michael Nausner, and Mayra Rivera (St. Louis: Chalice Press, 2004), 49–52.
38. Taylor, "Spirit and Liberation," 52–55.
39. Catherine Keller, *God and Power: Counter-Apocalyptic Journeys* (Minneapolis: Fortress Press, 2005), 100.
40. Keller, *God and Power*, 108–9.
41. Catherine Keller and John J. Thatamanil, "Is This an Apocalypse? We Certainly Hope So—You Should Too," ABC Religion and Ethics, April 15, 2020, https://www.abc.net.au/religion/catherine-keller-and-john-thatamanil-why-we-hope-this-is-an-apo/12151922.
42. Keller, *God and Power*, 99
43. Keller, *God and Power*, 101.
44. Miguel A. De La Torre, "Introduction," in *Faith and Resistance in the Age of Trump*, ed. Miguel A. De La Torre (Maryknoll, NY: Orbis Books, 2017), xxix.
45. De La Torre, "Introduction," xxxi.
46. "A Conversation with the Rev. Canon Kelly Brown Douglas," The Episcopal Diocese of Missouri, June 10, 2020, https://vimeo.com/427889957.
47. Kelly Brown Douglas, *Stand Your Ground: Black Bodies and the Justice of God* (Maryknoll, NY: Orbis Books, 2015), 16.
48. Douglas, *Stand Your Ground*, 19.
49. Douglas, *Stand Your Ground*, 31.
50. Douglas, *Stand Your Ground*, 62–63.
51. Douglas, *Stand Your Ground*, 63.
52. Douglas, *Stand Your Ground*, 71.
53. Douglas, *Stand Your Ground*, 101.
54. David P. Gushee, "After 30 Years, A Farewell Column," Religion News Service, September 14, 2017, https://religionnews.com/2017/09/14/gushee-ends-rns-column/.

55. David P. Gushee, *After Evangelicalism: The Path to a New Christianity* (Louisville, KY: Westminster John Knox Press, 2020), 151.
56. Gushee, *After Evangelicalism*, 143.
57. Professor Turman made this statement during a speech at the American Academy of Religion meeting in November 2019, see Gushee, *After Evangelicalism*, 151.
58. Gushee, *After Evangelicalism*, 158–61.
59. Gushee, *After Evangelicalism*, 83–101.
60. The 2019 deficit was 18 percent less than 2018's $418.9 billion deficit. See Kimberly Amaded, "U.S. Trade Deficit with China and Why It's So High," The Balance, October 12, 2020, https://www.thebalance.com/u-s-china-trade-deficit-causes-effects-and-solutions-3306277.
61. Martin Jacques, "Can the West's Democracy Survive China's Rise to Dominance?" *The Economist*, June 14, 2018, https://www.economist.com/open-future/2018/06/14/can-the-wests-democracy-survive-chinas-rise-to-dominance.
62. Fareed Zakaria, *The Post-American World: Release 2.0* (New York: Norton, 2012).
63. Fareed Zakaria, *Ten Lessons for a Post-Pandemic World* (New York: Norton, 2020), 187–209.
64. Reinhold Niebuhr, *The Children of Light and the Children of Darkness: A Vindication of Democracy and Its Traditional Defense* (New York: Charles Scribner's Sons, 1944).
65. Gary Dorrien, *Economy, Difference, Empire: Social Ethics for Social Justice* (New York: Columbia University Press, 2010), 39.
66. Niebuhr, *The Structures of Nations and Empires*, 202.
67. Niebuhr, *The Structures of Nations and Empires*, 22. See also R. S. Sugirtharajah, *Postcolonial Reconfigurations: An Alternative Way of Reading the Bible and Doing Theology* (St. Louis: Chalice Press, 2003), 143–48.
68. Wu Yaozong, "Gongchandang jiaoyu liao wo" (The Communist Party educated me) *Tian Feng* 271 (1951): 7, quoted in Ng Lee-ming, *Jidujiao yu Zhongguo shehui bianqian* (Christianity and Chinese social change) (Hong Kong: Chinese Christian Literature Council, 1981), 119. Translation mine.
69. Dorrien, *Economy, Difference, Empire*, 60.
70. Samuel P. Huntington, *The Clash of Civilizations and the Remaking of the World Order* (New York: Simon and Schuster, 1996).
71. Edward W. Said, "The Clash of Definitions," in *Reflection on Exile and Other Essays* (Cambridge, MA: Harvard University Press, 2000), 569–90.
72. Sidney Leng, "China's Dirty Little Secret: Its Growing Wealth Gap," *South China Morning Post*, July 7, 2017, https://www.scmp.com/news/china/economy/article/2101775/chinas-rich-grabbing-bigger-slice-pie-ever; and Christopher Ingraham, "The Richest 1 Percent Now Owns More of the Country's Wealth Than at Any Time in the Past 50 Years," *Washington Post*, December 6, 2017, https://www.washingtonpost.com/news/wonk/wp/2017/12/06/the-richest-1-percent-now-owns-more-of-the-countrys-wealth-than-at-any-time-in-the-past-50-years/.
73. Robert Frank, "Richest 1% Now Owns Half the World's Wealth," CNBC, November 14, 2017, https://www.cnbc.com/2017/11/14/richest-1-percent-now-own-half-the-worlds-wealth.html.
74. Michiko Kakutani, "Op-Ed: Democracies around the World Are under Threat. Ours Is No Exception," *Los Angeles Times*, October 31, 2020, https://news.yahoo.com/op-ed-democracies-around-world-101028070.html.
75. "A Conversation with the Rev. Canon Kelly Brown Douglas."

76. Roger S. Gottlieb, *A Spirituality of Resistance: Finding a Peaceful Heart and Protecting the Earth* (Lanham, MD: Rowman and Littlefield, 2005), 4.

5: Postcolonial Theology from an East Asian Perspective

1. To be consistent, I have put the surnames of Korean and Chinese names before their given names in the text. In their published works, some authors put their surnames after their given names, and I have not changed this so that readers can locate the sources easier.
    Nami Kim and Wonhee Anne Joh, "Introduction," in *Critical Theology against US Imperialism in Asia: Decolonization and Deimperialization*, ed. Nami Kim and Wonhee Anne Joh (New York: Palgrave Macmillan, 2016), xvi.
2. "March 1 Movement," *Encyclopedia Britannica*, https://www.britannica.com/event/March-First-Movement.
3. Edward W. Said, *Representations of the Intellectual* (New York: Vintage Books, 1996), 23.
4. See Kwok Pui-lan, Don H. Compier, and Joerg Rieger, eds., *Empire and the Christian Tradition: New Readings of Classical Theologians* (Minneapolis: Fortress Press, 2007).
5. William A. Dyrness, "Listening for Fresh Voices in the History of the Church," in *Teaching Global Theologies: Power and Praxis*, ed. Kwok Pui-lan, Cecilia González-Adrieu, and Dwight N. Hopkins (Waco, TX: Baylor University Press, 2014), 29.
6. Edward W. Said, *Culture and Imperialism* (New York: Knopf, 1994), 18.
7. The National Exhibit "Luther! 95 Treasures – 95 People" was held in Wittenberg, Germany, in 2017 in commemoration of the 500th anniversary of the 95 Theses.
8. Homi H. Bhabha, *The Location of Culture* (London: Routledge, 1994).
9. Frantz Fanon, *Black Skin, White Masks*, trans. Charles Lam Markmann (New York: Grove Press, 1967).
10. Ashis Nandy, *The Intimate Enemy: The Loss and Recovery of Self under Colonialism* (Delhi: Oxford University Press, 1983).
11. Gayatri Chakravorty Spivak, "Can the Subaltern Speak?" in *Marxism and the Interpretation of Culture*, ed. Cary Nelson and Lawrence Grossberg (Urbana: University of Illinois Press, 1988), 271–313. See also Spivak, *A Critique of Postcolonial Reason: Toward a History of the Vanishing Present* (Cambridge, MA: Harvard University Press, 1999), 308–11.
12. Enrique Dussel, "The Epistemological Decolonization of Theology," in *Postcolonial Theology*, ed. Hille Haker, Luiz Carlos Susin, and Eloi Messi Metogo (London: SCM Press, 2013), 29.
13. See Kwok, González-Adrieu, and Hopkins, eds., *Teaching Global Theologies*.
14. Nami Kim, "The 'Indigestible' Asian: The Unifying Term 'Asian' in Theological Discourse," in *Off the Menu: Asian and Asian North American Women's Religion and Theology*, ed. Rita Nakashima Brock et al. (Louisville, KY: Westminster John Knox Press, 2007), 28.
15. See Simon Shui-man Kwan, *Postcolonial Resistance and Asian Theology* (London: Routledge, 2014), 116–23.
16. Sebastian C. H. Kim, "The Word and the Spirit: Overcoming Poverty, Injustice, and Division in Korea," in *Christian Theology in Asia*, ed. Sebastian C. H. Kim (Cambridge: University of Cambridge Press, 2008), 143–44.
17. Y. T. Wu (Wu Yaozong), "China's Challenges to Christianity," *Chinese Recorder* 65 (1934): 10.

18. Y. T. Wu, "Christianity and China's Reconstruction," *Chinese Recorder* 67 (1936): 212.

19. For the development of the Three Self Patriotic Movement, see Alexander Chow, *Chinese Public Theology: Generational Shifts and Confucian Imagination in Chinese Christianity* (Oxford: Oxford University Press, 2018), 48–69.

20. Ahn Byung Mu, "Jesus and the Minjung in the Gospel of Mark," in *Minjung Theology: People as the Subjects of History*, ed. Kim Yong Bock (Singapore: The Commission of Theological Concerns, Christian Conference of Asia, 1981), 140–41.

21. Yong Bock Kim, "Doing Theology in Asia Today: A Korean Perspective," in *Asian Christian Theology: Emerging Themes*, ed. Douglas J. Elwood (Philadelphia: Westminster Press, 1980), 315–16.

22. Sebastian Kim, "Minjung Theology: Whose Voice, for Whom?" in *Asian Theology on the Way: Christianity, Culture and Context*, ed. Peniel Jesudason Rufus Rajkumar (London: SPCK, 2012), 112.

23. Wang Hsien-chih, *Taiwan xiangtu shenxue lunwen ji* (Collected essays of Taiwanese Homeland Theology), vol. 1, ed. Wang Hsien-chih (Tainan: Tainan Theological Seminary, 1988).

24. Kuan-Hsing Chen, *Asia as Method: Toward Deimperialization* (Durham, NC: Duke University Press, 2010), 17–20.

25. Chen, *Asia as Method*, 63.

26. Wai Ching Angela Wong, *"The Poor Woman": A Critical Analysis of Asian Theology and Contemporary Chinese Fiction by Women* (New York: Peter Lang, 2002), 23.

27. Wong, *"The Poor Woman,"* 3–5.

28. Choi Hee An, *A Postcolonial Self: Korean Immigrant Theology and Church* (New York: State University of New York Press, 2015), 51–54.

29. Hyun Ju Bae, "Embracing Life and the Bible: Toward a Hermeneutics of Compassion in Detachment," in *Korean Feminists in Conversation with the Bible, Church and Society*, ed. Kyung Sook Lee and Kyung Mi Park (Sheffield, UK: Sheffield Phoenix Press, 2011), 51.

30. Meehyun Chung, "Introducing Korean Feminist Theology," in *Breaking Silence: Theology from Asian Women's Perspective*, ed. Meehyun Chung (Delhi: ISPCK/EATWOT, 2006), 86–87.

31. Choi Hee An, *Korean Women and God: Experiencing God in a Multi-religious Colonial Context* (Maryknoll, NY: Orbis Books, 2005), 88.

32. Mi Kang Yang, "Lessons about Healing: Korean Comfort Women and the Hemorrhaging Woman of Mark 5," in *Korean Feminists in Conversation*, ed. Lee and Park, 123–26.

33. Yeong Mee Lee, "Motherhood as a Theological Model for Redemption in the Hebrew Bible," in *Korean Feminists in Conversation*, ed. Lee and Park, 22.

34. Lee, "Motherhood as a Theological Model," 22–24.

35. Seong Hee Kim, "Our (Neither) Mother and (nor) Father in Heaven: A Postcolonial Reading of the Lord's Prayer," in *Korean Feminists in Conversation*, ed. Lee and Park, 69–70.

36. Kim, "Our (Neither) Mother and (nor) Father in Heaven," 70.

37. Hisako Kinukawa, "Biblical Studies in the Twenty-first Century: A Japanese/Asian Feminist Glimpse," in *Feminist New Testament Studies: Global and Future Perspectives*, ed. Kathleen O'Brien Wicker, Althea Spencer Miller, and Musa W. Dube (New York: Palgrave Macmillan, 2005), 141.

38. Kinukawa, "Biblical Studies in the Twenty-first Century," 140.

39. Kinukawa, "Biblical Studies in the Twenty-first Century," 147–48.

40. Hisako Kinukawa, *Women and Jesus in Mark: A Japanese Feminist Perspective* (Maryknoll, NY: Orbis Books, 1994), 51–65.
41. Mari Yamamoto, *Grassroots Pacificism in Post-War Japan: The Rebirth of a Nation* (London: Routledge Curzon, 2004).
42. Kosuke Koyama, *Mount Fuji and Mount Sinai: A Pilgrimage in Theology* (London, SCM, 1984).
43. Koyama, *Mount Fuji and Mount Sinai*, 86–87.
44. Kim and Joh, "Introduction," xiv–xv.
45. Wonhee Anne Joh, "Postcolonial Loss: Collective Grief in the Ruins of Militarized Terror," in *Critical Theology against US Militarism in Asia*, ed. Kim and Joh, 8.
46. Joh, "Postcolonial Loss," 14–17.
47. In Soo Kim, "Toward Peace and Reconciliation between South and North Korean Churches: Contextual Analysis of the Two Churches," in *Peace and Reconciliation: In Search of Shared Identity*, ed. Sebastian C. H. Kim and Pauline Kollontai (Burlington, VT: Ashgate, 2008), 133–46.
48. Sebastian C. H. Kim, "Reconciliation Possible? The Churches' Efforts toward the Peace and Reconciliation of North and South Korea," in *Peace and Reconciliation*, ed. Kim and Kollontai, 170–76.
49. Kim, "Reconciliation Possible?," 170.
50. Chen, *Asia as Method*.
51. Huang Po Ho, "Uniting People of Asia through a Christian Movement: Ecumenical Movements in Pluralistic Asia," in *Mission from the Underside: Transforming Theological Education in Asia* (Bangalore: Programme for Theology and Cultures in Asia, 2010), 165.
52. Huang, "Uniting People of Asia," 166.

6: Transnationalism and Feminist Theology in Asia Pacific

1. Rita Nakashima Brock, "Cooking without Recipes: Interstitial Integrity," in *Off the Menu: Asian and Asian North American Women's Religion and Theology*, ed. Rita Nakashima Brock et al. (Louisville, KY: Westminster John Knox Press, 2007), 140.
2. For a discussion of various wars of the United States in Asia, see Philip West, Steven I. Levine, and Jackie Hiltz, eds., *America's Wars in Asia: A Cultural Approach to History and Memory* (Armonk, NY: M. E. Sharpe, 1998).
3. Edward W. Said, *Orientalism* (New York: Vintage, 1979).
4. Lisa Lowe, *Immigrant Acts: On Asian American Cultural Politics* (Durham, NC: Duke University Press, 1996), 5.
5. Rob Wilson, "Imagining 'Asia-Pacific' Today: Forgetting Colonialism in the Magical Free Markets of the American Pacific," in *Learning Places: The Afterlives of Area Studies*, ed. Masao Miyoshi and Harry D. Harootunian (Durham, NC: Duke University Press, 2002), 234.
6. Arif Dirlik, "The Asia Pacific Idea," in *What Is in a Rim? Critical Perspectives on the Pacific Region Idea*, ed. Arif Dirlik, 2nd ed. (Lanham, MD: Rowman and Littlefield, 1998), 15–36.
7. Gary Y. Okihiro, *Margins and Mainstreams: Asians in American History and Culture* (Seattle: University of Washington Press, 1994), 16.
8. Arif Dirlik, "The Asia-Pacific Idea: Reality and Representation in the Invention of a Regional Structure," *Journal of World History* 3 (1992): 66.
9. Harry D. Harootunian, *History's Disquiet: Modernity, Cultural Practice, and the Question of Everyday Life* (New York: Columbia University Press, 2000),

25–58; and Rey Chow, "Theory, Area Studies, Cultural Studies: Issues of Pedagogy in Multiculturalism," in *Ethics after Idealism: Theory, Culture, Ethnicity, Reading* (Bloomington: Indiana University Press, 1998), 1–13.

10. Maxine Hong Kingston, *The Woman Warrior: Memoirs of a Girlhood among Ghosts* (New York: Knopf, 1976).

11. Wilson, "Imagining 'Asia-Pacific' Today," 233.

12. Marianne Katoppo, *Compassionate and Free: An Asian Woman's Theology* (Geneva: World Council of Churches, 1979).

13. Naomi Southard and Rita Nakashima Brock, "The Other Half of the Basket: Asian American Women and the Search for a Theological Home," *Journal of Feminist Studies in Religion* 3, no. 2 (1987): 137–39.

14. Kwok Pui-lan, "Business Ethics in the Economic Development of Asia: A Feminist Analysis," *Asia Journal of Theology* 9, no. 1 (1995): 133–45.

15. Chalsa M. Loo, "Slaying Demons with a Sewing Needle: Gender Differences and Women's Status," in *Chinatown: Most Time, Hard Time* (New York: Praeger, 1991), 189–210; Miriam Ching Louie, "Immigrant Asian Women in Bay Area Garment Sweatshops: 'After Sewing, Laundry, Cleaning and Cooking, I Have No Breath Left to Sing,'" *Amerasia Journal* 18 (1992): 1–26; and Miriam Ching Louie, *Sweatshop Warriors: Immigrant Women Workers Take on Global Factory* (Cambridge, MA: South End Press, 2001). See also Saskia Sassen, "Notes on the Incorporation of Third World Women into Wage Labor through Immigration and Offshore Production," in *Globalization and Its Discontent* (New York: New Press, 1998), 111–31.

16. See Mary John Mananzan, "Sexual Exploitation of Women in a Third World Setting," in *Essays on Women*, rev. ed., ed. Mary John Mananzan (Manila, Philippines: St. Scholastica's College, 1991), 104–12; Nantawan Boonprasat Lewis, "When Justice Collapses: A Religious Response to Sexual Violence and Trafficking in Women in Asia," in *Off the Menu*, ed. Brock, et al., 217–30.

17. Samuel P. Huntington, *The Clash of Civilizations and the Remaking of World Order* (New York: Simon and Schuster, 1996).

18. Michael Chang, *Racial Politics in an Era of Transnational Citizenship: The 1996 "Asian Donorgate" Controversy in Perspective* (Lanham, MD: Lexington Books, 2004), xiii.

19. Aihwa Ong, *Flexible Citizenship: The Cultural Logic of Transnationality* (Durham, NC: Duke University Press, 1999).

20. Lowe, *Immigrant Acts*.

21. Nami Kim, "'My/Our' Comfort *Not* at the Expense of 'Somebody Else's,'" *Journal of Feminist Studies in Religion* 21, no. 2 (2005): 75–94.

22. Kwok Pui-lan, *Postcolonial Imagination and Feminist Theology* (Louisville, KY: Westminster John Knox Press, 2005).

23. Paul Gilroy, *The Black Atlantic: Modernity and Double Consciousness* (Cambridge, MA: Harvard University Press, 1993).

24. Edward W. Said, *Culture and Imperialism* (New York: Knopf, 1994), 51.

25. Michael Hardt and Antonio Negri, *Empire* (Cambridge, MA: Harvard University Press, 2000), xii–xiii.

26. Harootunian, *History's Disquiet*, 41.

27. Arjun Appadurai, "Grassroots Globalization and the Research Imagination," in *Globalization*, ed. Arjun Appadurai (Durham, NC: Duke University Press, 2001), 2; see also the discussion in Elizabeth A. Castelli, "Globalization, Transnational Feminisms, and the Future of Biblical Critique," in *Feminist New Testament Studies: Global and Future Perspectives*, ed. Kathleen O'Brien Wicker,

Althea Spencer Miller, and Musa W. Dube (New York: Palgrave Macmillan, 2005), 68.
28. Max Weber, *The Protestant Ethic and the Spirit of Capitalism*, trans. Talcott Parsons (New York: Scribner's, 1958).
29. Max Weber, *The Religion of China: Confucianism and Taoism*, trans. Hans H. Gerth (New York: Macmillan, 1964). The original in German was published in 1915. For a critique of Weber's view, see C. K. Yang's introduction to the 1964 edition of this book, xiii-xliii.
30. Tu Wei-ming, *Confucian Ethics Today: The Singapore Challenge* (Singapore: Federal Publications, 1984); see also his article "Cultural China: The Periphery as the Center," *Daedalus* 120, no. 2 (1991): 1–32; and Arif Dirlik, "Confucius in the Borderlands: Global Capitalism and the Reinvention of Confucianism," *boundary 2* 22, no, 3 (1995): 229–73.
31. Namsoon Kang, "Confucian Familism and Its Social/Religious Embodiment in Christianity: Reconsidering the Family Discourse from a Feminist Perspective," *Asia Journal of Theology* 18, no. 1 (2004): 171.
32. George Lakoff, *Moral Politics: How Liberals and Conservatives Think*, 2nd ed. (Chicago: University of Chicago Press, 2002), 166–67.
33. Kathryn Tanner, *Economy of Grace* (Minneapolis: Fortress Press, 2005).
34. John Milbank's work on gift exchange has been cited by Tanner and other scholars, see John Milbank, "Can a Gift Be Given?" *Modern Theology* 11, no. 1 (1995): 119–61.
35. I thank Rita Nakashima Brock for her input on the gift exchange model.
36. Aruna Gnanadason, *Listen to the Women! Listen to the Earth!* (Geneva: World Council of Churches, 2005), 90–91.
37. Gnanadason, *Listen to the Women!*, 96.
38. Rey Chow, "The Secrets of Ethnic Abjection," in *The Protestant Ethnic and the Spirit of Capitalism* (New York: Columbia University Press, 2002), 128.
39. Rey Chow, "The Interruption of Referentiality; or, Poststructuralism's Outside," in *The Age of the World Target: Self-Referentiality in War, Theory, and Comparative Work* (Durham, NC: Duke University Press, 2006), 45–69.
40. Castelli, "Globalization," 70.
41. Theologians and ethicists from these groups have debated vigorously how they use these terms to designate themselves. See Kwok Pui-lan and Rachel A. R. Bundang, "PANAAWTM Lives!" *Journal of Feminist Studies in Religion*, 21, no. 2 (2005): 147–58; the roundtable discussion "Must I Be Womanist?" *Journal of Feminist Studies in Religion* 22, no. 1 (2006): 85–134; and Michelle A. González, "'One Is Not Born a Latina, One Becomes One': The Construction of Latina Feminist Theologian in Latino/a Theology," *Journal of Hispanic/Latino Theology* 10, no. 3 (2002): 5–30.
42. Ivone Gebara, *Longing for Running Water: Ecofeminism and Liberation* (Minneapolis: Fortress Press, 1999), 12–13; Karen Baker-Fletcher, "The Erotic in Contemporary Black Women's Writings," in *Loving the Body: Black Religious Studies and the Erotic*, ed. Anthony B. Pinn and Dwight N. Hopkins (New York: Palgrave Macmillan, 2004), 199–200; Kwok, *Postcolonial Imagination and Feminist Theology*.
43. Harootunian, *History's Disquiet*, 46.
44. Appadurai, "Grassroots Globalization," 8
45. Appadurai, "Grassroots Globalization," 7–8.
46. Virginia Fabella, "A Common Methodology for Diverse Christologies?" in *With Passion and Compassion: Third World Women Doing Theology*, ed. Virginia

Fabella and Mercy Amba Oduyoye (Maryknoll, NY: Orbis Books, 1990), 108–17.

47. Wai-Ching Angela Wong, "Asian Theology in a Changing Asia: Towards an Asian Theological Agenda for the Twenty-first Century," *CTC Bulletin*, Special Supplement 1 (1997): 33.

48. This formulation of the uniqueness of Asia was presented by Aloysius Pieris in "Towards an Asian Theology of Liberation: Some Religio-cultural Guidelines," in *Asia's Struggle for Full Humanity*, ed. Virginia Fabella (Maryknoll, NY: Orbis Books, 1980), 75–76. Many Asian theologians have subsequently followed his characterization.

49. See the discussion of hybridity and interstitial third space in Wonhee Anne Joh, *Heart of the Cross: A Postcolonial Christology* (Louisville, KY: Westminster John Knox Press, 2006), 53–66.

50. Rita Nakashima Brock, "Interstitial Integrity: Reflections toward an Asian American Woman's Theology," in *Introduction to Theology*, ed. Roger A. Badham (Louisville, KY: Westminster John Knox Press, 1998), 190.

51. Chang, *Racial Politics*, xiii.

52. Wong, "Asian Theology in a Changing Asia," 37–39.

53. Lowe, *Immigrant Acts*, 30, emphasis added.

54. I benefit from the work of Ella Shohat in conceptualizing these complex phenomena. See Ella Shohat, "Area Studies, Gender Studies, and the Cartographies of Knowledge," *Social Text* 72 (Fall 2002): 67–78.

55. Kwok Pui-lan, ed., *Asian and Asian American Women in Theology and Religion: Embodying Knowledge* (Cham, Switzerland: Palgrave Macmillan, 2020).

56. Appadurai, "Grassroots Globalization," 16.

57. Catherine Keller, *God and Power: Counter-apocalyptic Journeys* (Minneapolis: Fortress Press, 2005), 116.

58. Edward W. Said, *Humanism and Democratic Criticism* (New York: Columbia University Press, 2004), 135.

59. Lowe, *Immigrant Acts*, 172.

60. In December 2006, Nicole won the case against Lance Corporal Daniel Smith, who was convicted and sentenced to forty years in prison by a Philippine court. The three other marines were acquitted of complicity. However, the court of appeals reversed the decision of the lower court in 2009 and ordered Smith's immediate release.

61. Shohat, "Area Studies," 78.

7: The Hong Kong Protests and Civil Disobedience

1. James Griffiths, "Chaos and Disruption across Hong Kong as Protesters Fortify University Campus," CNN, November 13, 2019, https://www.cnn .com/2019/11/12/asia/hong-kong-protests-chinese-university-intl-hnk/index .html.

2. The term "Hongkonger" refers to a native or inhabitant of Hong Kong. People call themselves "Hongkongers" when they want to claim their local identity with values and customs that are different from those of the Chinese.

3. Wing-sang Law, "Hong Kong Identity in Historical Perspective," in *Citizenship, Identity and Social Movements in the New Hong Kong: Localism After the Umbrella Movement*, ed. Wai-man Lam and Luke Cooper (New York: Routledge, 2018), 14.

4. Law, "Hong Kong Identity in Historical Perspective," 14.

5. Albert Sui-hung Lee, "Is Dialogue in the Church Still Feasible after the Hong Kong Protests?" in *The Hong Kong Protests and Political Theology*, ed. Kwok Pui-lan and Francis Ching-wah Yip (Lanham, MD: Rowman and Littlefield, 2021), 149–68.

6. For example, Kwok Pui-lan, ed., *1997 yu Xianggang shenxue* (1997 and Hong Kong theology) (Hong Kong: Chung Chi College Theology Division, 1983).

7. Archie C. C. Lee, "Returning to China: Biblical Interpretation in Postcolonial Hong Kong," *Biblical Interpretation* 7, no. 2 (1999): 156–73. The article was based on a presentation in 1997.

8. Francis Ching-wah Yip, *Xunzhen qiuquan: Zhongguo shenxue yu zhengjiao chujing chutan* (Chinese theology in state-church context: A preliminary study) (Hong Kong: Christian Study Centre on Chinese Religion and Culture, 1997).

9. Wai-ching Angela Wong, *"The Poor Woman": A Critical Analysis of Asian Theology and Contemporary Chinese Fiction by Women* (New York: Peter Lang, 2002); and Simon Shui-man Kwan, *Postcolonial Resistance and Asian Theology* (London: Routledge, 2014).

10. Beatrice Leung and Shun-hing Chan, *Changing Church and State Relations in Hong Kong, 1950–2000* (Hong Kong: Hong Kong University Press, 2003); and Kung Lap-yan "Politics and Religions in Hong Kong after 1997: Whether Tension or Equilibrium Is Needed," *Religion, State & Society* 32, no. 1 (2004): 21–36.

11. Justin K. H. Tse and Jonathan Y. Tan, eds., *Theological Reflections on the Hong Kong Umbrella Movement* (New York: Palgrave Macmillan, 2016); and Shun-hing Chan, "The Protestant Community and the Umbrella Movement in Hong Kong," *Inter-Asia Cultural Studies* 16, no. 3 (2015): 380–95.

12. Cliff Buddle, "Can Beijing's Power to Interpret Hong Kong's Basic Law Ever Be Questioned?" *South China Morning Post*, October 11, 2017, https://www.scmp.com/comment/insight-opinion/article/2114919/can-beijings-power-interpret-hong-kongs-basic-law-ever-be.

13. Lily Kuo, Verna Yu, and Helen Davidson, "'This Is the End of Hong Kong': China Pushes Controversial Security Laws," *The Guardian*, May 21, 2020, https://www.theguardian.com/world/2020/may/21/china-proposes-controversial-national-security-law-for-hong-kong.

14. Regina Ip, "Hong Kong Is a Part of China, Like It or Not," *New York Times*, October 1, 2020, https://www.nytimes.com/2020/10/01/opinion/hong-kong-china-security-law.html.

15. Chang Che, "The Nazi Inspiring China's Communists: A Decades-old Legal Argument Used by Hitler Has Found Support in Beijing," *The Atlantic*, December 1, 2020, https://www.theatlantic.com/international/archive/2020/12/nazi-china-communists-carl-schmitt/617237/.

16. Qi Zheng, "Carl Schmitt in China," *Telos* 160 (Fall 2012): 32–35.

17. Carl Schmitt, *Political Theology: Four Chapters on the Concept of Sovereignty*, trans. George Schwab (Cambridge, MA: MIT Press, 2005), 36.

18. Reinhold Niebuhr, *The Children of Light and the Children of Darkness: A Vindication of Democracy and a Critique of Its Traditional Defense* (1944; Chicago: University of Chicago Press, 2011), xi.

19. Chang Hao, *Youan yishi yu minzhu chuantong* (Dark Consciousness and the democratic tradition) (Taipei: Lien Ching Publisher, 1990).

20. Sungmoon Kim, *Confucian Democracy in East Asia: Theory and Practice* (Cambridge: Cambridge University Press, 2014).

21. Lee, "Return to China," 158.

22. Xin Liu, "'Too Simple and Sometimes Naïve': Hong Kong, Between China and the West," in *Routledge Handbook of Postcolonial Politics*, ed. Olivia U. Rutazibwa and Robbie Shilliam (New York: Routledge, 2018), 260–62.

23. Adela Suliman, Eric Baculinao, and Ed Flanagan, "China's Xi Jinping Spots Shenzhen as Future for Economic Growth, Hong Kong Given Back Seat," NBC News, October 14, 2020, https://www.nbcnews.com/news/world/china -s-xi-jinping-spotlights-shenzhen-future-economic-growth-hong-n1243298.

24. Agnes Shuk-mei Ku, "Identity as Politics: Contesting the Local, The National and the Global," in *Routledge Handbook of Contemporary Hong Kong*, ed. Tai-lok Lui, Stephen W. K. Chui, and Ray Yep (London: Routledge, 2018), 453.

25. Joshua Wong with Jason Y. Ng, *Unfree Speech: The Threat to Global Democracy and Why We Must Act, Now* (New York: Penguin Books, 2020), 240.

26. Wong, *Unfree Speech*, 241.

27. Hung Shin-fung, "'If Not Us, Who?' Youth Participation and Salient Aspects of the Protests," in *The Hong Kong Protests and Political Theology*, ed. Kwok and Yip, 65–67.

28. Ku, "Identity as Politics," 455.

29. Ciara Nugent, "From Chile to Hong Kong, the World Saw a Lot of Protests in 2019. Here's Why That Trend Is Going to Continue," *Time*, January 16, 2020, https://time.com/5766422/protests-unrest-2019-2020/.

30. "History," The Baltic Way, http://www.thebalticway.eu/en/history/.

31. "'March for the Beloved' Sung at the Hong Kong protests," YouTube, June 17, 2019, https://www.youtube.com/watch?v=2s3H_t6cTfg.

32. Nami Kim, "When the Minjung Events Erupt: Protest from Korea to Hong Kong," in *The Hong Kong Protests and Political Theology*, ed. Kwok and Yip, 179.

33. Judith Butler, *Notes toward a Performative Theory of Assembly* (Cambridge, MA: Harvard University Press, 2015).

34. For example, Francis L. F. Lee and Joseph M. Chan, *Media and Protest Logics in the Digital Era: The Umbrella Movement in Hong Kong* (New York: Oxford University Press, 2018); and Elizabeth Brunner, *Environmental Activism, Social Media, and Protest in China: Becoming Activists over Wild Public Networks* (Lanham, MD: Lexington Books, 2019).

35. Benny Y. T. Tai, "From Past to Future: Hong Kong's Democratic Movement," in *Citizenship, Identity and Social Movements in the New Hong Kong*, 157.

36. Martin Luther King Jr., *The Papers of Martin Luther King, Jr.*, vol. 4, *Symbol of the Movement, January 1957–December 1958*, ed. Clayborne Carson (Berkeley: University of California Press, 1992), 306.

37. See the discussion of the book in Sharon D. Welch, "The Power of Nonviolent Direct Action," in *The Hong Kong Protests and Political Theology*, ed. Kwok and Yip, 219.

38. John Rawls, *A Theory of Justice* (Oxford: Oxford University Press, 1972), 363–91.

39. Candice Delmas, *A Duty to Resist: When Disobedience Should Be Uncivil* (New York: Oxford University Press, 2018).

40. Delmas, *A Duty to Resist*, 29–30.

41. Delmas, *A Duty to Resist*, 106.

42. Candice Delmas, "Uncivil Disobedience in Hong Kong," *Boston Review*, January 13, 2020, http://bostonreview.net/global-justice/candice-delmas-uncivil -disobedience-hong-kong.

43. Sum Loi-kei, "Nearly a Fifth of Hong Kong Voters Say They Support Violent Actions by Protesters, such as Attacking Opponents or Hurling Petrol Bombs and Bricks," *South China Morning Post*, December 21, 2019, https://

www.scmp.com/news/hong-kong/politics/article/3043073/nearly-fifth-voters
-say-they-support-violent-actions.
44. Delmas, "Uncivil Disobedience." Emphasis hers.
45. Delmas, "Uncivil Disobedience."
46. Lai Tsz-him, "Understanding the Use of Violence in the Hong Kong Protests," in *The Hong Kong Protests and Political Theology*, ed. Kwok and Yip, 85–86.
47. John Howard Yoder, *The Politics of Jesus*, rev. ed. (Grand Rapids: Eerdmans, 1992).
48. Miguel A. De La Torre, *Decolonizing Christianity: Becoming Badass Believers* (Grand Rapids: Eerdmans, 2021), 208.
49. De La Torre, *Decolonizing Christianity*, 207–8.
50. De La Torre, *Decolonizing Christianity*, 208, contests the portrayal of Jesus as a pacifist.
51. Agence France-Presse, "Hong Kong Protests: Arrests as Thousands Sing Protest Anthem on Anniversary of Clashes," *The Guardian*, June 12, 2020, https://www.theguardian.com/world/2020/jun/13/hong-kong-protests-arrests-as-thousands-sing-protest-anthem-on-anniversary-of-clashes.
52. Shibani Mahtani, Timothy McLaughlin, and Theodora Yu, "With New Mass Detentions, Every Prominent Hong Kong Activist Is Either in Jail or Exile," *Washington Post*, February 28, 2021, https://www.washingtonpost.com/world/asia_pacific/hong-kong-arrests-national-security-law/2021/02/28/7e6cd252-77ea-11eb-9489-8f7dacd51e75_story.html.
53. Kung Lap-yan, "Crucified People, Messianic Time, and Youth in Protest," in *The Hong Kong Protests and Political Theology*, ed. Kwok and Yip, 136.
54. Kung, "Crucified People," 139.

8: Teaching Theology from a Global Perspective

1. bell hooks, *Teaching to Transgress: Education as the Practice of Freedom* (New York: Routledge, 1994), 8.
2. Gayatri Chakravorty Spivak, "How to Read a 'Culturally Different' Book," in *An Aesthetic Education in the Era of Globalization* (Cambridge, MA: Harvard University Press, 2012), 73–96.
3. Willie James Jennings, *After Whiteness: An Education in Belonging* (Grand Rapids: Eerdmans, 2020), 6.
4. Joerg Rieger and Kwok Pui-lan, *Occupy Religion: Theology of the Multitude* (Lanham, MD: Rowman and Littlefield, 2012), 5–6.
5. John Tomlinson speaks of globalization as "complex connectivity" in his *Globalization and Culture* (Chicago: University of Chicago Press, 1999), 2.
6. Anthony Giddens, *The Consequences of Modernity* (Stanford: Stanford University Press, 1990), 64.
7. Roland Robertson, "Glocalization: Time-Space and Homogeneity-Heterogeneity," in *Global Modernities*, ed. Mike Featherstone, Scott Lash, and Roland Robertson (London: Sage Publications, 1995), 25–44.
8. Harold A. Netland, "Introduction: Globalization and Theology Today," in *Globalizing Theology: Belief and Practice in an Era of World Christianity*, ed. Craig Ott and Harold A. Netland (Grand Rapids: Baker Academic, 2006), 25–27.
9. Gustavo Gutiérrez, *A Theology of Liberation: History, Politics, and Salvation*, trans. Caridad Inda and John Eagleson (Maryknoll, NY: Orbis Books, 1973).
10. Sergio Torres and John Eagleson, eds., *Theology in the Americas* (Maryknoll, NY: Orbis Books, 1976).

11. Robert J. Schreiter, *Constructing Local Theologies* (Maryknoll, NY: Orbis Books, 1985), 5.
12. Stephen B. Bevans, *An Introduction to Theology in Global Perspective* (Maryknoll, NY: Orbis Books, 2009).
13. Andrew Walls, *The Significance of African Christianity* (Edinburgh: St. Colm's Education Center and College, 1989), 3, quoted in Tite Tiénou, "Christian Theology in an Era of World Christianity," in *Globalizing Theology*, ed. Ott and Netland, 40.
14. Philip Jenkins, "The Next Christianity," *The Atlantic*, October 2002, http://www.theatlantic.com/magazine/archive/2002/10/the-next-christianity/302591/.
15. Lamin Sanneh, "Missionary Enterprise," in *Encyclopedia of African South of the Sahara*, ed. John Middleton (New York: Charles Scribner's Sons, 1997), 296.
16. Lamin Sanneh, *Whose Religion Is Christianity? The Gospel beyond the West* (Grand Rapids: Eerdmans, 2003), 22.
17. Walter Hollenweger, "Intercultural Theology: Some Remarks on the Term," in *Towards an Intercultural Theology: Essays in Honour of J. A. B. Jongeneel*, ed. Martha Frederiks, Meindert Dijkstra, and Anton Houtepen (Zoetermeer, Netherlands: Uitgeverij Meinema, 2003), 94, quoted in Tiénou, "Christian Theology," 42.
18. Soong-Chan Rah, *The Next Evangelicalism: Freeing the Church from Western Cultural Captivity* (Downers Grove, IL: IVP Books, 2009).
19. The syllabi can be found at the Wabash Center website, https://www.wabashcenter.wabash.edu/syllabi-topic/Theology/.
20. Kwok Pui-lan, Cecilia González-Andrieu, and Dwight N. Hopkins, eds., *Teaching Global Theologies: Power and Praxis* (Waco, TX: Baylor University Press, 2015).
21. William A. Dyrness, *Emerging Voices in Global Christian Theology* (Grand Rapids: Zondervan Publishing House, 1994), 13.
22. Veli-Matti Kärkkäinen, *Introduction to Ecclesiology: Ecumenical, Historical, and Global Perspectives* (Downers Grove, IL: InterVarsity Press, 2002); *Christology: A Global Introduction* (Grand Rapids: Baker Academic, 2003); *The Doctrine of God: A Global Introduction* (Grand Rapids: Baker Academic, 2004); *The Trinity: Global Perspectives* (Louisville, KY: Westminster John Knox Press, 2007).
23. Hans Schwarz, *Theology in a Global Context: The Last Two Hundred Years* (Grand Rapids: Eerdmans, 2005).
24. Namsoon Kang, "Re-constructing Asian Feminist Theology: Toward a Glocal Feminist Theology in an Era of Neo Empire(s)," in *Christian Theology in Asia*, ed. Sebastian C. H. Kim (Cambridge: Cambridge University Press, 2008), 210–11.
25. See the discussion in Dipesh Chakrabarty, *Provincializing Europe: Postcolonial Thought and Historical Difference* (Princeton, NJ: Princeton University Press, 2000).
26. Tiénou, "Christian Theology," 38.
27. Andrew Walls, "Globalization and the Study of Christian History," in *Globalizing Theology*, ed. Ott and Netland, 74.
28. For a detailed discussion of the stele, see P. Y. Saeki, *The Nestorian Monument in China* (London: Society for the Promotion of Christian Knowledge, 1916).
29. See chapter 2 in this volume.
30. Simon Shui-Man Kwan, *Postcolonial Resistance and Asian Theology* (London: Routledge, 2014).

31. Lai Pan-chiu, "Teaching Global Theology with Local Resources: A Chinese Theologian's Strategies," in *Teaching Global Theologies*, ed. Kwok, González-Andrieu, and Hopkins, 91–104.
32. Robert J. Schreiter, *The New Catholicity: Theology between the Global and the Local* (Maryknoll, NY: Orbis Books, 1997).
33. Schreiter, *The New Catholicity*, 132–33.
34. Schreiter, *The New Catholicity*, 16–20.
35. Orlando O. Espín, *Idol and Grace: On Traditioning and Subversive Hope* (Maryknoll, NY: Orbis Books, 2014), 17.
36. Espín, *Idol and Grace*, 10–13.
37. Mary McClintock Fulkerson and Sheila Briggs, "Introduction," in *The Oxford Handbook of Feminist Theology*, ed. Mary McClintock Fulkerson and Sheila Briggs (Oxford: Oxford University Press, 2012), 7–9.
38. Musa W. Dube, "Feminist Theologies of a World Scripture(s) in the Globalization Era," in *The Oxford Handbook of Feminist Theology*, ed. Fulkerson and Briggs, 387.
39. Ellen T. Armour, "Beyond the God/Man Duo: Globalization, Feminist Theology, and Religious Subjectivity," in *The Oxford Handbook of Feminist Theology*, ed. Fulkerson and Briggs, 371–81; and Sharon D. Welch, "Beyond Theology of Religions: The Epistemological and Ethical Challenges of Inter-Religious Engagement," in *The Oxford Handbook of Feminist Theology*, ed. Fulkerson and Briggs, 353–70.
40. Gayatri Chakravorty Spivak, *Other Asias* (Malden, MA: Blackwell, 2008), 1.
41. The Association of Theological Schools in the United States and Canada published the issue "Globalizing Theological Education in North America" in *Theological Education* in Spring of 1986, and other issues on globalization and theological education in Autumn of 1986, and Spring and Autumn of 1993.
42. Edward W. Said, *Orientalism* (New York: Vintage, 1979).
43. Dube, "Feminist Theologies," 394.
44. Gayatri Chakravorty Spivak was the first critic to use the term "transnational literacy" extensively.
45. Gutiérrez, *A Theology of Liberation*.
46. Rauna Kuokkanen, *Reshaping the University: Responsibilities, Indigenous Epistemes, and the Logic of the Gift* (Vancouver: University of British Columbia Press, 2007), 1.
47. William A. Dyrness, "Why Don't We Hear Much from the Global Church?" Teaching Theology in a Global and Transnational World, https://teachingtheology.blogspot.com/2011/11/why-dont-we-hear-much-from-global.html.
48. Althea Spencer Miller, "Feminist Pedagogies: Implications of a Liberative Praxis," in *Feminist New Testament Studies: Global and Future Perspectives*, ed. Kathleen O'Brien Wicker, Althea Spencer Miller, and Musa W. Dube (New York: Palgrave Macmillan, 2005), 34.
49. Miller, "Feminist Pedagogies," 35.
50. A helpful resource is Eleazar S. Fernandez, ed., *Teaching for a Culturally Diverse and Racially Just World* (Eugene, OR: Cascade Books, 2014).
51. The digital natives are those who were born into the culture of the Internet and digital media. Others are digital immigrants who have to learn the culture and catch up with the digital age. For the culture of the digital natives, see John Palfrey and Urs Gasser, *Born Digital: Understanding the First Generation of Digital Natives* (New York: Basic Books, 2010).

9: Postcolonial Preaching in Intercultural Contexts

1. Pablo A. Jiménez, "If You Just Close Your Eyes: Postcolonial Perspectives on Preaching from the Caribbean," *Homiletic* 40, no. 1 (2015): 28.

2. Lucy Atkinson Rose, *Sharing the Word: Preaching in the Roundtable Church* (Louisville, KY: Westminster John Knox Press, 1997).

3. Pablo Jiménez, "Toward a Postcolonial Homiletic: Justo L. González's Contribution to Hispanic Preaching," in *Hispanic Christian Thought at the Dawn of the Twenty-First Century: Apuntes in Honor of Justo L. González*, ed. Alvin Padilla et al. (Nashville: Abingdon Press, 2005), 159–67; Sarah Travis, *Decolonizing Preaching: The Pulpit as Postcolonial Space* (Eugene, OR: Cascade Books, 2014); the special issue of *Homiletic* 40, no. 1 (2015); and HyeRan Kim-Cragg, *Postcolonial Preaching: Creating a Ripple Effect* (Lanham, MD: Lexington Books, 2021).

4. Michael N. Jagessar and Stephen Burns, *Christian Worship: Postcolonial Perspectives* (London: Equinox, 2011); HyeRan Kim-Cragg, *Story and Song: A Postcolonial Interplay between Christian Education and Worship* (New York: Peter Lang, 2012); and Cláudio Carvalhaes, ed., *Liturgy in Postcolonial Perspectives: Only One Is Holy* (New York: Palgrave Macmillan, 2015).

5. Kwok Pui-lan, "Feminist Theology as Intercultural Discourse," in *The Cambridge Companion to Feminist Theology*, ed. Susan Frank Parsons (Cambridge: Cambridge University Press, 2002), 25.

6. Homi K. Bhabha, *The Location of Culture* (London: Routledge, 1994), 38, emphasis his.

7. Bhabha, *The Location of Culture*, 36–39.

8. Christopher Baker, *The Hybrid Church in the City* (Aldershot, UK: Ashgate, 2007), 125–35.

9. Baker, *The Hybrid Church in the City*, 154.

10. Rose, *Sharing the Word*, 15.

11. J. L. Austin, *How to Do Things with Words* (Cambridge, MA: Harvard University Press, 1962).

12. Eleazar S. Fernandez, "Orchestrating New Theological Overtures: Heterogeneity, Dissonance, and Fluidity vis-à-vis Imperial Monophony," *Journal of Race, Ethnicity, and Religion* 3, no. 2.1 (January 2012): 9, http://www.raceandreligion.com/JRER/Volume_3_(2012)_files/2%2013%201%20Intro.pdf.

13. Tat-siong Benny Liew, "Introduction: Intervening on the Postcolonial," in *Postcolonial Intervention: Essays in Honor of R. S. Sugirtharajah*, ed. Tat-siong Benny Liew (Sheffield, UK: Sheffield Phoenix Press, 2009), 15.

14. Travis, *Decolonizing Preaching*, 48.

15. Christopher Duraisingh, "Towards a Postcolonial Re-Visioning of the Church's Faith, Witness, and Communion," in *Beyond Colonial Anglicanism: The Anglican Communion in the Twenty-First Century*, ed. Ian T. Douglas and Kwok Pui-lan (New York: Church Publishing, 2001), 337.

16. Judith Butler, *Gender Trouble: Feminism and the Subversion of Identity* (New York: Routledge, 1990).

17. Judith Butler and Athena Athanasiou, *Dispossession: The Performative in the Political* (Cambridge: Polity Press, 2013), 178.

18. Butler and Athanasiou, *Dispossession*, 178.

19. Joerg Rieger and Kwok Pui-lan, *Occupy Religion: Theology of the Multitude* (Lanham, MD: Rowman and Littlefield, 2012), 111–32.

20. Jagessar and Burns, *Christian Worship*, 49.

21. Jagessar and Burns, *Christian Worship*, 52–53.

22. Martyn Percy discusses the development of vestments and clerical collar in *Clergy: The Origin of Species* (New York: Continuum, 2006), 88–91.
23. Jeffrey J. Meyers, "Why Does the Pastor Wear a Robe?" *Theologia*, http://www.hornes.org/theologia/jeffrey-meyers/why-does-the-pastor-wear-a-robe.
24. Glauco S. de Lima, "Preface," in *Beyond Colonial Anglicanism*, ed. Douglas and Kwok, 3.
25. For example, Richard L. Eslinger, *A New Hearing: Living Options in Homiletic Methods* (Nashville: Abingdon, 1987); and Thomas G. Long, *The Witness of Preaching*, 2nd ed. (Louisville, KY: Westminster John Knox Press, 2005).
26. Stephen Burns makes some suggestions to make preaching more dialogical in *SCM Studyguide to Liturgy* (London: SCM, 2006), 88–90.
27. Justo L. González, "Standing at the *Púlpito*," in *Púlpito: An Introduction to Hispanic Preaching*, ed. Justo L. González and Pablo A. Jiménez (Nashville: Abingdon, 2005), 57.
28. Virgilio Elizondo, "Seven Last Words," in *Púlpito*, ed. González and Jiménez, 89–94.
29. Elizondo, "Seven Last Words," 89.
30. Henry H. Mitchell, *Black Preaching: The Recovery of a Powerful Act* (Nashville: Abingdon, 1990), 88–97.
31. Evans E. Crawford, *The Hum: Call and Response in African American Preaching* (Nashville: Abingdon Press, 1995).
32. Timothy Jones mentioned at a conference that sometimes the dialogical or the call and response models can also reinforce the authority of the preacher and the context must be taken into consideration.
33. Teresa L. Fry Brown, *Weary Throats and New Songs: Black Women Proclaiming God's Word* (Nashville: Abingdon Press, 2003). See also Donna E. Allen, *Toward a Womanist Homiletic: Katie Cannon, Alice Walker and Emancipatory Proclamation* (New York: Peter Lang, 2013).
34. Eunjoo Mary Kim, *Preaching the Presence of God: A Homiletic from an Asian American Perspective* (Valley Forge, PA: Judson Press, 1999), 110.
35. Kim, *Preaching the Presence of God*, 111.
36. Kim, *Preaching the Presence of God*, 123.
37. Kim-Cragg, *Postcolonial Preaching*.
38. Jagessar and Burns, *Christian Worship*, 71-85; and Travis, *Decolonizing Preaching*, 109–26.
39. Musa W. Dube, *Postcolonial Feminist Interpretation of the Bible* (St. Louis: Chalice Press, 2000).
40. Musa W. Dube, "The Unpublished Letters of Orpah to Ruth," in *Ruth and Esther: A Feminist Companion to the Bible* (second series), ed. Athalya Brenner (Sheffield, UK: Sheffield Academic Press,1999), 145–50.
41. Dube, *Postcolonial Feminist Interpretation*; Laura E. Donaldson, "The Sign of Orpah: Reading Ruth through Native Eyes," in *Ruth and Esther*, ed. Brenner, 130–42; Kwok Pui-lan, "Finding Ruth a Home: Gender, Sexuality and the Politics of Otherness," in *Postcolonial Imagination and Feminist Theology* (Louisville, KY: Westminster John Knox Press, 2005), 100–121; Kwok Pui-lan, "Woman, Dogs, and Crumbs: Constructing a Postcolonial Discourse," in *Discovering the Bible in the Non-Biblical World* (Maryknoll, NY: Orbis Books, 1995), 71–83; and Laura E. Donaldson, "Gospel Hauntings: The Postcolonial Demons of Biblical Criticism," in *Postcolonial Biblical Criticism: Interdisciplinary Intersections*, ed. Stephen D. Moore and Fernando F. Segovia (London: T. and T. Clark, 2005), 97–113.
42. Dube, *Postcolonial Feminist Interpretation*, 111.

43. Kwok Pui-lan, "On Color-Coding Jesus: An Interview with Kwok Pui-lan," in *The Postcolonial Bible*, ed. R. S. Sugirtharajah (Sheffield, UK: Sheffield Academic Press, 1998), 176–88.

44. For example, Joseph A. Buttigieg and Paul A. Bové, "An Interview with Edward W. Said," *boundary 2*, 20, no. 1 (1993): 1–25; Jonathan Rutherford, "The Third Space: Interview with Homi Bhabha" in *Identity: Community, Culture, Difference*, ed. Jonathan Rutherford (London: Lawrence and Wishart, 1990), 207–21; and Gayatri Chakravorty Spivak, *The Post-colonial Critic: Interviews, Strategies, Dialogues* (London: Routledge, 1990).

45. Kwok, "On Color-Coding Jesus," 176.

46. Kwok, "On Color-Coding Jesus," 178.

47. Kwok Pui-lan, "Prologue," in *Discovering the Bible*, ix–xvi and "Epilogue," in *Discovering the Bible*, 96–100; and Kwok Pui-lan, "Worshipping with Asian Women: A Homily on Jesus Healing the Daughter of a Canaanite Woman," in *Feminist Theology from the Third World*, ed. Ursula King (Maryknoll, NY: Orbis Books, 1994), 236–42.

48. M. M. Bakhtin, *Dialogical Imagination: Four Essays*, ed. Michael Holquist (Austin: University of Texas Press, 1981).

49. Andrew Robinson, "Bakhtin: Dialogism, Polyphony and Heteroglossia," *Ceasefire*, http://ceasefiremagazine.co.uk/in-theory-bakhtin-1/.

50. "Inauguration of Frank Yamada," McCormick videos, February 9, 2012, http://videos.mccormick.edu/video/37628709.

51. Yamada, "Inauguration of Frank Yamada."

52. Rey Chow, *Not Like a Native Speaker: On Languaging as a Postcolonial Experience* (New York: Columbia University Press, 2014), 14.

53. Mitchell, *Black Preaching*, 81.

54. Mitchell, *Black Preaching*, 83.

55. González, "Standing at the Púlpito," 61.

56. Cited in Jesse Zink, "Returning to the Body," The Living Church, August 20, 2013, https://livingchurch.org/2013/08/20/returning-body/.

57. Edward Farley, "Toward a New Paradigm for Preaching," in *Preaching as a Theological Task: World, Gospel, Scripture*, ed. Thomas G. Long and Edward Farley (Louisville, KY: Westminster John Knox Press, 1996), 169.

10: Interreligious Solidarity and Peacebuilding

1. The Dalai Lama, "A Human Approach to World Peace," Dalailama.com, https://www.dalailama.com/messages/world-peace/a-human-approach-to-world-peace.

2. Al Jazeera, "Pope Francis Urges Iraq's Muslims, Christians to Unite for Peace," Al Jazeera, March 6, 202, https://www.aljazeera.com/news/2021/3/6/pope-francis-urges-iraqs-muslims-christians-to-unite-for-peace#:~:text=Pope%20Francis%20has%20urged%20Iraq%E2%80%99s%20Muslim%20and%20Christian,of%20the%20Prophet%20Abraham%2C%20father%20of%20their%20faiths.

3. Hans Küng, *Christianity and the World Religions: Paths of Dialogue with Islam, Hinduism, and Buddhism* (Garden City, NY: Doubleday, 1986), 442.

4. Samuel P. Huntington, *The Clash of Civilizations and the Remaking of World Order* (New York: Simon and Schuster, 1996).

5. Edward W. Said, *Orientalism* (New York: Vantage Books, 1979).

6. Edward W. Said, "The Myth of the 'Clash of Civilizations,'" YouTube, https://www.youtube.com/watch?v=aPS-pONiEG8&t=606s. A version of the presentation can be found in Edward W. Said, "The Clash of Definitions," in

Reflection on Exile and Other Essays (Cambridge, MA: Harvard University Press, 2000), 569–90.

7. Scott R. Appleby, *Ambivalence of the Sacred: Religion, Violence, and Reconciliation* (Lanham, MD: Rowman and Littlefield, 2000).

8. William T. Cavanaugh, *The Myth of Religious Violence: Secular Ideologies and the Roots of Modern Conflict* (New York: Oxford University Press, 2009).

9. Talal Asad, *Formations of the Secular: Christianity, Islam, Modernity* (Stanford: Stanford University Press, 2003).

10. Mohammad Yaseen Gada, "Islamophobia and Its Historical Roots: Content, Context, and Consequences," *Hamdard Islamicus* 40, no. 2 (2017): 42.

11. Gada, "Islamophobia and Its Historical Roots," 35.

12. Prashant Waikar, "Reading Islamophobia in Hegemonic Neoliberalism through a Discourse Analysis of Donald Trump's Narratives," *Journal of Muslim Minority Affairs* 38, no. 2 (2018): 153; Emily Cury, "Contesting Islamophobia and Securing Collective Rights: Muslim American Advocacy in the 2016 Elections," *Publics and Religion* 12 (2019): 710–11.

13. Stephen R. Prothero, *Religious Literacy: What Every American Needs to Know— and Doesn't* (San Francisco: HarperSanFrancisco, 2007); and "What Is Religious Literacy?" Harvard Divinity School Religion and Public Life, https://rpl .hds.harvard.edu/what-we-do/our-approach/what-religious-literacy.

14. Ajay Verghese, "British Rule and Hindu-Muslim Riots in India: A Reassessment," Georgetown University Berkley Center for Religion, Peace, and World Affairs, August 23, 2018, https://berkleycenter.georgetown.edu/responses /british-rule-and-hindu-muslim-riots-in-india-a-reassessment.

15. Chika Njideka Oguonu and Christian Chukwuebuka Ezeibe, "African Union and Conflict Resolution in Africa," *Mediterranean Journal of Social Sciences* 5, no. 27 (2014): 328.

16. Jeff Klein, "The Colonial Roots of Middle Eastern Conflicts," CounterPunch, October 22, 2015, https://www.counterpunch.org/2015/10/22/the-colonial -roots-of-middle-east-conflict/.

17. Rabbi Alan Lurie, "Is Religion the Cause of Most Wars?" *Huffington Post*, updated June 10, 2012, http://huffpost.com/entry/is-religion-the-cause-of-_b _1400766.

18. Leonard Swidler, *Theoria-Praxis: How Jews, Christians, and Muslims Can Together Move from Theory to Praxis* (Leuven, Belgium: Uitgeverij Peeters, 1998), 28.

19. David R. Smock, "Introduction," in *Interfaith Dialogue and Peacebuilding*, ed. David R. Smock (Washington, DC: United States Institute of Peace Press, 2002), 9.

20. Alexander Laban Hinton, Giorgio Shani, and Jeremiah Alberg, "Introduction: Rethinking Peace Studies," in *Rethinking Peace: Discourse, Memory, Translations, and Dialogue*, ed. Alexander Laban Hinton, Giorgio Shani, and Jeremiah Alberg (Lanham, MD: Rowman and Littlefield, 2019), xvi. Oliver Richmond has offered the notion of "hybrid peace," in addition to the negative/positive peace binary, in *Peace: A Very Short Introduction* (Oxford: Oxford University Press, 2014).

21. Pew Research Center, "Religious Landscape Study" (2014), Pew Research Center Religion & Public Life, https://www.pewforum.org/religious-landscape-study/.

22. Khyati Y. Joshi, *White Christian Privilege: The Illusion of Religious Equality in America* (New York: New York University Press, 2020), 2.

23. Jeannine Hill Fletcher, *The Sin of White Supremacy: Christianity, Racism, and Religious Diversity* (Maryknoll, NY: Orbis Books, 2017).

24. Sheryl Kujawa-Holbrook, "Postcolonial Interreligious Learning: A Reflection from a North American Christian Perspective," in *Postcolonial Practice of Ministry: Leadership, Liturgy, and Interfaith Engagement*, ed. Kwok Pui-lan and Stephen Burns (Lanham, MD: Lexington Books, 2016), 161–63.
25. Najeeba Syeed, "Interreligious Learning and Intersectionality," in *Asian and Asian American Women in Theology and Religion: Embodying Knowledge*, ed. Kwok Pui-lan (Cham, Switzerland: Palgrave Macmillan, 2020), 171.
26. Syeed, "Interreligious Learning and Intersectionality," 177.
27. Syeed, "Interreligious Learning and Intersectionality," 179.
28. Thich Nhat Hanh, "Please Call Me by My True Names," in *Call Me by My True Names: The Collected Poems of Thich Nhat Hanh* (Berkeley, CA: Parallax Press, 1999), 72. Used by permission.
29. Thich Nhat Hanh, "Please Call Me by My True Names," http://wtf.tw/ref/nhat_hanh.html.
30. Mohammed Abu-Nimer, *Nonviolence and Peace Building in Islam: Theory and Practice* (Gainesville: University of Florida Press, 2003), 2.
31. Abu-Nimer, *Nonviolence and Peace Building in Islam*, 30.
32. Marc H. Ellis, *Reading the Torah Out Loud: A Journey of Lament and Hope* (Minneapolis: Fortress Press, 2007), 142.
33. Regina M. Schwartz, *The Curse of Cain: The Violent Legacy of Monotheism* (Chicago: University of Chicago Press, 1997), ix.
34. Schwartz, *The Curse of Cain*, 176.
35. Marc Gopin, "Judaism and Peacebuilding," in *Religion and Peacebuilding*, ed. Harold Coward and Gordon S. Smith (New York: City University of New York Press, 2004), 113. See also his *Holy War, Holy Peace: How Religion Can Bring Peace to the Middle East* (New York: Oxford University Press, 2002).
36. Gopin, "Judaism and Peacebuilding," 114–24.
37. Martin Luther King Jr., "The Power of Non-violence" June 4, 1957, https://webs.wofford.edu/whisnantdm/Sixties/Civil-Rights/The%20Power_Non-violence.pdf.
38. Naim Stifan Ateek, *A Palestinian Christian Cry for Reconciliation* (Maryknoll, NY: Orbis Books, 2008), 180.
39. Ateek, *A Palestinian Christian Cry for Reconciliation*, 184.
40. Miguel A. De La Torre, *Decolonizing Christianity: Becoming Badass Believers* (Grand Rapids: Eerdmans, 2021), 191–92.
41. Molly Pascal, "Muslims Embraced Jews When We Were Slain at Worship. Now We Must Support Them," *Washington Post*, March 15, 2019, https://www.washingtonpost.com/opinions/muslims-embraced-us-jews-when-we-were-slain-at-worship-now-we-must-support-them/2019/03/15/f8bc612c-4749-11e9-8aab-95b8d80a1e4f_story.html.
42. Gayatri Chakravorty Spivak, "Can the Subaltern Speak?" in *Marxism and the Interpretation of Culture*, ed. Cary Nelson and Lawrence Grossberg (Urbana: University of Illinois Press, 1988), 271–313.
43. Susan Hayward and Katherine Marshall, eds., *Women, Religion, and Peacebuilding: Illuminating the Unseen* (Washington, DC: United States Institute of Peace Press, 2015).
44. Scilla Elworthy, "Dekha Ibrahim Abdi Obituary," *The Guardian*, August 9, 2011, https://www.theguardian.com/global-development/2011/aug/09/dekha-ibrahim-abdi-obituary.
45. "Spiritual leader of Thailand Mae Chee Sansanee on Strengthening the Mind," Wisdom from North, October 19, 2017, https://wisdomfromnorth.com/spiritual-leader-of-thailand-mae-chee-sansanee-on-strengthening-the-mind/.

46. Maria J. Stephan, "How the Catholic Church Can Bolster Alternatives to Violence," United States Institute of Peace, November 1, 2017, https://www.usip.org/publications/2017/11/how-catholic-church-can-bolster-alternatives-violence#:~:text=In%202001%2C%20Sister%20Marie-Bernard%20Alima%20created%20the%20Coordination,healing%20for%20victims%20of%20sexual%20and%20gender-based%20violence.

47. Wonchul Shin, "*Mama, Keep Walking for Peace and Justice*: Gender Violence and Liberian Mothers' Interreligious Peace Movement," *Religions* 11, no. 7 (2020): 11, https://doi.org/10.3390/rel11070323.

48. Tony Magliano, "Reflecting on Pope Francis' 2017 World Day of Peace Message," Catholic Online, January 3, 2017, http://www.catholic.org/news/hf/faith/story.php?id=72809.

49. Jean Zaru, "Active Nonviolence Is a Sign of Hope," Ramallah Friends Meeting (Quakers), September 13, 2016, http://www.rfmq.org/single-post/2016/09/13/Active-Nonviolence-is-a-Sign-of-Hope.

50. Zaru, "Active Nonviolence."

11: Christian Mission and Planetary Politics

1. Heather Eaton, "An Earth-Centric Theological Framing for Planetary Solidarity," in *Planetary Solidarity: Global Women's Voices on Christian Doctrine and Climate Justice*, ed. Grace Ji-Sun Kim and Hilda P. Koster (Minneapolis: Fortress Press, 2017), 43.

2. Lynn White Jr., "Continuing the Conversation," in *Western Man and Environmental Ethics: Attitudes toward Nature and Technology*, ed. Ian G. Barbour (Reading, MA: Addison-Wesley Publishing Company, 1973), 55.

3. Lynn White Jr., "The Historical Roots of Our Ecological Crisis," *Science* 155 (March 10, 1967): 1203–7.

4. White, "The Historical Roots of Our Ecological Crisis," 1205.

5. White, "The Historical Roots of Our Ecological Crisis," 1207.

6. See for example, Dieter T. Hessel, ed., *Theology for Earth Community: A Field Guide* (Maryknoll, NY: Orbis books, 1996); and Dieter R. Hessel and Rosemary Radford Ruether, eds., *Christianity and Ecology: Seeking the Well-Being of Earth and Humans* (Cambridge, MA: Harvard University Press, 2000).

7. "Ceylon Tea History," Tea Exportations Association, Sri Lanka, http://teasrilanka.org/history.

8. Elizabeth Hartfield and Leigh Ann Caldwell, "Obama: Climate Change 'Growing and Urgent Threat,'" CNN Politics, http://www.cnn.com/2014/09/23/politics/obama-un-climate-change/.

9. Jeff Goodell, "Will America Finally Lead on Climate?" *Rolling Stone*, March 1, 2021, https://www.rollingstone.com/politics/politics-features/john-kerry-climate-crisis-china-glasgow-1134293/.

10. CBS San Francisco Staff, "2020 in Review: The Day the Sky Turned Bloody Orange; Historical Wildfires Ravage Northern California," CBS SF Bay Area, January 1, 2021, https://sanfrancisco.cbslocal.com/2021/01/01/2020-historic-wildfires-wine-country-shaver-lake-rescue-orange-sky-san-francisco-deaths/.

11. Godell, "Will America Finally Lead on Climate?"

12. Pablo Mukherjee, "Surfing the Second Waves: Amitav Ghosh's Tide Country," *New Formations* 59 (2006): 144.

13. Alfred Crosby, *Ecological Imperialism: The Biological Expansion of Europe, 900–1900*, 2nd ed. (Cambridge: Cambridge University Press, 2015).

14. Janna Rose, "Biopiracy: When Indigenous Knowledge Is Patented for Profit," The Conversation, March 7, 2016, https://theconversation.com /biopiracy-when-indigenous-knowledge-is-patented-for-profit-55589.

15. I follow the characterization of the three forms of ecological imperialism in Graham Huggan and Helen Tiffin, *Postcolonial Ecocriticism: Literature, Animals, Environment*, 2nd ed. (New York: Routledge, 2015), 3–5.

16. James H. Cone, "Whose Earth Is It, Anyway?" in *Earth Habitat: Ecojustice and the Church's Response*, ed. Dieter Hessel and Larry Rasmussen (Minneapolis: Fortress Press, 2001), 23.

17. Gayatri Chakravorty Spivak, *Death of A Discipline* (New York: Columbia University Press, 2003), 72.

18. Kwok Pui-lan, "What Has Love to Do with It? Planetarity, Feminism, and Theology," in *Planetary Love: Spivak, Postcoloniality, and Theology*, ed. Stephen D. Moore and Mayra Rivera (New York: Fordham University Press, 2011), 33.

19. This artwork was used in the book cover of Anne Primavesi, *Gaia's Gift: Earth, Ourselves and God After Copernicus* (London: Routledge, 2003). The description of the artwork can be found on the back cover.

20. Catherine Keller. *Political Theology of the Earth: Our Planetary Emergency and the Struggle for a New Public* (New York: Columbia University Press, 2018), 6.

21. Dipesh Chakrabarty, *The Climate of History in a Planetary Age* (Chicago: University of Chicago Press, 2021), 68.

22. Chakrabarty, *The Climate of History*, 50–51.

23. Peter Brannen, "The Anthropocene Is a Joke," *The Atlantic*, August 13, 2019, https://www.theatlantic.com/science/archive/2019/08/arrogance-anthropocene /595795/.

24. Pope Francis, "Encyclical Letter *Laudato Si'* of the Holy Father Francis on Care for Our Common Home," The Vatican, May 24, 2015, #14, http:// www.vatican.va/content/francesco/en/encyclicals/documents/papa-francesco _20150524_enciclica-laudato-si.html.

25. Ecumenical Patriarch Bartholomew's closing remarks at the Halki Summit on "Global Responsibility and Ecological Sustainability," held in Istanbul, Turkey, June 20, 2012, cited in Pope Francis, *Laudado Si'* #9.

26. Bartholomew and Justin Welby, "Climate Change and Moral Responsibility," *New York Times*, June 19, 2015, https://www.nytimes.com/2015/06/20/opinion /climate-change-and-moral-responsibility.html.

27. Jonathan Ingleby, *Beyond Empire: Postcolonialism and Mission in a Global Context* (Central Milton Keynes, UK: AuthorHouse, 2010), 165–73; and Letty M. Russell, "God, Gold, Glory and Gender: A Postcolonial View of Mission," *International Review of Mission* 93, no. 368 (2004): 39–49.

28. Dana L. Robert, "Historical Trends in Mission and Earth Care," in *Creation Care in Christian Mission*, ed. Kapya J. Kaoma (Oxford: Regnum Books, 2015), 76–81.

29. Kapya John Kaoma, "Rethinking Mission," in Kenneth R. Ross, *Edinburgh 2010: Fresh Perspectives on Christian Mission* (Pasadena, CA: William Carey International University Press, 2010), 69.

30. George E. Tinker, *Missionary Conquest: The Gospel and Native American Cultural Genocide* (Minneapolis: Fortress Press, 1993).

31. Keller, *Political Theology*, 14.

32. Carl Schmitt, *Political Theology: Four Chapters on the Concept of Sovereignty*, trans. George Schwab (Cambridge, MA: MIT Press, 2005), 5.

33. Keller, *Political Theology*, 75–77.

34. Keller, *Political Theology*, 77.
35. Matthew Fox, ed., *Hildegard of Bingen's Books of Divine Works, with Letters and Songs* (Santa Fe, NM: Bear and Company, 1987), 10.
36. Thomas Berry, *Befriending the Earth: A Theology of Reconciliation between Humans and the Earth* (Mystic, CT: Twenty-Third Publications, 1991), 43.
37. Daniel R. DiLeo, "Introduction: The 'Climate Emergency' and the US Catholic Response to *Laudato Si*,'" *Journal of Moral Theology* 9, Special Issue 1 (2020): 9–10.
38. Daryl Balia and Kirsteen Kim, "Introduction," in *Edinburgh 2010: Witnessing to Christ Today*, ed. Daryl Balia and Kirsteen Kim (Eugene, OR: Wipf and Stock, 2010), 1.
39. "Edinburgh 2010 Common Call," http://www.edinburgh2010.org/fileadmin /Edinburgh_2010_Common_Call_with_explanation.pdf.
40. Eaton, "An Earth-Centric Theological Framing," 23.
41. Eaton, "An Earth-Centric Theological Framing," 26.
42. James W. Perkinson, *Political Spirituality in an Age of Eco-Apocalypse* (New York: Palgrave Macmillan, 2015), 7.
43. Chakrabarty, *The Climate of History*, 83.
44. Chakrabarty, *The Climate of History*, 83.
45. Anne Primavesi, *Sacred Gaia: Holistic Theology and Earth System Science* (London: Routledge, 2000).
46. Ivone Gebara, *Longing for Running Water: Ecofeminism and Liberation* (Minneapolis: Fortress Press, 1999), 137–71.
47. Carter Heyward, *Keep Your Courage: A Radical Christian Feminists Speak* (London: SCM, 2010), 112.
48. Chakrabarty, *The Climate of History*, 92.
49. Eaton, "An Earth-Centric Theological Framing," 42.
50. Christine Woodside, "The United Church of Christ and Climate Change," Yale Climate Connections, April 5, 2012, https://yaleclimateconnections .org/2012/04/the-united-church-of-christ-and-climate-change/.
51. Interfaith Power and Light website, https://www.interfaithpowerandlight.org.
52. John Vidal, "What Does the Arab World Do When Its Water Run Out," *The Guardian*, February 19, 2011, http://www.theguardian.com/environment /2011/feb/20/arab-nations-water-running-out.
53. Tommy Beer, "Top 1% of U.S. Households Hold 15 Times More Wealth Than Bottom 50% Combined," *Forbes*, October 8, 2020, https://www.forbes.com /sites/tommybeer/2020/10/08/top-1-of-us-households-hold-15-times-more-wealth -than-bottom-50-combined/?sh=51675bd45179.
54. Gabriele Dietrich, "The World as the Body of God: Feminist Perspectives on Ecology and Social Justice," in *Women Healing Earth: Third World Women on Ecology, Feminism, and Religion*, ed. Rosemary Radford Ruether (Maryknoll, NY: Orbis Books, 1996), 82–83.
55. Vandana Shiva, *Staying Alive: Women, Ecology, and Development* (London: Zed Books, 1989).
56. Balia and Kim, eds., *Edinburgh 2010*, 247.
57. Sharon A. Bong, "Not Only for the Sake of Man: Asian Feminist Theological Responses to *Laudato Si*,'" in *Planetary Solidarity*, ed. Kim and Koster, 91.
58. Danne Polk, "Ecologically Queer: Preliminaries for a Queer Ecofeminist Identity Theory," *Journal of Women and Religion* 19, no. 72 (2001): 84.
59. John R. Mott, *The Evangelization of the World in This Generation* (New York: Student Volunteer Movement for Foreign Missions, 1900).
60. Mary Evelyn Tucker, "Worldly Wonder: Religions Enter Their Ecological Phase," *Religion East and West* 2 (June 2002): 5.

61. Wai-Li Ho, "Rice, Medicine, and Nature: Women's Environmental Activism and Interreligious Cooperation in Taiwan," in *Off the Menu: Asian and Asian North American Women's Religion and Theology*, ed. Rita Nakashima Brock, et al. (Louisville, KY: Westminster John Knox Press, 2007), 231–51.
62. White, "Continuing the Conversation," 56.
63. Sandra Schneiders, "Spirituality as an Academic Discipline," *Christian Spirituality Bulletin* 1, no. 2 (Fall 1993): 11.
64. Ursula King, "Introduction: Spirituality, Society, and the New Millennium—Wasteland, Wilderness or New Vision?" in *Spirituality and Society in the New Millennium*, ed. Ursula King and Tina Beattie (Brighton, UK: Sussex Academic Press, 2001), 6.
65. Victoria Tauli-Corpuz, "Reclaiming Earth-based Spirituality: Indigenous Women in the Cordillera," in *Women Healing Earth*, ed. Ruether, 106.
66. John E. Carroll, *Sustainability and Spirituality* (Albany: State University of New York Press, 2004), 54–93.
67. This is summarized by Carroll in *Sustainability and Spirituality*, 52–53, based on Sr. Miriam Therese MacGillis, "To Know the Place for the First Time: Explorations in Thomas Berry's New Cosmology" (Sonoma, CA: Global Perspectives, 1991), a set of six audio-cassette tapes.
68. Sallie McFague, *A New Climate for Theology: God, the World, and Global Warming* (Minneapolis: Fortress Press, 2008), 3.

Epilogue

1. India TV News Desk, "India Records New High of 360,960 COVID Cases; Over 3,200 Fatalities in 24 Hours," India TV, April 28, 2021, https://www.indiatvnews.com/news/india/india-coronavirus-cases-death-toll-active-covid-cases-india-covid19-vaccination-registration-process-maharashtra-delhi-mumbai-701003.
2. Tedros Adhanom Ghebreyesus, "I Run the W.H.O., and I Know That Rich Countries Must Make a Choice," *New York Times*, April 22, 2021, https://www.nytimes.com/2021/04/22/opinion/who-covid-vaccines.html?action=click&module=RelatedLinks&pgtype=Article.
3. The Editorial Board, "The World Needs Many More Coronavirus Vaccine," *New York Times*, April 24, 2021, https://www.nytimes.com/2021/04/24/opinion/covid-vaccines-poor-countries.html.
4. "COVID-19 Vaccinations in the United States," COVID Data Tracker, Centers for Disease Control and Prevention, April 30, 2021, https://covid.cdc.gov/covid-data-tracker/#vaccinations; and Lauren Giella, "Just 1.5% of Indians Have Received Both COVID Vaccine Doses While the Country Tops 200K Deaths," *Newsweek*, April 28, 2021, https://www.newsweek.com/just-15-indians-have-received-both-covid-vaccine-doses-country-tops-200k-deaths-1587102.
5. Judith Butler, *Frames of War: When Is Life Grievable?* (New York: Verso, 2009), 38.
6. Lama Htoi San Lu, "Fierce Surviving and Collective Caring," (paper presented online at the 35th conference of Pacific, Asian, and North American Asian Women in Theology and Ministry, April 16, 2021), YouTube, April 20, 2021, https://www.youtube.com/watch?v=EtIg8WtOQF0.
7. "Glory to Hong Kong: Anthem of the Hong Kong Protests," YouTube, September 25, 2019, https://www.youtube.com/watch?v=6yjLIYNFKCg. I made some changes to the translation of the lyrics, based on the original Chinese

version. The Chinese version can be found in "Glory to Hong Kong," YouTube, September 11, 2019, https://www.youtube.com/watch?v=oUIDL4SB60g.

8. Traci C. West, *Solidarity and Defiant Spirituality: Africana Lessons of Religion, Racism, and Ending Gender Violence* (New York: New York University Press, 2019), 223.

Index

Abdel-Malek, Anwar, 25
Abrahamic faiths, 31, 36
Abu-Nimer, Mohammed, 177–78
activism, 26, 49, 53, 104, 113, 151, 184,
    190, 197–98
    in Hong Kong, 124–27, 131, 133, 136
Africa, 24–25, 28–30, 44, 47–48, 53–55,
    75–78, 86, 119, 143–45, 156–57,
    182–83, 197
    colonization of, 48, 75, 172, 188
    cultures, 54
    enslavement of African peoples, 30, 48,
        76–77
African Americans, 68, 83, 160–61, 203
Afrocentrism, 114
Ahmad, Aijaz, 25
Ahn Byung Mu, 98–99
alienation, 120, 176, 183, 199
Alima, Marie-Bernard, 183
al Qaeda, 110
alterity, 188–89
Althaus-Reid, Marcella, 14, 53, 59–61,
    64, 66–68
Alves, Rubem, 87
ambivalence, 20, 26, 73, 96, 111, 149, 170
American Academy of Religion (AAR), 9,
    13, 45–47
American Dream, 75

American empire
    building, 44–46
    and Christianity, 71–90
    theological critique of, 77–85
American exceptionalism, 44, 75, 77,
    81–85
Amin, Samir, 25
androcentrism, 7, 12, 159, 197
Anglican church, 6, 57–58, 160
Anglo-Saxon myth, 81–84
animals, 55, 186, 188, 192, 194, 200
animistic religion, 44
anthropic exceptionalism, 191, 200
Anthropocene era, 189–95, 200
    Christian mission in, 15, 190–93
anthropocentrism, 186, 191–94
anthropology, cultural, 8, 46
anti-Asian racism, 85, 202
    Trump presidency and, 1–2, 85
anti-immigration, 20, 77, 89, 170, 180
anti-Judaism, 10
anti-racism, 83, 175
anti-Semitism, 43
Anzaldúa, Gloria, 30
apartheid, 134, 188
apocalypse, 78, 80
    counterapocalypse, 80
Appadurai, Arjun, 15, 116, 119, 121–22

243

CPSIA information can be obtained
at www.ICGtesting.com
Printed in the USA
LVHW080734051121
702404LV00005B/121

9 780664 267490